Multiprocessor System Architectures

A Technical Survey of Multiprocessor/ Multithreaded Systems using SPARC®, Multi-level Bus Architectures and Solaris® (SunOS™)

Ben Catanzaro

sun microsystems

Editorial/production supervision
  and interior design: *Ann Sullivan*
Cover design: *TOMMYBOY*
Cover illustration: *Spilzen Inm Bogen* (Vasilly Kandinsky), 1927
Buyer: *Alexis Heydt*
Acquisitions editor: *Gregory G. Doench*
Editorial assistant: *Marcy Levine*

ISBN 0-13-089137-1

SunSoft Press
A Prentice Hall Title

Table of Contents

Multiprocessor System Architectures

Figures

≡

Tables

≡

Preface ≡

This book is the first of its kind to bring together in one volume a coherent description of the elements that provide for the design and development of multiprocessor systems architectures from Sun Microsystems, Inc.

During my years as SPARC® Marketing and Technology Licensing Manager at Sun, one of the most frequent requests was for documents that interrelated the various components and system technologies. To that end, this book is written for both hardware and software engineers interested in understanding these technologies and the design of a new array of multiprocessor system architectures.

The scope of the book includes SPARC hardware architecture, multi-level bus architectures including MBus, XBus, XDBus, and SBus, and the multiprocessing aspects of the software architecture of the Solaris® SunOS™ operating system. This book provides a concrete view of what is normally presented from a theoretical standpoint while providing concise, easy to understand descriptions and practical hands-on approaches to design issues related to multiprocessing, cache coherency, and cache protocols. Additional approaches discussed include multiprocessor system development using a behavioral simulator to model SPARC multiprocessor systems and an in-depth look at how to program within the new multithreaded programming environment of the Solaris SunOS multithreaded kernel architecture.

The book assumes that the reader has a prior knowledge of computer architecture. In fact, since a great deal of emphasis is placed on multi-level bus architectures, this book also provides detailed bus specifications and design guides to aid hardware designers in the design of high-performance bus systems.

This book is also appropriate as a supplementary text for a graduate-level computer architecture course or as the primary text for a class on multiprocessor system design utilizing a behavioral simulator.

How This Book is Organized

Although this book can be read in sequence from cover to cover, it can also serve as a reference guide to specific design components and procedures. The book is, therefore, intended to serve both as an overview of the technology as well as a reference handbook for designers interested in hands-on multiprocessor system design. In either case, it is recommended that Chapter 1 be read first.

Chapter 1, "Introduction to Multiprocessing," reviews design considerations associated with multiprocessor system design and sets the foundation for many practical approaches discussed later in the design of multiprocessor systems.

Chapter 2, "The SPARC Architecture," provides an in-depth study on the Scalable Processor ARChitecture (SPARC). This chapter focuses on SPARC versions 8.

Chapter 3, "SPARC Implementations," details the various SPARC implementations available today and provides details of system design using these chosen implementations.

Chapter 4, "System-level Resources," examines details of the SPARC memory model and SPARC Reference MMU from both software and hardware perspectives, while also examining Reference MMU implementations.

Chapter 5, "SPARC Multi-level Bus Architectures," introduces various multi-level bus architectures that allow for the design of multi-level multiprocessing systems. The bus architectures discussed include the SPARC MBus, a processor-level interconnection bus, XBus an intermediate-level interconnect bus, XDBus, a high-performance system backplane packet bus, and SBus, a system I/O expansion bus.

Chapter 6, "MBus Multiprocessor System Design," expands on the discussion in Chapter 5 on bus architectures by examining further practical approaches to multiprocessor system implementation via two-level MBus implementation and details the issues related to multiprocessing, cache coherency, and cache protocols. The second part of the chapter discusses the use of the SPARC MPSAS Behavioral Simulator to model SPARC multiprocessor systems. A number of system design examples are included to enhance the discussion.

Chapter 7, "SunOS Multithreading Architecture," focuses on the software aspects of multiprocessor system implementations and methods of achieving fine-grained parallelism through a new two-level multithreaded model provided by the Solaris (SunOS/SVR4) operating environment.

Chapter 8, "Multithread Programming Facilities for Implementing Multithreaded Applications," takes the reader deeper into the multithreaded environment by introducing multithreaded programming and examining the various programming facilities available to software developers. Chapters 7 and 8 impart a thorough understanding of how a multithreaded environment provides an efficient method for application developers to utilize the parallelism of the hardware. A number of code examples provide details on multithreaded applications.

Chapter 9, "Multiprocessor System Implementations," examines three multiprocessor system implementations from Sun Microsystems by highlighting the specific architectural features that provide for tightly coupled, shared-memory model architecture and performance enhancements furnished via multi-level bus implementations.

Chapter 10, "The Next Decade of Innovation," offers a glimpse of future technology—object and process-oriented messaging and distributed object-oriented application building.

Appendix A, "MBus Interface Specification," is the latest specification for the SPARC MBus. The specification provides designers with all the electrical and mechanical specifications needed for the design of MBus-based systems.

Appendix B, "MBus Module Design Guide," conveys the information needed to build MBus modules that will work in MBus-based systems. The appendix describes some significant aspects of designing 40 MHz MBus modules. Items include: PCB construction and routing, mechanical specifications and connector pin-out, skew management for clocks, timing specifications and their derivation for an MBus chip, and testability.

The **Glossary** defines unfamiliar terms.

The **Bibliography** provides a list of references used for writing this book. It also includes a list of references recommended for further reading.

Contacts provides the reader with a list of companies that are mentioned in the book.

Multiprocessor System Architectures

Acknowledgments

Special thanks go to the many individuals who provided technical input, information, guidance, and support in writing this book.

Elaine Miller, Sun Microsystems Computer Corporation, for allowing the MBus Interface Specification and the MBus Module Design Specification to be incorporated in this book,

Max Baron, Sun Microsystems Computer Corporation, for all of the SPARC information provided while strolling along the Avenue des Champs Elysées,

David Yen, Sun Microsystems Computer Corporation, for providing SPARCcenter 2000 material,

Adrian Cockroft and Lisa Sieker, Sun Microsystems Computer Corporation, for providing SPARCserver 1000 material,

Stan Head, Sun Microsystems Computer Corporation, for providing information and knowledge on a host of subjects,

Xuong Dang, Sun Microsystems Computer Corporation, for providing material on the MPSAS Behavioral Simulator,

Barry Barrett, Sun Microsystems Computer Corporation, for providing guidance during the early days of SPARC technology licensing,

Greg Blanck, Sun Microsystems Computer Corporation, for information on SuperSPARC,

Robert Gianni and Martin Sodos, Sun Microsystems Computer Corporation, for providing material on the SBus interface chips,

John Fetter, Edmund Kelly, and John Forehand, Sun Microsystems Computer Corporation, and Kevin Kitagawa for providing information on MBus and associated technical specifications,

Jim Ammon, Sun Microsystems Computer Corporation, for providing updates to the MBus module mechanical drawings,

Donna Pappachristou, John Bard, and Chuck Narad, Sun Microsystems Computer Corporation, for 6OOMP system architecture material,

Dan Stein, Joe Eykholt, Michael Sebrée, Sandeep Khanna, and Chris Prael, SunSoft, and Kuljeet Kalkat for their review and comments on the Multithread chapter, including the Realtime Scheduling material, with special thanks to Dan for setting me straight on multithreading,

John Zolnowsky, SunSoft, for providing SunOS real-time scheduling material,

Mache Creeger, SunSoft Object Products, for providing Project DOE information.

The writing of a book such as this requires the use of information and technical specification from several semiconductor, computer, and technology companies. I should like to extend a special thanks to the following companies and individuals for providing this critical material:

Bob Duncan and Greg Xenakis, SPARC International Inc., for providing permission to use material from the SPARC Architecture Reference Manual,

Prem V. Nath, LSI Logic Corporation, for SparKIT material,

Mathew Gutierrez, Cypress Semiconductor, for providing HyperSPARC material,

Michael Joplin, Texas Instruments, for providing SuperSPARC material,

Jean Castinel and Ronald E. Rider, Xerox Palo Alto Research Center, for the use of material from the XBus specification,

Patricia Shanahan and Alan Charlesworth, CRAY Research, for providing CRAY S-MP material,

Dr. Gary McMillan, System and Processes Engineering Corporation, for providing material on the Gallium Arsenide SPARC implementation,

Peter von Clemm, Fujitsu Microelectronics, Inc., for providing material on Fujitsu's SPARC implementations,

Institute of Electrical and Electronics Engineers (IEEE) for providing permission to use IEEE COMPCON material.

Many thanks to the editors, Greg Doench of Prentice Hall and Karin Ellison of SunSoft Press, for their editorial support. Someday I'll be able to pay back Karin Ellison with all the lunches owed for her help and assistance and for talking me into writing this book. Special thanks to Dianna Yee for her help with file translation.

Introduction to Multiprocessing 1

Multiprocessor system architectures—systems with several processing units—provide system designers with a method to increase available processing power by allowing more than one CPU per system. This method offers a significant source for performance improvement for a wide range of computer system applications.

Multiprocessor system architectures have been drawing attention as a means for computer makers to provide increased performance of their systems at reasonable cost. Over the past two decades, multiprocessor designs have resided in the realm of high-end computing, primarily because of low levels of silicon integration and lack of software that facilitates parallel execution. The advantages of Reduced Instruction Set Computer (RISC), including its ties to UNIX®, make RISC-based systems an ideal platform for exploring the strengths of multiprocessor system architectures. In addition, the availability of integrated devices containing multiprocessing support functions, such as memory management for microprocessor-based systems, provides the features and level of integration required for multiprocessing to move into mainstream computing.

From a cost perspective, the cost/performance range available today from microprocessors offers a cost-effective solution to the never-ending demand for computational power and speed. Add to this the increased performance capabilities and features provided with enhanced multiprocessing/multitasking operating systems, and it's easy to see why multiprocessor system implementations are becoming the predominant system architecture for high-performance computer systems.

Multiprocessing Benefits

Multiprocessing offers several benefits:

- Independent tasks can be handled by separate processors executing concurrently within the same kernel component, such as the file system or a device driver, thus increasing job throughput, the number of transactions, and/or the number of simultaneous users.

- Combining CPUs in one system lowers the overall cost of computing by sharing system resources like memory, disk, and network interfaces.

- Providing a high-speed interconnect between multiple CPUs achieves better coordination and faster interaction between related tasks.

- Depending on the type of application and tools available, a single large job can be decomposed into several smaller tasks that can run simultaneously for faster application time-to-completion.

Although the benefits are great, designing efficient multiprocessor systems is a complex undertaking, requiring considerable attention in both hardware and software integration. The considerations are discussed in the following sections.

Historical Perspective

In some respects, the computer industry is, and has always been, predictable in its requirement for computing power. Whether they be chip vendors, systems manufacturers, or end users, they all seek speed. The more megahertz and megaFLOPS, the better.

Traditionally, semiconductor and computer systems companies have poured massive resources into making their integrated circuits and machines run faster. Today, the quest for speed approaches the finite physical limitations of silicon. Chip manufacturers, hoping to yield microprocessors with clock speeds of 200+ MHz, use new technologies, such as gallium arsenide, to explore development of high-performance chips.

The end-users of these system products need and want more performance. Speed is but one factor in determining the overall performance of a system. For the vast majority of mid- and low-end users, however, speed (which translates into performance) has been the primary benchmark by which they have measured the performance of their machines. Suppliers of state-of-the-art microprocessor products know well that semiconductor and materials technologies alone cannot take the industry to the next level of performance. Instead, performance will depend more on advances in computer architecture and in operating systems technology. This realization has led over the last several years to a revolution in the computer industry—toward RISC and multiprocessing/multitasking operating systems.

RISC architectures have penetrated every major microprocessor and systems vendor's product line. Even established manufacturers of proprietary CISC (Complex Instruction Set Computing) processors and machines—have succumbed to the demonstrated advantages of RISC architectures and have embarked on RISC programs. Today, RISC machines continue to gain market share at an increasing rate. And SPARC (Scalable Processor ARChitecture) has emerged as the preferred RISC architecture for a wide range of computing applications.

However, RISC microprocessors are subject to the same laws of physics as other semiconductors. While recent RISC and CISC architectures have set new price/performance points for the computer industry, the insatiable appetite for performance will soon exceed the speed capabilities of today's most advanced microprocessors.

Enter multiprocessor system architectures.

Multiprocessing, in its broadest interpretation, is not new. The traditional minicomputer/server class of machines has employed multiple processing nodes for some time to provide a more economical alternative to expensive, single-processor, ECL implementations. Still, the majority of those products were built with discrete nMOS logic and often duplicated many expensive system resources (e.g., memory and I/O) and therefore confined multiprocessing to high-end systems.

Traditionally, in designing successive generations of microprocessor-based systems, designers have had to tackle problems associated with ways to make systems better, faster, and less expensive. Usually, extensive hardware changes to the system architecture introduced many costly improvements to the overall system.

Making systems faster meant either a redesign of the system to accommodate the faster clock speeds or an upgrade to a better (faster) microprocessor. While processor upgrades alone provided increased performance, there was no desire to extensively change the system architecture; thus, maintaining compatibility between both system and application software required minimum effort. In many instances however, obtaining more performance via extensive changes in the systems architecture proved to be an expensive upgrade solution, requiring extensive hardware changes to existing installed machines in order to take advantage of the performance gains. In turn, system and application software compatibility was put at risk.

With the remarkable advances in microprocessor technologies, some semiconductor chip vendors provide high-performance, pin-compatible upgrades for uniprocessor systems. That approach is still relatively expensive. These new (faster) implementations carry a high price, making their use in large numbers cost-prohibitive. Combining relatively inexpensive but powerful microprocessors to form multiprocessors holds much greater promise for increasing system performance.

In addition, multiprocessing support is now available in the form of integrated solutions that solve the complexities of shared-memory multiprocessing (where multiple CPUs share a common memory space) in VLSI firmware. With the range of integrated devices available, multiprocessing is now at an affordable level—affordable enough to penetrate a wide range of computing environments.

VLSI multiprocessing support is a natural step in the evolution of microprocessors. Traditionally, simply increasing the speed of a microprocessor has provided only a relatively linear increase in performance. Significant leaps in performance have resulted from enhancements in microprocessor architectures. Figure 1-1 offers a simplified representation of this trend.

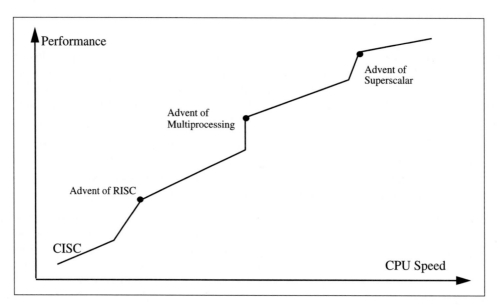

Figure 1-1   Microprocessor Evolution

Multiprocessing—Considerations and Practical Approaches

The move of multiprocessing into mainstream computing means more computing power for a wider range of systems and applications. A set of tasks (a task is a standalone application or a subprogram that runs as an independent entity) can be completed faster if several processing units (CPUs) are computing in parallel. But making the most of multiprocessing requires a thorough understanding of computer organization and software behavior. In other words, the way in which the CPUs are connected and the way in which the code that runs on them is written greatly influence the price and performance of a multiprocessing system.

Multiprocessing does bring significant gains in performance, but it also brings problems that make efficient multiprocessor systems difficult to design. Design constraints may allow only for a system design that maximizes overall application throughput or only speeds up the execution of a single application. Design and programming considerations involve synchronization of processes, data coherence, and scheduling, all of which must be addressed from the hardware design level up to the programming language and operating system level. In fact, putting hardware aside, the real challenges in designing efficient multiprocessing systems are synchronization, coherence, and the logical ordering of events.

Multiprocessing and Parallelism

The term *multiuser*, or *multiuser system*, is often associated with multiprocessing. A multiuser system is one that enables separate users to share a computer system simultaneously. This definition immediately implies some level of parallelism. Although several users are active at once, the majority of these systems are still only single-processor systems. Each user has the illusion of simultaneous operation as the operating system rapidly switches the processor among users, but, in fact, normally only a single instruction of a single user is being executed at one time.

The concept of *process* enables operating systems to distinguish among the concurrent activities of separate users. There tended to be a single process per user. In multitasking systems, each user can execute many concurrent tasks. The execution is normally accomplished in single-processor systems by switching the processor rapidly among the separate tasks or processes of the single user. SunOS (discussed further in Chapter 7), is an example of a multiuser, multitasking operating system in which each user can have many processes proceeding in parallel. As the level of parallelism increases, operating system overhead increases. More system resources are devoted to managing the parallel processes. The overhead is at times seen as a disadvantage, but has generally been considered worthwhile because of the added value of parallel computation.

Process-level parallelism can be implemented on uniprocessor or multiprocessor systems, but the real performance gains are realized on multiprocessors that execute parallel activities truly simultaneously. Processes are expensive. For example, considerable overhead is required to create and maintain separate virtual address spaces and to support interprocess communication (which of necessity occurs across address spaces), switching between processes to effect simultaneous execution, process synchronization, mutual exclusion, and so on.

Today, huge numbers of processes are normally supported on microprocessor systems, because not all the processes need to be active at once, and active processes rarely need all the processor's attention to make reasonable progress. The operating system rapidly switches among processes to give the illusion of continuous service. Strong protection must be enforced between processes; a malfunctioning process must not affect the proper operation of other processes. This protection contributes to the substantial overhead of maintaining separate concurrent activities.

Because processes require such great overhead, it is only practical to put them to work on the most substantial parallel tasks. But many problems consist of large numbers of simple parallel activities. For problems like these, it does not make sense to dedicate full processes to the independent activities.

As opportunities for large-scale hardware parallelism increase, it becomes feasible and attractive to enable processes to consist of huge numbers of threads. Threads operate in a cooperative and friendly manner, but without benefit of the rigid interactivity protection offered by processes. Now users can program highly parallel applications without incurring the substantial overhead of processes.

As is the case with most hardware innovations, realizing the maximum performance gains depends to a great extent on new developments in software, particularly in the operating system (OS). Multiprocessing extensions have already been incorporated into many new UNIX operating system releases [e.g., UNIX System V Release 4 (SVR4)] that provide coarse-grained parallelism (assigning multiple tasks to multiple processors) at the OS level. Application programs that are written to facilitate fine-grained parallelism (dividing a single application among multiple processors—or "multithreading") will allow multiprocessing machines to realize significant increases in overall system performance. Software developers, especially application programmers, have only begun to explore the performance improvements made possible with true parallel processing.

Scalability vs. Synchronization

Multiprocessor systems with up to 16 processors are typically classified as small-scale multiprocessing systems. Systems with thousands of processors, such as those developed by Thinking Machines Corporation, are classified as massively parallel machines. Table 1-1 shows a representative sample of parallel machines of the passed decade. The processing units used in massively parallel machines are usually less powerful than those in small-scale systems, as Table 1-1 illustrates.

Table 1-1   Representative Listing of Parallel Machine

Company/Product	Connectivity	Parallelism	Processor
Alliant Computer Systems/ FX18	Bus	Up to 20	64-bit CMOS gate array
Encore Computer/ Multimax	Bus	Up to 20	NS32032
Intel Scientific Computers/ iPSC	Hypercube	32 - 128	80286/287

Table 1-1   Representative Listing of Parallel Machine (Continued)

International Parallel Machines/ IP-1	Cross-barlike switch	Up to 8	32-bit
Ncube/Ncube/Ten	Hypercube	16 - 1024	Custom 32-bit
BBN Advanced Computers/ Butterfly	Packet-switched network	Up to 256	MC68020
Thinking Machines/ Connection Machine	Hypercube	64000 - 1,000,000	1-bit custom

Regardless of the actual number of CPUs, microprocessors incorporated in a multiprocessor system are basically asynchronous to begin with; explicit synchronization is needed between two or more CPUs in order to achieve a predictable outcome and the logical ordering of events. A microprocessor's instruction set architecture (ISA) must provide for adequate communications and synchronization in order for application processes to cooperate. In multiprocessing environments, communications and synchronization become so interleaved that they can be considered one and the same.

While communications are necessary for the exchange of data, synchronization provides a form of extended communications, turning specified data into control information. To this end, synchronization enforces correct sequencing of processes while also ensuring mutually exclusive access to certain shared writable data made possible through controlled sharing of data in memory.

In order to accomplish all of this, microprocessors intended for multiprocessing applications must provide efficient synchronization mechanisms to enforce atomic operations, atomic Loads and Stores. Synchronization and the outcome of concurrent applications are heavily dependent on the "atomic operations" performed by processors in a multiprocessor environment. Semaphores and message passing have traditionally provided the synchronization mechanism as well. Only after seamless integration of factors can efficient multiprocessing implementations result.

System Classifications

The mechanism by which a multiprocessing system is implemented can best be understood if we examine a classical description derived from a model that classifies computers into four types:

- *SISD*—Single Instruction, Single Data. One instruction stream operating on one data stream (e.g., personal computers)

- *SIMD*—Single Instruction, Multiple Data. One instruction stream operating on multiple pieces of data at the same time (e.g., array processors)

- **MISD**—Multiple Instruction, Single Data. Multiple instruction streams operating on one data stream at the same time (no useful implementations of such a machine)

- **MIMD**—Multiple Instruction, Multiple Data. Many instruction streams acting on many data streams at the same time

Within this classification, multiprocessing systems can best be categorized as MIMD architectures. That is, multiprocessing machines are computers with multiple, autonomous processing nodes, each of which can operate on its own set of data. All nodes are identical in function so that any node can operate on any task or portion of any task.

The way memory is connected to the processing nodes is the first level of distinction among multiprocessing systems. The two most common forms are "tightly coupled" and "loosely coupled" multiprocessing system architectures.

For tightly coupled multiprocessing all the processors share common memory and communicate with each other through shared memory (see Figure 1-2).

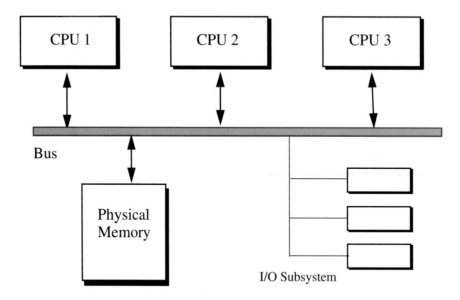

Figure 1-2   Tightly Coupled (Shared-bus) Architecture

Loosely coupled multiprocessors (also referred to as "distributed-memory multiprocessors") are characterized by processors that can access only their own memory (see Figure 1-3). Communication between processing nodes is required in order to coordinate activities and move data. Data can be exchanged, but not shared.

In loosely coupled systems, processors do not share a common address space. No problems are associated with having multiple copies of data, and the processors do not have to contend with each other to get to their data. Because each node is a complete computer system (including I/O devices if required) by itself, the only practical limit to the performance gains achieved by the addition of processing nodes is dictated by the topology used to connect the nodes. In fact, the interconnection scheme (e.g., rings, arrays, cubes) greatly impacts the performance of any loosely coupled multiprocessing system.

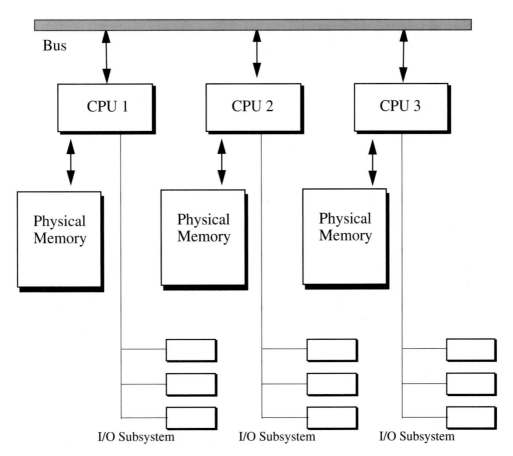

Figure 1-3   Loosely Coupled Architecture

Besides the complexity of the interconnections, one of the main disadvantages of a loosely coupled approach is the duplication of expensive system resources, primarily memory and I/O devices that are idle much of the time. For this reason, the most commercially attractive multiprocessing systems are tightly coupled (or "shared-memory") multiprocessors. Thc primary performance bottleneck in a tightly coupled system is typically *memory contention*. This issue is addressed later in this section as we examine methods of resolving memory contention.

Symmetric Multiprocessing vs. Asymmetric Multiprocessing

The software approaches used by tightly coupled and loosely coupled architectures vary between symmetric multiprocessing (SMP) and asymmetric multiprocessing (ASMP). Tightly coupled systems can be either asymmetric or symmetric.

Although the terms SMP and ASMP commonly refer to two types of multiprocessor systems, they mistakenly imply that symmetric multiprocessing is a binary condition. The degree of symmetry is more accurately portrayed as a continuum and not a binary condition; various systems fall all along this continuum.

Symmetric Multiprocessing

At one end of the spectrum is symmetric multiprocessing. Figure 1-4 illustrates the SMP approach.

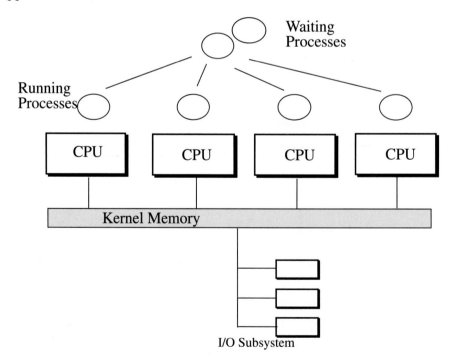

Figure 1-4   Symmetric Multiprocessing Approach

In symmetric multiprocessing systems, all processors are equals in that they can each run the operating system and user applications. That is, any work that needs to be done in the system can be performed by any of the processors. Each processor shares the kernel image in memory; all processors can run the kernel and can do so simultaneously. In particular, I/O requests and device-driver interrupts can be processed in parallel on several processors at once. Many user applications can run simultaneously on different processors.

Unlike ASMP, SMP is more difficult to define because a variety of systems can be called symmetric. However, all symmetric systems share the property that multiple processors can execute kernel-level code concurrently (hence the term "symmetric").

An accurate way of judging symmetrical multiprocessors is to understand the degree of symmetry. The degree of symmetry is best measured by the amount of concurrent execution that can take place in the operating system kernel. Symmetric systems tend to scale smoothly, up to some reasonable limit.

Asymmetric Multiprocessing

At the other end of the spectrum is asymmetric multiprocessing. Figure 1-5 illustrates the ASMP approach.

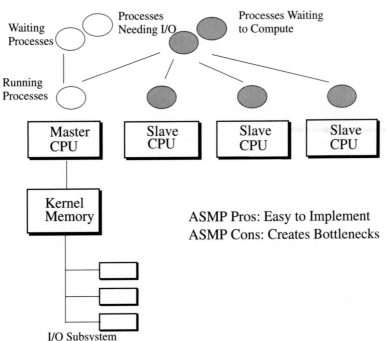

Figure 1-5   Asymmetric Multiprocessing Software Approach

In asymmetric multiprocessing, one of the processors is designated as master and the others are slaves to that master. The master performs all privileged operations such as I/O and the management of operating system resources. Only one processor can execute operating system code. The slaves run user applications, calling on the master when they need the services of the operating system.

The throughput (performance) of asymmetric systems decreases whenever the volume of operating system calls is high, certainly a possibility in large scale multiprocessing systems. Because adding processors tends to increase the demands on the master, which in turn tends to saturate the master, asymmetric master/slave systems do not scale well.

In shared-memory multiprocessing systems, multiple CPUs share a common memory space. The same data can be accessed by any processor, as can any I/O device.

Having multiple processors on the same bus limits the overall system performance gained with the introduction of additional processors. This fact is especially true with the majority of traditional bus architectures in use. The main reason is bus saturation—over-utilization of a bus. In a shared-bus system, this saturation results from the contention of the devices on the bus for use of the bus.

The three primary sources for contention are:

- Memory—Each CPU must use the bus for accesses to main (or second-level) memory.

- Communication—The bus is used by bus masters to communicate and coordinate.

- Memory latency—The memory subsystem must hold the bus during data transfers. Depending on how quickly memory can respond to requests, this factor could be significant.

In an effort to reduce the number of requests made by each CPU for the bus, multi-level memories (caches) are used. Caches are smaller, faster, and therefore more expensive memories that buffer data and/or instructions between the CPU and external memory. They rely on the principle of locality, which means that because of the sequential nature of programs, the next data or instruction needed is likely to be "located" close to the last one.

The data within caches is most often organized into blocks of data, called lines (see Figure 1-6). Cache lines are loaded into local caches as exact copies of the data in external memory. In order to reference data in cache memory, tags identify the cache lines. Cache tags use a portion of the data's physical address to compare against the address requested by the CPU. A cache "hit" occurs when addresses match exactly and other qualifiers are met (e.g., status, privilege, context); otherwise, a cache "miss" occurs and the data must be retrieved from memory.

The use of caches has become increasingly popular in uniprocessing systems to enable data flow to keep up with the speed of microprocessors. In multiprocessing architectures, caches provide the additional benefit of minimizing bus traffic (see Figure 1-7). Caching and cache protocols are examined in more detail in Chapter 6.

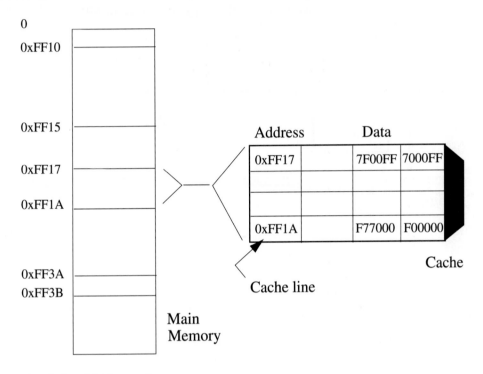

Figure 1-6   Cache with Memory Image

Multiprocessing Using SPARC, Multi-level Bus Architectures, and Solaris (SunOS)

Sun Microsystems and a growing number of independent SPARC system manufacturers are dedicated to the task of developing high-performance desktop and server systems. With SPARC, processing power increases with each new implementation, and future designs will continue to provide higher performance while maintaining binary compatibility. By coupling SPARC performance increases with advanced multiprocessor systems architecture, Sun is already delivering high-performance multiprocessing system platforms to power-hungry users. (Three such examples are discussed in Chapter 9, "Multiprocessor System Implementations".)

Multiprocessor (MP) products from Sun Microsystems and several other SPARC system manufacturers were introduced as a result of the move of multiprocessing technology from specialized high-end applications toward a wider range of desktop workstations. This change is indicated by two key trends: the inclusion of MP in UNIX standards and the development of UNIX database products that take advantage of MP.

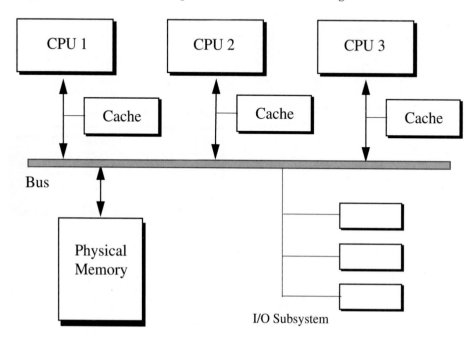

Figure 1-7   Minimizing Bus Contention with Caches

Many of these products are increasingly being used in the commercial computing environments and large technical departments, characterized by many users and large client/server networks. Extending the product line with MP systems provides the flexible range of solutions and configurations that customers are seeking to replace existing large, proprietary, centralized equipment. Tighter integration of CPU and memory technologies makes MP implementations more affordable.

Hardware: Solving the Hardware Complexity

The Sun MP implementation is based on a tightly coupled, shared-memory architecture. At the processor core level, processors are tightly coupled by a high-speed module interconnection bus, MBus, and share the same image of memory, although each processor has a cache where recently accessed data and instructions are stored (see Figure 1-7). In this implementation, the Solaris operating environment (a UNIX SVR4, based operating environment) coordinates the activities of all processors, scheduling jobs and coordinating access to common resources. All CPUs have equal access to system services, such as I/O and networking, unlike designs where specific resources are attached to a specific CPU.

The overall objective is a general-purpose system with sufficient computing and I/O resources to improve performance for a wide range of applications.

As you will come to realize later in this book, the implementation shown in Figure 1-8 satisfies one of Sun's original system design goals; that is, of separating CPU technology from the remainder of the system. For example, in this design a standard connector provides the interface between two separate boards.

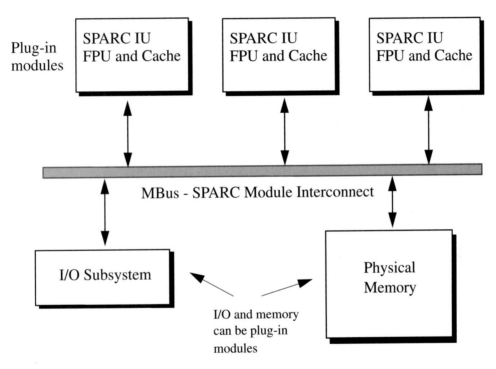

Figure 1-8   SPARC/MBus Multiprocessing Architecture

The main system functions and I/O are on the system board, while CPUs are located on modular daughtercards, called SPARC modules.

Providing a standard interface between CPUs and the rest of the system allows modular upgrade to future processor implementations. The interface also provides a convenient way to add more processors to a basic system, providing inexpensive scalability to increase system performance as application needs grow. Adding or changing processors is accomplished by installing a SPARC module (see Chapter 5, "SPARC Multi-level Bus Architectures"). As future CPUs become available, the SPARC modules can be swapped to achieve higher performance, thus providing a stable system platform for future needs.

SPARC modules attach to the MBus connectors on the system board. A module's processor core consists of a CPU, a floating-point unit (FPU), a memory management unit/cache controller (MMU/CC), and local cache. In its first multiprocessor implementation, SPARC modules contained two processor cores (each with a 64 Kbyte cache). A single system board supports one or two modules for two- or four-way multiprocessing. The specifics on using MBus for multiprocessor system implementations are discussed in Chapter 6.

In addition to MBus, XBus and XDBus provide yet another level of multiprocessor capability and offer multi-level bus architecture approaches for high-performance multiprocessor systems. XBus and XDBus are discussed in Chapter 5, "SPARC Multi-level Bus Architectures." In Chapter 9, "Multiprocessor System Implementations," multiprocessor systems using both MBus and XBus/XDBus are examined.

Software: Solving the Software Complexity

Undeniably, the UNIX operating system has grown to a position of prominence since its origins in the late 1960s. UNIX System V Release 4 (SVR4) multiprocessing extensions have provided developers with basic levels of coarse-grained parallelism. However, for fine-grained parallelism, enhanced application performance gains require that application programs be written to take advantage of multithreading. In addition, the goal of providing for symmetric multiprocessing is yet another significant requirement. These requirements are met by the Solaris 2.x operating environment from SunSoft, Inc., a Sun Microsystems, Inc. business.

Solaris, a SunOS 5.x/SVR4-based operating system environment, provides standard interfaces for multiprocessing applications, so that software developers can achieve unrestricted application portability and high performance. The gains are made possible by combining powerful 32-bit processing, industry-standard networking, a robust development environment, and a 3D multimedia desktop metaphor. Most of all, the Solaris environment uses the multitasking, multiprocessing and multithreaded capabilities of SunOS, in addition to multimedia and object management facilities and the ability to build a wide range of applications.

The Solaris Operating Environment

In addition to the SunOS 5.x/SVR4-based operating system, the Solaris operating environment consists of the following building block technologies: ONC+™, OpenWindows™, DeskSet™, and OPEN LOOK® and Motif® graphical user interfaces. These entries are discussed here, but first a brief historical perspective on UNIX System V Release 4.

UNIX System V Release 4 (SVR4)

AT&T's UNIX System V Release 4 is the result of evolution and conformance in the industry. While UNIX has been well established for many years, variants surfaced and application developers and users were not guaranteed that a software package would run on all versions of the operating system. Efforts began in the mid-1980s to unify the variants into a single UNIX operating system that would serve as an open computing platform for the 1990s. In 1987, Sun and AT&T formally announced a joint effort to develop this platform. In 1988, UNIX International was formed to provide industry-wide representation to the process of creating an evolving SVR4. As a result of these efforts, SVR4 complies with most existing industry standards and contains important functionality from the main variants of UNIX: SVR3, BSD 4.2/4.3, SunOS, and Xenix. Today UNIX belongs to the joint collaboration between UNIX Systems Laboratories and Novell (USL/Novell).

SVR4 is also fully compliant with POSIX 1003.1, the X/Open Portability Guide Issue 3 base (XPG3 Base), and ANSI C. AT&T has also defined a new version of the System V Interface Definition (SVID) for SVR4 called SVID3. SVID3 is a superset of POSIX and Application Binary Interface (ABI). (ABI is discussed further in the next sections.)

SVR4 features include:

- ABI—Permits application developers to develop "shrink-wrap" software.

- Memory management support—Provides greater efficiency in program execution through memory mapped files, shared memory, swapping to ordinary files, portable hardware address translation.

- Streams—Provides a uniform protocol independent communication interface.

- Virtual File System (VFS)—Offers greater flexibility, additional functionality, and improved performance. VFS, an enhanced file system, allows several different file systems to coexist on the same system. Different file types appear invisible to the programmer. As a result, programmers can design and install new file system types in a clean, straightforward manner. SVR4 defines several different file system types as standard options, including: S5, ufs, rfs, nfs, proc, fifo, specfs, and bfs.

- Real-time features—Include fixed priority real-time process, user process priority manipulation, and high resolution timers.

SVR4's Application Binary Interface (ABI) Standard

The SVR4 ABI comprehensively defines the interface between applications and System V Release 4. The ABI provides application binary compatibility across systems platforms with similar processor architecture and binary compatibility across all systems running SVR4 of the same architecture.

The ABI specifies the complete environment including system services, libraries, files, calling conventions—everything an application needs to run—plus the file formats, media types, and installation procedures to be used to package and install the application. The ABI is a contract: System vendors promise that their systems will run any software that conforms to the ABI, and software developers promise to write applications that will run on any ABI platform.

Since UNIX runs on many processor architectures, the ABI is actually a family of specifications consisting of two interacting parts: generic and processor-specific ABIs. The generic ABI describes those elements of the binary interface that are constant across all architectures. For a processor architecture to support the ABI, a processor-specific ABI must be defined. The SPARC ABI, for example, consists of two sections: the generic part and a SPARC-specific part. ABI specifications have also been developed for other architectures, including the 680X0, 88000, 80x86, and MIPS RISC.

The processor-specific ABI definition for SPARC is based on several standards, including POSIX 1003.1, ANSI C, X11, SVID 3, and X/Open[1]. The ABI specification includes a generic ABI with software packaging/media and installation, file formats, character representation, object file format (ELF - Executable and Linking Format), libraries (system, C, network, RPC, etc.), application environment, commands, file system structure, and window system (optional). The processor-specific ABI includes machine interface, data representation, function call sequence, operating system interface (address space, page size, process stack), coding examples, dynamic linking tables, and system data interfaces (header files).

The processor-specific SPARC ABI was developed by Sun, AT&T, and SPARC International Inc. SPARC system vendors are developing systems that support the SPARC ABI. Software developers have a wide range of platforms—from laptops to supercomputers—requiring only one version of their software for the entire SPARC market.

---

1. Consult the X/Open Portability Guide, Edition 3 (XPG3)

The SPARC ABI lets a developer write an application and "shrink-wrap" the software (that is, distribute it in its final, binary form), knowing that it will run on any SPARC machine, even those not yet built when the software was written. The ABI also means that a hardware developer can build a new SPARC computer, knowing that existing and future SPARC software will run on that machine. Most important, users will have an array of hardware and software combinations that best meet their needs.

SPARC Application Binary Interface

The SPARC ABI mandates dynamic linking and shared libraries, new features developed by Sun and part of SVR4, so that software built today can run far into the future. With dynamic linking, a program postpones the resolution of external references until runtime. The program knows which library routine it needs, and the system provides the right interface. As the ABI evolves (for example, to incorporate new industry standards), old software can be supported with compatibility libraries while new software can use the latest system features. As a side benefit, dynamic linking decreases the size of the executable files to be distributed and the amount of disk space required. Dynamic linking allows library code to be shared, making it possible to construct facilities out of shared libraries rather than implementing them in the kernel or server process. Window system tool kits are good examples of this sort of service.

The SPARC ABI is a detailed definition of the binary interface, including details such as calling sequence and object file format, meaning that even complex applications such as compilers and debuggers can be written. In contrast to standards that are controlled by a single company, the SPARC ABI has an explicit, industry-wide definition with verification suites defined by SPARC International to ensure conformance. Through SPARC International, the industry itself guides SPARC. This open definition leads to controlled evolution, since more interests are represented in changes to the standard.

The benefits brought on by a SPARC ABI include scalability of implementations and economics of scale.

Scalability

A key design goal for the SPARC architecture was the ability to have a wide range of implementations in a variety of technologies. Together, the SPARC ABI and the scalability of the SPARC architecture mean that the same binary program can run unchanged on platforms ranging from laptops to supercomputers. The SPARC architecture can move quickly into new technologies, and the SPARC ABI helps software move onto those new platforms. Dynamic linking is, once again, key. Rather than binding into the application all the details of the hardware configuration and system interface, dynamic linking accesses system- and platform-dependent services. When the application is started on a particular platform, the libraries best suited to that platform are linked with the program for optimum performance along with portability.

Economics

The standardization of the binary interface helps create larger markets for software vendors, making potential revenues larger while increasing the economics of scale, thereby lowering costs to users. Software suppliers can develop fewer versions of their software, reducing the costs of testing, distributing, and supporting software. Favorable economics leads to the availability of larger numbers of applications. More applications encourage more customers to use computer systems based on UNIX and SPARC. The synergy between platform vendors and applications vendors made possible by the SPARC ABI creates a positive feedback loop in which the number and choice of applications grow with the SPARC installed base; and the SPARC installed base growth accelerates as more applications are ported to SPARC/UNIX.

Although SunOS has significant new technology beyond UNIX, it remains fully compatible with UNIX SVR4. It complies with all the major industry standards including POSIX 1003.1, X/Open, and SVID level 3. Furthermore, SunOS preserves the UNIX SVR4 ABI.

SunOS 5.x, the Operating System Component of Solaris

While SVR4 consolidates the leading versions of UNIX—Xenix, BSD, SunOS, and System V—SunOS 5.x goes beyond SVR4 capability by introducing extensive new functionality, including symmetric multiprocessing with multithreads and real-time enhancements.

SunOS with symmetric multiprocessing (SMP) and a multithreaded kernel (discussed further in Chapter 7), significantly accelerates I/O processing and concurrency, increasing the performance of mission-critical, commercial, and technical applications.

SunOS 5.x is a highly symmetric operating system which allows multiple threads to execute concurrently in the operating system. In fact, several processors can even execute concurrently within the same kernel component, such as the file system, or a device driver (see Figure 1-9).

SunOS improves the underlying implementation of the next generation of SPARC systems by offering a multithreaded kernel to increase overall application throughput. Benefits of SunOS multithreading include increased application responsiveness, enhanced process-to-process communications, the ability for programmers to create efficiently structured programs, and efficient use of system resources. In addition, SunOS system software provides standard interfaces for MP applications, so that software developers can achieve unrestricted application portability. Chapter 7, "SunOS Multithreading Architecture," elaborates on these benefits.

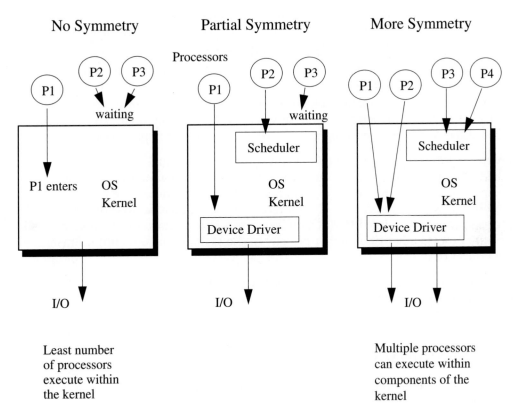

Figure 1-9   *Symmetry with the SunOS 5.x Kernel*

In addition to symmetric multiprocessing and two-level thread control, SunOS 5.x contains the real-time extensions of UNIX SVR4, with additional enhancements from SunSoft™. These capabilities make SunOS ideal for applications that depend on split-second response, such as on-line transaction processing. These features include the following:

- Fixed priority real-time processes (also in standard UNIX SVR4). SunOS allows processes to be classified as real-time processes. These processes have fixed priorities that are not affected by the system's heuristic priority adjustment algorithm.

- User process priority manipulation (also in standard UNIX SVR4). Users can increase or decrease the priority of processes by issuing a system call `pnocntl()`. This feature gives the user control over system response.

- High resolution timers (also in standard UNIX SVR4). The timers in SunOS can be programmed to provide microsecond granularity notifications. This feature is particularly useful for monitoring real-time events.

- Completely preemptive scheduling (SunOS value-added). As a result of using locks for mutual exclusion (see "Synchronization Architecture" in Chapter 7), the SunOS kernel has also been made completely preemptive. Since all critical data structures are protected by locks, interrupts can be serviced as soon as they occur, and, if necessary, scheduling can be initiated immediately after the interrupt is processed.

- Process priority inheritance (SunOS value-added). As a result of preemptive scheduling, processes in the kernel could suffer from starvation or indefinite postponement. In such a scenario, a high priority process could need a critical resource held by a low priority process, yet not receive that resource because the low priority process is never scheduled to run. SunOS corrects such occurrences by making the low priority process inherit the higher priority of the waiting process until it finishes with the critical resource.

- Deterministic and guaranteed dispatch latency (SunOS value-added). SunOS provides deterministic scheduling response and guarantees various dispatch latencies on different hardware platforms.

Solaris Value-added Features

SunSoft has added the following features to enhance the Solaris operating environment.

ONC+

The phrase *"The Network is the Computer"*™ which has its origins in the early days of Sun's Open Network Computing (ONC), more than any other phrase symbolizes one of the key technologies—ONC+— that brings the Solaris operating environment into the forefront of computing technology.

ONC+ is a second-generation, distributed-computing environment consisting of a set of core services for high-performance, enterprise-wide distributed computing. The ONC+ core services in Solaris 2.x include:

- Transport-independent Remote Procedure Call (TI-RPC)—Provides runtime transport independence, allowing a single binary version of a distributed application program to run on multiple transports.

- eXternal Data Representation (XDR)—Provides an architecture-independent method of representing data, resolving differences in data byte ordering, data type size, representation and alignment.

- Transport Layer Interface (TLI)—the communications layer underneath ONC+ in Solaris 2.x—Makes RPC protocol-independent, allowing RPC programs to run across multiple network transports (e.g., TCP/IP, OSI).

- NFS, a multithreaded distributed file system—Provides transparent access to remote file systems on the network.

- Network Information Service Plus (NIS+)—a hierarchical enterprise naming service—Simplifies the management of a changing network environment. NIS+ provides a secure, extensible information base for storing system information, such as host names, network addresses, and user names. It serves as a central point for implementing changes to the network, such as addition, removal, and relocation of resources.

- Lock Manager (LM)—Allows users to coordinate and control access to information by supporting file and record locking across a network. It can prevent two or more users from simultaneously modifying the same file or record and possibly destroying valuable data.

- Automounter—Automatically mounts and unmounts remote directories on an as-needed basis, providing increased transparency and availability of NFS file systems. The Automounter supports replication of frequently read and rarely written files, such as system binaries, by allowing remote mount points to be specified with a set of servers rather than with a single server.

- PC-NFS Daemon, a small program that runs on the ONC-based server—Provides authentication and print-spooling services to PCs running a DOS implementation of ONC.

OpenWindows

The developer environment of Solaris features an upgraded version of the popular OpenWindows applications development platform, OpenWindows V3 (OWV3). OWV3 provides application developers with the technologies and products to accelerate user-interface development and to create networked applications that are easy to use and adapted for the international market.

The Solaris environment builds on X11, the industry's most widely adopted network-based windowing technology, by integrating it with NeWS®, based on the PostScript imaging model, to create a powerful new X11/NeWs™ core. This new core allows developers to create WYSIWYG (what you see is what you get) applications across the network.

ToolTalk®, an integral part of OpenWindows V3, is a message-based application interoperability solution. ToolTalk allows applications to exchange information and automatically to update each other by means of procedural or object-oriented messaging technology.

OPEN LOOK Graphical User Interface

The Solaris 2.x user environment is defined by DeskSet V3, a full range of productivity applications and utilities based on the OPEN LOOK graphical user interface.

OPEN LOOK provides simple and efficient use of windows, menus, and a mouse. The OPEN LOOK interface describes the look and feel of the desktop, so the user works intuitively with buttons, pointers, scrollbars, and icons instead of with complex UNIX commands.

DeskSet provides an enhanced set of applications including Workgroup Calendar Manager, Multimedia Mail, Network File Manager and Magnify Help™. The Workgroup Calendar Manager enables users to schedule their own appointments as well as to access colleagues' calendars to schedule time with them.

Multimedia Mail offers users the ability to attach text, graphics, sound and video to mail messages and send to them across networks.

The Network File Manager features an easy-to-use and consistent graphical front-end, allowing users to represent files on the screen and to access them anywhere on the network with a simple point and click of the mouse.

Magnify Help allows users to click on a specific icon to see a brief help message on the screen. For more help, users can access the help handbooks that provide on-line detailed help on the use of a specific icon or application. In addition, users can access a hypertext-based, on-line tutorial that provides a walk-through of the Solaris environment.

DeskSet provides icons that are internationally understood by users, a crucial feature for conducting business in the worldwide commercial markets. The Solaris environment also enables users in other countries to customize their desktops with date and time format and local language messages, enabling them to use the simple desktop metaphor within a local context.

Part of the Solaris family is a product group called the Commercial Extensions Products. It provides additional support for network security and system administration, and consists of Account Resource Management, Online: DiskSuite, and Online: Backup facilities.

- Account Resource Management is a set of administrative security features that enhances account protection and usage control. Supplementing the standard UNIX login and password mechanisms, ARM provides the account protection and access denial that are critical in many environments.

- Online: DiskSuite allows system administrators to improve file availability, conserve disk space, and facilitate systems management. On-line DiskSuite provides a number of technologies, including: disk mirroring, that is the system "mirrors" a user's file on another disk and automatically uses it in case of a system failure; disk striping, which increases application performance by spreading the I/O load across several disks; and disk concatenation, which enables system administrators to easily move large files around the network without interrupting users.

- On-line: Backup provides for safe and automatic on-line backup of all files across the network. It reduces the time and cost of backup and contributes to system availability.

For application developers, the Solaris environment provides the Open Windows Developer' Guide (called Devguide). This user interface builder significantly reduces development time and costs. Devguide enables developers to interactively construct an OPEN LOOK-based interface for their application, complete with menus, scrollbars, buttons, and other objects, without developers writing a line of code. Devguide includes code generators which generate the appropriate toolkit code to define the user interface, significantly increasing developers' productivity while reducing time to market.

MOTIF for Solaris 2.2 (SPARC)

The Motif graphical user interface provides application developers, end-users and system vendors with standardized application presentation on a wide range of platforms, which support the X-Window System (X11R5).

Motif 1.2.2 Developer's Toolkit provides software developers with a a comprehensive set of tools to create applications with a Motif look-and-feel GUI. It includes the Motif 1.2.2 libraries, Motif Window Manager, and User Interface Language (UIL) compiler.

Some of the key benefits are:

- Standard, widely available API, portable across many platforms

- Based on X11R5 libraries, with support for internationalization

- Support for drag-and-drop operations, allowing software developers to provide graphically rich user models for selecting and transferring data within and between Motif applications

- Easy-to-use PC windowing-style interactive behavior

- UIL, which provides a means of describing the initial state of a Motif application in a set of modules outside the application code, facilitating fast prototyping, easy localization and logical separation of the functionality of the application from the user interface

The technical survey that follows highlights the SPARC building blocks and SunOS features that contribute to the development of advanced high-performance multiprocessor system architectures.

1

The SPARC Architecture 2

SPARC (Scalable Processor ARChitecture) is an open, scalable Reduced Instruction Set Computer (RISC).

SPARC is an open architecture, which means that the technology is available to multiple semiconductor vendors. Developers have access to everything necessary to build SPARC systems, including the processor architecture, integrated support chips, system software, development tools such as silicon and system design packages, and engineering support. With the freedom to choose from a variety of SPARC implementations, system developers are not locked into the prices, performance, and rate of innovation associated with a proprietary architecture.

In addition, in October 1990, SPARC International submitted a proposal to the IEEE for the formation of an IEEE committee to standardize the SPARC architecture. SPARC is now on its way towards becoming the first, and possibly only, IEEE standardized RISC architecture, IEEE standard number 1754. SPARC International is an independent, nonprofit corporation founded in January of 1989; it consists of software, hardware (systems), semiconductor vendors and users who want to influence the evolution of the SPARC architecture as an open standard.

SPARC is scalable, allowing implementations to be designed using a variety of semiconductor technologies (from CMOS to gallium arsenide). Various chip implementations (from low-cost, low-integration devices to highly integrated compute engines) and system configurations (from uniprocessor to multiprocessor systems) are possible with SPARC. For example, SPARC implementations have scaled from 10 VAX MIPS in the first SPARC implementations to the current level of 65 MIPS. SPARC gallium arsenide implementations offering up to 250 VAX MIPS are currently in development.

To ensure that system vendors have the broadest possible choice of SPARC components, several semiconductor manufacturers, including Bipolar Integrated Technology, Cypress Semiconductor, Fujitsu Microelectronics, LSI Logic Corporation, and Texas Instruments, are each using their particular skills to develop various implementations of the architecture. For example, several SPARC vendors are designing multiprocessor versions of SPARC; others are working on higher levels of integration; some are focusing on embedded applications; still others are designing SPARC peripherals (see Chapter 3 "SPARC Implementations"). For the SPARC-compatible and clone system developer, vendors provide completely integrated SPARC chip sets. The availability of this technology from multiple vendors leverages the resources of multiple Research and Development teams who work in parallel, providing solutions across a wide spectrum. Technological breakthroughs are readily incorporated.

SPARC as a binary standard ensures the binary compatibility of application programs across different SPARC platforms as a result of the creation of a standard application binary interface (ABI). This move toward an ABI reflects the proliferation of compatible software for all SPARC-based systems. The growing software base, in turn, has attracted more end-users and hardware manufacturers, further increasing production SPARC chip volumes. An advanced architecture designed for future growth—which is open and standard—broadens the market for SPARC vendors. Competition ultimately meets the most important need of end-users—long-term computing solutions at lower prices.

SPARC: Architecture vs. Implementation

The terms architecture and implementation are often discussed as if they meant the same thing. In fact, each is distinct. The single SPARC architecture was carefully defined to permit select semiconductor vendors to develop and market numerous but different implementations.

The SPARC *architecture* is defined by the instructions, data types, register model, and interrupt and trap models. These are defined for the integer unit (IU) and floating-point unit (FPU). Instruction format and a standard interface are defined for a coprocessor unit (CP). The architecture provides the interface between software programs and the computer hardware.

Implementation refers to the gates, logic blocks, caches, memory management units, execution units, and buses. It also refers to process technology, circuit partitioning, and integration levels. While implementation-specific features have a significant bearing on performance, these features are invisible to application software programs, ensuring binary compatibility (sometimes called instruction set compatibility) across multiple implementations.

For example, SPARC's register window model is part of the architecture. Whether separate instruction and data caches or a unified cache is used is a difference germane only to a particular implementation and does not affect binary compatibility.

Architecture Conformance

An implementation that conforms to the definitions and algorithms given in the SPARC Architecture Reference Manual (a SPARC architecture specification) is an implementation of the SPARC instruction set architecture (ISA).

The SPARC architecture is a model which specifies unambiguously the behavior observed by software on SPARC systems. Therefore, it does not necessarily describe the operation of the hardware in any actual implementation.

An implementation is not required to execute every instruction in hardware. An attempt to execute a SPARC instruction that is not implemented in hardware generates a trap. If the unimplemented instruction is nonprivileged, then it must be possible to emulate it in software. If it is a privileged instruction, whether it is emulated by software is implementation-dependent. Appendix L, "Implementation Characteristics," of the *SPARC Architecture Reference Manual* Version 8, details which instructions are not hardwired in existing implementations.

Compliance with the SPARC specification shall be claimed only by a collection of components which is capable of fully implementing all SPARC opcodes, through any combination of hardware or software. Specifically, nonprivileged instructions that are not implemented in hardware must trap to the software such that they can be implemented in software. For the implementation to be complete, by default the implementation must trap and report all undefined, unimplemented, and reserved instructions.

Some elements of the architecture are defined to be implementation-dependent. These elements include certain registers and operations that can vary from implementation to implementation and are explicitly identified in this document.

Implementation elements (such as instructions or registers) that appear in an implementation but are not defined in the SPARC Architecture Manual Version 8 (or its updates) are not considered to be SPARC elements of that implementation.

A "SPARC Architecture Test Suite" is available from SPARC International, Inc., and a "SPARC Architectural Simulator" (SPARCsim™) and Multiprocessing SPARC Architecture Simulator (MPSAS) are available from Sun Microsystems Computer Corporation (SMCC). These tools can serve both to verify a SPARC implementation and to simulate a SPARC uniprocessor and multiprocessor system environment. MPSAS Behavioral Simulator is discussed further in Chapter 6.

Semiconductor Technology Scalability

Three key parameters for achieving performance are the processor's instruction set architecture (ISA), compiler efficiency, and semiconductor technology. To maintain software compatibility, the instruction set must remain fixed. For example, the same instruction set is used for all implementations of the SPARC architecture, ensuring binary compatibility. With today's reliance on high-level language programming, compilers are key to achieving high performance. SPARC compilers including C, C++, FORTRAN 77 with extensions, and Pascal and are optimized and tuned to support SPARC developments. Semiconductor technology is the area where dramatic processor performance improvements have been and continue to be achieved by taking advantage of the latest semiconductor technologies.

SPARC—Multi-level Scalability

As its name implies, the Scalable Processor ARChitecture (SPARC) is designed to be implemented across a broad range of semiconductor technologies, chip implementations, and system configurations. The combination of semiconductor scalability and architectural scalability of SPARC permits system developers to design computers ranging from laptops to high-end multiprocessor systems that all run the same software applications.

As new semiconductor technologies are developed, they have tight restrictions on the number of transistors that can be put on a chip. Complex processor designs, such as those found in Complex Instruction Set Computer (CISC) architectures, require large numbers of transistors, exceeding the capabilities of the latest semiconductor technologies, which limits the processor's scalability. Further, CISC processors have long design cycles and are often not debugged until the technology for which they were designed is nearly obsolete. Because of the complexity of CISC machines, speed improvements (e.g., pipeline enhancements or reduction of the number of cycles per instruction) made possible because of SPARC's simple and scalable architecture, are difficult to implement in CISC.

The simplicity of the SPARC design allows it to be implemented with fewer transistors than most other architectures. For example, the first SPARC integer unit (IU) was implemented in a single 20K CMOS gate array. The simplicity of its design means that SPARC can easily and quickly be implemented, allowing it to take advantage of emerging semiconductor technologies ahead of most other architectures. Currently, systems implemented in gate array, semi-custom, and full custom CMOS and ECL process technologies are available, with BiCMOS and gallium arsenide (GaAs) chips in development.

As new semiconductor technologies mature, permitting larger numbers of transistors on a chip, SPARC implementations can achieve high levels of integration. The simplicity of SPARC frees scarce chip-area resources for additional functions (e.g., memory management, floating point, coprocessor, and cache). For example, developments are under way that will place the entire compute engine of a computer system on a single chip. For embedded applications, additional SPARC support devices are available with integrated functionality (e.g., memory control, I/O interface, DMA, interrupt control, programmable wait states, and memory protection). The freedom of designers to choose from a variety of implementations (from the modularity of chipsets to highly integrated SPARC devices) results in a wide range of systems across the price/performance spectrum as well as low-cost embedded solutions.

Examples of SPARC Scalability

The IU and optional FPU and coprocessor (CP), illustrated in Figure 2-1, make up the core of the SPARC architecture, which can accommodate a variety of implementations and levels of integration. For example, the FPU can be external to the IU or integrated on the same chip. In addition, standard off-the-shelf FPUs from companies such as Texas Instruments and Weitek can be used.

The CP can also be located on the same chip as the IU, or it can be external, depending on the implementation. Today, most implementations provide a CP interface to an external coprocessor. System developers can design and build their own custom CP or use vendor-supplied coprocessors. Alternatively, building block CP designs can be licensed from Sun Microsystems Computer Corporation (SMCC).

Multiprocessor support is built into the SPARC instruction set. This feature is unique among all RISC architectures. Two instructions (swap and "Atomic Load and Store Unsigned Byte") support tightly coupled multiprocessors. With SPARC's multiprocessor capability, systems can be scaled to extremely high performance levels.

The organization and operation of the register windows (discussed later) is clearly defined by the architecture but the number of windows is implementation-dependent, that is, scalable. The IU can contain from 40 to 520 general-purpose registers. This range corresponds to a grouping of the registers into 2 to 32 overlapping register windows, where the actual number of registers and windows depends on the implementation.

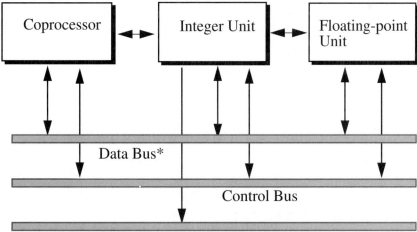

Figure 2-1   SPARC Conceptual Diagram

To maximize scalability, SPARC does not define system components that are visible only to the operating system and that are unseen at the user application level. For example, the SPARC architecture does not specify a memory management unit (MMU). This is an important feature of SPARC. A personal computer may not need an MMU, while a supercomputer definitely does. Furthermore, a multiprocessor system such as a vector machine requires specialized memory management facilities. The SPARC architecture can be implemented with a different MMU configuration for each of these purposes without affecting binary compatibility. System designers are given the freedom to use the appropriate memory management unit for the specific system they are designing, optimizing this important feature of the system.

Sun has defined a Reference MMU for SPARC (see "SPARC Reference MMU" in Chapter 4). The Reference MMU architecture serves as a guideline for system designers on how a preferred MMU for SPARC-based systems should behave. Like the SPARC architecture, the Reference MMU offers scalability, and high performance across different implementations. It is currently available from chip manufacturers in various VLSI implementations and integration levels from MMU-only devices to highly integrated chips containing the MMU, cache controller, and cache tag RAM (see "Reference MMU Implementations" in Chapter 4).

Version 8: Technical Specifications

This section discusses Version 8 of SPARC. For those who are familiar with, or have design experience with Version 7 of SPARC, note that the following information supersedes that of Version 7 of SPARC. Since the availability of Version 7 specifications, several commercial sources have released SPARC processors. All of them conform to the Version 7 architecture.

SPARC Version 8 is upward-compatible from Version 7; all Version 7-conformant software will run on Version 8-conformant processors, with one minor exception discussed in a following section. The Version 8 changes are enhancements to the architecture; the most obvious is the addition of Integer Multiply and Divide instructions. The following sections present a detailed list of changes introduced in Version 8.

Changes to the SPARC architecture since Version 7 are in four main areas: memory model, trap model, data formats, and instruction set.

Enhanced Memory Model

The Version 8 memory model is an upward-compatible extension of the Strong Consistency model implicitly assumed in Version 7. The new model allows building of higher-performance memory systems in either uniprocessor or shared-memory multiprocessor SPARC applications.

Enhanced Trap Model

Trap categories have been renamed since Version 7; the correspondence is as follows:

SPARC Version 7	SPARC Version 8
Synchronous Trap	Precise Trap
Asynchronous Trap	Interrupting Trap
Floating-point/Coprocessor Trap	Deferred Trap

The Version 8 trap model enhancements give SPARC chip implementation designers more latitude in their designs. The privileged and essentially user-code-transparent trap architecture includes some new trap types. It also allows for new, implementation-specific traps.

A given trap may be implemented as either "precise" or "deferred," although each implementation must provide a way to handle traps precisely. For more detail on the trap model refer to the SPARC Architecture Reference Manual Version 8, Chapter 7.

Data Formats

Quad- (128-bit) precision data format replaces the extended- (96-bit) precision format. No existing SPARC application code uses extended-precision floating-point arithmetic. So, although this one change is not strictly upward-compatible with SPARC Version 7, the impact is insignificant.

Instruction Set

Version 8 modifies the definitions of some SPARC instructions as follows:

- Extended-precision floating-point operations are now quad-precision operations.

- IFLUSH has been renamed FLUSH; its definition has expanded to encompass multiprocessor systems and processor implementations with separate instruction and data memories.

- FQ Optional—The floating-point queue (FQ) is optional for SPARC implementations that choose to make floating-point traps precise instead of deferred.

- New FSR.*ftt* Value—A new value, invalid_fp_register, is defined for the FSR.*ftt* field. Use of the new register is optional. If implemented, its use indicates attempted execution of an instruction that refers to an invalid floating-point register number.

A few instructions have been added to the Version 8 architecture:

- Store Barrier instruction (STBAR)

- Integer Multiply instructions (SMUL, SMULcc, UMUL, UMULcc)

- Integer Divide instructions (`SDIV`, `SD1Vcc`, `UDIV`, `UD1Vcc`)

- Floating-point Multiply Single to Double (`FsMULd`)

- Floating-point Multiply Double to Quad (`FdMULq`)

- Ancillary State-Register access instructions (`RDASR`, `WRASR`), of which `RDY`/`WRY` and `SBAR` are subcases

- NOP ("promoted" from being a pseudo-instruction)

SPARC Architecture Overview

The SPARC architecture was defined at Sun Microsystems between 1984 and 1987; it was derived from the RISC work done at the University of California at Berkeley from 1980 through 1982. A team of Sun engineers with operating system, compiler, and hardware experience enhanced the Berkeley design for commercial use. The enhancements included new floating-point support, multiprocessor support, and a small but significant change to a portion of the register architecture to expand the support for optimizing compilers.

SPARC defines the instructions, register structure, and data types for the integer unit (IU) and IEEE standard floating-point unit (FPU). It allocates opcodes and defines a standard interface for a coprocessor unit (CP). It assumes a linear, 32-bit virtual address space for user application programs. The data bus size is implementation-dependent. As Figure 2-2 illustrates, SPARC does not define system architecture components, such as I/O interface, cache architecture, or memory management unit (MMU) that are visible only to the operating system and that are unseen at the user application level.

The SPARC architecture defines simple instructions, all 32-bits long, in three formats, with single-cycle execution for most instructions. Integer, IEEE floating-point and coprocessor instructions can be executed concurrently with architectural support for program concurrence and precise traps. Multiprocessor support is built into the instruction set. This feature is unique among RISC architectures.

SPARC has technical features that set it apart from other RISC architectures. Contributing to SPARC's high performance are its overlapping register windows. Register windows allow for multiple register use without the time-consuming saves and restores to main memory characteristic of fixed register set designs found in other RISC architectures.

Register windows and tagged arithmetic, found in SPARC systems but not in other commercial RISC machines, can support excellent performance for expert system applications developed with object-oriented languages such as Lisp and Smalltalk.

In SPARC, an 8-bit address space identifier field (ASI) can be used to manage system resources. This field allows the system address space to be divided into 256 separate 4 Gbyte areas.

Architecture Level

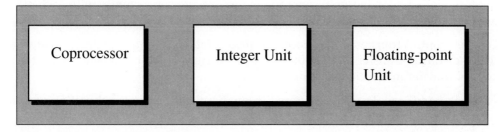

System-level Architecture Extensions

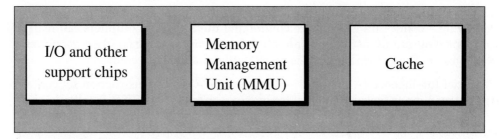

Figure 2-2   SPARC On-chip and System Level Resources

The SPARC architecture has the following features:

- A linear, 32-bit address space

- Few and simple instruction formats—All instructions are 32 bits wide, and are aligned on 32-bit boundaries in memory. Three basic instruction formats feature uniform placement of opcode and register address fields. Only load and store instructions access memory and I/O.

- Single cycle execution—Most instructions execute in a single cycle.

- Few addressing modes—A memory address is given by either "register + register" or "register + immediate."

- Triadic register addresses-—Most instructions operate on two register operands (or one register and a constant) and place the result in a third register.

- A large "windowed" register file—Unique to SPARC, the processor has access to a large number of registers configured in overlapping sets.   This access permits compilers to automatically cache values and pass parameters in registers. At any one instant, a program sees eight global integer registers plus a 24-register window into a larger register file. The windowed registers can be described as a cache of procedure arguments, local values, and return addresses.

- A separate floating-point register file—Software configures the file into 32 single-precision (32-bit), 16 double-precision (64-bit), 8 quad-precision registers (128-bit), or a mixture thereof. Floating-point operations can execute concurrently with each other and with integer (IU) and coprocessor instructions.

- Delayed control transfer—The processor always fetches the next instruction after a delayed control-transfer instruction. It either executes it or not, depending on the control-transfer instruction's "annul" bit.

- Fast trap handlers—Traps are vectored through a table and cause allocation of a fresh register window in the register file.

- Tagged instructions—The tagged add and subtract instructions assume that the two least-significant bits of the operands are tag bits.

- Enhanced delayed control transfer—The processor fetches the next instruction following a control transfer before completing the transfer. Compilers can rearrange code, placing useful instructions after a delayed control transfer, thus maximizing throughput. The delayed branch is an example of a delayed control.

- Artificial Intelligence (AI) support—Unique to SPARC, the instruction set contains tagged arithmetic instructions for use by languages such as LISP, Smalltalk, and Prolog.

- Multiprocessor support—Unique to SPARC, two special instructions (swap and "Atomic Load and Store Unsigned Byte") support tightly coupled multiprocessor systems. One instruction performs an atomic read-then-set-memory operation; the other performs an atomic exchange-register-with-memory operation.

- Coprocessor support—The architecture defines a straightforward coprocessor instruction set, in addition to the floating-point instruction set. Coprocessor operations can execute concurrently with integer (IU) and floating point (FPU) instructions.

- Scalability for speed—Speed scalability refers to chip geometry (the size of the smallest lines on a chip). As lines become smaller, chips become faster. When an architecture is too complicated, it becomes more difficult to shrink the size of the lines. The simplicity of SPARC makes it scale well. Consequently, SPARC systems can become faster as semiconductor technology advances. Further, speed scalability also allows for quicker implementation in different technologies.

- Scalability of systems—Unique to SPARC, flexible integration of cache, MMU, FPU, multiprocessor, bus size, and the number of register windows allow implementations at a price/performance suitable for systems ranging from laptops to supercomputers.

Figure 2-3 illustrates the SPARC register set.

A complete specification of the architecture is available in the *SPARC Architecture Reference Manual, Version 8.0*. Copies can be obtained from SPARC International Inc.

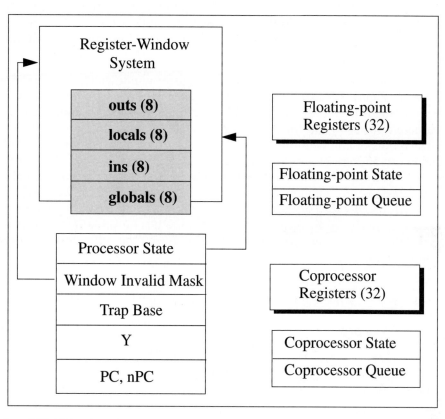

Figure 2-3   SPRAC Register Set

Integer Unit Architecture

SPARC matches the needs of high-level languages by supporting exploratory programming languages and environments, such as Lisp, Prolog, and Smalltalk. To achieve these benefits, Sun selected a windowed-register model for the integer unit (IU). Although the register structure is defined by SPARC, component manufacturers have the freedom to implement the optimum number of register window sets to meet price/performance requirements of their target market.

The IU can contain from 40 to 520 general-purpose registers. The registers are organized into conceptual groups called register windows. The register windows overlap, allowing certain registers between adjacent windows to be shared. The actual number of register windows ranges from 2 to 32, as defined by the architecture, and is dependent upon the implementation. The number of windows is not discernible by a compiler or application program. Note that a chip with only two windows (40 registers) functions as a fixed (nonwindowing) set of registers. In this case, code (not able to take advantage of the higher performance provided by windowed registers) would execute properly, although more slowly.

Figure 2-4 illustrates the circular stack nature of register windows for a seven window implementation. Figure 2-5 also illustrates the register windows structure but from a flat perspective. At any time, a program can address 32 integer registers: 8 ins, 8 locals, and 8 outs of the active window, and the 8 global registers that are addressable from any window. The 8 outs of one window are also the 8 ins of the adjacent window. Although an instruction can address 24 windowed registers, a single window actually comprises 16 registers—8 ins and 8 locals. The overlapping nature of the register windows makes them ideal for multitasking environments like UNIX, where parameters can be quickly passed between procedures. Because of the overlapping nature of the register windows where specific registers are shared between the windows, there is no actual movement of parameters. Rather, parameters are simply shared between the caller and callee register windows (see Figure 2-6).

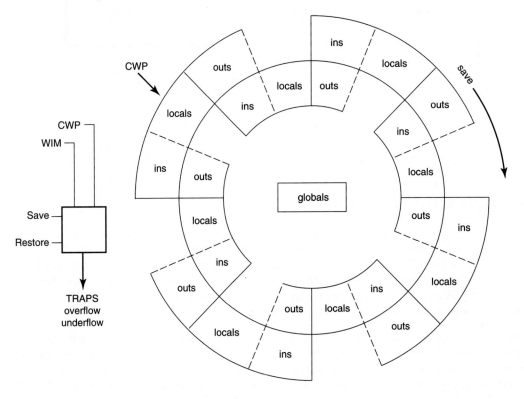

Figure 2-4   SPARC Register Windows

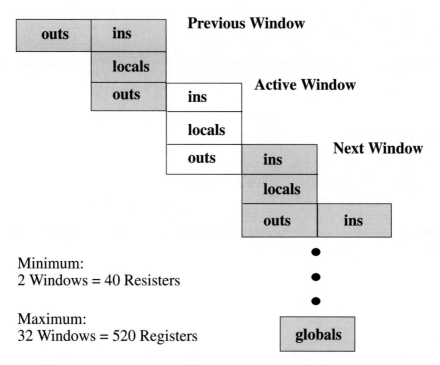

Minimum:
2 Windows = 40 Resisters

Maximum:
32 Windows = 520 Registers

Figure 2-5   Register Windows (another perspective)

Register windows can be managed in several ways to tailor the operation of SPARC to specific application needs. For example, real-time applications require fast context switching and deterministic behavior. One approach used in real-time systems is to use the register windows in a non-overlapping cache-like manner (Figure 2-7). Windows are saved only if no window is available to load the initial window of the required process. Thus, if a window is available at the time of the interrupt, no registers need be saved. Under these conditions, context switching can occur multiple times between high and low priority processes without any memory references if both tasks fit in the register windows at the same time.

Another register window management approach for real-time is to allocate a register window to a specific task or groups of tasks. For example, a high-speed task might be allocated its own set of register windows. Context switching to or from that task would *never* require saving or restoring its register windows.

In addition to the windowed registers, the IU contains several other processor status registers. The window invalid mask register (WIM) controls the size of the window stack. The program status register (PSR) holds a user/supervisor bit, condition codes (negative, zero, overflow, and carry), the 4-bit processor interrupt level, floating point and coprocessor unit disable bits, the current window pointer (CWP), and an 8-bit version/implementation number. The trap base register (TBR) holds a programmable base address for the trap table and an 8-bit field that identifies the type of the current trap. Like the WIM, the PSR and TBR are accessible only to the operating system. One other special register, the Y register, is used in multiplication and division operations. The Y register is accessible to application code.

Instruction Set

The instruction set of SPARC was designed for fast execution of compiled code, especially code generated by compilers that optimize register usage. Unnecessary instructions, (e.g., complex instructions common to CISC machines) are not implemented in the SPARC architecture. All instructions are hardwired, and most execute in a single machine cycle. In addition, specific instructions are included for multiprocessor applications and support of AI languages.

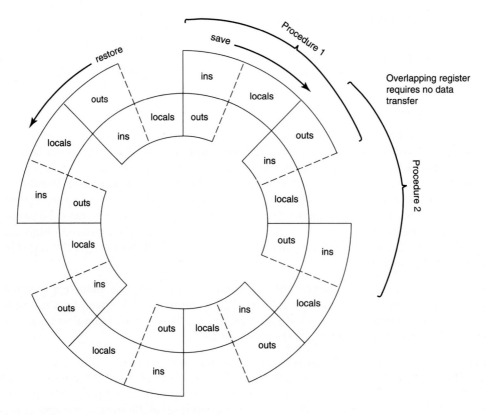

Figure 2-6   Parameter Passing Between Processes

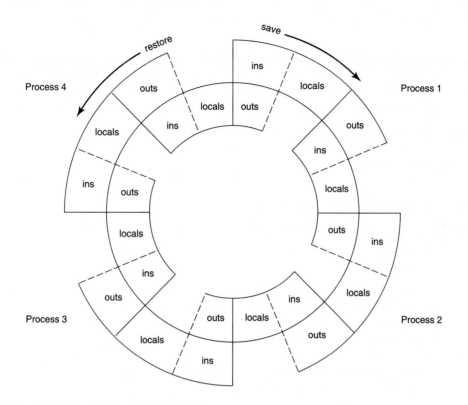

Figure 2-7   Cache-like Register Window Model

The SPARC architecture instructions fall into the following basic categories:

- **Load and Store instructions**—These instructions are the only ones that access memory. They use two registers or a register and a constant to calculate the memory address involved. Half-word accesses must be aligned on 2-byte boundaries, word access on 4-byte boundaries, and double-word accesses on 4-byte boundaries. The alignment restrictions greatly speed up memory access.

- **Arithmetic/logical/shift instructions**—These instructions compute a result that is a function of two source operands in registers and place the result in a register. They perform arithmetic, tagged arithmetic, logical, or shift operations. Tagged arithmetic is useful for implementing AI languages.

- **Coprocessor operations**—These operations include floating-point calculations, operations on floating-point registers, and instructions involving the optional coprocessor. Floating-point operations execute concurrently with IU instructions, with other floating-point operations, and with coprocessor operations. This architectural concurrence hides coprocessor implementation details from the applications programmer.

- **Control-transfer instructions**—These instructions include jumps, calls, traps, and branches. Control transfers are usually delayed until after execution of the next instruction, so that the pipeline need not be flushed every time a control transfer occurs. Compilers can, therefore, produce code optimized for delayed branching.

- **Read/write control register instructions**—These include instructions to read and write the contents of various control registers. Generally, the source or destination is implied by the instruction.

Floating-point Architecture

SPARC systems are designed for optimal floating-point performance and support single-, double-, and quad-precision operands and operations, as specified in the ANSI/IEEE 754 floating-point standard.

The FPU has thirty-two, 32-bit registers. Double-precision values occupy an even-odd pair of registers, and quad-precision values occupy an aligned group of four registers. The floating-point registers can hold a maximum of either 32 single-, 16 double-, or 8 quad-precision values. The FPUs registers are accessed externally only via memory load and store instructions. The SPARC IU does not contain instructions to allow for the transfer of operands directly between the IU itself and the FPU. Floating-point load and store double instructions improve the performance of double- and quad-precision programs.

Coprocessor Architecture

SPARC supports additional coprocessors. Like the FPU, the coprocessor (CP) has its own set of registers, executes instructions concurrently with the IU and FPU, and can be disabled by a state bit in the PSR of the IU. Like the FPU, which supports precise trapping, the CP includes a coprocessor queue that records all pending coprocessor instructions and their addresses at the time of a coprocessor exception.

Multiprocessor (MP) Support

SPARC defines a uniprocessor, "single thread of control" architecture, but SPARC has special support instructions for MP systems. Programs running on a SPARC implementation execute only a few more instructions than on a CISC chip and have fewer data memory references, so SPARC chips are ideal for high-performance, tightly coupled multiprocessor systems.

Two special instructions support tightly coupled multiprocessors: swap and "Atomic Load and Store Unsigned Byte" (ldstub). These instructions provide an efficient synchronization mechanism to enforce atomic operations in MP environments by providing the means to develop complex synchronization protocols. The following examples demonstrate swap and ldstub instructions.

```
example:SWAP (%r1.M)
{
        temp := memory (M);
        memory (M) : = %r1;
        %r1 : = temp;
        return (temp);
}

example:LDSTUB (%r1,M)
{
        temp := memory (M);
        memory (M) := 0xff;
        %r1 := temp;
}
```

The swap instruction exchanges the contents of an IU register with a word from memory, while preventing other memory accesses from intervening on the memory or I/O bus. It can be used in conjunction with a memory-mapped coprocessor to implement other synchronization instructions, such as the non-blocking "fetch and add" operation, which fetches a word and adds a value supplied by the processor to the word in memory.

The ldstub instruction reads a byte from memory into an IU register and then writes the same byte in memory to all 1s (see preceding examples), also while precluding intervening accesses on the memory or I/O bus. The ldstub instruction can be used to construct semaphores. It operates on a byte, rather than a word, because a byte suffices and is the smallest addressable unit on SPARC. Also, memory-mapped device registers with which ldstub is sometimes used may be only 8 or 16 bits wide.

SPARC Architecture Version 9

SPARC Architecture Version 9 specification offers performance and feature enhancements beyond those of Version 8 while maintaining upward binary compatibility.

Version 9 was developed cooperatively by leading SPARC microprocessor architects from over a dozen companies including Amdahl Corporation, Ericsson, Fujitsu Limited, HaL Computer Systems, Hyundai, ICL, Interactive Systems, LSI Logic, Matsushita, Oracle Corporation, Philips International, Ross Technology, Sun Microsystems, and Texas Instruments.

2

Version 9 contains new instructions, enhanced support for the UNIX operating system, and continued enhancements in multiprocessor support. Version 9 offers complete 64-bit extensions to the SPARC Architecture Version 8, on which current superscalar SPARC implementations, such as Texas Instrument's SuperSPARC™ and Cypress Semiconductor's HyperSPARC™, are based. These SPARC implementations are discussed further in Chapter 3.

At the time of this book's development, SPARC International announced availability of the SPARC Version 9 specification. Since no Version 9 chip implementations are available as of this writing, the remainder of the book will focus on currently available Version 8 implementations. SPARC Version 9 features include the following enhancements.

64-bit Extension

All Version 8 integer registers have been extended to 64 bits in Version 9, and all register commands work on the full 64-bit register, with full hardware support for 64-bit arithmetic, including multiplication and division. Addressing is via a 64-bit linear address space, enabling next generation SPARC machines to more efficiently handle very large applications. The architecture provides dual integer condition codes to enable 32-bit and 64-bit code to co-exist efficiently and reliably. Other enhancements include support for a 128-bit floating-point format, and addition of four floating-point condition registers.

New Instructions

Several new instructions, specifically for SPARC superscalar implementations, were added in Version 9. New conditional move instructions minimize branches and increase performance in both superscalar and superpipelined machines. New atomic memory access instructions and a more flexible memory model allow more efficient synchronization in large scale multiprocessors. Also, 64-bit integer multiply and divide instructions were added, as well as load and store quad-word instructions to load and store 128 bits at a time. Other instructions were added for branch prediction, since branches are typically difficult to implement. The new branch prediction instructions eliminate many of the delays associated with branches by reducing the total number of instructions executed, thereby speeding up program execution.

UNIX Operating System Support

Version 9 was enhanced to simplify development of fast, modular client/server or microkernel UNIX implementations. These enhancements provide support for new microkernel models of operating systems with support for lightweight threads. A new privileged registers structure is included, enhancing the ability to access important control bits faster while also being transparent to the user-level applications.

To improve context switch and trap handling speed and reliability, Version 9 includes a hardware trap stack and improves SPARC register window handling. Some of the benefits include more efficient code execution and faster context switching through a more flexible register window structure. This new window structure allows for context switching between different processes. The register windows are used as banks of registers to achieve no-overhead context switching. Version 9 also includes support for object-oriented software.

Multiprocessor Enhancements

The Version 8 architecture pioneered a formal model of the interaction of a processor with memory. Version 9 continues this formalism and has added a more relaxed execution order. Individual processors can now synchronize efficiently using a new Memory Barrier instruction.

Version 9 allows processors employing superscalar and superpipeline techniques to use any valid order of execution. Version 9 also adds an atomic compare-and-swap instruction that pioneers the use of wait-free multiprocessing algorithms.

Support for Advanced Compiler Optimization Instructions

Version 9 includes support for conditional move instructions. Conditional moves eliminate branch delays. Support for advanced compiler optimizations is included as well, in order to take advantage of new optimizing compiler techniques. One of these new enhancements includes instructions that perform pre-fetching of data and instructions that reduce the memory latency, thus preventing a program from waiting for the memory to respond.

The 64-bit Application Binary Interface (ABI)

Concurrent with the development of Version 9, SPARC International is developing the Version 9 ABI, and is now cooperating with UNIX International to adopt that work. This work represents an extension of the Version 8 ABI, enabling both Version 8 and Version 9 binaries to run on any Version 9-compliant machine. The Version 9 ABI will be the basis of the SPARC International work to extend the scope of the SPARC Compliance Definition for applications and platforms based on Version 9 technology.

Support for Advanced Superscalar Processors

Version 9 includes support for advanced superscalar processor designs such as SuperSPARC and HyperSPARC (discussed in Chapter 3). Version 9 supports superscalar processors in several ways. Having more floating-point registers available allows computation of more things in parallel. Support for speculative loads is important, and having multiple condition codes allows more things to occur in parallel. Using branch prediction cuts down on branch penalties.

Support for Reliability and Fault Tolerance

Version 9 provides some features for enhanced reliability and fault-tolerance demands. One of these is a specific instruction called compare-and-swap which is useful in fault tolerant applications. It also provides an efficient mechanism for handling multiprocessor synchronization.

Version 9 Development Tools

SPARC International and HaL Computer Systems are working together to make available tools that will assist in the development of Version 9-compliant products. These tools include a full Version 9 instruction set simulator that will run on existing SPARC Version 8 and Version 7 systems, a Version 9 architectural test suite, an automated test vector generator, and a Version 9 assembler and linker. Contact SPARC International for further details.

In the next chapter, we'll examine some of the SPARC implementations and of the architecture.

SPARC Implementations 3≡

Implementation refers to the gates, logic blocks, caches, memory management units, execution units, and buses. It also refers to process technology, circuit partitioning, and integration levels.

SPARC chip sets with various implementations of the integer unit, floating-point unit, memory management unit, and cache functions, which form the compute engine of many systems, are available from various SPARC semiconductor manufacturers. Table 3-1 lists some of the implementations that have made their way into systems manufactured by Sun Microsystems Computer Corporation along with several others which are used in a wide range of applications.

SPARC Embedded Controller implementations have found great use in a wide range of embedded applications while others, like the SPARC ECL implementation from Bipolar Integrated Technology (B5000), have found suitable applicability in high performance systems from CRAY® Research. Still others, such as the KAP implementation from Solbourne Computer Corporation, have remained proprietary in their use.

The wide range of SPARC implementations offers designers versatility in system design. Designers can begin with a single SPARC chip to serve as a compute engine of a uniprocessor system and incrementally migrate to a multiprocessor system by implementing a SPARC MBus Module architecture. MBus modules are basically subsystems which at a minimum contain a single SPARC processor. Other, more advanced, higher performance MBus modules contain dual processors, cache, FPU, arbitration logic, clock, and synchronization circuitry. MBus modules open new ways for developing multiprocessor systems by eliminating problems associated with using a different processor/memory bus for different processor implementations. The end benefit to the SPARC system designer is realized by cost-effective processor migration/evolution without the time and expense associated with hardware redesign. More on MBus in Chapter 5.

Table 3-1   SPARC Implementations

Implementation	Vendor	Comments/Application
MB86900	Fujitsu	Sun 4/100, 4/200
MB86901	Fujitsu	Sun SPARCstation™ 1, 1+

Table 3-1   SPARC Implementations   (Continued)

Implementation	Vendor	Comments/Application
L64801	LSI Logic	Sun SPARCstation1, 1+
CY7C601	Cypress/Ross	Sun SPARCstation2, Sun SPARCserver™ 490 & 690
L64811	LSI Logic	Sun SPARCstation2
MB86930	Fujitsu	Embedded controller
L64901	LSI Logic	Embedded controller
CY7C611	Cypress/Ross	Embedded controller
MB86903	Fujitsu	Combined IU/FPU, Sun SPARCstation IPC & ELC
L64831	LSI Logic	Combined IU/FPU SparKIT™-40/MBus
HyperSPARC™	Cypress/Ross	Superscalar CMOS
TMS390Z50 Superscalar BiCMOS	Texas Instruments SuperSPARC™	Sun 600 Series MP and Sun SPARCstation10 SPARCserver 1000 SPARCcenter 2000
TMS390S10	Texas Instruments microSPARC™	Low cost workstations, X-terminals, SPARC portables
B5000	Bipolar Integrated Technology	ECL Implementation CRAY S-MP Supercomputer
SPEC	SPEC, Inc.	Gallium arsenide 200MHz
KAP™	Solbourne Computers	Solbourne S4000

Current SPARC Implementations

From the list of SPARC implementations shown in Table 3-1, an overview of a selected few, including their associated support devices, follows. Most of the implementations have been incorporated into uniprocessor and multiprocessor SPARC systems from Sun Microsystems Computer Corporation.

The Fujitsu MB86900

The MB86900 was the first implementation of the SPARC architecture. The MB86900 SPARC implementation (also referred to as the Fujitsu S-16 chipset) was used in the original Sun 4/100 and 4/200. The MB86900 was designed in a single 20,000 gate CMOS gate array from Fujitsu. Cycle time was 60 ns.

Since the SPARC architecture allows different implementations to have different numbers of register windows, the MB86900 provides 120 general purpose registers, eight of which are global registers and the rest of which are divided into seven overlapped windows of 24 registers each.

From a system design perspective, the MB86900 employs a single 32-bit data bus (D<31:0>) and a single 32-bit address bus (A<30>) for interface to the cache or memory. In the MB86900, the low portion of the address bus is sent (unlatched) a cycle earlier than the high portion. In a cache-based system, this timing would allow the system designer to latch the low address externally and use the output of the latch directly to access the cache data and cache tag RAMs. The high portion of the address is not as critical as the low portion and therefore is latched on the chip before it is sent out. The external latch in this scheme also functions as a buffer for driving the heavily loaded cache address lines. Once the cache tags are read, the high portion of the address is used to compare the tags in that cycle and to send a cache miss/hit signal to the processor. The missed address must be saved and regenerated externally during a cache miss. Other features of this early implementation include:

- Use of the D<31:0> bus for fetching instructions as well as data. This use results in two-cycle execution of single-word load and three-cycle execution of double-word load instructions.

- A four-stage pipeline.

- Execution of taken branch instructions in one cycle; non-executed branches take two cycles. The control logic is designed so that all branches are assumed to be taken and the target instruction is fetched immediately. The processor, however, ignores the target instruction if the condition code evaluation resulted in false condition.

- Tight coupling of the floating-point unit with the integer unit; integer instructions can execute concurrently with floating-point operations.

- Use of a separate 32-bit F bus (F<31:0>) for dispatching floating-point instructions to the floating-point unit.

The MB86900 works with a companion floating-point controller chip and can be interfaced to either Weitek W1164/W1165 or Texas Instruments TI-8847 arithmetic units capable of delivering 1.1 to 1.8 MFLOPS for double-precision Linpack benchmark.

MB68900 System Configuration

Figure 3-1 shows a basic system configuration using the MB68900, a floating-point controller chip, the Weitek 1164 multiplier chip, and Weitek 1165 ALU chip. These four chips are the core of any system designed around MB68900 processor.

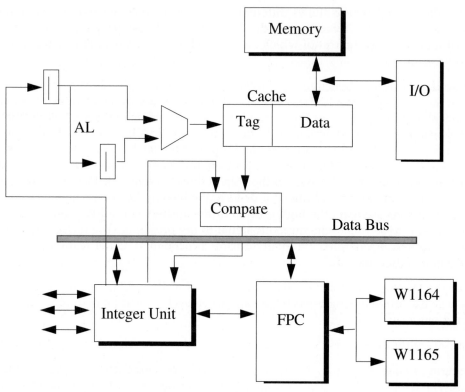

Figure 3-1   MB86900 Basic System Block Diagram

As shown, two separate 32-bit buses are used for address and data to access the storage. The cache is an essential part of the system and must be capable of delivering one instruction to the processor in every cycle. The processor bus cycles and the timing of I/O signals are optimized for cache-based systems. For example, the address bits are divided into two groups: low-address bits and high-address bits. The low-address bits (bits 17...00) are available earlier than the high-address bits (bits 31...16). In a cache-based system this scheme allows the designer to use the lower address bits to read the cache RAMs and cache tags and to use the higher address bits to compare the tags later. The low-order and high-order bits of the address are overlapped in bits 16 and 17, allowing direct addressing of a virtual cache with a size up to 256K bytes.

From a hardware point of view, the higher 16-bits of the address bus are taken directly from an on-chip memory address register that holds the address of the instruction or data to be fetched in that cycle. The lower 18-bits of the address are "un-latched" and sent a cycle earlier.

The bits are latched in an external memory address register before they are used. The processor provides necessary control signals that synchronize the internal and external memory address registers.

The processor also sends out an 8-bit address space identifier (ASI) field for the instruction or data. Normally, these eight bits carry information such as processor mode (user/superuser) and the type of fetch (instruction/data). During the execution of alternate load and store instructions, these bits carry the ASI for load or store data.

Every processor cycle in this system is either an instruction fetch cycle, a load cycle, or a store cycle. When the processor sends out an instruction address, the cache is accessed and the instruction is fetched into the processor in the same cycle. This instruction may or may not be the correct instruction, depending on whether the instruction actually existed in the cache. Within the same cycle the cache tags are read and checked.

In the case of a cache hit, the processor treats the fetched instruction as a correct instruction and continues to fetch the next instruction in the following cycle. However, if the cache is missed, the external cache controller logic must hold the processor operation in the cycle following the cycle in which the instruction is fetched. This can be done by asserting one of the MHOLD input signals. Assertion of the MHOLD signal forces the processor pipeline into a WAIT state for the duration of the time that the signal is asserted. During this period, the cache controller fills the missed cache line and strobes (using MDS signal), writing the missed instruction into the processor's instruction register when ready. The processor, in this case, ignores the previous instruction and uses the new instruction as the correct instruction to be executed. Since a new instruction address is sent every cycle before the tag comparison for the previous address is made, the cache address must be saved by the external circuitry for one extra cycle. This delayed address will be needed by the cache in the case of a cache miss; otherwise it is ignored.

The MB68900 bus request/grant operations are implemented in a simple manner. Basically, the processor can be forced into a WAIT state in any cycle for any duration of time by means of a BHOLD signal. A LOCK signal is provided and is asserted when the processor is in the middle of a multicycle bus transaction that should not be aborted. Normally, a device that needs the bus simply asserts the BHOLD signal in the first cycle in which it sees that the LOCK signal is inactive. Once the processor is in the WAIT state, AOE and DOE control signals can be used to turn off the output drivers of the chip during the bus grant period.

All I/O devices are memory-mapped and normal load/store instructions are used to read from or write into the I/O devices. The 8-bit ASI output signals determine the mapping of user space, superuser space, MMU, cache tags, and other I/O devices in the system. A set of alternate load and store instructions are defined which are privileged and which can be used to access any address space between 0 and 256 in the system.

Interrupts are vectored. An on-chip trap base address register is used to point to the interrupt table. External interrupts are given to the processor through four interrupt input signals. Any logic level other than zero on these four inputs is detected by the processor as an external interrupt request. This value is compared with the current processor interrupt level, which can be set in the processor status register; the interrupt is taken if the external interrupt request level is greater than the processor interrupt level. The highest level interrupt (level 15) is defined to be nonmaskable.

The Cypress/Ross SPARC Chipset

The Cypress SPARC chipset consists of the CY7C601 integer unit, the CY7C602 floating-point unit, the CY7C604 cache controller and memory management unit, the CY7C605 cache controller and memory management unit for multiprocessing, and the CY7C157 cache storage unit. Figure 3-2 illustrates the chipset.

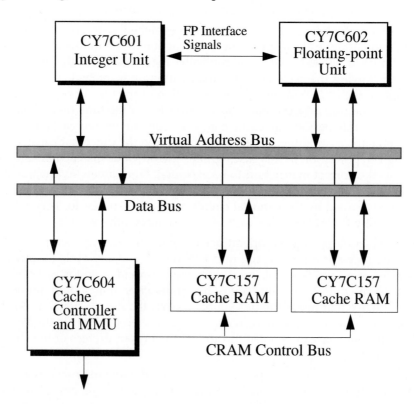

Figure 3-2   CY7C601 Uniprocessor System Configuration (Courtesy Cypress Semiconductor Corporation)

The CY7C601 Integer Unit

The CY7C601 Integer Unit (IU) is a high-performance, full-CMOS microprocessor delivering up to 29 MIPs of computing power at 40 MHz. It is a complete implementation of the SPARC integer instruction set and fully supportive of a multitasking operating system. It derives its high throughput from a four-stage pipeline in which instructions start every clock cycle.

Contained in the CY7C601 is a large register file comprising a total of 136 registers divided into overlapping register windows and global registers. Each of the eight register windows contains 24 registers, and 16 are shared with adjacent windows for passing parameters between routines, significantly decreasing main-memory accesses. Eight global registers are available to all processes at any time.

The CY7C602 Floating-point Unit

The CY7C602 floating-point unit (FPU) is a complete implementation of the SPARC floating-point instruction set. It combines a floating-point processor and controller, for a full 64-bit floating-point engine that interfaces directly to the CY7C601and memory. The CY7C602 delivers over six double-precision Linpack MFLOPs.

The CY7C604 Cache Controller and Memory Management Unit

The CY7C604 cache controller and memory management unit (CMU) is a complete implementation of the SPARC Reference MMU architecture, with a 4K page size and large linear mappings of 256K, 16 Mbytes, and 4 Gbytes. The CY7C604 has an on-chip, 64-entry, fully associative translation look-aside buffer (TLB) and hardware support for table-walking. In addition, the CY7C604 contains all the logic necessary on chip to create a direct-mapped 64K virtual cache using the CY7C157 Cache Storage Unit. On-chip, the CY7C604 has 2K direct-mapped virtual-cache tag entries and provision for 4096 multiple contexts. The CY7C604 offers both write-through with no-write-allocate and copy-back with write-allocate cache policies. It also has separate, full-cache line read and write buffers.

The CY7C604 can lock entries in the on-chip TLB and can also lock the cache, preventing critical translations and code from being replaced. This double-locking feature is essential for real-time applications in order to have deterministic response time. No other RISC or CISC microprocessor has this capability. The CY7C604 is in production at 25, 33, and 40 MHz.

The CY7C157 Cache RAM

The CY7C157 cache storage unit (CSU) is a 16K x 16 synchronous SRAM. It features a common I/O architecture and has a self-timed byte-write mechanism. The CY7C157 has registers for all addresses, a chip enable, write enables, and latches for data input and data output. The CY7C604/CY7C157 cache and MMU combination gives users two additional benefits. First, both chips are designed to scale in clock frequency with the CY7C601 and CY7C602 throughout their lifetime. Multiprocessor chip manufacturers who do not have a tightly coupled and integrated cache and MMU will not be able to provide this capability. At higher frequencies, other architectures will incur wait states and deliver lower performance than at the lower frequencies without wait states. The second benefit of the CY7C604/CY7C157 combination is the ability to cascade several chips together to provide up to 256K of cache and 256 TLB entries. The CY7C157 is in production at 25 MHz (33 ns), 33 MHz (24 ns), and 40 MHz (20 ns).

The CY7C601 chip set is discussed in more detail in Chapter 9 as we examine specific system configurations that make up high performance MP systems.

The Fujitsu MB86901

In 1988, Fujitsu introduced the S-25 family, a multichipset targeted at entry-level systems. The S-25 family consists of the MB86901 IU and the MB86920 MMU. The MB86901 IU, used in the first generation of Sun SPARC workstations and servers, provided 12- and 15-MIPS versions. The floating-point unit available for the S-25 is the Weitek 3170. Figure 3-3 illustrates the S-25 chipset.

The Fujitsu MB86920 MMU is one of the VLSI implementations of the SPARC reference MMU and is designed to be closely coupled to the MB86901 IU. The MB86920 MMU offers 4 Gbytes of virtual address space and 64 Gbytes of physical address space, with up to three levels of page tables supporting a 4 Kbyte page size. The MB86920 also supports up to 256 contexts, selective flushing and probing, automatic miss processing, and 36-bit physical addresses.

Because the MMU performs protection and permission checking on every access, it can be used in both on-line and off-line virtual caches. The MMU provides additional features, such as reporting of external bus errors and caching of intermediate table entries, which go beyond the scope of the basic reference MMU. The MB86920 replaces many discrete components on the system board and provides certain cache-control functions, such as cache-access checking.

The LSI Logic L64801 and L64811

LSI Logic introduced its first microprocessor based on the SPARC architecture in December 1988. The L64801 was designed in conjunction with Sun Microsystems for use in the desktop SPARC workstations and servers product line.

The high performance of the L64801 and its relatively low cost were major factors contributing to the early success of SPARC in general, as evidenced by the demand for the new Sun workstation at that time. The L64801 has also seen use in many other products, from Sun-compatible workstations manufactured by other vendors to board-level and controller products used for data communications and other embedded/real-time applications.

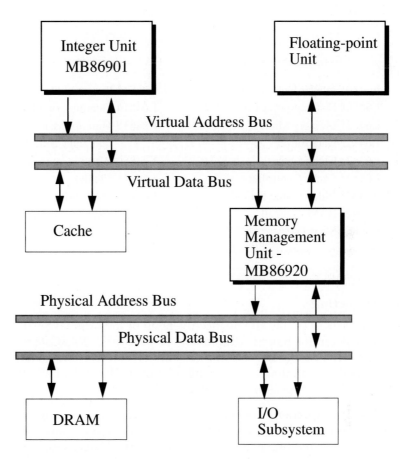

Figure 3-3   Basic MB86901 System Core

LSI Logic has since brought forward two complete families of matched and co-designed chips that work together with no extra glue logic, to allow straightforward and easy design of a SPARC compatible workstation. These SPARC chipset families—SparKIT-20 and SparKIT-25—consist of two complete and distinct chipsets (see Figure 3-4).

Both the SparKIT-20 and SparKIT-25 chipsets provide a complete system-level solution with one-stop shopping for all the required silicon, including all the motherboard chips, color and monochrome monitor interface, and SBus graphics card. Each of the kits also includes a design package with schematics, bill of materials, films, and Gerber tapes (manufacturing kit).

SparKIT-20	SparKIT-25
L64801 Integer Unit	L64811 Integer Unit
L64804 Floating-point Unit	L64814 Floating-point Unit
L64821 Memory Management Unit	L64815 Memory Management
L64822 Data Buffer	Unit and Cache Tags
L64823 Clock Chip	L64850 DRAM Controller
L64824 Cache Controller	L64851 STDIO
L64825 Video Frame Buffer	L64852 M2S (MBus to SBus)
L64826 RAM Controller	L64853 SBus DMA Controller
L64853 SBus DMA	L64855 Frame Buffer

Figure 3-4   LSI LogicSparKIT 20/25 Chipsets

The L64801 Integer Unit

The L64801 Integer Unit (IU) is an enhanced version of the original SPARC microprocessor used in the Sun SPARCstation1 (Figure 3-5), SPARCstation1+, SLC, and IPC workstations. The L64801 SPARC implementation contains 120-general purpose working registers divided into 7 overlapping windows. The 20 and 25 MHz versions delivered 12- and 15-MIPS performance, respectively.

Most of the L64801 instructions execute in a single cycle because of a four-stage pipeline that minimizes interlocks, a bus structure that allows single-cycle instruction/data accesses, and an optimized branch handler. Other L64801 features include:

- High-performance operation of 12 VAX-equivalent MIPS at 20 MHz
- Conformity to Scalable Process Architecture (SPARC) Version 7.0
- Open architecture to support multiple vendors
- Optimization for high-level languages
- Up to 4 Gbytes of direct address space with 32-bit SBus
- Simple instruction format with fast instruction cycle using four-stage pipeline
- Large central register file divided into seven overlapping windows of 24 registers each
- Pipeline interlocks in hardware
- High-performance interface to L64804 FPU for concurrent execution of floating-point instruction
- Multitasking support with user/supervisor mode and privileged instructions

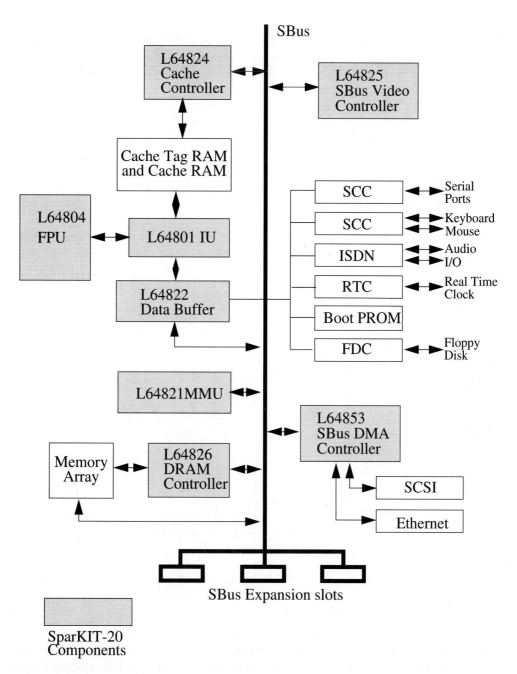

Figure 3-5   *L64801 System Configuration, SPARCstation1*

The L64801 uses a simple, but efficient, four-stage pipeline as shown in Figure 3-6.

Most L64801 instructions flow through the pipeline in four cycles during which three additional instructions may enter the pipeline. Execution of instructions overlaps, so that effective execution time is a single cycle per instruction. The processor achieves its maximum throughput of one instruction per cycle when a stream of these single-cycle instructions flows through the pipeline.

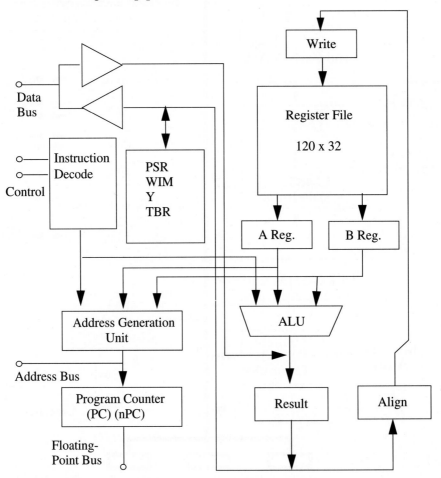

Figure 3-6   L64801 Four-Stage Pipeline

The four pipeline stages are designated Fetch, Decode, Execute, and Write. The Decode, Execute, and Write stages each have an instruction register and an instruction decoder. Each instruction decoder generates signals that control operations later during its own stage and early in the next stage.

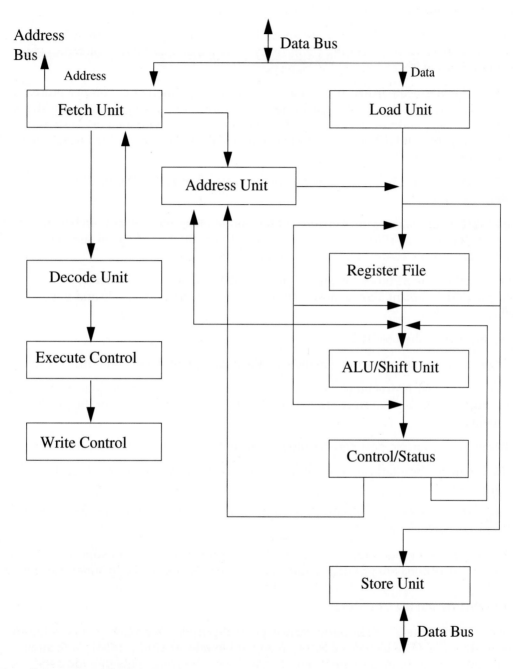

Figure 3-7   L64811 IU Block Diagram

3

The L64811 Integer Unit

The L64811 Integer Unit (IU) is a high-speed implementation of the SPARC 32-bit RISC architecture available in operating frequencies of 40, 33, and 25 MHz, which provide execution rates of 29, 23, and 18 MIPS, respectively.

The L64811 can execute instructions at a rate approaching one instruction per processor clock cycle. The L64811 provides hardware support for multitasking operating systems and fast interrupt and trap processing. The IU communicates with memory systems via a 32-bit address bus and a 32-bit data/instruction bus. Figure 3-7 shows the L64811 internal architecture.

The L64811's pipeline is a four-stage pipeline consisting of Fetch, Decode, Execute, and Write.

The L64811 is compatible with Version 7 of the Sun Microsystems SPARC architecture and executes five types of SPARC instructions: load/store, arithmetic/logical shift, control transfer, read/write control register, and miscellaneous.

All instructions are 32 bits wide and aligned on 32-bit boundaries in memory. A register-to-register arrangement allows most instructions to execute in one cycle and lowers bus traffic.

Other features of the L64811 include:

- Tagged arithmetic instructions to indicate the data type of the operand in AI languages

- Control transfer instructions that allow compilers to rearrange code, placing a useful instruction after a delayed control transfer to take better advantage of the processor pipeline

- Large 136 x 32 triple-port register file for efficient register-to-register operations

- Two coprocessor interfaces, one for a floating-point unit and one for a user-definable coprocessor

- Support for asynchronous traps (interrupts) and synchronous traps (error conditions and trap instructions)

- Support for a multitasking operating system by providing user and supervisor modes (some instructions are privileged and can only be executed while in supervisor mode)

The L64811 IU and the CPU Core

A SPARC CPU Core is a high-performance, general-purpose, reprogrammable computer. The SPARC CPU Core includes a SPARC-compatible Integer Unit (L64811), a floating-point unit, a memory management unit, and a cache. These elements provide data, integer, and floating-point arithmetic processing power and the flexible, fast memory management required to support multiple processes running simultaneously from a large physical memory. Together, these elements are referred to as the CPU Core. Figure 3-8 shows the relationship of the elements in the CPU Core. Figures 3-9 and 3-10 show the L64811 core as the heart of both SBus- and MBus-based systems implementations.

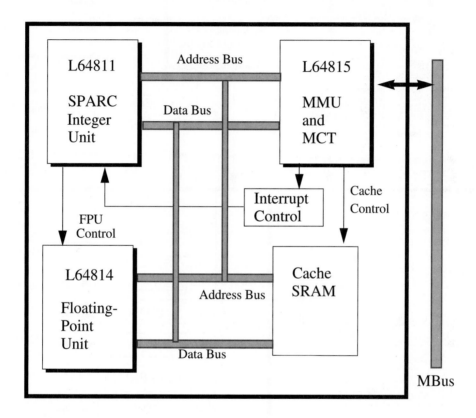

Figure 3-8   L64811 "SPARCORE" Configuration

The L64831 SPARC Integrated IU/FPU

The L64831 was LSI Logic's next-generation, highly integrated SPARC implementation. The L64831 SPARC Integrated IU/FPU combines the functionality of the L64811 Integer Unit (IU) with the L64814 FPU in a single die, thus increasing performance while reducing chip count, board space, and cost. The on-chip FPU complies with the ANSI/IEEE 754-1985 standard for floating-point arithmetic. The L64831 operates at clock speeds up to 40 MHz, which provides execution rates of 29 MIPS.

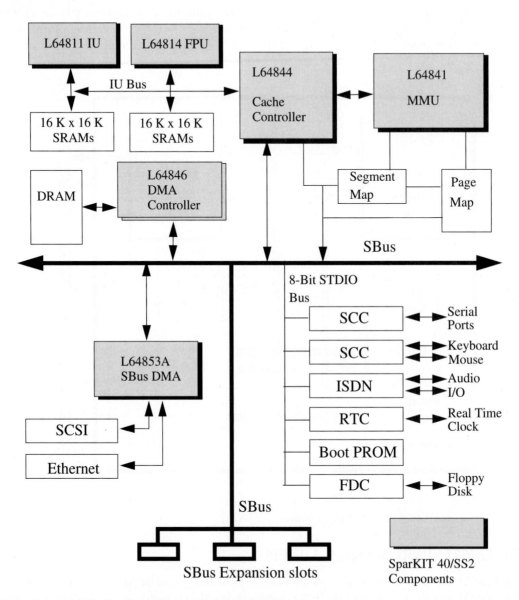

Figure 3-9   L64811 SBus-based System (SparKIT-40/SS2)

The L64831 is socket-compatible with the L64811. Users can replace the L64811 with the L64831 and can easily add floating-point capability to existing systems. The L64831 can replace the L64811 IU and the L64814 FPU in the 40 MHz SPARCstation2 (SS2) and 40 MHz MBus systems as illustrated in Figure 3-11.

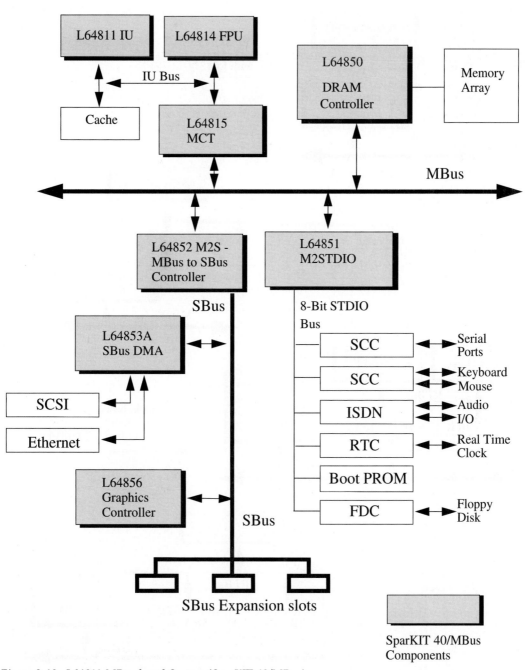

Figure 3-10   L64811 MBus-based System (SparKIT-40/MBus)

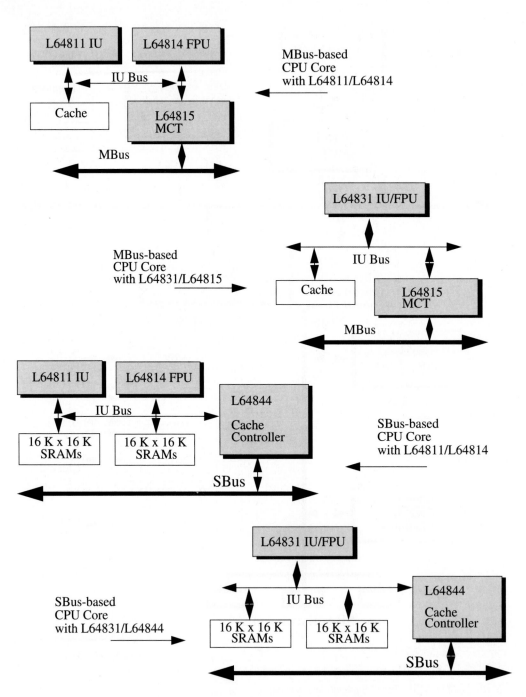

Figure 3-11   L64831 Core System Comparisons (Courtesy LSI Logic Corporation)

Multiprocessor System Architectures

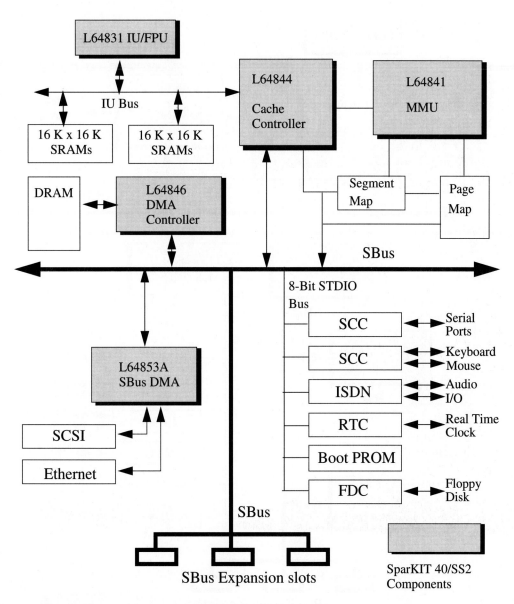

Figure 3-12 L64831 SBus System Architecture

Figure 3-12 shows a block diagram of a typical SparKIT-40/SS2 system incorporating the L64832. Figure 3-13 shows a block diagram of a typical SparKIT-40/MBus system incorporating the L64831.

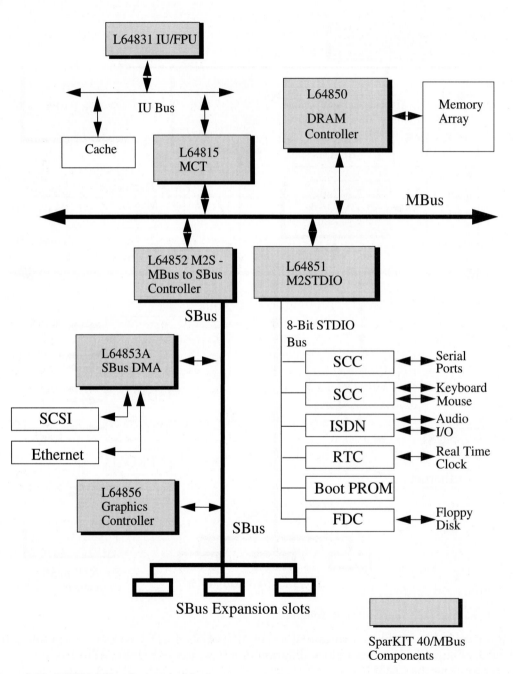

Figure 3-13   L64831 MBus System Architecture

The key features of the L64831 SPARC Integrated IU/FPU include:

- Full 32-bit operation—The L64831 communicates with memory systems via a 32-bit address bus and a 32-bit data/instruction bus.
- 64-bit-wide internal floating-point data path—Provides efficient double-precision performance for floating-point operations.
- Four-stage pipeline—Allows the L64831 to process several instructions (both integer and floating-point) at the same time.
- Two sets of register files—Used when processing either integer or floating-point operations.
- SPARC instruction set—Conforms to Version 7.0 of the SPARC architecture. Floating-point operations implement the ANSI/IEEE 754-1985 standard for floating-point arithmetic. As a RISC-based processor, the L64831 executes the majority of its instruction set in one processor cycle.
- Floating-point queue—Pipelines and sequences operand automatically. This queue allows the L64831 to execute floating-point operations in parallel with integer operations.

SPARC Superscalars

Superscalar architectures boost performance by launching and executing instruction in parallel while circumventing the problems of system with clock speeds of 100 MHz. These processors typically launch two to four instructions in parallel, in a single clock cycle. Superscalar architectures achieve their performance gains from multiple pipelines, as opposed to superpipelined architectures which offer a single, deeper (5 to 10 stages) pipeline.

While superscalar architectures are scalable in frequency and parallelism, they need not increase cycle time as traditional architectures have frequently done to increase performance. They do require more hardware, thus contributing to processor complexity. On the other hand, superpipelined architectures have limited frequency scalability and require reduced cycle time in order to achieve performance gains. Essentially, superscalar architectures allow multiple instructions per clock cycle.

The scalability afforded by SPARC has introduced two superscalar implementations: the Texas Instruments TMS390Z50 SuperSPARC CPU chip and the Cypress CY7C620 HyperSPARC processor. Each of these SPARC superscalar implementations allows virtual drop-in performance upgrades (owing to their plug-in module design approach) for existing system designs and will run existing binary code with significant performance gains.

The TMS390Z50 and the CY7C620 (hereafter referred to as SuperSPARC and HyperSPARC, respectively) processor family of modules offers a simple and efficient modular (via MBus modules) plug-and-play mechanism for increasing performance. However, they differ significantly in their internal architecture and in the manner in which they interface to the MBus.

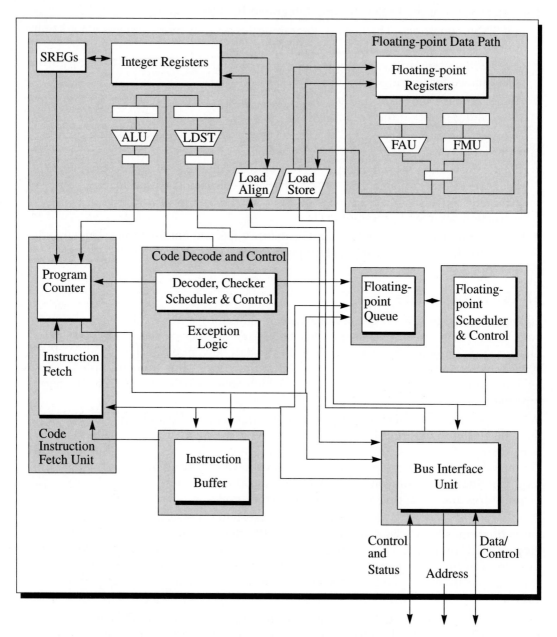

Figure 3-14 The HyperSPARC Processor (Courtesy Cypress SemiConductor)

Multiprocessor System Architectures

HyperSPARC

The HyperSPARC is the central processor that makes up the family of Cypress SuperCore™ MBus Modules. It is integrated on an MBus module along with the CY7C625 cache controller/MMU tag unit (CMTU) and two or four CY7C627 cache data units. Different modules offer one or more CPUs and two or four cache units (128 Kbytes or 256 Kbytes, respectively).

HyperSPARC includes integer and floating-point units and an 8-Kbyte two-way set instruction cache; it can launch two 32-bit instructions per cycle. It contains 1.2 million transistors. The cache controller/MMU unit controls the cache memory units that are not integrated on the CPU and also interfaces to the MBus at 40 MHz. Figure 3-14 illustrates the HyperSPARC processor.

The HyperSPARC Core Unit data path includes the arithmetic and logic unit (ALU) that handles integer arithmetic, logical, and shift instructions. The core unit data path also contains the integer register file (IREGS). The load and store unit (LSU) handles loading and storing of both integer and floating point data. The special register unit (SRU) handles instructions that read and write the SPARC special registers (SRECS).

The floating-point unit data path (FPDP) handles all SPARC floating-point instructions. The FPDP includes the floating-point queue (FPO), the floating-point arithmetic unit (FAU), the floating-point multiplier unit (FMU), the floating-point register file (FREGS), and the floating-point status register (FSR).

The CMTU (CY7C625) is a combined secondary cache controller and memory management unit optimized for multiprocessing systems. Its contains a secondary cache controller, a memory controller, and on-chip physical cache tag memory. The CY7C625 is a high-speed CMOS implementation of the SPARC Reference MMU and supports the SPARC MBus Level-2 protocol for multiprocessing systems. The CMTU is discussed in more detail in "SPARC Reference MMU" in Chapter 4.

The CY7C627 CDU is organized as four arrays of 16-Kbyte static memory with a built-in, one-deep write buffer pipeline, byte write logic, registered inputs, data-in and data-out latches, and data forwarding logic for the write buffer. Writing into the RAM core is delayed until the next write access. To allow data forwarding, the CY7C627 incorporates a comparator to compare the address of the write-buffer to the incoming read address. If a match occurred, data is forwarded from the write-buffer to the current read cycle. The CY7C627 also includes byte-write enables. The CY7C627 requires no glue logic for interfacing to the HyperSPARC (CPU) and the CY7C625 (CMTU).

SuperSPARC

SuperSPARC is a single chip implementation with clock speeds up to 50 MHz. Figure 3-15 illustrates the processor.

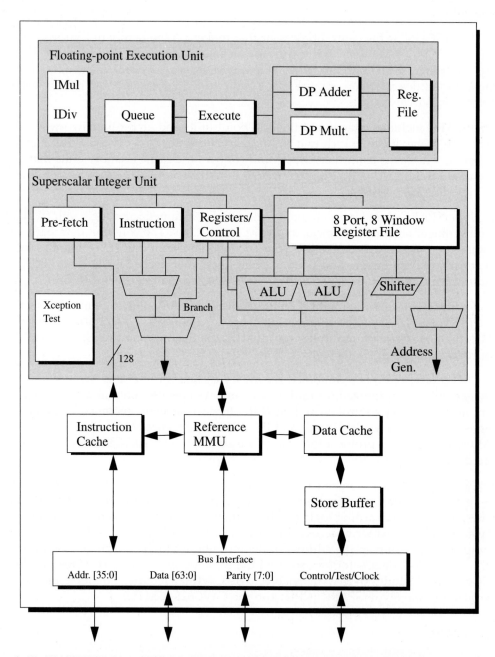

Figure 3-15 TMS390Z50 SuperSPARC Processor (Courtesy of Texas Instruments Corporation)

SuperSPARC includes a tightly-coupled integer unit [capable of up to three instructions per clock cycle (average CPI = 0.75)] and 64-bit floating-point unit, memory management unit, separate fully coherent 20-Kbyte instruction cache, and 16-Kbyte data cache. SuperSPARC also supports a second-level (1Mbyte) cache with the aid of the multi-cache controller (MXCC) chip, while also providing support for circuit and packet switched buses: MBus & XBus respectively, (see Chapter 5, SPARC Multi-level Bus Architectures).

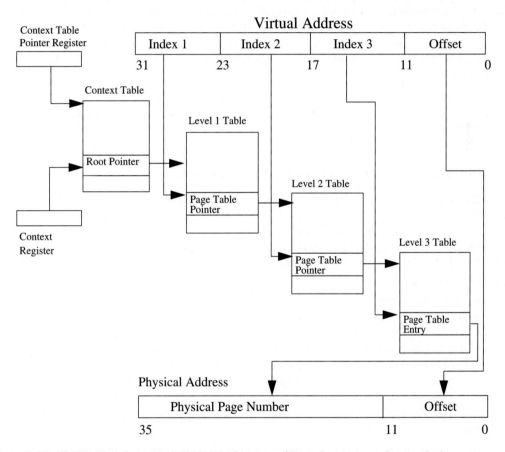

Figure 3-16   TMS390Z50 SuperSPARC MMU (Courtesy of Texas Instruments Corporation)

Integrated within the processor's 3.1 million transistors are most of the support functions normally required to build large-scale multiprocessor systems, low-cost single-user workstations and high-performance embedded controllers. These features include: integer unit, memory management unit, floating-point unit, instruction cache, data cache, store buffer, external cache support, multiprocessor cache coherence support, MBus and XBus support, hardware breakpoints, JTAG emulation, and full testability.

The MMU is an implementation of the SPARC Reference Memory Management Unit (see Chapter 4, "SPARC Reference MMU"). The MMU provides a 64-entry TLB to translate virtual to physical addresses. A second-level page table pointer (PTP) cache and a root pointer cache are included to reduce TLB miss penalties. Figure 3-16 illustrates the MMU.

The external cache support provides a flexible external cache (E-Cache) interface. The MXCC also provides a complete implementation of a large, direct-mapped, physically addressed external cache. The MXCC provides a single-chip interface to the SPARC MBus standard Level 2. It also provides a general purpose packet-switched interface (the XBus) that can be used to interface to a variety of packet bus standards. Typically, the MXCC is employed when a large secondary cache or an interface to a non-MBus system is required.

SuperSPARC and the MXCC are independently optimized to work with fully pipelined cache RAMs, and they both support the SPARC TSO (Total Store Ordering) and PSO (Partial Store Ordering) memory models (see "Software Architecture" in the "SPARC Reference MMU" of Chapter 4).

The Texas Instruments TMS390S10 microSPARC

As of this writing, the TMS 390S10 microSPARC microprocessor (hereafter referred to as microSPARC) represents the latest SPARC implementation resulting from a joint collaboration between Sun and Texas Instruments, with the goal of bringing workstation performance to the world of the desktop for less than the cost of a comparable high-end PC CPU. In fact, the microSPARC implementation resulted from a scaled-down version of SuperSPARC.

The microSPARC is the latest and most highly integrated member of the Texas Instruments TMS390 family. It combines a complete SPARC-compatible processor with critical system logic on a single chip, including built-in instruction and data caches, integer and floating-point units, memory management, and DRAM and SBus control. This level of integration allows manufacturers to produce highly interactive workstations with the fewest components. For example, compared to the previous SPARCstation configurations, with microSPARC a SPARC SBus-compatible system can be built using only microSPARC and two ASICs. Essentially, the workstation manufacturer need only add memory and peripherals.

A reduced parts count means enhanced reliability, less power and heat dissipation, and smaller boards and boxes. microSPARC introduces a new standard of integration —workstation on a chip. In addition, microSPARC provides a cost-effective solution for SPARC-compatible X-Windows (X-terminals) applications (Figure 3-17).

microSPARC features include:

- 32-bit SPARC Version 8 integer unit, fully SPARC-Compliant

- 40 dhrystone MIPS performance

- Economical floating-point unit

- Glueless interface to SBus (5 slots) and memory

- SPARC reference MMU

- Separate instruction and data caches

- IEEE1149.1 (JTAG) boundary scan testability

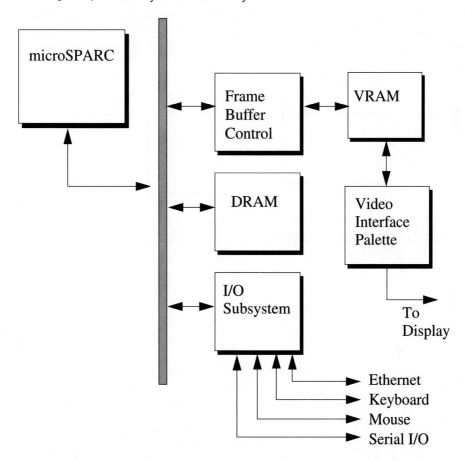

Figure 3-17   Simple X-Terminal Configuration

The processor delivers over 40 dhrystone MIPS of integer performance for commercial users and ample floating-point performance for CAD users. Separate internal cache systems—4 Kbytes for instructions and 2 Kbytes for data—differentiate microSPARC from other SPARC processors. A five-stage pipeline supports single-cycle accesses to cached data. Through its on-chip SBus controller, microSPARC can support up to five SBus devices.

The internal MMU not only provides the functions of I/O and reference memory management as specified by the SPARC Reference MMU architecture, but also contains most of the required memory arbitration logic. With support for system memories of up to 128 Mbytes, microSPARC's memory interface provides complete control and data signals for memory systems with either 32- or 64-bit data buses. These integrated system functions result in a smaller footprint, smaller box, fewer components, enhanced reliability and—most important—lower costs to both the system manufacturer and the end-user.

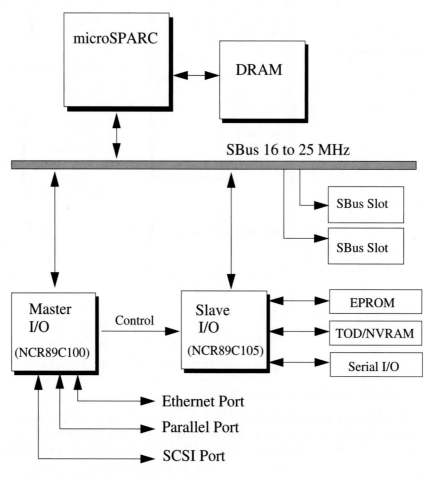

Figure 3-18 Three-chip Workstation Configuration

Figure 3-18 shows a three-chip system combined with NCR's NCR89C100 and NCR89C105 peripheral controllers and microSPARC. This simple configuration allows design engineers to build a workstation around just three integrated circuits plus base memory and peripherals. Because fewer components are required, systems employing microSPARC can offer significant time-to-market advantages and increased reliability.

The Bipolar Integrated Technology Inc. (BIT) B5000 ECL SPARC Implementation

At the time of its introduction, the B5000 SPARC ECL microprocessor delivered new levels of performance to the market and demonstrated the scalability of the SPARC architecture. With an 80 MHz clock rate and up to 65 MIPS performance, the B5000 demonstrated exceptionally fast performance, achieving the objectives of the Sun/BIT joint-development team, that being, increased clock rate and reduced cycles per instruction of the processor relative to previous SPARC implementations.

The B5000 includes a combined 32-bit instruction and data cache with a 2-word interface and instruction prefetching. The B5000 delivers high floating-point performance and reduced integer performance by less than 10%. For real applications, the combined cache can sustain higher integer performance because of the reduced miss cost of a double-word cache interface.

At 80 MHz, the processor-to-cache interface became one of the critical paths in the design and was optimized by selecting:

- directional buses, to reduce wire delay and simplify board layout

- complementary sets of 30-ohm address drivers, to allow two tightly packed cache arrays, which also reduced wire delay

- an early clock for the cache-address register, to offset wire delay

- matched on-chip delay paths for the cache address, cache write enable, and system clock, to reduce skew effects on cycle time

Figure 3-19 illustrates the processor-to-cache interface.

With the clock buffer on the chip, the B5000 compensates for process variations, eliminating the system-by-system tuning normally associated with ECL systems running at this clock rate. Figure 3-20 shows the B5000 block diagram.

The double-word instruction fetch has the additional instruction bandwidth necessary for the single-cycle loads and two-cycle stores. A five-stage pipeline facilitated cycle-count reduction for loads, but increases the number of bypass paths. As a result, the load data and ALU results are written to the register file during their respective write (fifth) stage of the pipeline.

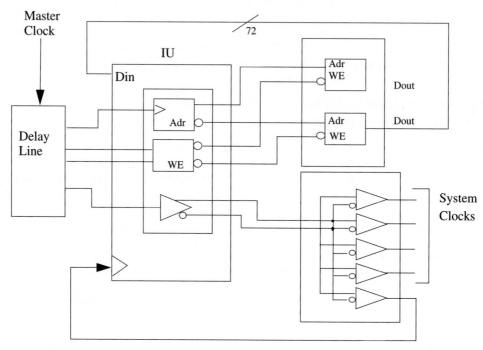

Figure 3-19   B5000 Cache Interface

Using a double-word interface to the cache achieves several other advantages; for example, double-precision floating-point loads and stores can finish in a single cycle. As mentioned earlier, cache fills are faster, taking half as many cache writes to update a cache block as would a 32-bit interface.

Single-cycle, double-precision loads and stores, combined with the BIT floating-point chip set, yield exceptional floating-point performance. As with other SPARC processors, floating-point operations can be dispatched by the integer unit, and integer processing can continue while the floating-point operations run in parallel. The B5100 floating-point controller (FPC) has a four-deep floating-point queue, allowing up to four floating-point instructions to be pending, while integer operations continue.

Although the BIT SPARC chipset has the highest available performance possible, system-integrity issues are not ignored. Soft memory errors can occur in any system, whether it is CMOS or ECL. Most vendors do not provide the needed support for cache and register-file parity. By contrast, the BIT SPARC chipset provides byte parity on all system data paths and register files in both the integer and floating-point units.

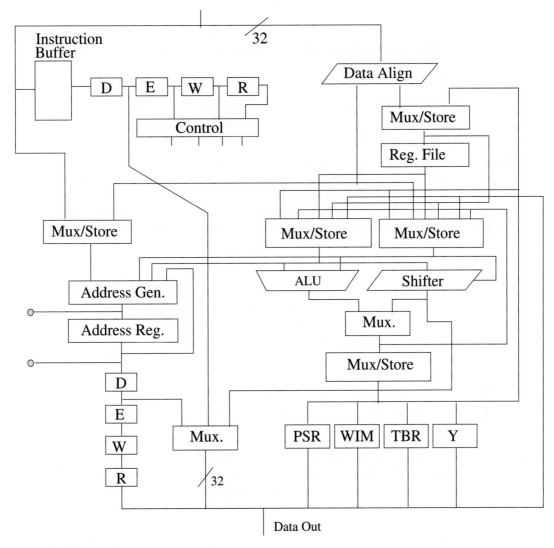

Figure 3-20 B5000 Internal Block Diagram

The B5000's synchronous parity-error traps enable the processor to determine precisely which instruction contained the parity error and, in many cases, to recover from the error. For example, if a cache read contains a parity error, but that cache block has not been modified, the parity-trap routine can invalidate that block and restart the instruction. Processing would then continue without error.

The B5000 supports two coprocessor interfaces. One of them is a dedicated floating point interface, the other one could be used to interface to a user-defined coprocessor. Both coprocessors can operate concurrently with the integer unit. Control signals are provided to branch on condition codes generated by the coprocessors. All exceptions detected by the coprocessors are communicated to the integer unit. The store data bus dispatches instructions from the integer unit to the coprocessors.

Coprocessors maintain their own copies of the program counter which are managed by the integer unit. In case of control transfer instructions, the new program counter is sent to the coprocessors over the store data bus.

The B5000 integer unit dissipates a maximum of 22 watts of power. The package-heat sink assembly is designed to be cooled with forced air. The chip is housed in a ceramic pin grid array (PGA) package that gives users maximum flexibility in thermal management. These PGA packages use a cavity down configuration and incorporate a copper-tungsten slug brazed into the cavity. The silicon die is mounted directly to the slug with a silver glass paste. A path of low thermal resistance is thus provided from the silicon chip to the external area of the slug.

The B5000 is the first commercial single-chip 32-bit microprocessor to be designed in bipolar ECL technology. It is a low-cost approach to achieving mainframe performance in desk-side machines. Cray Research superservers has incorporated the B5000 as the core of their S-MP Supercomputer, as shown in Figure 3-21.

The Cray S-MP system is a SPARC-based superserver. It consists of a four-bus system interconnect implemented as a centerplane (vs. the usual backplane) to both sides of which various system modules can be connected. These modules include:

- Up to eight ECL 67 MHz SPARC processors, each with a 128-Kbyte virtually addressed primary cache and a 512-Kbyte physically addressed secondary cache.

- Up to two vector processors each with a peak 267 MFlops in 64-bit IEEE arithmetic and 128 Kbytes of vector registers arranged in four sets of 16 registers each with 256 64-bit elements. Each vector processor is tightly coupled to a scalar processor, but has an independent direct access to memory. A vector processor occupies the space of two scalar processors.

- Up to four Gbytes of interleaved physical memory supported by a virtual memory system that includes a 16 K-entry address translation cache and 16 Kbyte pages.

- I/O processors, including support for standard I/O buses such as the VME bus. An option for a direct HIPPI connection to the centerplane supports two dual-simplex HIPPI channels, resulting in four HIPPI paths, each with a peak 100 Mbyte/s bandwidth.

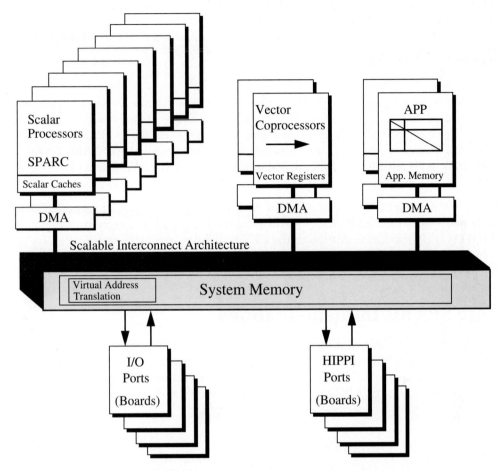

Figure 3-21   Cray Research S-MP System (Courtesy Cray Research Superservers)

As a shared resource, the CRAY S-MP superserver provides resource scheduling, accounting, and hierarchical storage management software, and achieves high utilization rates. The CRAY S-MP operates under the Solaris operating environment SunOS 5.x.

200 MHz Gallium Arsenide SPARC Implementation

Advancements in development tools and process technology during the last decade have changed the role of gallium arsenide (GaAs) technology in digital and analog design. GaAs costs, traditionally dominated by overhead rather than materials, have reduced to the point where GaAs is competing with sophisticated silicon designs in many areas;

wafer sizes have increased while geometries have been reduced to less than 1-micron processes, reducing costs substantially. Increasing experience with GaAs process technology is producing sophisticated, easier-to-use, blindingly fast GaAs designs.

Among these is the first GaAs SPARC implementation by Systems and Processes Engineering Corporation (SPEC), located in Austin, Texas.

SPEC is developing a complete SPARC Version 8 implementation for use in applications by the National Aeronautic and Space Administration Space Data Systems Technology program. The end-product from SPEC is a three-chip 200 MHz GaAs SPARC core with an integer unit, floating-point unit, and memory management unit. This SPARC GaAs chipset along with additional cache SRAM and ECL I/O will constitute a GaAs SPARC module.

As of this writing, SPEC has developed an ALU test chip consisting of compiled data-path elements with measured delays, indicating a critical path through the ALU at 2 ns, 500 MHz ALU performance. Although the CPU will have an S-class certification for space applications, SPEC hopes to market versions of the module for commercial applications such as low power GaAs computers and communications applications.

Future SPARC Implementations

The list of SPARC implementations shown in Table 3-1 will expand considerably during the next decade. Sun Microsystems Computer Corporation is committed to SPARC and (as of this writing) has nine SPARC CPU designs, within three families, currently under development. The microSPARC and SuperSPARC families will be joined by a third family, called UltraSPARC™, a 64-bit SPARC implementation.

The microSPARC Design Family

The microSPARC design family—a "workstation on a chip"—will meet CPU requirements for the low-cost desktop and server, portable and embedded markets. These requirements include high system-level integration on-chip, volume-oriented packaging, strong integer performance, low power consumption, and low cost.

The microSPARC design family is composed of three design "points," called microSPARC, microSPARC II, and microSPARC III. Each point will result in multiple CPU implementations. The microSPARC family is expected to deliver performance scaling to 150 dhrystone MIPS and 100 SPECint 92.

A new floating-point unit, an enhanced integer unit, and power management features are design enhancements to microSPARC II, targeted for 1994. The microSPARC III designs, slated for 1995, will use faster transistors and add external cache memory.

The single-scalar, single-pipeline microSPARC designs are 32-bit architectures based on Version 8 of the SPARC architecture published by SPARC International, thus preserving end user investment in SPARC application software. MicroSPARC processors, manufactured by Texas Instruments, power Sun's recently announced SPARCclassic™ and SPARCstation LX workstations.

The SuperSPARC Design Family

Like microSPARC, the SuperSPARC family also includes three design points, called SuperSPARC, SuperSPARC+ and SuperSPARC II. They are 32-bit Version 8 designs optimized for high-volume multiprocessing, high-performance per clock cycle (SPECint/MHz) and an integer/floating point balance for outstanding application performance. Resulting CPU implementations will include versions beyond 100 SPECint 92 and approaching 200 SPECfp 92.

SuperSPARC+ designs, available in late 1993, will incorporate faster transistors. SuperSPARC II designs, slated for 1994, will incorporate enhanced integer and new floating-point units, plus a dual-launch floating point, increasing overall floating-point performance. SuperSPARC will continue to provide integrated multiprocessing features, and MBus or XDBus upgradeability which offers up to 20-way multiprocessing.

The UltraSPARC Design Family

The UltraSPARC design family is SMCC's next-generation 64-bit SPARC technology, based on the Version 9 architecture specification from SPARC International. The Version 9 architecture supports upward compatibility with all current 32-bit SPARC applications. Resulting CPU implementations will power future Sun workstations and servers. UltraSPARC microprocessors are four-scalar, four-level metal designs, featuring dual-launch floating-point units and providing both uni- and multiprocessor support.

The family features three design points, UltraSPARC I, UltraSPARC II and UltraSPARC III. Each will include multiple CPU implementations. UltraSPARC I and II will utilize .5 micron CMOS processes, while UltraSPARC III uses advanced .5 to .4 micron BiCMOS process technology. This family will ultimately scale in performance, ranging from 700 to 1000 SPECint 92/SPECfp 92 and beyond. CPU implementations based on these designs are expected to arrive between 1995 and 1997.

3

SPARC System-level Resources

4

In addition to SPARC, Sun has defined a memory management unit (MMU) architecture designed specifically for use with SPARC processors. The MMU specification is available to anyone wanting to develop SPARC systems or board-level products. In order to fully understand the SPARC memory system architecture, we first examine the SPARC memory model followed by a detailed discussion of the SPARC Reference MMU.

SPARC Memory Model

The SPARC memory model defines the semantics of memory operations, such as load and store, and specifies how the order in which these operations are issued by a processor is related to the order in which they are executed by memory. It also specifies how instruction fetches are synchronized with memory operations.

The model applies both to uniprocessor and to shared-memory multiprocessors.

In the case of multiprocessor systems, the nondeterministic aspect of the memory model (see below) requires that the result of executing a program on a given implementation must be a possible result of executing the same program on the model machine defined by the architecture. This requirement allows for unspecified (and unpredictable) timing-dependent effects of interprocessor interaction. Note that other events, such as interrupts and I/O, can also cause nondeterministic behavior.

The SPARC architecture is a model which specifies the behavior observed by software on SPARC systems. Therefore, access to memory can be implemented in any manner in hardware, as long as the model described here is the one observed by software. The standard memory model is called *Total Store Ordering (TSO)*. All SPARC implementations must provide at least the TSO model. An additional model, called *Partial Store Ordering (PSO)* is defined, allowing higher performance memory systems to be built. If present, this model is enabled via a system mode bit; if a SPARC Reference MMU is used, this bit is the PSO mode bit in the MMU control register (discussed in "SPARC Reference MMU Architecture").

Machines that implement *Strong Consistency* (also called Strong Ordering) automatically support both TSO and PSO because the requirements of Strong Consistency are more stringent than either model. In Strong Consistency, the loads, stores, and atomic load-stores of all processors are executed by memory serially in an order that conforms to the order in which these instructions were issued by individual processors. However, a machine that implements Strong Consistency may deliver lower performance than an equivalent machine that implements TSO or PSO. Although particular SPARC implementations may support Strong Consistency, software must not rely on having this model available on all machines. Strong Consistency is not the standard SPARC memory model.

Programs written using single-writer-multiple-readers locks are portable across PSO, TSO, and Strong Consistency. Programs that use write-locks but read without locking are portable across PSO, TSO, and Strong Consistency only if writes to shared data are separated by STBAR instructions. If these STBAR instructions are omitted, then the code is portable only across TSO and Strong Consistency. The guidelines for other programs are as follows:

- Programs written for PSO work automatically on a machine running in TSO mode or on a machine that implements Strong Consistency

- Programs written for TSO work automatically on a machine that implements Strong Consistency

- Programs written for Strong Consistency may not work on a TSO or PSO machine

- Programs written for TSO may not work on a PSO machine

Multithreaded programs in which all threads are restricted to run on a single processor behave the same on PSO and TSO as they would on a Strongly Consistent machine.

Basic Definitions

Memory is the collection of locations accessed by the load/store instructions (refer to Appendix B, Sections B.l through B.8 of the SPARC Architecture Manual, Version 8). These locations include traditional memory, as well as I/O registers, and registers accessible via address space identifiers.

Real Memory

Real (or main) memory is defined to be those memory locations accessed when either:

- The ASI field is 8, 9, 0xA, or 0xB

or:

- The ASI field, together with a field in a corresponding MMU entry, implies a reference to real memory. For example, when the Reference MMU is used, physical address pass-through ASIs 0x20-2F refer to real memory.

Real memory should not be accessed by any other ASI, be it a coprocessor register or an ancillary state register. The exact ASI assignments and MMU implementation details that define a real memory access are implementation-dependent.

A defining characteristic of real memory is that operations defined on it are free of side effects; that is, a load, store, or atomic load-store to a location in real memory has no observable effect except on that location. All of the semantics of operations defined on real memory are captured by the memory model.

Input/Output Locations

I/O registers are locations that are not real memory. In contrast to operations on real memory, load, store, and atomic load-store operations on these locations may have observable side effects. The semantics of operations on I/O locations are not defined by the memory model, since these semantics are typically implementation-dependent. All of the axioms of the memory model that constrain the ordering of operations apply equally to operations on real memory and I/O locations. In addition, the order in which operations to I/O locations by a given processor are executed by memory must conform to the "program order" of these operations for that processor. In other words, references to I/O locations are "strongly ordered" among themselves, but behave like TSO or PSO (whichever is applicable) when compared with references to real memory.

I/O locations include the following:

- Those memory locations accessed when the ASI field is not 8, 9, 0xA, 0xB,or 0x20-2F

- Those memory locations accessed when the ASI field is 8, 9, 0xA, or 0xB and a field in a corresponding MMU entry (such as the cacheable bit in the Reference MMU, which identifies the access as an I/O access)

- Possibly, coprocessor registers

- Possibly, ancillary state registers

SPARC assumes that I/O registers are accessed via load/store alternate instructions, normal load/store instructions, coprocessor instructions, or read/write ancillary state register instructions (RDASR, WRASR). In the case of the load/store alternate instructions, the VO registers can only be accessed by the supervisor. If coprocessor instructions are used, whether the I/O registers can be accessed outside of supervisor code is implementation-dependent.

The contents and addresses of I/O registers are implementation-dependent.

Overview of Model

Memory is byte-addressed, with half-word accesses aligned on 2-byte boundaries, word accesses aligned on 4-byte boundaries, and double-word accesses aligned on 8-byte boundaries. The largest datum that is atomically read or written by memory hardware is a double-word. Also, memory references to different bytes, half-words, and words in a given double-word are treated for ordering purposes as references to the same location. Thus, the unit of ordering for memory is a double-word.

Memory is modeled as an N-port device, where N is the number of processors. A processor initiates memory operations via its port in what is called the *issuing order*. Each port contains a Store Buffer used to hold stores, flushes, and atomic load-stores. A switch connects a single-port memory to one of the ports at a time, for the duration of each memory operation. The order in which this switch is thrown from one port to another is nondeterministic and defines the *memory order* of operations. Figure 4-1 illustrates the model.

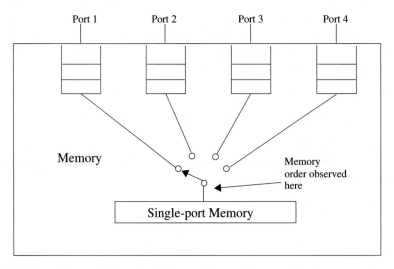

Figure 4-1   Conceptual Model of Memory

For purposes of the memory model, a processor consists of an idealized processor IP and an instruction buffer IBuf. Figure 4-2 illustrates the processor.

IP executes instructions one at a time as specified by the ISP, without overlap, in what is called program order. For each instruction, IP fetches the instruction from IBuf and then executes it, issuing any data loads and stores directly to the processor's memory port. For such a given instruction fetch, IBuf issues an instruction load via the processor's memory port if the instruction is not already in IBuf. The distinction between instruction fetches and instruction loads is important; confusing the two will lead to incorrect conclusions about the memory model.

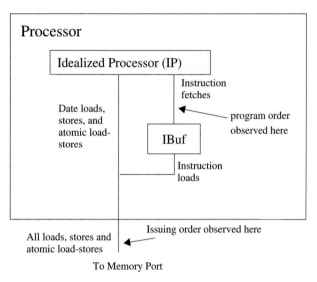

Figure 4-2   Model of Processor

IBuf may also prefetch instructions via the memory port. Thus, IBuf models the effects of instruction pipelining, FIFO instruction buffering, and/or a nonconsistent instruction cache in a processor implementation. Note that the issuing order of data loads and stores conforms to the order of the corresponding instructions in program order. However, in general, the issuing order of instruction loads does not conform to the order of instruction fetches, which defines program order. Also, the interleaving of instruction loads relative to data loads and stores is, in general, not known.

The FLUSH instruction synchronizes instruction fetches with data loads and stores; when a processor executes FLUSH *A*, the data corresponding to location *A* is removed from the IBufs of all processors in the system some time after the execution of the flush. An implementation may choose to flush any portion of IBuf as long as location *A* is included.

Total Store Ordering (TSO)

Total Store Ordering guarantees that the store, flush, and atomic load-store instructions of all processors appear to be executed by memory serially in a single order called the memory order. Furthermore, the sequence of store, flush, and atomic load-store instructions in the memory order for a given processor is identical to the sequence in which they were issued by the processor. Figure 4-3 shows the ordering constraints for this model graphically.

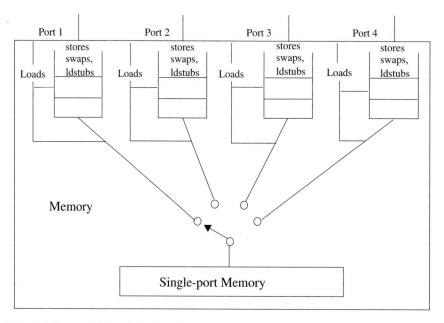

Figure 4-3   *Total Store Ordering Model of Memory*

Stores, flushes, and atomic load-stores issued by a processor are placed in its dedicated Store Buffer, which is FIFO. Thus, the order in which memory executes these operations for a given processor is the same as the order in which the processor issued them. The memory order of these operations corresponds to the order in which the switch is thrown from one port to another.

A load by a processor first checks its Store Buffer to see if it contains a store to the same location (atomic load-stores do not need to be checked for because they block the processor). If it does, then the load returns the value of the most recent such store; otherwise the load goes directly to memory. Since not all loads go to memory, loads, in general, do not appear in the memory order. A processor is blocked from issuing further memory operations until the load returns a value.

An atomic load-store (`swap` or `ldstub`) behaves like both a load and a store. It is placed in the Store Buffer like a store, and it blocks the processor like a load. In other words, the atomic load-store blocks until the Store Buffer is empty and then proceeds to memory. A load therefore does not need to check for atomic load-stores in the Store Buffer because this situation cannot arise. When memory services an atomic load-store, it does so atomically; no other operation can intervene between the load and store parts of the load-store.

Programming Note – In the definition of TSO, the term "processor" may be replaced everywhere by the term "process" or "thread" as long as the process or thread switch sequence is written properly. See Appendix J, "Programming with the Memory Model" of the SPARC Architecture Manual Version 8 for the correct process switch sequence.

Partial Store Ordering (PSO)

Partial Store Ordering guarantees that the store, flush, and atomic load-store instructions of all processors appear to be executed by memory serially in a single order called the memory order. However, the memory order of store, flush, and atomic load-store instructions for a given processor is, in general, not the same as the order in which they were issued by that processor. Conformance between issuing order and memory order is provided by use of the STBAR instruction; if two of the above instructions are separated by an STBAR in the issuing order of a processor, or if they reference the same location, then the memory order of the two instructions is the same as the issuing order. Figure 4-4 shows the ordering constraints for this model graphically. A complete formal specification appears in Appendix K, "Formal Specification of the Memory Model" of the SPARC Architecture Manual Version 8.

Flushes and atomic load-stores issued by a processor are placed in its dedicated Store Buffer. This buffer is not guaranteed to be FIFO as it was in TSO; it does maintain the order of stores and atomic load-stores to the same location, but otherwise it is partitioned only by the occurrence of STBAR instructions. These instructions are shown in Figure 4-4 as *S*. Thus, the order in which memory executes two stores or atomic load-stores separated by an STBAR for a given processor is the same as the order in which the processor issued them. The memory order of these operations corresponds to the order in which the switch is thrown from one port to another.

Loads first check the Store Buffer for the processor to see if it contains a store to the same location (atomic load-stores don't need to be checked for because they block the processor). If it does, then the load returns the value of the most recent such store; otherwise, the load goes directly to memory. Since not all loads go to memory, loads in general do not appear in the memory order.

A processor is blocked from issuing further memory operations until the load returns a value.

An atomic load-store (swap or ldstub) behaves both like a load and a store. It is placed in the Store Buffer like a store, and it blocks the processor like a load. A load therefore does not need to check for atomic load-stores because this situation cannot arise. When memory services an atomic load-store, it does so atomically; no other operation can intervene between the load and store parts of an atomic load-store.

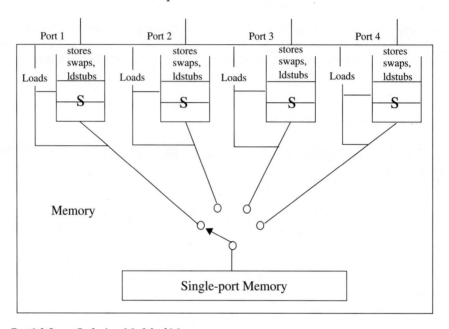

Figure 4-4   Partial Store Ordering Model of Memory

Implementation Note – The advantage of PSO over TSO is that it allows an implementation to have a higher-performance memory system. PSO therefore should be thought of as a performance optimization over TSO.

Implementation Note – See Appendix L, "Implementation Characteristics" of the SPARC Architecture Manual Version 8 for information on which of the various SPARC implementations support the PSO mode.

Programming Note – In the definition of PSO, the term "processor" may be replaced everywhere by the term "process" or "thread" as long as the process or thread switch sequence is written properly. See Figure J-2, Section J.4, in Appendix J of the SPARC Architecture Manual Version 8 for the correct process switch sequence.

Mode Control

The memory model seen by a processor is controlled by the PSO bit in the MMU control register for that processor, if the processor has a SPARC Reference MMU. PSO = 0 specifies Total Store Ordering, while PSO = 1 specifies Partial Store Ordering. See "SPARC Reference MMU" for the location of this bit.

The STBAR instruction must execute as a NOP on machines that implement Strong Consistency, machines that implement only TSO, and machines that implement PSO but are running with PSO mode disabled.

Implementation Note – A given SPARC implementation must provide TSO, but it may or may not provide PSO. In implementations that do not provide PSO, setting the PSO mode bit has no effect.

Programming Note – Programs written for PSO will work automatically on a processor that is running in TSO mode. However, programs written for TSO will not, in general, work on a processor that is running in PSO mode. See Appendix J, "Programming with the Memory Model" of the SPARC Architecture Manual Version 8 for a more detailed discussion of portability.

Synchronization of Instruction Fetches with Memory Operations

The FLUSH instruction ensures that subsequent instruction fetches to the target of the flush by the processor executing the flush appear to execute after any loads, stores, and atomic load-stores issued by that processor prior to the flush. In a multiprocessor configuration, FLUSH also ensures that stores and atomic load-stores to the target of the flush issued by the processor executing the flush prior to the flush become visible to the instruction fetches of all other processors some time after the execution of the flush. When a processor executes a sequence of store or atomic load-stores interspersed with appropriate FLUSH and STBAR instructions (the latter are needed only for PSO), the changes appear to the instruction fetches of all processors to occur in the order in which they were made. Figure 4-5 shows the operation of FLUSH graphically, assuming Processor 1 is the one executing the flush. A complete formal specification of FLUSH appears in Appendix K, "Formal Specification of the Memory Model" of the SPARC Architecture Manual Version 8.

The IBuf of each processor consists of three elements: a five-instruction local flush (*Iflush*) delay that delays the execution of locally generated flushes by at most five instructions; the IBuf data; and a remote flush (*rflush*) FIFO that contains flushes generated by remote processors. Processor 1 executes a FLUSH *A* by issuing a local flush (*Iflush*) command to its IBuf and placing a remote flush (*rflush*) command in its store buffer and then proceeds to execute the next instruction. Processor's IBuf executes the *Iflush* after at most a five-instruction delay by invalidating the contents of address *A* in IBufl. The *rflush* placed in the Store Buffer is treated exactly like a store for ordering purposes; it appears in the global memory order by going through the single port to memory and is then placed in the *rflush* FIFOs of processors other than the one executing the flush. The *rflush* has no effect on the contents of memory. A remote processor's IBuf invalidates the contents of address *A* when the *rflush* comes to the head of that processor's *rflush* FIFO.

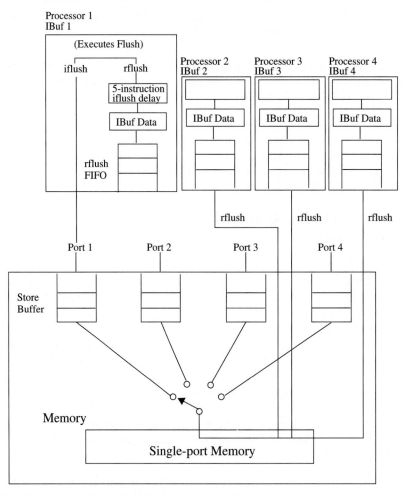

Figure 4-5   FLUSH Instruction Operation by Processor 1

The *Iflush* guarantees that an instruction fetch to address *A* issued five instructions or more after the FLUSH *A* by Processor 1 will miss the IBuf and turn into an instruction load that will appear in the issuing order defined at Processor 1's memory port. Given the guarantees provided by the memory model, the instruction fetch will observe the value of a store done to *A* before the flush. Note also that the order of *Iflush*es is preserved, so that if a processor executes the sequence ST *A*, FLUSH *A*, STBAR, ST *B*, FLUSH *B*, the instruction fetches of this processor will observe the two stores in the order in which they were issued. In TSO mode the STBAR is superfluous.

The guarantee provided by *rflush* is weaker; copies of *A* in the IBufs of remote processors are invalidated some time after the flush is executed by Processor l. In particular, Processor 1 *cannot* assume that the remote IBufs have been invalidated at the time when it starts the execution of the instruction just after the flush. Also note that since *rflushes* are ordered just like stores, the two stores in the sequence ST *A*, FLUSH *A*, STBAR, ST *B*, FLUSH *B* are observed by the instruction fetches of remote processors in the issuing order. In TSO mode the STBAR is superfluous, of course.

A complete formal specification appears in Appendix K, "Formal Specification of the Memory Model" of the SPARC Architecture Manual Version 8. For copies of the SPARC Architecture Manual Version 8, contact SPARC International, Inc.

SPARC Reference MMU

The SPARC Reference MMU Architecture is a memory management architecture for use with SPARC processors. The architecture is designed so that single-chip MMU implementations can provide general-purpose memory management that efficiently supports a large number of processes running a wide variety of applications.

The Reference MMU Architecture serves as a guideline for system designers, describing how a preferred MMU for SPARC-based systems should behave. Actual Reference MMU implementations may employ different pin-outs and different internal organizations (see reference MMU implementations). The Reference MMU Architecture primarily describes (for software) a common architecture for memory management. This section's purpose is that of a guide to implementors and users.

The goal of the Reference MMU Architecture is to promote standardization. Use of a standard MMU architecture by manufacturers will reduce the time taken to port an operating system to new hardware and reduce the likelihood of introducing new hardware bugs. The portability of user-level and application programs is not affected by the MMU design.

The Reference MMU Architecture can be implemented as a single chip in CMOS, BiCMOS, ECL, GaAs, or even on the same chip as the CPU in some technologies. (Examples of single-chip MMU implementation are presented in "Reference MMU Implementations.") The MMU uses three levels of page tables in main memory to store full translation information, and page table entries are cached in the MMU to provide quick translation.

Among the features offered by the MMU are:

- 32-bit virtual address
- 36-bit physical address
- Fixed 4-Kbyte page size
- Support for sparse address spaces with three-level map
- Support for large linear mappings (4 Kbytes, 256 Kbytes, 16 Mbytes, 4 Gbytes)
- Support for multiple contexts
- Page-level protections
- Hardware miss processing

The Reference MMU Architecture specifies both the behavior of the MMU hardware and the organization and contents of the tables in main memory required to support it.

Software Architecture

A SPARC Reference MMU provides three primary functions:

1. It performs address translation from the virtual addresses of each running process to physical addresses in main memory (see Figure 4-6). This mapping is done in units of 4-Kbyte pages so that, for example, an 8-Mbyte process does not need to be located in a contiguous section of main memory. Any virtual page can be mapped into any available physical page.

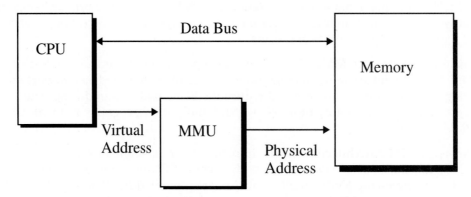

Figure 4-6   Basic SPARC Configuration with MMU

2. It provides memory protection, so a process cannot read or write the address space of another process. This protection is necessary for most operating systems to allow multiple processes to safely reside in physical memory at the same time.

3. It implements virtual memory. The page tables track which pages are in main memory; the MMU signals a page fault if a memory reference occurs to a page not currently resident.

Physical Page Number	Page Offset

35   12 11   0

Figure 4-7   Physical Address Format

The MMU translates virtual addresses from the CPU into physical addresses. A 32-bit virtual address translates to a 36-bit physical address, providing for a 64-Gbit physical address space to support large physical memories and memory mapping of 32-bit buses (for example, VME or MultiBus II). A physical address is logically composed of an offset into a 4-Kbyte page and a Physical Page Number as illustrated in Figure 4-7.

Pages are always aligned on 4-Kbyte boundaries; hence, the lower-order 12 bits of a physical address are always the same as the low-order 12 bits of the virtual address and do not require translation. For every valid virtual page resident in memory there is a corresponding page table entry that contains the physical page number for that virtual page. Translating a virtual address to a physical address replaces the virtual page number with the physical page number.

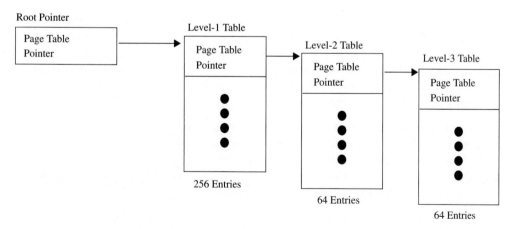

Figure 4-8   Basic SPARC Configuration with MMU

All the address translation information required by the SPARC Reference MMU resides in physically addressed data structures in main memory. The MMU fetches translations from these data structures, as required, by accessing main memory. Mapping a virtual address space is accomplished by up to three levels of page tables, in order to efficiently support sparse addressing. The first and second levels of these tables typically (though not necessarily) contain descriptors (called page table descriptors) which point to the next-level tables. A third-level table entry is always a page table entry (PTE) that points to a physical page. A first- or second-level entry may also be a PTE. A representation of the full three levels of mapping is shown in Figure 4-8.

The Root Pointer page table descriptor is unique to each context and is found in the context table. See "Contexts."

A virtual address is divided into index fields as shown in Figure 4-9.

Index 1	Index 2	Index 3	Page Offset

```
31          24 23          18 17          12 11          0
```

Figure 4-9   Virtual Address Format

Each index field provides an offset into the corresponding level of page table. A full set of tables is rarely required, as the virtual address space is usually sparsely populated. In some cases, the full three levels of page tables are not required to obtain the page table entry. This happens when a 256-Kbyte, 16-Mbyte, or 4-Gbyte section of linear memory is mapped with a single page table entry. See the description of page table entries in this section for details.

CPU memory references would be too slow if each one required following the three levels of page tables in main memory in order to translate a virtual address to a physical address. Consequently, page table entries are cached in the MMU's page descriptor cache, or PDC (often called a translation look-aside buffer, or TLB). The cached entries are usually all that is needed to perform a translation, reducing significantly the need to fetch translation information from main memory.

Figure 4-10 is a simplified block diagram of the major components of a possible MMU implementation. The virtual address comes in to the MMU and is latched in an internal register. It is then compared with the virtual address tags stored in the PDC. A match against one of the tags indicates that the correct page table entry is already stored in the MMU, and the physical address is generated directly.

If there is no match, miss processing occurs. During miss processing, the MMU automatically takes over the address and data buses from the CPU and fetches page table descriptors until it reaches the needed page table entry, or incurs an error. That page table entry is then cached in the MMU, translation occurs and the original memory request continues from the latched address. Memory access permissions are checked for each translation; if the requested access violates those permissions, then a trap is generated. If an error occurs, the appropriate status information is stored in the fault status register and the fault address register, and a fault is generated to the processor.

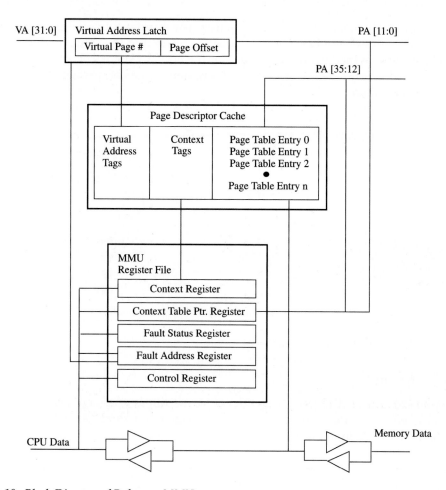

Figure 4-10 Block Diagram of Reference MMU

Contexts

The SPARC Reference MMU can retain translations for several process address spaces at the same time. This speeds up context switching between processes. Each address space is identified by a "context" number, which may also be used by the system to maintain several processes in a virtual cache. The management of multiple contexts, including the assignment of contexts to processes, the reclamation of unused contexts and the reassignment of contexts, is the responsibility of the memory management software. Context numbers are used to index into the context table (Figure 4-11) in main memory to find the root of the page table hierarchy (root pointer page table descriptor—see Figure 4-8) for a process.

At any one time only one address space is active. The current active address space is identified by its context number. This provides the offset into the context table used to retrieve the pointer to the Level-l page table for the address space.The size of the context table is implementation-dependent. See the discussion of the context register in "Hardware Architecture."

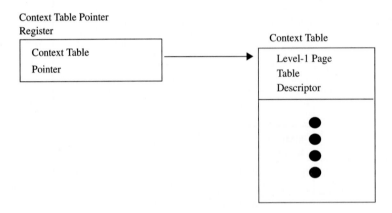

Figure 4-11   Reference MMU Context Table

Page Table Descriptor

A page table descriptor (PTD) contains the physical address of a page table and defines the format of entries in the context table, Level-1 page tables, and Level-2 page tables. A PTD is defined as shown in Figure 4-12.

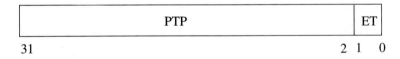

Figure 4-12   Page Table Descriptor

The fields have the following definitions.

PTP: Page Table Pointer

> Physical address of the base of a next-level page table. The PTP appears on bits 35 through 6 of the physical address bus during miss processing. The page table pointed to by a PTP must be aligned on a boundary equal to the size of the page table. The sizes of the three levels of page tables are summarized in Table 4-1.

Table 4-1   Page Table Size

Level	Page Table Size (Bytes
1	1024
2	256
3	256

ET: Entry Type

> This field differentiates a PTD from a PTE. For a PTD, it must contain the value 1. Table 4-2 list the possible values in the ET field and their meanings.

Table 4-2   Field Values and Meanings

ET	Entry Type
0	Invalid[1]
1	Page Table Descriptor
2	Page Table Entry
3	Reserved

1. "Invalid" means that the corresponding range of virtual addresses is not currently mapped to physical addresses.

Page Table Entry

> A page table entry (PTE) specifies both the physical address of a page and its access permissions as shown in Figure 4-13.

Figure 4-13 Page Table Entry Format

The fields have the following definitions.

PPN: Physical Page Number

> The high-order 24 bits of the 36-bit physical address of the page. The PPN appears on bits 35 through 12 of the physical address bus when a translation completes.

C: Cacheable

> If this bit is one, the page is cacheable by an instruction and/or data cache.

Programming Note – All Input/Output (I/O) locations mapped by the MMU should have the C bit in their corresponding PTEs set to 0.

M: Modified

> This bit is set to 1 by the MMU when the page is accessed for writing (except when the access is via a Reference MMU pass-through ASI. Refer to Appendix I, "Suggested ASI Assignments for SPARC Systems" of the SPARC Architecture Manual Version 8).

R: Referenced

> This bit is set to 1 by the MMU when the page is accessed (except when the access is via a Reference MMU pass-through ASI. Refer to Appendix I, the SPARC Architecture Manual Version 8, "Suggested ASI Assignments for SPARC Systems").

ACC: Access Permissions

> These bits indicate whether access to this page is allowed for the transaction being attempted. The address space identifier used in an access determines whether it is a data access or an instruction access, and whether the access is being attempted by user or supervisor software. Table 4-3 list the ACC field interpretations.

Table 4-3   ACC Field Interpretations

ACC	User Access (ASI = 0x8 or ASI = 0xA)	Supervisor Access (ASI = 0x9 or ASI = 0xB)
0	Read Only	Read Only
1	Read/Write	Read/Write
2	Read/Execute	Read/Execute
3	Read/Write/Execute	Read/Write/Execute
4	Execute Only	Execute Only
5	Read Only	Read/Write
6	No Access	Read/Execute
7	No Access	Read/Write/Execute

ET: Entry Type

> This field differentiates a PTE from a PTD. See "Page Table Descriptors," above. For a PTE, it must contain the value 2.

I1	I2	I3	Offset

31   24 23   18 17   12 11   0

Figure 4-14   Virtual Address

If a PTE is found in the Context Table or a Level-1 or Level-2 Page Table, the address translation process stops and that PTE is used. Virtual addresses, from the first virtual address corresponding to the PTE through the last virtual address corresponding to the PTE, are mapped linearly to physical addresses as specified by the PPN. The physical address specified by the PPN must be aligned on a boundary equal to the size of the region mapped by the PTE. For example, given a virtual address (see Figure 4-14) and given that the 12 entry of the appropriate Level 2 Page Table is a PTE (rather than a PTD) with a physical page number field containing the value PPN, the corresponding physical address (see Figure 4-15) is the bit-wise OR of the register contents.

And

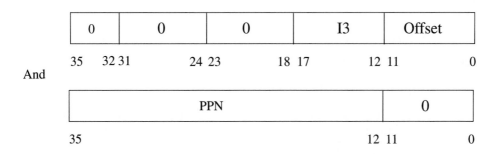

Figure 4-15   Corresponding Physical Address

Implementation Note – A page table entry with an ACC field value of 6 or 7 represents a supervisor page. Translating supervisor addresses is more efficient if the page descriptor cache ignores the context number used to fetch the PTE when matching cache tags for such references.

Implementation Note – Thc MMU should use one PDC entry for a Level-1 or Level-2 PTE to provide a large linear address mapping for buses, coprocessors, and kernels without requiring many translation cache entries.

Note that the low-order six bits of PPN must all be zeros, to satisfy the alignment requirement on the region mapped by the PTE.

The sizes of the regions mapped by different levels in the page tables are summarized in Table 4-4.

Table 4-4   Size of Region Mapped by MMU

Level	Mapping Size
3	4 Kbytes
2	256 Kbytes
1	16 Mbytes
Root	4 Gbytes

MMU Flush and Probe Model

The privileged load and store alternate instructions are used to flush entries from the MMU's Page Descriptor Cache (PDC) and to probe for entries in the MMU. In an alternate address space used for flushing and probing, an address is composed as shown in Figure 4-16.

VFPA	Type	Reserved

31   12 11   8 7   0

Figure 4-16   Flush/Probe Address, in Alternate Space

The fields have the following definitions.

VFPA   Virtual flush or probe address.

Type   The Type field indicates either the object(s) to be flushed from the PDC or the object to be probed. Encoding of the Type field is described in Table 4-5. (Note that Types 5-0xF are ignored. Probe Types 0-3, in the table, are optional.)

reserved   This field is reserved and should be supplied as zero by software.

Flush Operations

A flush operation removes from the PDC a PTE or PTD that matches the criteria implied by the Type field[1]. A flush is accomplished by executing a store alternate instruction to the appropriate address (given by the VFPA field), with the appropriate type (given by

---

1. It may remove more than one PTE or PTD, as long as it removes the indicated one.

the Type field), with the appropriate context (given by the Context register), and with the appropriate address space identifier (ASI), which is implementation-dependent. The data supplied by the store alternate instruction is ignored.

Table 4-5   Type Field Assignments

Type	Probe Object	Flush PDC Object(s)
0 (page)	Level-3 entry [1]	Level-3 PTE
1 (segment)	Level-2 entry [1]	Level-2 and -3 PTE/PTDs
2 (region)	Level-1 entry [1]	Level-1, -2, -33 PTE/PTDs
3 (context)	Level-0 entry [1]	Level-0, -1, -2, -3 PTE/PTDs
4 (entire)	Level-n entry	All PTEs/PTDs
5 0xF	none (reserved) [2]	none (reserved) [2]

1. Implementation is optional for this probe type

2. This probe/flush should be ignored in current MMU implementations.

A flush operation removes the object(s) specified by the Type field from the PDC. The following paragraphs delineate the flush criteria. Since a flush operation in a particular implementation may remove more entries from the PDC than specified by the Type field, a "precise" flush is defined as one that removes the minimum number of entries implied by the Type field.

A page, segment, or region flush (Types 0-2) removes a PTE if the PTE's access code indicates a supervisor page (PTE.ACC = 6 or 7). A precise page, segment, or region flush removes a user page (PTE.ACC = 0-5) if the PTE's context tag equals the context register. Furthermore, a precise page, segment, or region flush removes a PTE if the PTE's address tag equals the corresponding bits of the VFPA field. Also, a precise page flush removes a PTE if the level tag indicates that the PTE was fetched from a level-3 page table; a precise segment flush removes a PTE with a level-2 or -3 tag; and a precise region flush removes a PTE with a level-1, -2, or -3 tag.

A precise context flush (Type 3) removes a PTE if its context tag equals the context register and the PTE's access code indicates a user page (PTE.ACC= 0-5). An imprecise context flush may also remove a supervisor entry. The PTE's address and level tags are ignored. An entire flush (Type 4) removes PTEs regardless of the values of their address tags, context tags, level tags, and ACC codes. In other words, the entire PDC is flushed.

A PTD is flushed if its context tag equals the context register and the level tag corresponds to the flush type. A precise segment flush removes a PTD with a Level-2 tag. A precise region flush removes a PTD with a Level-l or -2 tag. A precise context flush removes a PTD with a Level-0, -1, or -2 tag. An entire flush removes all PTDs from the PDC.

The PTE flush match criteria are summarized in Tables 4-6 and 4-7. Note that these criteria are the same as those for PTEs, except there are no access code checks.

Table 4-6   Page Table Entry Flush Match Criteria

VA [11:8]	Flush Type	Precise PTE Flush Match Criteria
0	page	((ACC 6) or Context_equal) and V A [31:12]_equal
1	segment	((ACC ≥ 6) or Contexts_equal) and V A [31:18]_equal
2	region	((ACC 6) or Contexts_equal) and V A [31:24]_equal
3	context	((ACC £ 5) and Contexts_equal)
4	entire	....
5-0xF	reserved	....

Table 4-7   Page Table Descriptor Flush Match Criteria

VA [11:8]	Flush Type	Precise PTE Flush Match Criteria
0	page	Contexts_equal and VA [31:12]_equal
1	segment	Contexts_equal and VA [31:18]_equal
2	region	Contexts_equal and VA [31:24]_equal
3	context	Contexts_equal
4	entire	....
5-0xF	reserved	....

Probe Operations

A probe returns an entry from either the PDC or from a page table in main memory or generates an error. A probe is accomplished by executing a privileged load alternate instruction with the appropriate address (given by the VFPA field), type (given by the Type field), context (given by the Context register), and address space identifier (ASI)—the last of which is implementation-dependent.

Two classes of errors can occur during a probe operation:

- An entry with ET not equal to 1 (PTD) is encountered before the level being probed is reached.
- A memory error occurs. No memory access exception is signaled to the processor, but the fault registers are updated (see Fault Status Register).

If either of the preceding errors occurs, the probe operation returns a zero value. If the probe operation succeeds, it returns the corresponding entry from a page table at the level implied by the Type field.

The value returned by a probe operation is specified in Table 4-8. For a given probe type, the table is read left-to-right. "0" indicates that a zero is returned, "†" indicates that the page table entry itself is returned, and "‡" indicates that the next-level page table entry is examined.

Table 4-8   Return Value From Reference MMU Probe

Probe Type	Upon a Memory Error	If no Memory Errors Occur															
		Level-0 Entry Type				Level-1 Entry Type				Level-2 Entry Type				Level-3 Entry Type			
		2 PTE	3 res	0 inv	1 PTD	2 PTE	3 res	0 inv	1 PTD	2 PTE	3 res	0 inv	1 PTD	2 PTE	3 res	0 inv	1 PTD
0 (page)	0	0	0	0	‡	0	0	0	‡	0	0	0	‡	†	0	†	0
1 (segment)	0	0	0	0	‡	0	0	0	‡	†	0	†	†	----------			
2 (region)	0	0	0	0	‡	†	0	†	†	----------				----------			
3 (context)	0	†	0	†	†	----------				----------				----------			
4 (entire)	0	†	0	0	‡	†	0	0	‡	†	0	0	‡	†	0	0	0
5 - 0xF	(undefined)																

Page, segment, and region probes should not update a PTE's Referenced bit, although an implementation can set the PTE.R bit for a Type 4 (entire) probe.

Probe types 5-0xF are reserved for future use. They return an undefined value. Also, the presence of page, segment, region, and context probes is implementation-dependent; that is, an implementation may not provide these probe operations. If not implemented, the value returned is undefined.

Implementation Note – It is recommended that probe operations check the PDC before walking the page tables in main memory. Also, it is recommended that a Type 4 (entire) probe bring the accessed PTE into the PDC. Updating the PDC is not recommended for probe Types 0 through 3.

Hardware Architecture

This subsection describes the hardware architecture for the Reference MMU.

Access to MMU Registers

Five internal registers are defined in the Reference MMU. The Control register contains general MMU control and status flags. The current process identifier is stored in the context register, and a pointer to the base of the context table in memory is stored in the context table pointer register. If an MMU fault occurs, the address causing the fault is placed in the fault address register and the cause of the fault can be determined from the fault status register. All the internal MMU registers can be accessed directly by the CPU through peripheral accesses. The peripheral address map for the MMU is shown in Table 4-9. Note that the least significant 8 bits of the virtual address, VA[7:0], are unused; software should set these bits to zero.

Table 4-9   MMU Internal Register Virtual Addresses

VA [31:0]	Register
0x000000xx	Control Register
0x000001xx	Context Table Pointer Register
0x000002xx	Context Register
0x000003xx	Fault Status Register
0x000004xx	Fault Address Register
0x000005xx to 0x00000Fxx	Reserved
0x00010xx to 0xFFFFFFxx	Unassigned

It is intended that the MMU be mapped via an alternate address space of the CPU (refer to Appendix I, "Suggested ASI Assignments for SPARC Systems" in the SPARC Architecture Reference Manual Version 8). However, the MMU definition only assumes the existence of a chip-select signal indicating that a peripheral access to the MMU is in progress.

Control Register

The MMU control register is defined as shown in Figure 4-17.

IMPL	VER	SC	PSO	Reserved	NF	E
31 28	27 24	23 8	7	6 2	1	0

Figure 4-17 MMU Control Register

The fields have the following definitions.

IMPL　　　　This field identifies the specific implementation of the MMU. It is hardwired into the implementation and is read-only.

VER　　　　This field identifies a particular version of this MMU implementation and is typically a mask number. It is hardwired into the implementation and is read-only.

SC   The system control bits are implementation-defined. They may be reflected in a variable number of signals external to the MMU and need not all be implemented. If a bit is not implemented, it reads as zero and writes to it are ignored.

PSO   The PSO bit controls whether the memory model seen by the processor is Partial Store Ordering (PSO=1) or Total Store Ordering (PSO=0).

reserved   This field is reserved and must be zero.

NF   NF is the "No Fault" bit. When NF=0, any fault detected by the MMU causes FSR and FAR to be updated and causes a fault to be generated to the processor. When NF=1, a fault on an access to ASI 9 is handled as when NF=0; a fault on an access to any other ASI causes FSR and FAR to be updated, but no fault is generated to the processor. If a fault on access to an ASI other than 9 occurs while NF=1, subsequently resetting NF from 1 to 0 does not cause a fault to the processor (even though FSR.FT is not equal to 0 at that time). A change in value of the NF bit takes effect as soon as the bit is written; a subsequent access to ASI 9 will be evaluated according to the new value of the NF bit.

E   The Enable bit enables or disables the MMU as shown in Table 4-10.

Table 4-10 MMU Enable/Disable

Ebit	MMU State
1	Enabled
0	Disabled

When the MMU is disabled:

- All virtual addresses pass through the MMU untranslated and appear as physical addresses

- The upper 4 of the 36 bits of the physical address are zero

- The MMU indicates that all virtual addresses are noncacheable. The E bit reads as zero.

On MMU reset, the MMU is disabled and the PSO bit is set to zero.

Context Table Pointer Register

The context table pointer register is defined as shown in Figure 4-18.

Context Table Pointer	Reserved

31   2   1   0

Figure 4-18   Reference MMU Context Table Pointer Register

The context table pointer points to the context table in physical memory. The table is indexed by the contents of the context register (see below). The context table pointer appears on bits 35 through 6 of the physical address bus during the first fetch occurring during miss processing. The context table pointed to by the context table pointer must be aligned on a boundary equal to the size of the table.

For example, if the number of bits used in the context register is 8, then the table must be aligned on a 1024-byte (that is, 2^{8+2}-byte) boundary.

The *reserved* field is reserved and must be zero.

Context Register

The Reference MMU context register is defined as shown in Figure 4-19.

The context register defines which of the possible process virtual address spaces is considered the current address space. Subsequent accesses to memory through the MMU are translated for the current address space until the context register is changed. Each MMU implementation may specify a maximum context number, which must be one less than a power of 2.

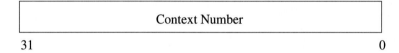

Context Number

31   0

Figure 4-19   Reference MMU Context Register

Diagnostic Register

A SPARC Reference MMU may provide access to diagnostic registers through an alternate address space (refer to Appendix I, "Suggested ASI Assignments for SPARC Systems" in the SPARC Architecture Reference Manual Version 8). If present, their operation is implementation-dependent. The following describes a suggested operation.

Accessing an MMU diagnostic register reads or writes a PDC entry or performs a diagnostic PDC hit/miss operation. Suggested decoding of the virtual address VA[31:0] presented to the MMU is shown in Table 4-11.

Table 4-11 MMU Diagnostic Register Address Decoding

Bits	Decode as
VA [31:12]	Virtual address
VA [11:4]	PDC entry
VA [3:2]	Register (see Table 4-12)

Table 4-12 indicates further decoding of VA[3:2].

Table 4-12 Reference MMU Diagnostic Register Selection

VA [3:2]	Register
0	D [31: 20] : context D [19: 0] : address
1	PTE
2	Control bits (e.g., V, Level, LRU)
3	Load: Start compare in every PDC entry; if hit, return the PTE; if miss, return 0 Store: For each PDC entry: if the content of its LRU counter is less than the "stored" data value, increment counter. Otherwise, leave unchanged. In any case, zero the LRU counter of the addresse PDC entry.

Fault Status Register

The fault status register is defined as shown in Figure 4-20.

The fault status register provides information on exceptions (faults) issued by the MMU. Since the CPU is pipelined, several faults can occur before a trap is taken. The faults are grouped into three classes: instruction access faults, data access faults, and translation table access faults. If another instruction access fault occurs before the fault status of a previous instruction access fault has been read by the CPU, the MMU writes the status of the latest fault into the fault status register, writes the faulting address into the fault address register, and sets the overwrite bit (OW) to indicate that the previous fault status has been lost.

Reserved		EBE	L	AT	FT	FAV	OW
31	18		10	8	5	2	1	0

Figure 4-20 Reference MMU Fault Status Register

The MMU and CPU must ensure that if multiple data access faults can occur, only the status of the one taken by the CPU is latched into the fault status register. If data fault status overwrites previous instruction fault status, then the OW bit is cleared, since the fault status is represented correctly. An instruction access fault may not overwrite a data access fault.

A translation table access fault occurs if an MMU page table access causes an external system error. If a translation table access fault overwrites a previous instruction or data access fault, then the OW bit is cleared. An instruction or data access fault may not overwrite a translation table access fault.

The fields have the following definitions.

reserved This field is reserved and must be zero

EBE Bits in the external bus error field are set when a system error occurs during a memory access. The meanings of the individual bits are implementation-dependent. Examples of system errors are: time-out, uncorrectable error, and parity error. The MMU need not implement all the bits in EBE. Unimplemented bits read as zeros.

L The level field (see Table 4-13) is set to the page table level of the entry which caused the fault. If an external bus error is encountered while fetching a PTE or PTD, the level field records the page table level of the page table containing the entry.

Table 4-13 Level Field Assignments

L	Level
0	Entry in context table
1	Entry in Level-1 page table
2	Entry in Level-2 page table
3	Entry in Level-3 page table

AT The access type field (see Table 4-14) defines the type of access which caused the fault. (Loads and stores to user/supervisor instruction space can be caused by load/store alternate instructions with ASI = 8 or 9).

Table 4-14 AT Field Assignments

AT	Access Type
0	Load from user data space
1	Load from supervisor data space
2	Load/Execute from user instruction space
3	Load/Execute from supervisor instruction space
4	Store to user data space
5	Store to supervisor data space
6	Store to user instruction space
7	Store to supervisor instruction space

FT   The fault type field defines the type of the current fault (see Table 4-15). Invalid address, protection, and privilege violation errors (see Table 4-16) depend on the access type field of the fault status register and the ACC field of the corresponding PTE. A translation error is indicated if an external bus error occurs while the MMU is fetching an entry from a page table, a PTD is found in a level-3 page table, or a PTE has ET=3. The L field records the page table level at which the error occurred, and the EBE field records the type of bus error (if any). Access bus error is set when an external bus error occurs during memory access that is not a page table walk access. The EBE field records the type of bus error. Internal error indications are set when the MMU detects an internal inconsistency. This situation should be considered a fatal error by software, requiring system reset.

Table 4-15 Fault Type Field Assignments

FT	Fault Type
0	None
1	Invalid address error
2	Protection error
3	Privilege violation error
4	Translation error

Table 4-15 Fault Type Field Assignments (Continued)

5	Access bus error
6	Internal error
7	Reserved

Table 4-16 Error Definitions

AT	PTE. V=0	FT Value							
		PTE. V=1							
		PTE. ACC =							
		0	1	2	3	4	5	6	7
0	1	-	-	-	-	2	-	3	3
1	1	-	-	-	-	2	-	-	-
2	1	2	2	-	-	-	2	3	3
3	1	2	2	-	-	-	2	-	-
4	1	2	-	2	-	2	2	3	3
5	1	2	-	2	-	2	-	2	-
6	1	2	2	2	-	2	2	3	3
7	1	2	2	2	-	2	2	2	-

FAV   The fault address valid bit is set to 1 if the contents of the fault address register are valid. The fault address register need not be valid for instruction faults. The fault address register must be valid for data faults and translation errors.

OW   The overwrite bit is set to 1 if the fault status register has been written more than once by faults of the same class since the last time it was read. If an instruction access fault occurs and the OW bit is set, system software must determine the cause by probing the MMU and/or memory.

Table 4-17 Reference MMU Fault Priorities

Priority	Error
1	Internal error
2	Translation error
3	Invalid address error
4	Privilege violation error
5	Protection error
6	Access bus error

Table 4-17 shows the order (from highest to lowest) in which faults are recognized if a single access causes multiple errors.

The highest priority fault is recorded in the fault type field. Reading the fault status register clears it. Writes to the fault status register are ignored.

Fault Address Register

The fault address register is defined as shown in Figure 4-21.

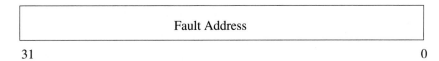

Figure 4-21 Reference MMU Fault Status Register

The fault address register contains the virtual memory address of the fault recorded in the fault status register. Fault addresses are overwritten according to the same priority used for the fault status register. Writes to the fault address register are ignored.

Implementation Note – It is not required that the MMU latch the full address. It need only latch the virtual page number for which the fault occurred. In this case, the low-order address bits are set to zero.

In the case of a translation error, the contents of the fault address register will be the original virtual memory address for which translation was requested.

Programming Note – After a translation error, the table can be walked by software to find the entry that triggered the fault.

MMU Operation

This subsection describes the operations of the Reference MMU.

Reset

Upon detection of a reset, the MMU sets the enable and PSO bits in the control register to zero (that is, the MMU is disabled and total store ordering is in effect). All other MMU state is unaffected.

Miss Processing

If the MMU does not have the required information to perform a requested translation in the PDC, it initiates miss processing to retrieve the required page table entry from the page tables. The retrieved page table entry is then cached in the MMU, and the MMU completes the permission checking and address translation.

Referenced and Modified Bit Updates

A successful translation of any kind results in the Referenced bit (R) in the page table entry being examined. If the R bit is zero, then the MMU sets the R bit of both the cached page table entry and the page table entry in memory to 1.

A successful translation of a write operation results in the Modified bit (M) in the page table entry being examined. If the M bit is zero, then the MMU sets the M bit of both the cached page table entry and the page table entry in memory to 1.

Implementation Note – The MMU must provide signals that make it possible for the R and M bits in memory to be atomically updated with respect to other system accesses to the page tables. In addition, updating these bits must be synchronous with the access that caused the update. Specifically, the M bit must be set before a store to a location in a page becomes visible. This applies equally to store, `ldstub`, `ldstuba`, `swap`, and `swapa` instructions.

Reference MMU Implementations

The SPARC Reference MMU architecture has been adopted by several SPARC chip vendors and designed into various MMU implementations. In this section, two single-chip implementations are discussed briefly. These include the LSI Logic L64815 MCT and the Cypress CY7C625 CMTU. In comparison, the SuperSPARC TMS390Z50 on-chip memory management mechanism is examined in more detail. For more details on each of these MMU implementations, refer to the manufacturers' data sheets.

L64815 Memory Management, Cache Control, and Cache Tag Unit

The L64815 includes a memory management unit and cache controller with on-chip cache-tag memory. The MCT provides system designers with a low chip count and an efficient method of implementing a fully functional computing module to power a SPARC-based workstation or general-purpose computer. The L64815 MCT implements both the MBus interface specification (see Appendix A) and the SPARC Reference MMU specification.

The L64815 incorporates the cache ASIC, the MMU ASIC, and the cache-tag RAM used in the initial Sun Microsystems SPARCstation1 into one combined unit consisting of four main functional units: memory management, cache-control logic, cache-tag memory, and MBus interface and control unit, as shown in Figure 4-22.

The L64815 MMU's virtual address translation can have up to 256 contexts and incorporates a 64-entry translation look-aside buffer (TLB) to translate from the 32-bit virtual address generated by the IU to the 36-bit physical address of the MBus. TLB replacement is done by using a true Least Recently Used (LRU) replacement algorithm within the TLB. LRU provides an efficient method of replacing TLD entries since those entries that have not been used recently are replaced with new entries needed in the TLB to perform a translation.

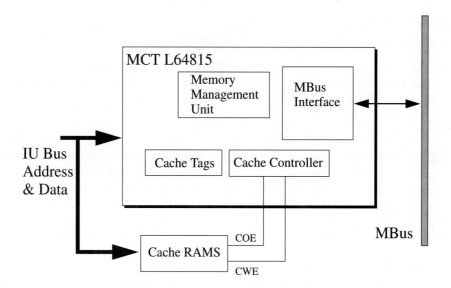

Figure 4-22   LSI L64815 MCT Block Diagram

The MMU also supports three levels of table mapping, and all table walking is performed directly in hardware; the MMU also supports different modes that allow bypassing the address translation when needed. The L64815 cache controller unit supports cache sizes of 32, 64, 128, and 256 Kbytes of combined instruction and data cache in a write-through configuration without requiring extra MCTs. Line sizes of 32, 64, and 128 bytes are supported, and to minimize memory delays, the longer line sizes are broken down into sub-blocks. Sub-blocks break up long cache lines, such that when a cache line needs to be filled, only the particular sub-block is filled. Subsequent sub-blocks are filled only when needed. This scheme provides an efficient mechanism for maintaining delays at an absolute minimum whenever a cache line is filled.

The 64-bit MBus Interface and Control (L64815 MCT) provides the control signals and interface to the MBus. The MCT handles the multiplexing of data and address and supports burst transfer capabilities of up to 32 bytes and meets other MBus Level-1 requirements.

The MCT also handles packing and unpacking of data from 32-bit wide IU bus to double-words for the 64-bit MBus.

The MCT cache-tag RAMS provide 2 Kbyte cache tags on chip, saving board space and SRAM costs, speeding up processing, and eliminating the need for an extra (expensive) "Tag SRAM" chip.

The Cypress CY7C625 Cache Control, Memory Management, and Tag Unit (CMTU)

The CMTU is also an implementation of the SPARC Reference MMU and supports the SPARC MBus Level-2 protocol for multiprocessing systems. Figure 4-23 illustrates the implementation.

The CMTU consists of a secondary cache controller, a memory controller, and on-chip physical cache-tag memory and connects directly to the CY7C620 CPU and CY7C627 cache data unit without any external circuitry. The CY7C625 is designed to use two or four CY7C627 CDUs for 128 Kbyte or 256 Kbyte, respectively, of zero-wait-state, direct mapped virtual cache memory (the actual number of CY7C627 CDUs utilized varies from module to module). Each CY7C627 is a 16 Kbyte x 32 SRAM with on-chip address and data latches and timing control.

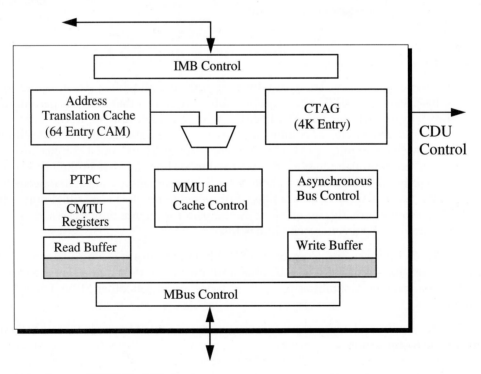

Figure 4-23   Cypress CMTU Block Diagram

The MMU portion of the CMTU provides translation from a 32-bit virtual address (4 Gbytes) to 36-bit physical address (4 Gbytes). Virtual addresses are further extended with the use of a context register, which is used to identify up to 4096 contexts or tasks. The TLB entries contain context numbers to identify tasks or processes, thus minimizing necessary TLB entry replacement during task switching.

The CMTU performs its address translation task by comparing a virtual address supplied by the CY7C620 through the intra-module bus (IMB) to the address tags in the TLB entries. If a "hit" occurs, the physical address stored in the TLB translates the virtual to physical address. If the virtual address does not match any valid TLB entry, a "miss" occurs. This causes a table walk (a search performed by the MMU through the address translation tables stored in main memory) to be performed by the MMU. Upon finding the PTE, the MMU translates the address and selects a TLB entry for replacement.

The CMTU cache controller supports two modes of caching: write-through with no write allocate and copy-back with write allocate.

The 4 Kbyte cache-tag entries in the CMTU reflect the physical address.The cache directory can be accessed from both the processor and MBus.

A 64-byte write buffer and a 32-byte read buffer are provided in the CMTU to fully buffer the transfer of cache lines. This feature allows the CMTU to simultaneously read a cache line from main memory as it flushes a modified cache line from the cache.

The CMTU supports the SPARC MBus interface standard and the SPARC MBus Level 2 cache coherency protocol. The CMTU supports data transfers in transaction sizes of 1, 2, 4, 8, or 32 bytes. These data transfers are performed in either burst or nonburst mode, depending upon the size. Data transactions larger than eight bytes are transferred in burst mode. Bus mastership is granted and controlled by an external bus arbiter.

The CMTU also supports the MBus module identifier feature of the MBus, in which the CMTU accepts the module identifier input from the MBus and embeds it in the MBus address phase of all MBus transactions initiated by the CMTU.

The CMTU also provides support for systems with reflective memory controllers and is able to recognize a cache-to-cache data transfer and can automatically update itself without delaying the system.

The SuperSPARC TMS390Z50 MMU

The SuperSPARC processor employs an on-chip MMU. The SuperSPARC cache controller is an optional external device used in designs with a large secondary (2nd level) cache.

The SuperSPARC processor implements a 64-entry fully associative MMU compatible with the SPARC Reference MMU Specification. The MMU translates 32-bit virtual addresses into 36-bit physical addresses. The mapping is done in units of 4 Kbyte page,

256 Kbyte segment, 16 Mbyte region, or 4 Gbyte context. Physical addresses are composed of an offset within a page and a physical page number (PPN), while virtual addresses are composed of an offset within a page and a virtual page number (VPN).

The MMU translates 32-bit virtual addresses and 16-bit context numbers into 36-bit physical addresses by accessing up to four levels of page tables in memory. Normally, this translation is cached in the on-chip 64-entry TLB. When the translation entry is missing from the TLB, the MMU table-walk hardware automatically retrieves the translation from the page tables in memory. Figure 4-24 illustrates the architecture.

Each virtual address space is identified by a context number that is kept in the context register. Virtual addresses kept in the TLB are tagged with a 16-bit context number. The effective size of the context register is variable between 10 and 16 bits, so that page tables can be smaller in systems with less memory.

The page tables can contain page table pointers (PTP) or page table entries (PTE). A PTE is distinguished from a PTP by the two low-order bits of the table entry. A PTP contains the physical address of the next page table level, while a PTE contains the physical address of the page with its access rights.

The MMU has 64 TLB entries. When a new PTE entry is brought into the MMU on a TLB miss, it must be stored in the TLB. If one or more entries are invalid, the new translation is stored in the lowest-numbered invalid entry. When all entries are valid, one of the valid entries must be selected for replacement by the new entry. SuperSPARC's TLB uses a limited-history LRU policy.

Each TLB entry has a used bit associated with it. Initially, when a demap-all operation is done to invalidate all TLB entries, all used bits are cleared. The used bit is then set for any valid TLB entry that has a TLB hit. When all entries have their used bits set, all used bits (except the last one to be set and those that are locked) are cleared. This is the case when all past history is lost. To select an entry to be replaced when all TLB entries are valid, the lowest-numbered entry for which the used bit is not set will be chosen. This represents the least recently used entry based on the limited history available, since a TLB hit causes the used bit to be set.

When an entry is invalidated or flushed from the TLB, its corresponding used bit is cleared. In addition to the used bits, the replacement policy also checks the corresponding lock bit (one per TLB entry). If a lock bit for an entry is set, then, regardless of the used bits, that entry will never be replaced. An invalid entry with its lock bit set can still be replaced, and the newly written entry becomes locked, since the lock bit remains set. If all entries have their lock bits set, no replacement takes place, and the newly brought-in PTE is not stored in the TLB. Locking all the entries in the TLB must be avoided, since a translation finishes only after a table-walk operation has completed, thus causing an infinite table-walk loop.

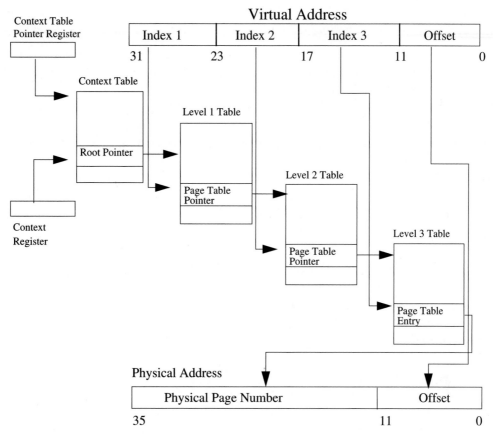

Figure 4-24   SuperSPARC on-chip MMU architecture

4

SPARC Multi-level Bus Architectures 5≡

No system is complete without much consideration and design time in the various bus architectures required for reliable high speed transfer of data between the processor and memory, to other processor boards/modules, and for communication to external peripherals.

For a variety of reasons, traditional minicomputer and mainframe manufacturers have exploited the concept of mixing buses in a single system. Multiple buses have been used by a host of minicomputer and workstation manufacturers to separate very high-speed processor-to-memory functions from slower, more routine external I/O and peripherals.

Back in Sun's early days, traditional open buses, such as VME, made significant performance contributions to Sun's workstation architecture. More recently, high-speed, processor-to-memory, processor module to processor module, secondary I/O bus, and new packet-switched back-plane buses have taken Sun workstations to new high-performance bus architectures—MBus, SBus, XBus, and XDBus. These buses create technical partitions within a system architecture that allow the designer to focus more attention on achieving the highest performance possible while providing the flexibility needed for simple, cost-effective system evolution. As we examine each of these bus architectures you will see that each bus scheme clearly adheres to the model of system partitioning.

The following section provides an overview of these multi-level bus architectures which are not only transforming the traditional workstation architecture but also introducing to the industry new approaches to achieving very high performance while maintaining a cost-effective, flexible multiprocessor system architecture.

SPARC MBus

MBus is a high-speed interface bus that connects SPARC compute modules (comprised of integer unit, floating-point unit, MMU, and cache controller) to physical memory modules and special purpose I/O modules. It is a high-speed local interconnect bus that can accommodate up to 16 modules on a single printed circuit board. Figure 5-1 illustrates the architecture.

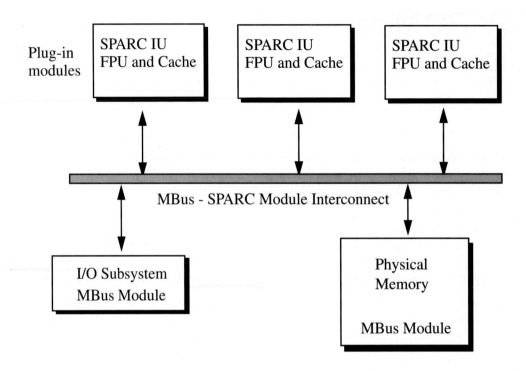

Figure 5-1   MBus Level-1 Architecture

MBus is a processor module interconnect bus. MBus provides a short physical connection medium between processor modules, synchronous operation with clock rates to 40 MHz, 64-bit data transfers, and support for uniprocessor (Level-1 protocol) and multiprocessor (Level-2 protocol) system implementations.

This section provides an overview of the MBus, its features and the many benefits realized by system designers in pursuit of efficient and flexible multiprocessing system configurations. A complete SPARC MBus Interface Specification is provided in Appendix A; additional copies and information can be obtained from SPARC International Inc. A complete MBus module design guide is provided in Appendix B.

MBus technical specifications include:

- Fully synchronous operation at 40 MHz

- 64 Gbytes physical address space

- Multiplexed address/control with 64 bits of data

- Burst transfers up to 128 bytes

- Centralized arbitration, reset, interrupt, clock distribution, and time-out

- Uniprocessor and multiprocessor module interconnect through pin-compatible interface

- Multimaster operation, overlapped arbitration with "parking," no driver overlap

- CMOS and BiCMOS compatibility, TTL voltage levels

- Multiprocessor support, arbitration with parking, signals, and transactions to support write-invalidate cache coherency schemes

MBus provides system designers with considerable benefits:

- Eliminates costly components through backplane bus technology that can be built on a single board

- Provides a module interconnect mechanism that allows for critical subsystems to be integrated more cleanly and more cost effectively

- Opens new ways for development of more economical desktop and server systems

- Eliminates problems associated with having a different processor/memory bus for different processor implementations; supports new processor migration/evolution,

- Provides designers the assurance offered by incorporating an open industry standard bus

- Provides a roadmap for system evolution without hardware redesign

- Provides an opportunity for system and module developers to add value more easily

MBus Design Goals

The primary reason for the development of MBus resulted from a critical need for a standard interface between the processor plus the cache and the rest of the system. This interface is key to satisfying the high-performance requirements and variety of protocol constraints in system architectures, in particular MP architectures. Once implemented, this interface creates a technical partition, allowing for enhanced development by independent groups with different requirements and capabilities.

MBus provides a common microprocessor pin-out standard, which has created a move among several different semiconductor manufacturers to design SPARC processor implementations to this standard. In addition, this move towards a common pin-to-pin interface has allowed SPARC chip vendors to also develop SPARC-compatible support devices, cache controllers, for example, independently of Sun. The first chips to appear which integrate an interface to the MBus include the Cypress/Ross Technology 7CY604 SPARC cache controller/MMU for uniprocessor systems, the Cypress/Ross Technology

7CY605 SPARC cache controller/MMU for MP systems, and the LSI Logic L64815 SPARC cache controller/MMU. Figure 5-2 illustrates a Cypress CY7C601/605-based multimodule MP system configuration. Other implementations of SPARC chips are following the MBus standard as well.

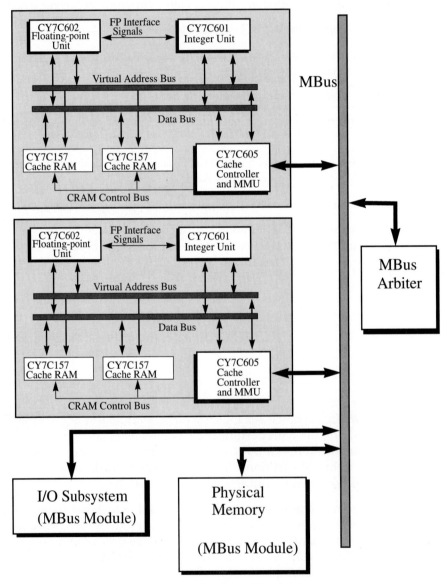

Figure 5-2   Cypress CY7C601/605 MBus MP Configuration

MBus provides a rapid process to integrate new processors into systems because of the levels of compatibility provided. Systems incorporating MBus can take advantage of new higher performance processors much sooner, without the need for hardware redesign often required by other architectures.

One of the primary goals of the MBus definition was to define a physical bus carefully at a specific point within the overall system architecture such that Sun, and other system manufacturers, could avoid the problems associated with having a different processor/memory bus for different processor implementations. By defining the bus carefully at the memory side of the cache and memory management unit, the problem of having a different physical bus with each SPARC implementation was solved. The same benefits apply to SPARC system manufacturers. The majority of new SPARC implementations provide for MBus pin-compatibility, communication, and migration to higher levels of system performance without any modifications to the system hardware.

MBus was designed with enough bandwidth to accommodate SPARC processor evolution for several years. With 40 MHz bus operation and 64-bit data transfer capability, MBus can achieve a sustained bandwidth of 80 Mbytes per second as well as a peak bandwidth of 320 Mbytes per second. In addition to providing high-performance levels, the other major consideration was that the MBus also achieve levels of simplicity and cost constraints for system developers. To this end MBus uses TTL input voltage levels, allowing designers to use standard off-the-shelf CMOS devices while also providing for high-speed operation.

MBus provides 36 bits for physical addressing, permitting an addressing capability of 64 Gbytes.

MBus Centralized Functions

MBus centralized functions are those functions that are not controlled within a specific MBus module but instead supported as central functions on the bus (see Figure 5-3). These functions (signals) include Bus Arbitration, Interrupts, Reset, Clock, and Time-out. MBus centralized functions are discussed in more detail later in Chapter 6.

Bus Classifications

MBus Level-1 protocol has many characteristics of partitioning which are similar to SBus, Sun's I/O System Expansion Bus. This similarity is due to the fact that MBus serves explicitly for processor/memory interconnect, where SBus serves only as a system expansion bus. MBus and SBus can, however, be used in the same system configuration, thus providing a high-performance computer system with separate and distinct buses (see Figure 5-4).

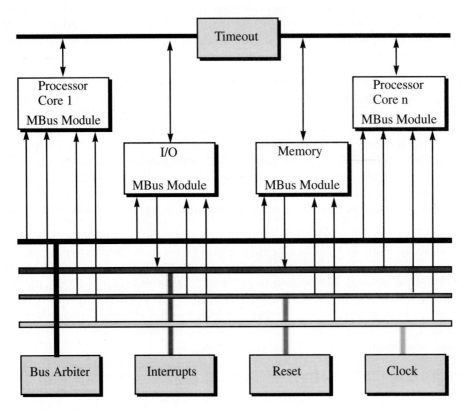

Figure 5-3   MBus Centralized Functions - Logical Representation

In this MBus Level-2 example, MBus provides a 40 MHz, high-speed, pin-compatible interface for multiple MBus processor modules with a direct connection to physical memory. SBus is used only as the I/O interconnect to expansion slots where optional expansion I/O can be inserted for added system level functionality. In this example, the interconnection between MBus and SBus is accomplished by an LSI Logic L64852 MBus-to-SBus Controller (M2S). The LSI Logic L64852 provides a high-performance interface from the 64-bit 40 MHz MBus to the 25 MHz 32-bit SBus while also supporting major MBus functions.

MBus Level 1 and Level 2 Protocols

The MBus Interface Specification defines two levels of compliance, Level 1 and Level 2. A uniprocessor system implementation conforms to the Level 1 specification while Level 2 describes the signals, transactions, and protocols for building cache coherent, shared-memory multiprocessing systems.

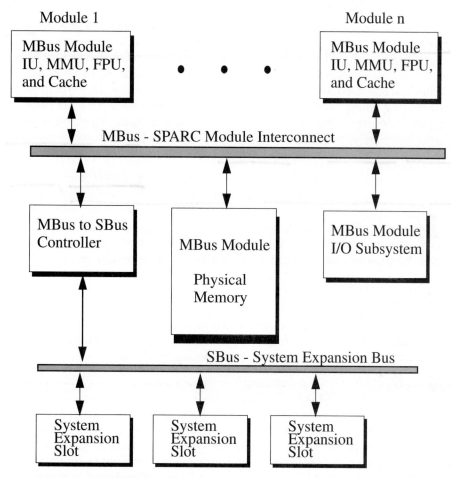

Figure 5-4   MBus Level-2 Configuration

Compliance Level 1: Uniprocessors

The Level-1 MBus supports two transactions: read and write. These transactions read or write a specified number of bytes from a specified physical address. The read and write transactions are supported through a subset of the MBus signals (a 64-bit multiplexed address/data bus, an address strobe signal, and an encoded three-signal acknowledge protocol). In addition, signals are available to support arbitration of modules, interrupts, reset, asynchronous errors, module identification, and the MBus reference clock. It is assumed that there are central functional elements to perform reset, arbitration, interrupt distribution, time-out, and MBus clock generation (refer back to Figure 5-3).

Compliance Level 2: Multiprocessors

The Level-2 MBus includes all Level-1 transactions and signals while adding four transactions and two signals to support cache coherency. These additions facilitate the design of symmetric, shared memory multiprocessor systems. In Level 1, details of the caches inside modules are not visible to the MBus transactions. In Level 2, many aspects of the caches are assumed as part of the new MBus transactions. To participate in cache consistent sharing using Level-2 transactions, a cache must have a "write back" caching capability, an "allocate" capability on write misses, and a block or sub-block size of 32 bytes. Cache lines are assumed to have at least five states (invalid, exclusive clean, exclusive dirty, shared clean, and shared dirty).

The additional transactions present in Level-2 systems are *Coherent Read*, *Coherent Invalidate*, *Coherent Read* and *Invalidate*, and *Coherent Write* and *Invalidate*. The two additional signals are *Shared* and *Inhibit*. *Coherent Read* and *Invalidate*, and *Coherent Write* and *Invalidate* are simply the combination of a *Coherent Invalidate* and either a *Coherent Read* or *Write*. Its use reduces the number of MBus transactions. Refer to "MBus Transactions," MBus Interface Specification, provided in Appendix A.

MBus Modules

MBus modules are basically subsystems which at a minimum contain a single SPARC processor. Other, more advanced, higher performance modules contain dual processors, cache, FPU, arbitration logic, clock, and synchronization circuitry.

In designing MBus modules, designers will typically need to run SPICE simulations (SPICE is an acronym for "Simulation Program with Integrated Circuit Emphasis") when building modules that have not been analyzed, such as the MBus-compatible modules available from licensed SPARC vendors (discussed further in Chapter 6). Designers are encouraged to reference the MBus Module Design Guide provided in Appendix B. The Module Design Guide conveys the necessary information needed to build an MBus module that will work at 40 MHz in Sun Microsystems MBus-based systems. The guide includes PCB construction and routing, mechanical specifications and connector pin-out, skew management for clocks, timing specifications and their derivation for an MBus chip, and testability considerations.

Depending on the application, specific ASIC devices may be required in order to interface to the MBus. Figure 5-5 illustrates an MBus system configuration with ASICs providing the interface to special purpose high performance devices such as a Digital Signal Processor (DSP) and a 100 Mbit-per-second Fiber Distributed Data Interface (FDDI) to an FDDI network. The high data-transfer capability requirements of DSP and FDDI devices can be accommodated by the MBus's 64-bit data-transfer capability and sustained bandwidth of 80 Mbytes per second as well as a peak bandwidth of 320 Mbytes per second.

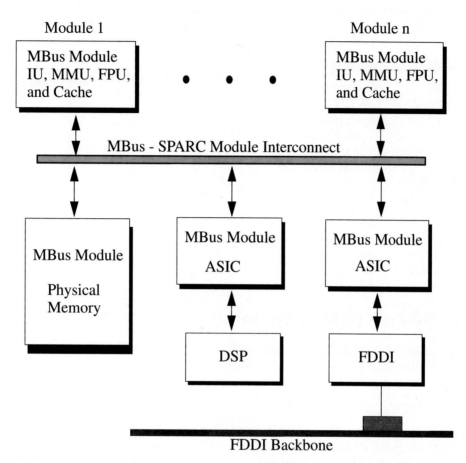

Figure 5-5   MBus Configurations with ASICs

Table 5-1 lists the bandwidth specifications of optional I/O expansion devices. Not all of these would be appropriate for interface to MBus. In fact, the majority of them are more suited for connection to SBus (discussed in the next section).

MBus Clock Rates

MBus provides for a fully synchronous 40 MHz clock rate; however, processors with clock rates above 40 MHz can also be incorporated to run asynchronously in an MBus system. In such an application, additional clock circuitry and synchronization logic on the processor module maintains complete synchronization with the bus. The advantage here is the performance enhancement realized from the move to higher performance SPARC processors as they become available. A 50 MHz SPARC processor, for example, with cache, can run independently from the rest of the system. In so doing, MBus allows the designer to buffer the system architecture from processor changes, thus avoiding costly system redesign to accommodate new processors.

Table 5-1 . I/O Device Specifications

I/O	Bandwidth
Ethernet	1.25 to 1.5 Mbytes/sec
FDDI	12.5 Mbytes/sec
Token Ring	2 Mbytes/sec
SCSI	1 to 5 Mbytes/sec
Video Cards	2 to 30 Mbytes/sec
Coprocessor (DSP)	5 to 20 Mbytes/sec
8-bit NTSC Video	6.5 Mbytes/sec
Laser Printers	0.2 to 5 Mbytes/sec
Digital Audio	352 Kbytes/sec
Local Talk/Flask Talk	30 to 100 Kbytes/sec
ISDN (Primary Rate)	200 Kbytes/sec
ISDN (Basis Rate)	16 Kbytes/sec
MIDI	4 Kbytes/sec

SBus - System I/O Expansion Bus

SBus is a high-performance I/O interconnect that is optimized for high-speed I/O expansion for desktop and other high performance workstations and servers.

SBus Overview

SBus provides a flexible, microprocessor-independent architecture that can be implemented in many different configurations. The two most common are host-based and symmetrical; they are differentiated by the connection between the CPU and SBus. In host-based systems, the CPU has both special access to the MMU and a special path through the SBus controller that bypasses the MMU. The host-based configuration saves the CPU the clock cycles required for the address translation, but increases the cost of the SBus controller. SBus machines such as the SPARCstation 1+ use the host-based model, with their main memory located on the SBus (refer to Figures 3-5 and 3-9).

In symmetric SBus systems, all masters on SBus use the SBus controller to translate virtual addresses to physical addresses. With this configuration, the CPU can have a private memory bus in order to increase its performance while allowing an optimized I/O interface.

SBus provides the memory bandwidth necessary for low-latency access by I/O devices such as Ethernet and SCSI. It features low-static power dissipation, so that it can be used in both desktop and portable machines.

SBus provides for both synchronous and asynchronous operations. SBus interrupt lines are allowed to be asynchronous; the other 75 signals are sampled on the rising edge of a fixed frequency clock, which must be in the range of 16.67 MHz to 25 MHz.

The advantages of SBus being synchronous with the main CPU are well worth preserving, since running the I/O bus asynchronously to the processor greatly increases the complexity of logic needed in the interface. This is why SBus is designed to run at any frequency between 16.67 MHz and 25 MHz. On systems where the CPU operates at a frequency greater than 25 MHz, SBus can be clocked at some integer division of the processor frequency. For example, in a 40-MHz MBus system, the SBus frequency can be set at 20 MHz (refer to Figure 5-4).

SBus allows use of virtual addresses at the hardware level by all masters on the bus to specify the source and destination of data. This usage eliminates the need for software to translate addresses for all I/O tasks. An MMU in the SBus controller has the responsibility of translating these addresses to the appropriate SBus slot and physical address.

In addition, SBus allows any master to talk to any slave on the bus. Thus, in any transfer between two I/O devices, SBus automatically provides a two-fold performance improvement over other bus architectures that require all traffic to "stop over" in main memory.

The 64-byte burst transfers provided by SBus are a good compromise between bus bandwidth and latency, as increasing bus bandwidth by even 10% would double the latency. By requiring all transfers to complete within 255 clock cycles, the worst-case latency—with a maximum of eight masters (assuming three clock cycles for address translation)—is only about 124 microseconds at 16.67 MHz [8 * (256 + 3) clock cycles].

While some SBus applications may need 64 bytes of buffer memory, most SBus devices will not require much, if any, buffer memory because of the ability of SBus slaves to regulate the rate at which data is transferred.

The ability of any SBus master to talk to any slave makes synchronous operation simpler and more reliable than if all messages had to be placed in system memory.

SBus allows users to expand the types and quantity of I/O devices connected to the system without affecting the host motherboard. These features allow SBus developers to build cards that attach directly to the platform as newer, faster technologies evolve. For example, SBus could conceivably be used as a high-bandwidth connection between a portable CPU and a desktop expansion unit containing disks and other I/O devices.

SBus expansion cards use a 96-pin high-density connector (see Figure 5-6) of which 82 pins are used for signalling and 14 pins are used for +5V, +12V, -12V and ground. To keep power supply requirements down to a reasonable level in desktop or portable machines, each expansion card is limited to 2 amps at +5V and 0.03 amps each at +12V and -12V. By limiting the power consumption to about 11 watts per SBus expansion board, no cooling is inherently necessary, unlike most other bus architectures, in which some amount of airflow is required.

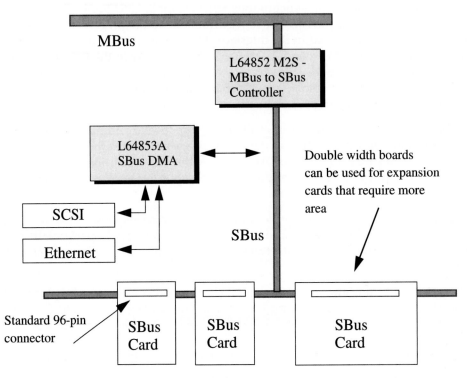

Figure 5-6   Basic SBus Configuration with SBus Cards

While the expansion boards are small, SBus height specifications allow active components to be placed on both sides of the board, resulting in a surface area of 38.28 square inches. Double-width boards are possible if more space is needed. This small form factor means that up to four SBus options can reside on the 9U, double-height Eurocard used with VME. In contrast, other bus architectures restrict component heights so that the bottom surface of the card is all but unusable for most active components.

SBus Features

SBus features include:

* High performance access to memory and I/O

* Completely synchronous operation (except interrupts)

- 80-100 Mbyte/second burst bandwidth

- Master, slave, and interrupt capability

- 32-bit shared virtual address space for masters

- 28-bit physical address space per slave

- 32-bit data bus

- Jumperless addressing for auto-configuration

- Standardized device IDs for auto-configuration

- Boot architecture for future boot devices

- Support for 1-, 2-, 4-, 8-, 16-, 32-, and 64-byte transfer

- Seven sharable interrupt requests

- Support for up to eight masters

SBus provides for device auto-configuration. Installing SBus expansion boards is easy for end-users, thanks to the use of a configuration PROM containing machine-independent FORTH code on each expansion board (see Figure 5-7). Since SBus cards have the FORTH program starting at address zero (0), the system retrieves configuration information from the expansion boards upon power-up, thereby initializing all devices connected on the SBus.

SBus Devices and Implementations

Designing products to meet the SBus specification is facilitated with the various VLSI chips that provide SBus interface and SBus controller functions.

Typically, an SBus system is composed of three major types of devices: a single SBus controller, SBus master devices, and SBus slave devices. The SBus controller is responsible for providing central clocking, address translation through a memory management unit (MMU), bus arbitration, reset, and power to the SBus. The SBus masters initiate all bus transactions in accordance with the SBus protocol, and the SBus slaves respond to these transactions.

VLSI devices that support these functions include the L64853 SBus DMA Controller and the L64852 MBus to SBus Controller (M2S) from LSI Logic Corporation. Other, more recent, devices include the MC92001 SBus DMA Interface Controller and the MC92005 Slave Interface chip from Motorola Inc.

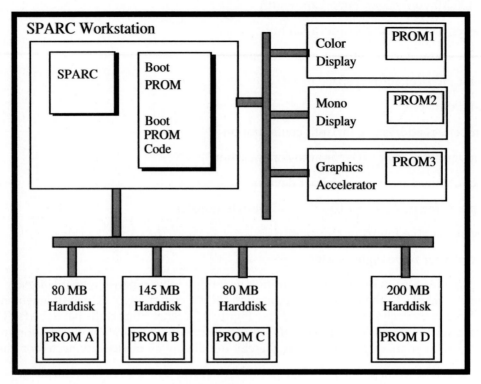

Figure 5-7   SBus OpenBoot Auto-configuration PROMs

The LSI Logic L64853 and L64852 Controllers

The LSI L64853 Direct Memory Access (DMA) interface chip, designed by Sun for SBus, was the first generation of SBus VLSI devices. The L64853 SBus DMA controller enables vendors to quickly develop intelligent functions, such as graphics accelerators and high-speed I/O controllers. With the L64853, an easy, single-chip interface between the SBus and Ethernet, SCSI, and many other peripheral controllers can be designed.

Figures 5-8 and 5-9 illustrate four of the interfaces incorporating the L64853.

The L64852 MBus-to-SBus Controller (M2S) provides a high-performance interface from the 40 MHz 64-bit MBus to the 20-25 MHz 32-bit SBus. Major functions like MBus arbitration, SBus arbitration, SBus control functions, and bus protocol conversions are provided in the M2S to allow a glueless interface from the MBus to the SBus (refer to Figure 5-4.)

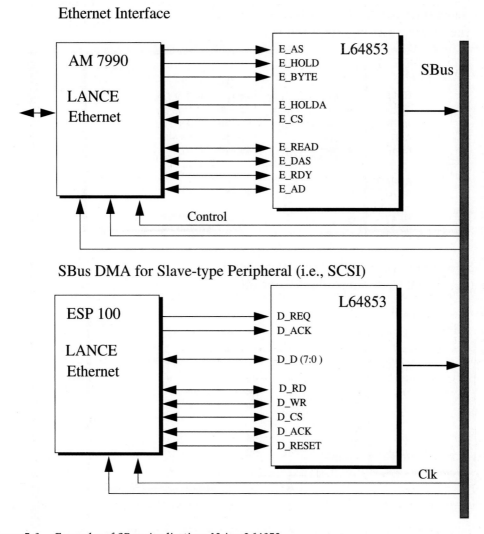

Ethernet Interface

SBus DMA for Slave-type Peripheral (i.e., SCSI)

Figure 5-8   Examples of SBus Applications Using L64853

Since the MBus consists of 64 bits that are multiplexed as 36 address bits and 28 control bits, during the first cycle and, as 64 bits of data during the second cycle, packing and unpacking of the data needs to be done whenever interfacing with 8-, 16-, or 32-bit wide I/O devices (like SCSI or Ethernet or graphics boards). The M2S handles all these functions.

SBus Interface for Master-type Peripherals
(i.e., Compression/Expansion Processors)

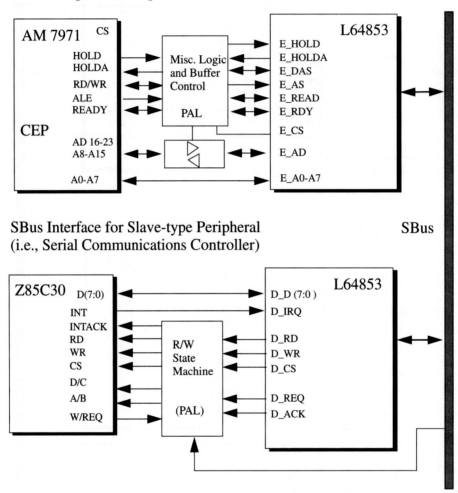

Figure 5-9   More Examples of SBus Applications Using L64853

The M2S chip also handles the address translation from the 32-bit virtual addressing of the SBus to the 36-bit physical addressing of the MBus. In order to do this, the M2S chip has an on-board I/O memory management unit (MMU) with a 16-entry translation look-aside buffer (TLB). The MMU is coordinated by the OS with the other MMU in the MCT chip (the L64815). As with the other MBus devices, slower I/O peripherals can pack their data into the M2S, which then efficiently bursts the data across the high speed MBus.

The Motorola MC92001 Interface Controller

The Motorola MC92001 SBus DMA Interface Controller is a complete 64-bit SBus master/slave interface and DMA controller. It provides a complete master/slave interface, which connects directly to the SBus and fully implements the SBus protocol. The MC92001 meets all SBus timing and bus loading constraints of the B.0 SBus specifications.

Figure 5-10 presents a block diagram of the MC92001. The MC92001 consists of an SBus interface, a local bus (LBus) interface, and several FIFOs which decouple the two interfaces and allow them to operate asynchronously. Alternate SBus master devices and slave peripheral devices attach to the LBus side of the MC92001, resulting in a fully SBus-compliant board.

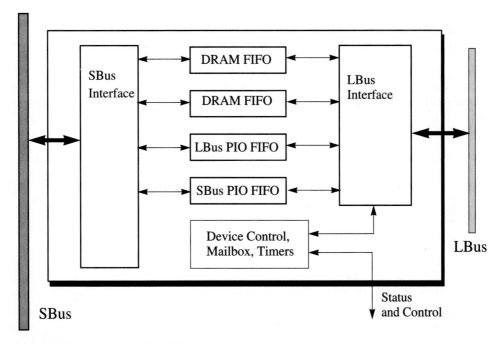

Figure 5-10   MC92001 Internal Block Diagram

Other notable features include:

- Four programmable chip selects on local bus

- Programmable local bus characteristics

- Big/little endian conversion

- Eight independent DMA channels

- Two programmable interval timers

- Four mailbox registers with interrupts

- 160 Mbyte/sec transfer rate

The eight-channel DMA controller can transfer data either to or from the SBus, and a direct programmed I/O (PIO) path is also provided to allow local devices to connect directly to the SBus. Both master and slave devices can be connected to the LBus. The DMA controller can transfer data to and from the SBus and LBus in a variety of combinations of direction and protocol.

All SBus transfer modes are supported, including 64-bit wide, 128-byte burst transfers, resulting in a sustainable data transfer rate of 160 Mbytes/sec. The local bus protocol is fully configurable and will interface to most devices with little or no glue logic.

MC92005

The MC92005 slave interface chip (SLIC) provides a complete, general purpose, 32-bit slave interface to the SBus. The SLIC interface seeks to minimize and ideally eliminate any external hardware required to interface with a large family of peripheral devices, as shown in Figure 5-11.

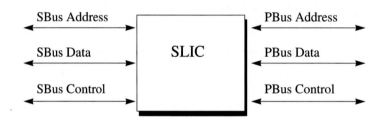

Figure 5-11   SLIC System Interface

By interpreting SBus slave accesses, SLIC allows the simple connection of a variety of peripheral devices to the SBus. The SLIC interfaces two buses, the SBus and a private bus (PBus), to which various devices (PROM, RAM, peripheral chips, etc.) can directly attach, as shown in Figure 5-12.

The SLIC supports byte, half-word, and word transfers either via packing/unpacking or via SBus dynamic-sizing protocol. Devices connect to the SLIC PBus interface, which generates a separate chip select per device. Interrupts from up to six devices are channeled through the SLIC, which selectively masks and propagates the interrupts as an SBus interrupt.

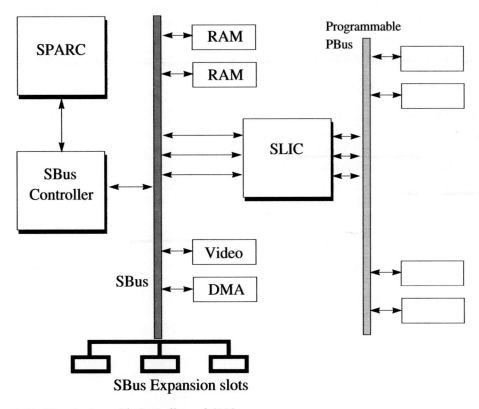

Figure 5-12   SBus System with Controller and SLIC

The SLIC PBus interface provides for 128 Kbytes of address for each of up to six external devices. Devices requiring a larger address space (up to 128 Mbytes) can be supported (in extended address mode) with the addition of a single external address buffer.

The SLIC propagates SBus slave read and write requests onto the local PBus. The SLIC complies with all SBus timing and bus loading constraints, while providing an asynchronous programmable private bus interface. This compliance leaves the hardware designer free to explore SBus board design without the bother of having to design to and meet the SBus specification.

Sun Services for SBus Developers

Sun Microsystems offers SBus third-party system and peripheral developers the services of its SBus Technical Support Group and SBus Design Center. To accelerate the development of third party SBus-based boards, Sun also offers an SBus Developers Kit. The kit contains: The SBus specification (version B.0) with design principles and protocols, and technological, electrical, and mechanical considerations; guidelines for writing UNIX device drivers for SBus boards; guidelines for writing FORTH programs to create ID PROM and to implement auto-configuration on SBus boards; application notes and examples of slave and master interfaces.

For further information on these SBus devices, contact the appropriate vendors.

XBus[1] and XDBus

XBus and XDBus bring the next level of system partitioning and performance to the basic SPARC/MBus multimodule architecture. XBus and XDBus are both high-performance synchronous, packet-switched buses developed jointly by Sun Microsystems and Xerox Corporation Palo Alto Research Center.

Packet switching refers to the switching of data by means of addressed packets (typically a short block of data—1K to 2K bits) whereby a channel (in this case XBus and XDBus) is occupied only for the duration of transmission of the packet. The bus is then available for the transfer of other packets. In contrast with circuit switching, the bus logic determines the routing during, rather than prior to, the transfer of a packet. Figure 5-13 illustrates packet switching vs. circuit switching bus characteristics.

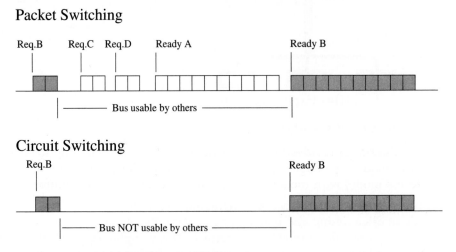

Figure 5-13   Packet Switching vs. Circuit Switching

XBus is similar to XDBus, but has additional control information which permits the exchange of private data between the core processing units and the XDBus interface; much like the MBus provides an interconnect between processor modules. The XBus also uses an arbitration mechanism which ensures the ordering of incoming packets from the various XDBus. This guarantees proper serialization of events.

---

1. Portions © Xerox Corporation XBus Specification, reproduced with permission from Xerox Corporation.

While providing an additional layer in the hierarchy of buses, the two buses differ in the manner in which they provide system interfaces; XBus is an interchip interconnect designed to provide low latency, high-bandwidth communication between subsystem modules. The main advantage of the XBus interconnect bus is that it provides a standard interface, allowing migration to new components independently without requiring changes to other components.

Within SuperSPARC's external cache, the XBus connects MXCC Cache Controller chip to one or more bus watcher (BW) chips, each of which is connected to a separate system bus, XDBus (Figure 5-14). The MXCC provides independent processor-side access to the cache, while the bus watchers handle functions related to XDBus snooping. The data RAMs are connected directly on the SuperSPARC bus to ensure low latency access for the processor. The MXCC, BWs, and static RAMs comprise a 1 Mbyte fully coherent, write-back, second-level cache. XBus provides a simple set of data transfer and cache-tag manipulation commands. Tag commands are used in situations where dual tags are split across multiple chips, as in a high-performance multiprocessor system.

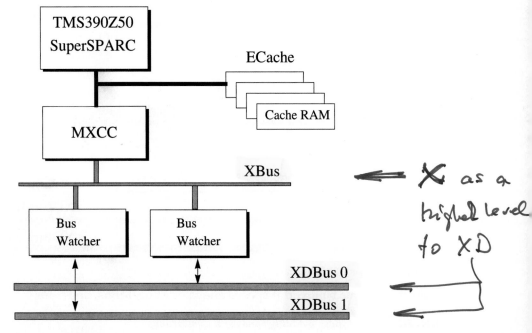

Figure 5-14 XBus Processor Subsystem

In addition to providing packet-switched features, other XBus specifications include:

- 64-bit data path
- Synchronous (25 ns cycle, scalable to 10 ns)

- High data bandwidth (232 Mbytes/sec, scalable to 580 Mbytes/sec)
- Low latency
- Cache coherence support
- RAS support (half-word parity, error reporting)

In comparison to MBus and SBus, XBus differs in the following ways:

- It is packet-switched, not circuit-switched
- It connects subsystem components: processor to cache and I/O to I/O (see Figure 5-15)
- It interfaces to a variety of system buses and I/O buses
- It is not itself a system bus or I/O expansion bus
- It does not provide a modular "MBus-like" plug-and-play capability

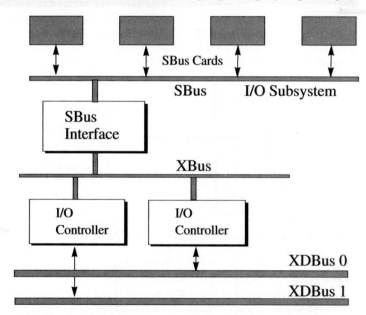

Figure 5-15   XBus I/O Subsystem

Table 5-2 lists the bandwidth specifications of XBus, MBus, and SBus.

Table 5-2   XBus, MBus, and SBus Bandwidth Comparisons

	XBus	**MBus**	**SBus**
Raw bandwidth (Mbytes/sec)	320	320	160
Data bandwidth (Mbytes/sec)	232	80	40

XDBus[2]

XDBus is a high-performance, synchronous, packet-switched bus designed for shared memory MP systems. XDBus provides system designers with the flexibility needed to implement a wide variety of system architectures including:

- Small, single board systems with a single bus segment

- Medium, multiple-board systems with one backplane bus segment or two on-board bus segments per board (I/O)

- Large, multiple-board systems with multiple parallel backplane bus segments or two on-board bus segments per backplane segment

- Second-level cache-based systems with one top-level bus or one bus per second-level cache

The range of flexibility afforded by XDBus is augmented by an additional feature: A conceptually simple cache model guarantees that each processor sees a consistent view of memory, one that reflects all caching and I/O transactions. Built-in hardware functions ensure that multiple copies of read/write data in caches are consistent and that both input and output devices are able to access cached data.

Other XDBus specifications include:

- 64-, 128-, 256-bit data transfers

- Synchronous (25 ns cycle, scalable to 10 ns)

- High data bandwidth (250 Mbytes/sec to 1700 Mbytes/sec)

- Multi-level cache coherency

- Error detection and reporting

Most of the advantages of XDBus stem from the synergy between an efficient packet-switched protocol layered on top of a fast, low-voltage-swing signalling scheme. Implementations based on XDBus are low cost for these reasons: a smaller number of wires switching at lower frequencies is needed to achieve a given level of performance; the signalling scheme uses ordinary CMOS technology and consumes little power, obviating the need for expensive cooling or exotic packaging; and finally, high integration ensures a small parts count and, therefore, low cost.

Implementations based on XDBus deliver high speed because the signalling scheme allows bus cycle time to be made extremely short, while protocol efficiency ensures that most of the raw bus bandwidth is delivered as useful data bandwidth to applications.

P. Sindhu et al.

2. Portions reprinted by permission of IEEE. "XDBus, A High Performance, Consistent, Packet-Switched VLSI Bus", COMPCON, San Francisco, Feb. 1993. © IEEE

Digord of Papers, pp. 338 – 344

22-26 Feb. '93

XDBus's physical and protocol layers interact to promote a high level of integration. Complex devices, including memory controllers, cache controllers, high speed network controllers, and external bus controllers that traditionally required entire boards can be integrated onto a single chip connected to the XDBus. The result is a high-performance, compact, and cost-effective system.

A unique advantage of XDBus is the broad range of architectural and packaging configurations it can support. Because of its low power and its ability to be pipelined, the XDBus can be used at the chip, board, and backplane levels. Its scalable performance can support systems with bandwidth needs from a few hundred Mbytes/sec to a few Gbytes/sec through the use of bus pipelining and bus replication. Finally, XDBus also provides support for multi-level caches, which localizes bus traffic and enables many more processors to be combined into a single system.

XDBus provides an efficient protocol for maintaining multiprocessor cache coherency. With this protocol, the hardware ensures that multiple cached copies of data are kept consistent and that both input and output devices take cached data into account. The protocol is fundamentally write update, but can emulate the spectrum of algorithms from write update to write invalidate. This flexibility enables applications to best utilize precious bus bandwidth. The coherency scheme also supports multi-level caches although no existing implementation uses this feature.

The XBus/XDBus-based configuration shown in Figure 5-15 has several advantages:

- The SuperSPARC bus is kept physically small so that SuperSPARC, CC, and the RAMs can operated at a high frequency despite the presence of multiple system buses.

- The functionality of the chips on either side of the XBus is modular in that each side can be modified without completely redesigning the other. A given CC can be used for different system buses by replacing just the BW, and conversely, the processor can be upgraded by changing just the CC.

- A larger cache can be supported because the processor and bus tags are spread over two chips.

- XDBus on the two sides of XBus can be run at different frequencies, which provides flexibility in system design. In both organizations, the XBus runs synchronous to the XDBus, while all of the CC except for its XBus interface runs synchronous to the processor.

- A module containing SuperSPARC, the CC, and the RAMs becomes more attractive because the XBus provides an interface that is common across multiple implementations.

The one disadvantage of a bus hierarchy is a small latency penalty due to the extra chip crossings and bus arbitrations. The performance impact of this added latency is negligible since it affects only second-level cache misses.

The advantage of using a hierarchy of buses allows XBus to remain small while in some cases operating at higher frequencies than the XDBus. Additional flexibility is realized from cache functions being distributed between two chips—the CC and XBus bus watcher. Distributed cache control allows larger caches than those of processor-side cache to be implemented, allowing off-module memory accesses via XBus.

XDBus Multiprocessing

The XDBus provides a number of carefully selected features for multiprocessor support. Simple but efficient hardware coherency protocol keeps cached data consistent. Support is also provided for maintaining TLB (translation look-aside buffer) consistency. A dedicated interrupt transaction removes the need for the usual jumble of wires to communicate interrupts from devices to processors. Two schemes are provided for multiprocessor synchronization: a simple efficient SWAP primitive and a more general locking mechanism.

The cache coherency protocol is a generalization of the well known multicopy write-broadcast protocol. The first generalization is to adapt the algorithm to a packet-switched bus. The main difficulty here is that bus transactions are no longer atomic, since they are broken up into request and reply packets. The XDBus scheme resolves this difficulty by conceptually treating a read as if all the work were performed on the request packet, and a write as if all the work were performed on the reply packet. Snooping information that tells whether an address that appears on the bus is present in one or more caches is collected by the arbiter and logically ORed to give a single result. This result is then returned in a reply packet to the device that sent the corresponding request.

The second generalization enables the hardware to effectively emulate any coherency scheme between pure write update and write invalidate. The basic idea is to remove a cached copy probabilistically when a foreign write is done to it. Setting the probability close to 1 yields a write invalidate scheme, while setting it close to 0 yields write update. This scheme can be easily implemented by means of a free running modulo N counter, a register that contains a value between 0 and N-1, and a comparator. The counter is updated on each clock, so its value is essentially uncorrelated with the arrival of packets.

When a foreign write arrives, the value of the counter is compared with that of the register, and the update is turned into an invalidate if the counter's value is less than that of the register. As shown in Figure 5-16, setting the register to N-1 gives write invalidate; setting it to 0 gives write update; and setting it to intermediate values gives intermediate schemes. This idea can be implemented cheaply, but has the potential for significantly improving performance when an application's sharing patterns are known.

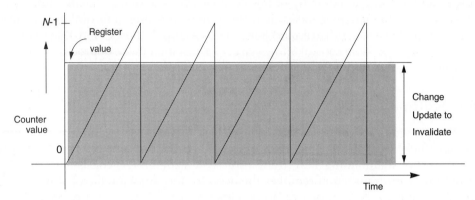

Figure 5-16   Probabilistic Conversion of Write Updates to Write Invalidates

The third generalization is the support of cache coherency in a multi-level hierarchy of caches. Surprisingly, this adds little complexity to the basic single-level algorithm: just one additional transaction called KillBlock is needed. Multi-level caches provide localization of data traffic and have the potential for supporting hundreds of processors in a single system.

Most multiprocessor systems provide no hardware support for consistency of address mapping information. This information is typically kept in main memory tables and copies are kept in TLB's, inside each processor. The copies must, however, be kept consistent; this is usually done in software at a substantial cost in system performance. XDBus supports a single operation called DeMap, which forces a given address translation to be flushed synchronously from all TLBs. Since all new translations must use main memory tables, the software can safely change an entry by first locking it and then using DeMap to flush the TLB entries. This scheme provides a simple and efficient way to solve the TLB consistency problem.

In traditional bus designs, interrupts are communicated from I/O devices to processors via dedicated wires. This scheme has the obvious problem of connectivity when multiple I/O devices must communicate with multiple processors. It also has the drawback that the communication paths are fixed and interprocessor interrupts are not handled the same way as I/O interrupts. XDBus provides a single transaction to transport an interrupt from an I/O device or a processor to one or more processors. The transaction either specifies that a particular processor is to be interrupted or all processors are to be interrupted. Besides providing a single mechanism for transporting all interrupts, this transaction facilitates dynamic interrupt targeting: since the target processor is determined dynamically, an interrupt can be dispatched to the least loaded processor in the system.

The synchronization primitive supported directly by XDBus is SWAP. The implementation of SWAP is efficient in that non-local operations are done only in case the target of the SWAP is marked shared. For nonshared locations SWAP is performed local to the cache, and is therefore much faster. Although only SWAP is supported directly, any `FetchAndOp` type of primitive could be implemented with equal efficiency.

Also, a set of two transactions, Lock and Unlock, allow any sequence of bus transactions to be made atomic. Atomicity can be provided with respect to a single location or any contiguous, self-aligned region in memory that is a power of two in size.

XDBus Physical Characteristics

XDBus uses low voltage-swing GTL[3] transceivers connected to a terminated transmission line to achieve both fast switching speeds and low power consumption. The speed and power advantages of GTL do not compromise noise immunity, however, and noise immunity is as good as that of ECL, the industry benchmark.

Figure 5-17 illustrates the signalling scheme. It shows two GTL transceivers connected to a single wire terminated at both ends at its characteristic impedance.

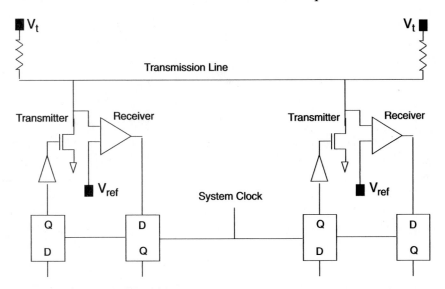

Figure 5-17 XDBus GTL Signalling Scheme

The terminated transmission line, combined with a small 800 mV voltage swing ensures fast switching times. Furthermore, as shown in the figure, data is transferred synchronously from a flip-flop in the sender to a flip-flop in the receiver, so no time is wasted in synchronization and a complete system clock period is available for data

---

(39th)

3. "A CMOS Low-Voltage-Swing Transmission-Line Transceiver" See Gunning, B., Yuan, L., Nguyen, T., Wong, T., in *Proceedings of the 1992 IEEE International Solid State Circuits Conference.* © IEEE

Digest of Tech. Papers, pp. 58-59
Frisco 19-21 Feb. '92

transfer. That is, the clock rate is limited essentially only by signal transition time. Since one bit is transferred per clock for each wire, the data rate is as fast as possible under the given constraints.

A low voltage swing also ensures low power consumption, because power varies as the square of voltage swing. An important aspect of the low-power design is the use of simple open drain drivers. These drivers consume no power in the off state and very little power when on, so virtually all the power for the bus is consumed off-chip in termination resistors. This low on-chip power consumption is mainly responsible for the high levels of integration possible in XDBus-based designs.

A final aspect of the signalling scheme is that it can be pipelined naturally: If the bus settling time is too long, the bus can be broken up into shorter segments connected via pipeline registers (which are present anyway for speed). As shown in Figure 5-18, each of these shorter segments can switch several times faster than the original long segment, and the pipelined bus can be thus run much faster.

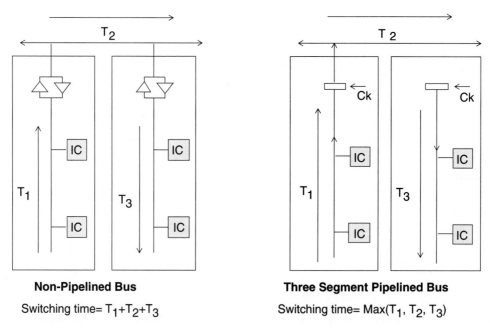

Non-Pipelined Bus

Switching time= $T_1 + T_2 + T_3$

Three Segment Pipelined Bus

Switching time= $Max(T_1, T_2, T_3)$

Figure 5-18   XDBus Pipelining Alternatives

XBus/XDBus Operation

The XBus consists of 73 bused wires, along with three point-to-point arbitration wires per device. Most of the bused wires (64) constitute a multiplexed, data/address path. XBus signals are divided into *Control*, *Arbitration*, and *Data*.

XBus operation can be understood in terms of three levels: cycles, packets, and transactions. A bus cycle is one period of the bus clock; it forms the unit of time and one-way information transfer. A packet is a contiguous sequence of cycles that constitutes the next higher unit of transfer. The first (header) cycle of a packet carries address and control information, while subsequent cycles carry data (see Figure 5-19). Packets come in two sizes: two cycles and nine cycles. A transaction consists of a pair of packets (request, reply) that together perform some logical function. Packets usually come in request-reply pairs, although there are a few exceptions.

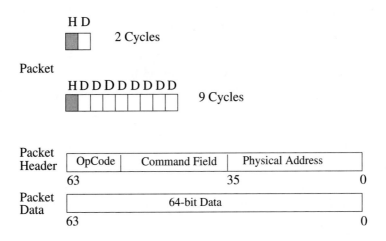

Figure 5-19   *XBus Packet Format*

Each chip on the XBus has several XBus devices, each identified by a unique *XBusId*. An arbiter permits the bus to be multiplexed among the various devices. Before a device can send a packet, it must obtain bus mastership from the arbiter. Once it has the XDBus, it puts the packet on the XDBus one cycle at a time without interruption. The arbiter is implemented in the CC and is specialized to provide low latency for misses and to handle flow control for packet-switched system buses. Since packet transmission is point-to-point, only the recipient identified in a packet typically takes action on the packet.

Packet headers contain a data command, some control bits, a tag command, source and destination *XBusId*, and an address. The data command transfers data between BWs and the CC, while the tag command keeps the bus and processor side copies of cache tags consistent with each other. The data command and address in a reply packet are the same as those for the corresponding request packet. These commands, along with the control bits, provide sufficient flexibility to accommodate a variety of system buses. For instance, block access to non-cacheable data is supported, as are references to I/O devices, locked references over circuit-switched buses, and buffered references over packet-switched buses.

While XBus is flexible in the above respects, it was not designed to be a general-purpose system bus. For example, connection of arbitrary devices that do not fit the BW/CC model may be awkward or impossible. Also, XBus was not designed to accommodate caches built using lower levels of integration than that is suggested in Figure 5-14. For instance, a design using MSI parts would be bulky because of the buffering requirements imposed by noninterruptible packet transmission.

XDBus consists of 88 signal lines, 64 of which are multiplexed data and address lines. The remaining signal lines are used for control, arbitration, parity, and clock signals. As a system backplane bus, XDBus operation is based on requesting bus nodes gaining access from the arbiter before the node can place packets on the bus. A transaction is completed when bus mastership is assumed by the bus node answering the request. The new bus master sends a reply packet to the requesting node. Request and reply packets can be separated by an arbitrary number of cycles, during which time the bus is free to handle other traffic—provided a predefined time-out period has been reached. Packet transmission, once begun, is noninterruptible—no other devices can take the bus away during this time, regardless of priority.

XBus characteristics are summarized as follows:

- High data bandwidth
    - 232 Mbytes/sec at 25 ns
    - Scalable to 580 Mbytes/sec at 10 ns
    - "Default Grantee" absorbs arbitration cost most of the time—Important in processor subsystem application
- Packet-switched
    - Multiple outstanding operations
    - Support of very high performance processors (e.g., SuperSPARC)
    - Easy connection to bridges and slow devices
- RAS features
    - Half-word parity on data wires
    - Error-with-data for memory errors
    - Error replies for all other non-fatal errors
    - XError for fatal errors
- Cache coherency support
    - Can incorporate variety of snooping algorithms
    - Independent bus and processor tags yield high performance
- General transaction set
    - Can be applied in a variety of environments
    - Processor subsystem components
    - I/O subsystem components

XBus and XDBus Interface

XBus signals are divided into *Control, Arbitration,* and *Data.* The control group contains complementary clocks and an error signal; the arbitration group contains a pair of request and grant signals per device; and the data group contains 64 bits of data and 8 bits of parity.

Bused bidirectional data signals carry the bulk of the information being transported on XBus. During header cycles they carry address and control information; during other cycles they carry data.

The XBus arbiter allows the bus to be multiplexed between the bus watchers (BW) and the cache controller (CC) as shown in Figure 5-20. When a chip has a packet to send, it makes a request to the arbiter via its dedicated request lines, and the arbiter grants the bus, using that chip's dedicated grant line. The arbiter implements four priority levels for flow control and deadlock avoidance. Service at a given priority level is round-robin among contenders, while service between levels is based strictly on priorities. The arbiter is implemented in the CC because this is simpler and more efficient.

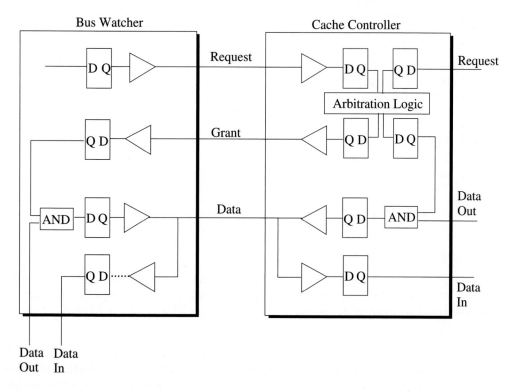

Figure 5-20 XBus BW and CC Interface

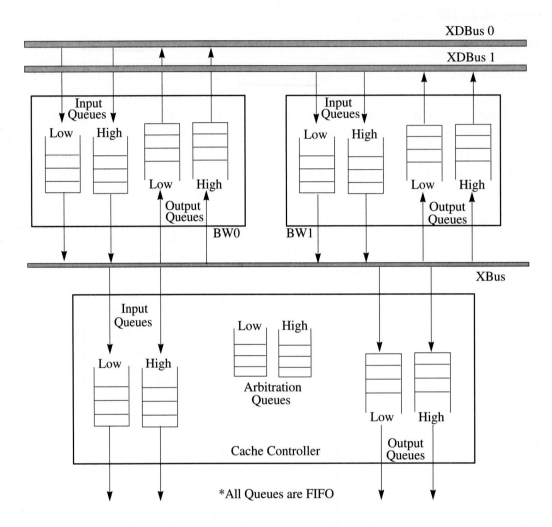

Figure 5-21   XBus BW and CC Queue Structures

XBus data transfers are maintained by a queue structure within the BW and CC chips (all queues are FIFO). Each BW has four XDBus queues, two for output and two for input. The queues are used to send or receive packets between XBus and the XDBus, as shown in Figure 5-21.

The CC also has four packet queues, two for input from the XBus and two for output to the XBus. Additionally, CC has two arbitration queues used to hold arbitration requests from each BW. These queues ensure that packets from multiple system buses are serviced by the XBus arbiter in system bus arrival order. The XBus arbiter also provides a flow control mechanism to guarantee that queues receiving packets or arbitration requests over the XBus never overflow.

XDBus was conceived and initially implemented in the Computer Science Laboratory at the Xerox Palo Alto Research Center. The bus technology is currently in its third generation of design; several commercial multiprocessors systems, including Sun Microsystem's new SPARCcenter 2000 series (see Chapter 9), are using it as their main system interconnect.

5

MBus Multiprocessor
System Design

The SPARC MBus provides an elegant systems upgrade path to take advantage of the latest microprocessor technology as a result of a simple modular plug-and-play capability. MBus connects SPARC processor modules, physical memory, and I/O modules. (Refer to Figures 5.1 and 5.4 for MBus level-1 and level-2 system configurations, respectively.) As a result, MBus allows the building of high-performance, shared-memory multiprocessor systems where system memory is a shared resource allowing both instructions and data to be shared among processors. The price/performance ratio is favorable for multiprocessor systems, since it allows the interconnection of multiple, relatively low-cost microprocessors. The price of a uniprocessor-based system of equal performance would be much greater.

Hardware Implementation

The SPARC MBus interface is a fully synchronous 64-bit, multiplexed address and data bus that supports multiple masters at 40 MHz. It supports data transfers of up to 128 bytes and can support up to 64 Gbytes of physical address space. Data transfers larger than eight bytes occur as burst transfers, allowing MBus to achieve a peak bandwidth of 320 Mbytes/sec. Bus arbitration among masters is defined to be handled by a central bus arbiter. Requests from MBus modules are sent to the arbiter, and ownership is granted to the module with the highest priority. System reset, bus arbitration, interrupt distribution, bus time-out, and MBus clock are centralized functions that must be supported by the system. That is, they do not belong to any particular module. A module ID mechanism allows each module to be uniquely identified and addressed to aid in system configuration.

A typical MBus cycle begins after an MBus module requests and is granted the bus. The module then initiates a transaction by supplying an address during an address phase. The bus slave that responds to the transaction either sources or sinks the data and then supplies an encoded acknowledgment to the bus master, signifying either a successful or unsuccessful data transfer. Figure 6-1 shows the timing of a typical MBus transaction (for an accurate interpretation of MBus transaction timing, refer to the MBus Interface Specification provided in Appendix A).

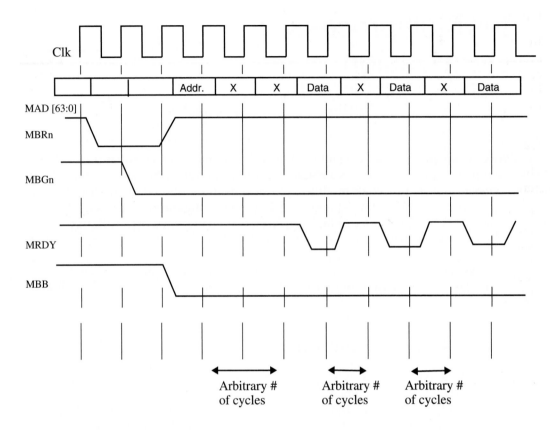

Figure 6-1   MBus Transaction Timing

The data rate is controlled by the slave. The master must be able to accept a burst read, or source a burst write, of the requested size, at the maximum data rate of the bus. The arbitrary number of cycles is dependent on the data rate and can be zero for the maximum data rate on MBus.

When a successful data transfer is acknowledged, the bus master releases the bus. Multiple acknowledgments are sent in the case of burst mode on each bus cycle. An unsuccessful data transfer can be stopped immediately, and the slave can signal for the master either to retry or relinquish and retry. A retry tells the master to stop the current transaction and restart it by reissuing the transaction from the beginning. A relinquish and retry tells the master to give up the bus and try to regain ownership before reissuing the transaction.

Cache Coherency Considerations

In multiprocessing system implementations with multiple caches, as in MBus-based systems, some mechanism must be included to ensure that local copies of data remain consistent. In order to maintain this data consistency, all caches in the system participate in a multiprocessor *cache coherence* (consistency) protocol. The SPARC MBus provides transactions that make it possible to implement such coherence in a simple way.

Cache Protocols

The way in which memory is updated by the local caches can have a great impact on the performance of a multiprocessing system.

The simplest protocol is a *write-through* protocol. Write-through policies require all updates to cache to also be "written through" to memory (see Figure 6-2). In this way, main memory always has the latest copy of the data—it is never inconsistent with the cache(s). However, this protocol results in relatively frequent accesses to memory, which are unnecessary since software is modifying the same piece of data many, many times (e.g., when operating in a loop) before the cache line needs to be flushed.

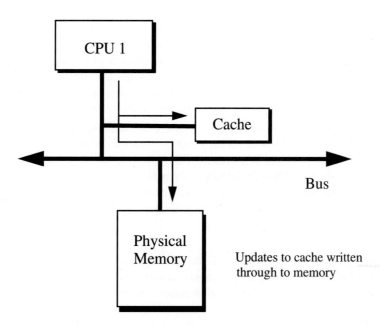

Figure 6-2   Write-through Policy

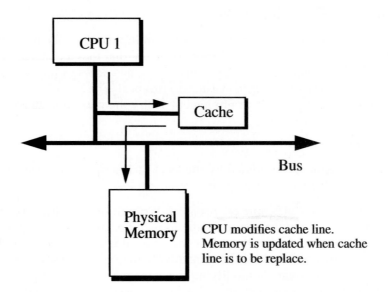

CPU modifies cache line.
Memory is updated when cache
line is to be replace.

Figure 6-3   Copy-back Policy

<u>Copy-back</u> protocol is a more efficient memory update protocol, but is also more complex and therefore more difficult to implement. In a copy-back system, the CPU is allowed to modify a cache line without having to update memory immediately (see Figure 6-3). The data is written out to memory only when the cache must replace the modified cache line with a new one. This protocol not only minimizes bus traffic, of vital importance to the other CPUs on the bus, but also frees the individual processor from the task of having to write to main memory so that it can accomplish more meaningful work.

The introduction of copy-back caches into a shared-bus architecture does not come without a price. Although they help reduce the bottleneck on the bus between the CPUs and main memory, copy-back caches also introduce a new level of complexity—*coherency* (also referred to as data or cache *consistency*). Because each cache can operate on a copy of the data from main memory, the challenge is to ensure that the data remains consistent among all caches with a copy. There are two popular methods for a cache to keep other caches apprised of changes being made to shared data: *Write-broadcast* and *Write-invalidate* protocols.

<u>Write-broadcast</u> protocols require the CPU modifying shared data in its cache to update the other caches. The address of the data and the data itself are placed on the bus for all interested parties to capture. This protocol ensures that every cache line in the system is an exact copy of the others.

<u>Write-invalidate</u> protocols mandate that a CPU cannot modify shared data in its cache until other caches invalidate their copies. Once other caches invalidate their cache lines, the modifying cache effectively has the only copy. In this manner, only one cache at a time

is guaranteed to write to a shared cache line. Write-invalidate implementations have the advantage of conserving bus bandwidth because the modified data does not have to be sent to other caches.

Both protocols rely on caches to be able to identify requests on the bus that affect their data. This is accomplished with *bus snooping,* whereby each cache monitors, or "snoops," the bus for requests to memory from other CPUs. Each snooping cache compares the address of the request on the shared bus against the address of the data in its own cache, using the cache tags. This is the mechanism by which broadcasts and invalidations take place.

With snooping, however, more than a single set of cache tags is needed. With only one cache tag directory, the processor is prevented from accessing the cache during bus snoop operations; bus snooping operations must have priority to the tags to maintain data consistency. This results in frequent processor stalls and, consequently, lower throughput.

Adding a second set of cache tags to a cache control unit is not a trivial task. In addition to the extra control and translation logic required, the physical size of these memory cells (i.e., the tags themselves) can pose a serious challenge to a semiconductor's transistor budget. As a result, an integrated commercial VLSI solution has not previously been available. That is, until now. Recent developments in VLSI multiprocessing support devices bring significant features to MP technology. One of these devices is the Cypress CY7C605 cache controller and MMU for MP systems (examined in detail in Chapter 9, Multiprocessor System Implementations").

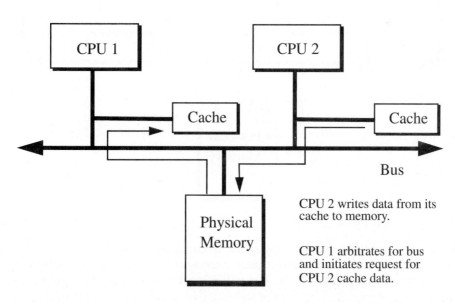

CPU 2 writes data from its cache to memory.

CPU 1 arbitrates for bus and initiates request for CPU 2 cache data.

Figure 6-4   Indirect Data Intervention

Several protocols are associated with bus snooping for moving data and messages between caches. These include *Indirect Data Intervention, Direct Data Intervention,* and *Memory Reflection.*

Indirect data intervention is the simplest method of exchanging data between CPUs. It is also the most inefficient. A typical example of this transaction is depicted in Figure 6-4. CPU #1 makes a request for data (by placing an address on the bus) that is snooped by the cache for CPU #2. A "snoop hit" results if the data requested is owned by the cache for CPU #2. CPU #2 must gain control of the bus and signal CPU #1 to retry later. CPU #2 then writes the data from its cache to memory. CPU #1 arbitrates for the bus again and re-initiates its request. The data is then provided by memory.

In a direct data intervention, scenario, the data is supplied directly from CPU #2 to CPU #1 (see Figure 6-5). This protocol is primarily applicable to systems offering the advantages of copy-back caching policies. Although direct data intervention can save dozens of clock cycles compared to an indirect data intervention process, main memory remains incoherent after the transaction and must be updated when the cache line is flushed.

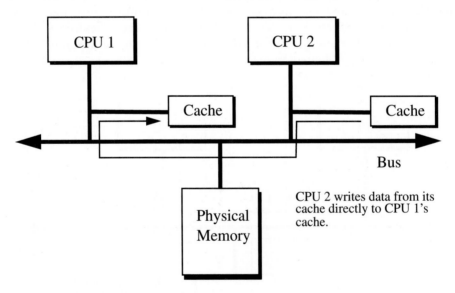

Figure 6-5   Direct Data Intervention (DDI)

The most efficient method of providing cache-to-cache data transfers is to incorporate memory reflection together with direct data intervention. In such a transaction, memory captures the data being placed on the bus while it is being sent to the requesting CPU. If the cache line is not modified before the last such *direct data intervention* transaction takes place, it need not be written out to memory when it is being replaced, conserving valuable bus bandwidth. This updating of the requesting cache and memory can take place in the same, single clock-cycle (see Figure 6-6).

Because cache coherency is supported both in the MBus Interface Specification and in the cache control logic, there is little overhead and little impact on the performance of individual CPUs. With caches snooping the MBus for coherent transactions and intervening to maintain consistency, copy-back (or write-back) operation is possible. The copy-back cache (Figure 6-3) only issues stores to memory when flushing or reallocating a modified cache line, reducing MBus occupancy significantly compared to a write-through cache (Figure 6-2). Since all CPU-to-CPU and CPU-to-memory transactions occur on the MBus, it is much less expensive and complex than the specialized synchronization buses used on older MP implementations.

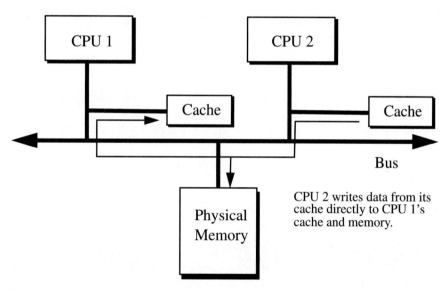

Figure 6-6   DDI with Memory Reflection

MBus Level-1 and Level-2 Operation

This section examines MBus Caching and Caching Protocols in further detail.

Level-1 Signals and Transactions

The MBus Interface Specification has defined two levels of compliance. Level 1 includes the basic signals and transactions needed to design a complete uniprocessor system. Level 1 allows for the operations of *read* and *write* of sizes ranging from 1-128 bytes.

MAD [63:0]   Address Phase

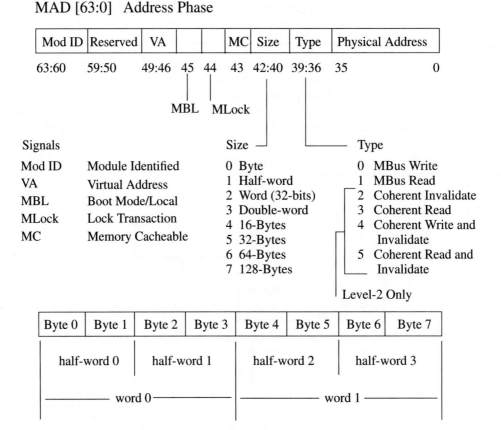

Figure 6-7   Memory Address and Data—MAD [63:0]

MBus Level-1 signals are summarized in section 2.1 of the MBus Interface Specification provided in Appendix A. MBus defines a 64-bit multiplexed address and data bus, MAD [63:0], as shown in Figure 6-7. During the data phase, this bus contains the data of the transaction. During the address phase, the lower 36 bits contain the physical address of the transaction. The upper bits during this phase contain transaction-specific information, such as transaction type and data size.

Level-1 MBus supports two transactions, Read and Write.

A Read transaction merely reads a specified size of data, where size is from 1 to 128 bytes. Reads of greater than eight bytes occur as burst transfers. Reads of less than eight bytes will have undefined data on the unused bytes. A module that issues a Read transaction must be able to receive the data at the maximum rate of the MBus for the duration of the transaction.

A Write operation writes a specified size of data, where size is from 1 to 128 bytes. Writes of greater than eight bytes occur as burst transfers. Writes of less than eight bytes will have undefined data on the unused bytes. A module that issues a Write transaction must be able to source the data at the maximum rate of the MBus for the duration of the transaction.

Level 2—Cache Coherency and MBus

Level 2 adds the additional signals and transactions needed to design a fully symmetric, cache-coherent, shared-memory multiprocessor system. The transactions—*coherent read, coherent read and invalidate, coherent write and invalidate,* and *coherent invalidate*—make it possible to implement caches that maintain a consistent (or coherent) image of memory at all times.

The system performance bottleneck in designing a shared memory MP system tends to be bus bandwidth (refer to "Multiprocessing—Considerations and Practical Approaches" in Chapter 1). Reducing the amount of memory accesses over the bus is, therefore, essential. Using private caches for each processor significantly reduces the bus traffic, since most memory references will access only the cache without the need of a bus transaction. The choice of memory update policy can also affect system performance. As illustrated in Figure 6-3, a write-back (or copy-back) memory updated policy is one in which stores only modify the cache line and do not immediately update main memory. The data are written out only when required. A write-through, memory update policy stores the data to the cache and immediately updates main memory. Since the amount of memory accesses on the bus are significantly reduced, the write-back policy further enhances system performance.

MBus modules include a private cache in order to reduce memory bus traffic. Either write-back or write-through caches are supported, but in order to be cache-consistent in Level 2, the caches in MBus systems must be write-back. MBus caches must also have a write-allocate policy where the contents of the cache line are updated on a write miss.

While a write-back cache reduces bus traffic, it also introduces a problem, since a cache can have a modified line that is inconsistent with memory. When another module requests that line, the most up-to-date copy must be provided. This problem is solved by MBus implementing a write-invalidate, ownership-based protocol modeled after that used by the IEEE Futurebus. A line of data is said to be owned when one (and only one) cache in the system is responsible for writing it back to memory as well as supplying the line when requested by another cache. If no cache is the owner, memory is considered the owner. This protocol allows any cache to read a given line, but allows only the cache that owns the line to be able to write to it. Each cache listens to (snoops) each bus transaction and takes actions, if necessary, to maintain the consistency of any local copies of the line.

Cache States

A cache line can be in one of the following states:

- Invalid (I)—Cache line is not valid.

- Exclusive Clean (EC)—Only this cache has a valid copy of this cache line, and it is consistent with memory.

- Exclusive Modified (EM)—Only this cache has a valid copy of the cache line, but the data has been modified and is different from memory. This cache is the owner of the cache line and supplies the data whenever there is a request for this memory location or when memory needs to be updated.

- Shared Clean (SC)—This cache line exists in one or more other caches. This line is consistent with the most up-to-date copy of this memory location, which is held by the owner of this cache line.

- Shared Modified (SM)—This cache line exists in one or more other caches. This cache is the owner of the cache line and supplies the data whenever there is a request for this memory location or when memory needs to be updated.

Please refer to Appendix A, Figure 3, "Simplified Cache Block State Diagram," which illustrates the cache coherency states.

Level-2 Signals and Transactions

Level-2 MBus adds the Coherent Read, Coherent Invalidate, Coherent Read and Invalidate, and Coherent Write and Invalidate transactions, as well as two additional signals, MBus Share ($\overline{\text{MSH}}$) and MBus Inhibit ($\overline{\text{MIH}}$). All Coherent transactions have SIZE=32 bytes.

The Cache Block Shared signal ($\overline{\text{MSH}}$) is asserted by all caches that have a valid copy of data requested in a Coherent Read. It is asserted in the second cycle after the address is received.

The Memory Inhibit signal ($\overline{\text{MIH}}$) is asserted by the owner of a cache line to tell the main memory module not to supply the data for the current Coherent Read or Coherent Read and Invalidate. The owner will supply the data to the requesting cache. It is asserted in the second cycle after the address is received.

Coherent Read

The Coherent Read transaction is similar to the Read transaction with a data size of 32 bytes (MBus line size). It also maintains cache consistency in the system. When a Coherent Read is issued by a module, all other modules "snoop" the bus. If another cache has a copy of the data and owns it, that cache asserts $\overline{\text{MSH}}$ and $\overline{\text{MIH}}$ during the A+2 cycle and supplies the data no sooner than cycle A+6. If there are multiple copies of the data, only the cache that owns the data will supply the data. All caches that have a copy of the data will assert MSH active and mark their copies as SHARED if they have not already done so. Otherwise, main memory supplies the data, and the requesting cache marks its data as EXCLUSIVE. An example of when Coherent Reads are issued by a module is in response to a cache miss on a processor read.

Coherent Invalidate

The Coherent Invalidate transaction invalidates all copies of a line in a system. When a Coherent Invalidate is issued by a module, all other modules snoop the bus. If a module has a valid copy of the cache line, it immediately invalidates the line. Caches do not have to assert $\overline{\text{MSH}}$. One module (normally a memory controller) is responsible for acknowledging a Coherent Invalidate transaction. The Coherent Invalidate MBus transaction is issued when a processor is writing to a cache line that is marked shared. Because MBus follows the write-invalidate cache consistency protocol, the module must invalidate all other copies of the line in the system. Doing so, the module takes ownership of the cache line, and the write is performed.

Coherent Read and Invalidate

The Coherent Read and Invalidate combines a Coherent Read and a Coherent Invalidate. This combining reduces the number of Coherent Invalidate transactions on the bus. When a Coherent Read and Invalidate transaction is issued on the bus, and if a cache owns the line, it will assert $\overline{\text{MIH}}$ to inhibit memory and supply the data. Once the data has been transferred successfully, the cache then invalidates its entry. All other caches that have a valid copy of the cache line immediately invalidate their cache line upon seeing this transaction on the bus. The Coherent Read and Invalidate transaction is issued, for example, on a processor write miss to read data from the current owner for write allocation. The module knows that it needs to fill the line and invalidate all other entries before the processor write can take place.

Coherent Write and Invalidate

A Coherent Write and Invalidate combines a Coherent Write and a Coherent Invalidate. Again, this combining reduces the number of Coherent Invalidate transactions on the bus. When a Coherent Write and Invalidate transaction is issued, any system cache with a valid copy of the line will immediately invalidate its entry. The cache that issued the transaction will then transfer the line to main memory. Software flush, block copy, or block fill are examples of when this transaction is issued.

Transaction Acknowledgments

A master that has issued a transaction must be able to accept any acknowledgment. Normally, the slave will acknowledge a Valid Data Transfer, but can indicate that an error has taken place. Acknowledgments for any transaction are encoded on the $\overline{\text{MERR}}$, $\overline{\text{MRDY}}$, and $\overline{\text{MRTY}}$ signals. Table 6-1 lists the encoding of these three bits. An Idle Cycle indicates that either there is no bus activity or the bus is not transferring data. This situation can occur when there is a need to insert wait states or during dead cycle to prevent driver overlap.

Table 6-1   Transaction Acknowledgment Bit Encoding

MERR	MRDY	MRTY	Definition
H	H	H	Idle Cycle
H	H	L	Relinquish and Retry
H	L	H	Valid Data Transfer
H	L	L	Reserved
L	H	H	ERROR1 (Bus Error)
L	H	L	ERROR2 (Time-out)
L	L	H	ERROR (Uncorrectable)
L	L	L	Retry

Relinquish and Retry occurs when a slave device cannot accept or supply data immediately. The occurrence tells the requesting master to release the bus immediately, giving another master an opportunity to use the bus. The suspended transaction waits until bus ownership is attained. Once the slave regains the bus, the same transaction is issued again from the beginning. An exception is for the Coherent Invalidate, which turns into a Coherent Read and Invalidate.

Valid Data Transfer indicates that valid data has arrived. On writes, it indicates that the data has been accepted and that the writing master shall stop driving the accepted data. The next data during a write burst is driven onto the bus in the cycle immediately following MRDY being asserted.

ERROR1 indicates that an external bus error has occurred. ERROR2 indicates that a time-out has occurred, for example, from a system watchdog timer. ERROR3 indicates that an uncorrectable error has occurred and is mainly used by memory controllers.

Retry is similar to the Relinquish and Retry acknowledgment except the master will not relinquish control of the bus. The master immediately retries the transaction.

MBus System Issues

Developers must address the following concerns:

- Centralized functions
- System interrupts

- Memory subsystems
- Reflective memory
- MBus connector

Centralized Functions

System reset and bus arbitration are handled externally on behalf of the MBus.

System Reset

MBus systems must provide a mechanism for system reset. All modules should have a reset input ($\overline{\text{RSTIN}}$) from some central reset logic that resets all the logic on a module to its initial state and drives its external signals inactive or tristate. Level-1 modules can also have a reset-out signal (RSTOUT) that will perform a system reset.

Bus Arbitration

Bus arbitration among masters is handled by an external bus arbiter. MBus does not specify the algorithm used by the arbiter and assumes that the system designer will choose one that best suits the application. The only requirement is that fair bandwidth allocation be maintained. Arbitration is overlapped with the current bus cycle.

A requesting module requests the MBus by asserting its dedicated MBR signal and then waits for assertion of its dedicated grant signal $\overline{\text{MBG}}$. Upon receiving its grant, the requesting master can start using the bus as soon as the previous master releases the bus busy signal ($\overline{\text{MBB}}$). The requesting master asserts $\overline{\text{MBB}}$ immediately to acquire and hold the bus. A requesting master will not own the bus if it does not immediately assert $\overline{\text{MBB}}$ as soon as it is granted the bus. The requester, upon receiving a grant, immediately removes its request for the bus on the next clock edge. The arbitration protocol creates a dead cycle between transactions to ensure there will be no bus contention among back-to-back reads or writes from different masters.

The bus arbiter prioritizes requests and issues grants accordingly. A grant remains asserted until at least one cycle after the current master has deasserted $\overline{\text{MBB}}$, and it may be removed at any time after this in response to assertion of requests from other masters. Bus parking is implemented, and if no other requests are asserted, the grant to the current owner remains asserted.

System Interrupts

Each module has a dedicated set of interrupt request lines. A central system interrupt handler takes care of the distribution, status, priority, and level of system interrupts. Corresponding interrupt levels to the module correspond to the SPARC interrupt levels and are level-sensitive. Refer to the SPARC Architecture manual for more detail on the SPARC interrupt levels.

Bus time-out and MBus system clock should also be implemented as centralized functions.

Memory Subsystems

During an MBus transaction, all caches snoop the bus to see whether they have a valid entry in their cache that needs to be modified in some way. For example, if a Coherent Read or Coherent Read and Invalidate is issued by an MBus module, all other modules are required to inhibit memory ($\overline{\text{MIH}}$ asserted) and supply the data (owned), or to mark their copy shared. Memory controllers will react to the assertion of $\overline{\text{MIH}}$ by immediately aborting the transaction, allowing the owner to supply the correct data. Memory controllers are also responsible for acknowledging Coherent Invalidate transaction.

MBus does not specify system details on how memory controllers handle memory errors, but it does provide mechanisms to report such errors. For example, a memory controller that supports error detection and correction may send a Retry Acknowledgment for a correctable error. Any of the error acknowledgments or the asynchronous error signal (AERR) can be used to signal an error.

<table>
<tr><th colspan="6">Present Cache States</th></tr>
<tr><th></th><th>Invalid
(I)</th><th>Exclusive Clean
(EC)</th><th>Shared Clean
(SC)</th><th>Exclusive Modified
(EM)</th><th>Shared Modified
(SM)</th></tr>
<tr><td rowspan="2">Read hit</td><td>N/A</td><td>None</td><td>None</td><td>None</td><td>None</td></tr>
<tr><td></td><td>EC</td><td>SC</td><td>EM</td><td>SM</td></tr>
<tr><td rowspan="2">Read miss</td><td>Coherent Read</td><td>Coherent Read</td><td>Coherent Read</td><td>Coherent Read and Write</td><td>Coherent Read and Write</td></tr>
<tr><td>EC/SC</td><td>EC/SC</td><td>EC/SC</td><td>EC/SC</td><td>EC/SC</td></tr>
<tr><td rowspan="2">Write hit</td><td></td><td>None</td><td>Coherent Invalidate</td><td>None</td><td>Coherent Invalidate</td></tr>
<tr><td></td><td>EM</td><td>EM</td><td>EM</td><td>EM</td></tr>
<tr><td rowspan="2">Write miss</td><td>Coherent Read and Invalidate</td><td>Coherent Read and Invalidate</td><td>Coherent Read and Invalidate</td><td>Coherent Read Invalidate + Write</td><td>Coherent Read Invalidate + Write</td></tr>
<tr><td>EM</td><td>EM</td><td>EM</td><td>EM</td><td>EM</td></tr>
</table>

(Processor Transaction)

Cache State after Transaction

MBus Transaction Issued

Figure 6-8   Transaction Effect on Cache States

Present Cache States

MBus Transaction	Invalid (I)	Exclusive Clean (EC)	Shared Clean (SC)	Exclusive Modified (EM)	Shared Modified (SM)
Coherent Read Reflective Memory		MSH	MSH	MSH/MIH send data	MSH/MIH send data
	N/A	SC	SC	SC	SC
Coherent Read Non-Reflective Memory		MSH	MSH	MSH/MIH send data	MSH/MIH send data
	N/A	SC	SM	SM	SM
Coherent Invalidate					
	I	I	I	I	I
Coherent Read & Invalidate					
	I	I	I	I	I
Coherent Write & Invalidate					
	I	I	I	I	I

Cache State after Transaction	Snooping Cache Action

Figure 6-9   MBuS Transaction Effects on Cache States

Reflective Memory

Main memory can react to a Coherent Read in two ways. If the memory controller supports reflective memory, it updates main memory when the cache that owns the data sends it across the bus. The cache controllers must know that the memory controller supports reflective memory in order to mark their cache entries correctly. When the system has a memory controller that supports reflective memory, the cache entries will be marked clean, since they now reflect the most recently modified data. If the memory controller does not support this feature, the memory will not be updated, and the cache entries will be marked modified.

Figure 6-8 shows the MBus transaction that is issued on the bus, depending on the actions of the local cache. The vertical axis lists the processor-cache action, and the horizontal axis shows the state of that cache. The intersection of the axes shows two things: the transaction that is issued and the state of the cache after the transaction is completed.

Figure 6-9 shows the cache states and actions in response to an MBus transaction. The vertical axis shows the MBus transaction issued and the horizontal shows the state of a cache that is snooping the bus. The intersection shows which signals are asserted as well as the change in cache state due to the transaction.

MBus Connector

The MBus specifies a standard connector, pin-out, and full mechanical specifications for the module printed circuit boards for easy future module upgrades (see Figure 6-10. Also see Appendix B, MBus Module Design Guide). The 100-pin AMP "Microstrip" style connector (AMP part # 121354-4 and Fujitsu part #FCN-264P100G/C) were selected to provide high reliability, ease of installation, and a foolproof keying scheme. Two sizes of modules, illustrated in Figure 6-10 are defined for more flexibility: a full-size MBus module and a half size MBus module. The connector placement and width of the modules are constant between the two and can, therefore, be used within the same system.

Having examined MBus operation, cache protocols, and MBus module mechanical specifications, we provide in the next section an in-depth example of the process steps and considerations when designing an MBus module.

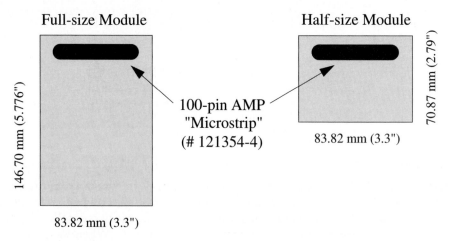

Figure 6-10   MBus Module Connector

MBus System Example

To illustrate the dynamics of MBus, let's use a simple system, as shown in Figure 6-11. Our example includes a physical nonreflective memory module (MEM) and three processor modules (PM), each having a processor, floating-point unit, cache controller and cache RAM, and a SPARC Reference memory management unit. For simplicity, the memory module is only 32 bytes large, and each processor module only has one cache line (32 bytes) corresponding to the memory address.

The example presents series of events to illustrate both MBus transactions and the cache line state changes that take place. Each event causes an MBus transaction and state change. Note that in a real MBus system, this situation would not occur, since most events will not cause a module to issue an MBus transaction. Please refer to Figures 6-8 and 6-9 for explanations of which transactions are being issued and how the caches are being affected.

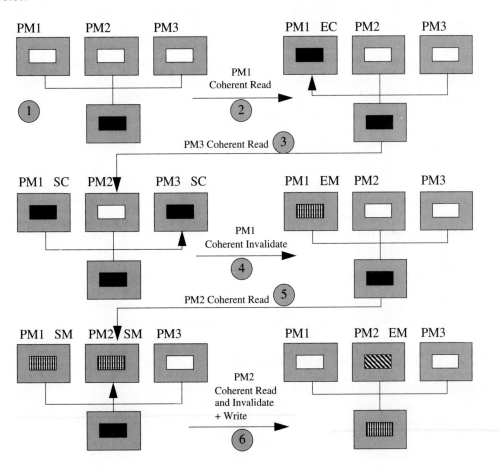

Figure 6-11   System State Changes (Example)

The following numbered steps walk through the system example in Figure 6-11.

1. Initially, the cache line in all processor modules have an invalid state, and memory owns the data.

2. Processor 1 executes a read and gets a read miss. In response to this, PM1 issues a Coherent Read, obtains data from memory, and marks the line Exclusive Clean.

3. Now, Processor 3 wants the data, so PM3 issues a Coherent Read. Memory supplies the data, PM1 plus MSH active, and both PM1 and PM3 mark their entries as Shared Clean.

4. Processor 1 needs to write data into the cache and needs to own the cache line in order to do so. PM1 issues a Coherent Invalidate to invalidate any other copy of the data to take ownership. It also updates its cache and marks its entry as Exclusive Modified. PM3, with a valid copy of the data, immediately invalidates its entry.

5. A read miss occurs in PM2 and a Coherent Read is issued. PM1 snoops the bus and sees that it owns the requested data. It then asserts MIH to inhibit memory from supplying the data and supplies the data to the requester. MSH is also asserted at this time. Both PM1 and PM2 mark their caches Shared Modified.
If this particular system had supported reflective memory, the caches would have been marked Shared Clean, since memory would have been updated at this time.

6. Finally, PM2 experiences a write miss and issues a Coherent Read and Invalidate and a Write transaction. The Coherent Read and Invalidate causes the memory to supply the new data to PM2 and causes PM1 to invalidate its entry. The Write causes the previous cache line to be written into memory. These two transactions occur automatically. Processor 2 updates the new line with the data from the write miss and marks the line Exclusive Modified.

In the next section we'll examine how to model an MBus/SPARC-based computer systems with the aid of the MPSAS behavioral simulator. The term "simulator" refers to a tool (typically a system and its software which imitate the operation of another computer system) that allows you to model SPARC-based computer systems.

MPSAS Behavioral Simulator

The MPSAS behavioral simulator is a SunOS Application written in C++ and SPARC assembly language. It allows you to model SPARC-based computer systems at the instruction or transaction level. The system being simulated is independent of the computer on which the simulation is running. When run on a SPARCstation, it typically simulates thousands of SPARC instructions per second.

The goal of instruction-level simulation is to model the programmer's view of a computer system. This modeling entails simulations of the execution of processor instructions, system and device registers, interrupts, and the memory hierarchy. The structure of the simulator need not directly correspond to the structure of the hardware.

The goals of transaction-level simulation are to model the major components (e.g., each ASIC and bus) of the computer system hardware, to model the transactions between those components, and to support the programmer's view. Transaction-level models are more difficult to develop and run more slowly than instruction-level models, but they more accurately model the computer hardware.

The sample architectures supplied with MPSAS are modelled at the instruction level. These sample architectures are discussed further later in this chapter.

The simulator aids the following activities:

• Porting machine-dependent code; for example, SunOS kernel, boot PROM, diagnostics. The target computer system hardware need not be available for code testing to begin. Also, the simulator provides a software environment that is more easily controlled and observed than real hardware.

• Estimating performance. Accurate instruction counts of a benchmark program can be obtained with an instruction-level simulation. Accurate cycle counts require a timing-accurate, transaction-level simulation.

• Verifying the correctness of a design; for example, testing a cache coherence protocol.

• Verifying the correctness of a lower-level simulation; for example, gate-level. The lower-level simulation and MPSAS simulation of the same computer system are run simultaneously with the same test program, and their results are compared periodically.

• Exploring design trade-off by simulating the different configurations of interest.

The MPSAS user interface is inspired by the UNIX C shell (csh) and the SunOS dbx debugger. It supports a rich set of commands to allow the user to control and observe the simulation. It provides batch facility to combine commands in a text file. It provides on-line help for the commands.

Modular Structure

To build a system, a hardware design engineer selects instances of integrated circuits from a catalog and connects their pins via printed-circuit board traces. Similarly, a user of MPSAS selects instances of "module classes" compiled into the simulator executable and connects their "interfaces." All of the information about instances of module classes and interface connections is located in a configuration file.

A "module class" is the code which simulates some hardware. An MPSAS module class may represent part of an integrated circuit or several boards full of integrated circuits. Instances of a module class are called "module instances." This MPSAS discussion uses the term "module" by itself in many cases where the distinction between class and instance is either unimportant or obvious.

Modules are written as necessary to simulate a computer system. For simplicity, several sample modules come with MPSAS, including a SPARC integer unit, SPARC floating-point unit, MMUs, memory, I/O devices, and assorted buses. The sample modules can be used along with custom modules in a simulation.

The configuration file is an ASCII text file. Different "systems" made from the same set of modules can be simulated by invoking the same simulator executable with different configuration files. For example, a cache module could be included in or excluded from a simulation by using different configuration files.

In addition to the code for the various module classes, a simulator executable contains code that sets up the module classes and their instances calls each module instance every "cycle" to do its next increment of work, handles communications between module instances, and provides an interface by which the user can control and observe the simulated system. This software is collectively called "the Framework." A "cycle" is the notion of simulation time used in MPSAS. Its closest hardware analogy is the system clock.

An "architecture" is a simulator executable combined with one or more configuration files and any files required by the modules in the configuration files. Each configuration file is used to specify a "system" that uses module classes included in an architecture. MPSAS comes with four sample architectures:

- Sun4c—SPARCstation1
- Sun4e—SPARCengine™ 1
- MBus—a generic multiprocessor MBus machine
- Simple—a "bare bones" machine (CPU, FPU, RAM, and serial ports)

Communications—Messages

Module instances communicate by sending messages to each other. For example, a module simulating a processor might send a message to a module simulating a memory device to fetch an instruction.

Sending a message (message passing) takes place over a "channel." A channel is a mechanism provided by the Framework to transport messages. There are two types of channels: *simulation and debug*. The simulation channel is active only when the simulation is running (the simulator cycles are being incremented). It is used by module instances to transfer information needed by the simulation (e.g., a memory request). The debug channel is always active. It is used by module instances to support user interface commands.

Messages can contain data. No message size or content restrictions are enforced by the Framework. However, there is a set of message formats that most modules use.

Each message has a type associated with it (a 32-bit value). The type implies the message protocol (format of message data and its use). The type is used as an aid in the debugging modules and to multiplex more than one protocol on a connection.

Associated with each message is an optional cycle delay. This delay allows a module instance to send a message to another instance such that it is not received immediately but rather is delayed by a specified number of cycles.

Communications—Interfaces

Interfaces provide module instances with access to the simulation and debug channels. An interface is similar in concept to a group of pins on an integrated circuit. Interfaces are visible to the user in the configuration file and in some user interface commands.

Each interface belongs to a module instance. For two module instances to communicate, their interfaces must be connected. Figure 6-12 shows two module instances, each with an interface (the circles) that is connected to the other. The line between the interfaces represents the simulation and debug channels. Module instance *A* owns interface *iA* and module instance *B* owns interface *iB*. When module instance *A* sends a message to its interface, it is received by module instance *B* on its *iB* interface.

Each interface has a name and a type associated with it (e.g., bus of type slave). Each module supports a fixed number of interface types. A module instance can have multiple interfaces of the same type, so the name is used to uniquely identify each interface. Modules can enforce restrictions on the number of interfaces of each type.

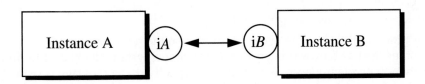

Figure 6-12   Interface Connections

Working with MPSAS Modules

In MPSAS, a computer system is modelled by a group of autonomous units called "modules." Each module contains code and state to model the behavior of a hardware component. Typically, each module's state is private, although portions of it may be shared with other modules. Modules communicate with each other by passing messages and through shared state. A module updates its state based on messages it receives and as time elapses.

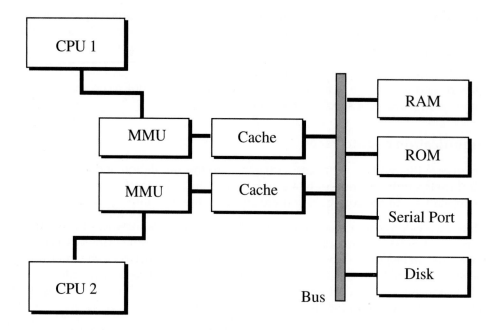

Figure 6-13 Abstract View of A Basic Computer System

Figure 6-13 shows an abstract view of a basic computer system. The rectangles are modules and the lines between them represent their communication paths. The system depicted has two processors, each with a memory management unit and a cache. These two processors share a serial port, disk controller, RAM, and ROM. The bus arbitrates between the requests of the two processors.

The unit of time in MPSAS is the cycle. Modules use the notion of a cycle to synchronize with each other (just as hardware synchronizes using a system clock) and to divide their work into time-dependent pieces. A module may specify that a message is to be delivered some number of cycles in the future. This delay feature is useful in simulating the response time of a device or communication delays.

Simulation Levels

A module can simulate the behavior of its hardware at different levels of detail. As the level of detail increases, a module more accurately simulates all of the behaviors of its hardware, the performance of the simulator decreases, and the effort to develop a module increases.

Modules of different levels of detail can be mixed in a system to provide the required level of accuracy and speed. Two common levels of simulation detail for a module are called "instruction-accurate" and "transaction-accurate."

Instruction-Accurate Modules

An instruction-accurate module simulates its hardware at a low level of detail. It correctly simulates the functions of its hardware, but its timing and transactions may not be correct.

The structure of a system modelled by instruction-accurate modules can be quite different than the structure of the system hardware, because of the simulation's level of abstraction.

The order in which instructions are executed by the processors in the system may in some cases differ from the order in which they would be executed on actual hardware. Quite often these inaccuracies are acceptable since they are not of interest to the users of the simulator.

Transaction-Accurate Modules

A transaction-accurate module accurately simulates the transactions involving the module and the module's state. It is more detailed than an instruction-accurate module.The structure of a system modelled by transaction-accurate modules is very similar to the structure of the system hardware.

Modularization Criteria

In MPSAS, a computer system is modelled as a collection of modules. Thus, the functions of the system must be decomposed into a set of modules. Various trade-offs are involved in decomposing the system.

The functions of a module should be as cohesive as possible. Typically there is a large degree of sharing of data and communications between them.

The degree of interdependence between modules should be minimized to decrease the overhead of message passing. Sharing of state can reduce the message passing overhead.

Typically a computer system has a hardware block diagram that shows the integrated circuits and how they are connected. Hardware designers follow a set of modularization criteria similar to those followed by the module programmer, so their block diagram is a reasonable starting point for decomposing the system into modules. The blocks can be decomposed into several MPSAS modules, or some of the blocks can be combined into one module since hardware constraints differ from simulation constraints. Each bus in the hardware block diagram that has more than one reader should be modelled by a module.

Some of the negative characteristics of a too coarsely decomposed system are:

- Runtime configurability is reduced
- Reuse of modules is decreased
- Complexity of debugging the system simulation is increased (because larger modules are more complex)
- Opportunities for parallel development by multiple programmers are reduced

The negative characteristics of a too finely decomposed system are:

• More states are needed by the modules

• Performance is degraded by excess message passing

MPSAS Framework

In addition to the code implementing the modules, MPSAS contains code to implement the Framework. The Framework performs several key functions:

• Supports module classes and module instances

• Controls the configuration of the modules

• Implements the message-passing facility

• Implements the cycle paradigm

• Implements the concept of layers

• Provides support functions for the modules

The Framework also provides several additional services to modules. These services include data types, interaction with the user, and asynchronous input. In addition, the Framework provides commands that allow the user to print module variables, set them, dump them out to trace files (MPSAS includes a built-in simulator trace facility which allows any module variables and messages to be traced), and use them in expressions. The Framework also allows asynchronous input from SunOS file descriptors to be accessed independently by modules.

The Framework can be thought of as surrounding the modules. It provides the environment in which the modules exist. This concept is analogous to the SunOS kernel providing an environment in which applications exist.

The operation of the Framework proceeds in two distinct phases: configuration and simulation.Soon after the simulator is started, the Framework enters the configuration phase. The configuration phase parses a configuration file and then initializes the modules specified in it. The simulation phase starts immediately after the configuration phase finishes. During the simulation phase, the simulation is said to be "running," if activities related to simulating the computer system are occurring, that is, the message passing facility is active and cycles are advancing. The user can start and stop the simulation at will; the modules and the Framework can stop the simulation as well, with breakpoints.

Module Classes and Module Instances

The Framework supports module classes and module instances. To the Framework, a module class is a set of entry points (pointers to C routines). These entry points are called module entry points. A module class is analogous to a C data type; it specifies the behavior of an object. A module instance is analogous to a C variable; it is an instance of some C data type and has state associated with it. A module instance is associated with a module class but it also includes a state.

Note – The use of the term "module" by itself in many cases indicates where the distinction between class and instance is unimportant or obvious.

The Framework can support an unlimited number of module classes and module instances. The Framework is designed so that increasing the number of module instances in a simulation does not increase the Framework's overhead; that is, the Framework imposes no speed penalty for large number of module instances.

The Framework deals with module classes and module instances during the configuration phase. During the simulation phase, the Framework only deals with the module instances.

The Framework controls which module executes at any time. It calls a module entry point to have it perform some function related to that module's configuration or simulation. The module entry point can call routines in the Framework (called Framework routines) to help it complete its task, but eventually the module entry point returns control to the Framework.

Module Configuration

The configuration of the modules in the system is divided into six steps:

1. Initialize the module classes.

2. Initialize each module instance of each module class.

3. Initialize each interface of each module instance.

4. Create each shared object of each module instance.

5. Look up each shared object used by each module instance.

6. Verify the final configuration of each module instance.

The Framework performs each configuration step for all modules before it proceeds to the next step. For example, all module classes are initialized, and then all module instances of all module classes are initialized. Each module must support the first step of configuration; the other steps are optional, but most modules support some of them. Each module provides a routine to perform each step it supports. These routines are called "module configuration entry points."

The Framework calls the module configuration entry points to aid in the configuration of the system specified by the configuration file. Each entry point can have several parameters associated with it; some parameters are passed to the entry point when the Framework calls it; others are obtained by the entry point calling an appropriate Framework routine.

The module configuration entry points pass information to the Framework by a combination of the entry point's return code and a call to the appropriate Framework routines. Table 6-2 shows how the Framework and module configuration code interact during the configuration phase. The *mod name* prefix in the module entry point names represents the name of some arbitrary module class. Note that only module classes that have instances defined in the configuration file are involved in the configuration process.

Message Passing

Modules communicate by sending messages to each other much like two integrated circuits communicate. The source chip drives its output pins and the destination chip samples its pins some time later. Of course, the pins of the two chips must be connected by wires in order for them to communicate.

Instead of pins, modules have interfaces. An interface provides a module with access to the Framework message-passing facility as a pin provides the die of a chip access to the printed circuit board wires. Like a pin, each interface belongs to a single module instance.

A message sent by a module to an interface it owns is received by the module connected to the remote interface. One-to-one interfaces are bidirectional. The interface that originated the message is called the "source interface" or the "local interface" and the interface that receives the message is called the "destination interface" or the "remote interface."

The Framework allows each module instance to have any number of interfaces. The Framework assigns a unique 32-bit opaque value (called the "interface handle") to each interface during the configuration phase. The module can store this handle for later operations involving the interface.

During configuration, the module can examine the interface type and the interface arguments of each of its interfaces specified in the configuration file. From those two sources, it determines how each interface is to behave.

For example, an MMU module may require two types of interfaces: one to connect to the processor and one to connect to the memory system. In this case, a different type could be assigned to each interface, and the MMU would examine the interface type of each interface to identify it.

Several topics related to message passing are channels, message composition, and interface operations.

Channels

The Framework message-passing facility is composed of three independent channels: positive-phase simulation, negative-phase simulation, and debug. Interfaces may support message passing on all channels.

Table 6-2   Configuration Phase

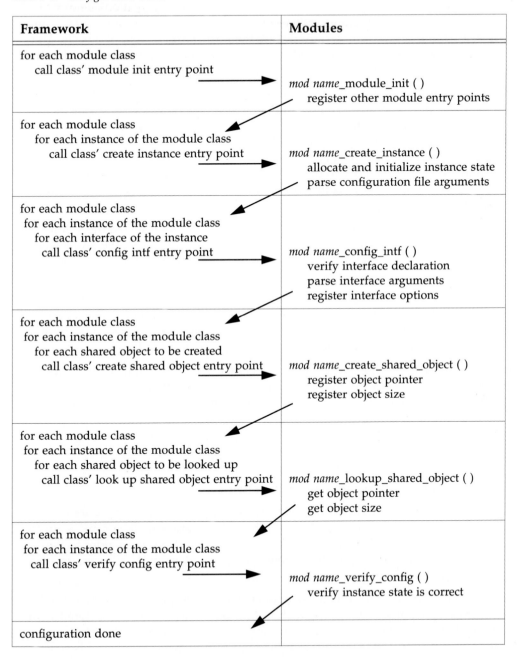

Framework	Modules

for each module class
    call class' module init entry point
	*mod name*_module_init ( )
	    register other module entry points

for each module class
    for each instance of the module class
        call class' create instance entry point
	*mod name*_create_instance ( )
	    allocate and initialize instance state
	    parse configuration file arguments

for each module class
  for each instance of the module class
    for each interface of the instance
      call class' config intf entry point
	*mod name*_config_intf ( )
	    verify interface declaration
	    parse interface arguments
	    register interface options

for each module class
  for each instance of the module class
    for each shared object to be created
      call class' create shared object entry point
	*mod name*_create_shared_object ( )
	    register object pointer
	    register object size

for each module class
  for each instance of the module class
    for each shared object to be looked up
      call class' look up shared object entry point
	*mod name*_lookup_shared_object ( )
	    get object pointer
	    get object size

for each module class
  for each instance of the module class
    call class' verify config entry point
	*mod name*_verify_config ( )
	    verify instance state is correct

configuration done	

Modules use the simulation channels to communicate information relevant to the simulation. For example, a processor may send a message on a simulation channel to fetch an instruction from the memory subsystem. The positive-phase simulation channel is used to send a message to an interface during the positive (first) half of a cycle. The negative-phase simulation channel is used to send a message to an interface during the negative (last) half of a cycle.

Modules use the debug channel to communicate information on behalf of the simulator user. For example, the user enters a command that causes the processor to send a message on the debug channel to fetch an instruction from the memory subsystem and then display it. Debug channel accesses should not change the simulation state unless the user specifically asks the simulator to change the simulation state. For example, If a user requests an instruction in memory to be disassembled, the simulator should not mark the cache as referenced; if the user asks to write to an address in memory, the state of the cache may have to be changed.

Simulation channel messages are delivered by the Framework only when the simulation is running. However, debug channel messages are always delivered by the Framework. Thus users can stop the simulation and still have the modules communicate on their behalf.

Each simulation channel message has a cycle delay associated with it. Depending on the characteristics of the destination interface, the Framework may deliver the message immediately (ignoring the delay) or may delay the transmission of the message by the specified number of cycles. All debug channel messages have zero delay.

The Framework has a message queue for each channel. The simulation channel message queues accept messages with an arbitrary positive delay. A delay of zero is not allowed in certain situations (described later). The debug channel message queue only accepts messages with zero delay.

Message Composition

A message is composed of a size, a data pointer, and a message type.

The size specifies the size of the message data in bytes.

The data pointer points to a dynamically allocated contiguous block of memory of "size" bytes if the message size is nonzero; otherwise the data pointer can be any value. In the first case, a message pass transfers the ownership of the data from the sender to the receiver. The receiver may free the data or reuse it. The sender must not access the data even though it may still have a pointer to the data.

The message type specifies how the message data is to be interpreted. Each message type has a unique opaque pointer associated with it. Message types must be registered with the Framework. If the format of the data for a message type is described to the Framework, the simulator user can observe the fields of the message when it is sent between interfaces.

Interface Operations

Three message-passing operations are associated with an interface: sending messages, receiving messages, and queuing messages. Each of these operations can occur over the simulation or debug channels.

Figure 6-14 illustrates how the three interface operations interact with the Framework message-passing facility. The rectangles are module instances, the rounded rectangles are interfaces, and the objects that look like ladders are queues. In the figure, interface "a" of module instance A is connected to interface "b" of module instance B.

The figure shows only one of the three message channels; the diagram applies equally to all of them. Note that an interface can be connected to itself. A message sent to such an interface is received by the same interface; that is, the interface is both source and destination.

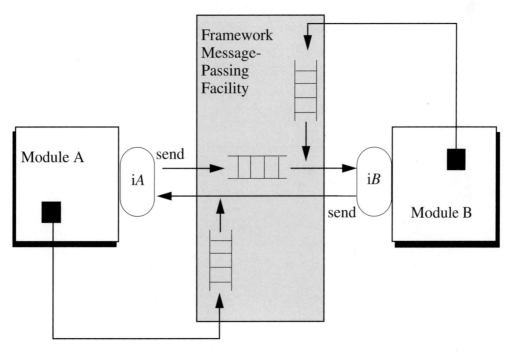

Figure 6-14   Interface Operations

Configuration File

The simulator parses a configuration file, which is a readable ASCII text file when it is started. The configuration file specifies which module instances are involved in the simulation and how they are connected. The configuration file is composed of module class declarations. The classes must be chosen from the available module classes contained in a simulator binary. The class declarations are composed of module instance declarations. Most classes can have any number of instances declared.

Each instance declaration is composed of three optional components: instance arguments, interface declarations, and global declarations.

Instance arguments provide a mechanism for the configuration file to control features of a module instance. For example, a memory module may have an instance argument to specify the size of its memory. This argument would allow different instances of the same memory module class to have different sizes.

Interface declarations specify the interfaces of a module instance. Besides a name and a type, interface declarations are composed of connectivity information, optional arguments, and optional read-only/write-only flags.

Global declarations provide a mechanism for modules to share portions of their state.

Here is a example of a configuration file entry for a fictional processor module class:

```
module processor {
      instance processor {
            args "NUM_REGISTER_WINDOWS 7";
            args "PREFETCH enabled";

            interface ram of type master {
                  connected to ram1:slave;
                  args "ASI 0-250";
            }
            interface control of type master {
                  connected to control1:slave;
                  args "ASI 251-255";
            }
            interface interrupt of type interrupt {
                  unconnected;
            }
            interface cmd_done of type cmd_done {
                  connected to ui1:cmd_done;
                  write-only;
            }
      }
}
```

The module class processor has one instance called processor1. Its arguments specify that the instance should have seven register windows, and prefetching is enabled.The processor1 instance has three interfaces.

The RAM interface is of type master and is connected to the slave interface of the RAM 1 module instance. The ASI argument controls the behavior of the master interface. The control interface is also of type master. The configuration file syntax allows multiple interfaces of the same type, as long as they have different interface names (ram and control in this case).

User Interface

At the MPSAS prompt, the user can enter any of dozens of commands. The on-line help facility shows the available commands or details about a particular command.

At any time, the user interface is "focused" on a particular module instance. The name of that module instance, followed by a colon, provides a prompt. Being focused on a module instance has the following ramifications:

- While many commands are independent of the modules and are universally available, some commands are associated with a particular module class and can only be executed with regard to an instance of that class. By focusing on a module instance, you temporarily add any of its commands to the user interface repertoire.

- The help command shows commands defined by the currently focused module instance, in addition to those which are universally available.

- In referring to the variables of the currently focused module instance, you need not specify the module instance name.

The MPSAS MODULE_CMD_PATH environment variable can be created to specify the order of module instances the user interface examines to match for module commands. If it does not exist, only the currently focused module instance is examined.

MPSAS Commands

MPSAS provides an extensive array of commands. Commands comprise several different groups including:

- Universal Commands

- Module Commands

- CPU Commands

- FCPU Commands

- FPU Commands

- Sun4c/Sun4e MMU Commands

- CMU Commands

The MPSAS User Manual provides complete details of MPSAS commands; the following sections provide a brief overview of each group.

MPSAS also supports a command history facility which provides a subset of the features provided by the UNIX C shell history mechanism.

Universal Commands

Universal commands include: `help, focus, status, delete, version load, load_section, list, quit, print, cycle, step, msg, set, when, snoop, echo, onstop, setenv, alias/unalias, history, if, flush`.

MPSAS initially has its focus on the instance of the user interface (UI) module, but the focus can be changed at any time with the `focus` command.

MPSAS also provides a powerful facility for automatically executing commands when certain conditions, called "triggers," occur. The `when` command specifies a trigger to be checked at the end of each cycle, along with a list of commands to be executed if the trigger "fires." The `snoop` command also specifies a trigger and a list of commands, but in this case the trigger is checked when a message is transmitted between modules. The `snoop` command is useful when debugging newly written modules, since it allows the user to see messages (when combined with the `msg` command). The `snoop` command can also be used to modify the contents of messages (when combined with the `set` command). The `onstop` command specifies a list of commands to be executed whenever the simulation stops.

Some commands provide features similar to those available in various UNIX shells. The `setenv` command associates text with a name; thereafter, the name is expanded in a command to that text. The `echo` command simply prints out its arguments to the screen. The `alias` command associates a list of commands with a name, in effect creating a new command. The `unalias` command removes an alias. The `history` command displays the last few MPSAS commands typed by the user.

MPSAS commands can be stored in files and then executed, with parameters by using the `file` command. Such files of MPSAS commands are called "scripts." You can use the `echo` command to cause commands from scripts to be echoed as they are executed. The `if` command allows you to conditionally execute a list of commands. If a script finds some problem, it can prevent ensuing commands in the script from being executed by using the `flush` command.

The `sh` command executes Bourne shell commands or starts a shell.

Module Commands

Module commands add to the base set of commands described above. These commands are immediately available whenever you are focused on an instance of the module which defines them or they are present in a module instance specified in the MODULE_CMD_PATH environment variable.

Refer to the MPSAS User's Guide, document number 800-6795-02 for the details on each command and for more information on the MPSAS Behavioral Simulator.

CPU and FCPU Commands

The CPU module's breakpoint command allows you to set, delete, and list breakpoints for a CPU.

The FCPU module supports all of the CPU module commands listed above.

FPU Commands

The FPU module show_fpq command displays the contents of the floating-point queue. The finish_fpop command finishes execution of the oldest floating-point operation in the queue.

Sun4c/Sun4e MMU Commands

The MMU module used in the Sun4c and Sun4e architectures defines a single command, xlate, which takes a virtual address and MMU context number and displays the physical address and memory type to which they map.

CMU Commands

The CMU module of the MBus architecture also has an xlate command to translate a virtual address to the corresponding physical address. In addition, a number of commands exist to display the various internal and external data structures used by the CMU. The *tables* command displays translation tables, and the *ranges* command shows how they map memory. The *contexts* command shows MMU contexts that have valid mappings, and *lines* shows valid cache lines.

The CMU module keeps extensive statistics. The *sstat* command, for example, displays statistics about activity on the processor bus and MBus. The *clstat* command shows statistics for all cache lines, such as hits and misses for reads, writes, and read-modify-writes, while *cstat* shows those same statistics for the cache as a whole. The *alias_cnt* command tells how many virtual address aliases were detected on reads and writes. The *mstat* command displays statistics about the MMU, such as how many tablewalks it had to do at each level, and the hit rate on the TLB.

Sample Architectures

MPSAS includes four sample architectures: Simple, Sun4c, Sun4e, and MBus.

The files of each architecture are contained in a directory whose name matches that of the architecture. These directories are located in the top of the MPSAS source tree. Each directory contains:

- C++ language source code for any module classes specific to that architecture
- A makefile (called Makefile) used to build the simulator executable
- A configuration file for each system the architecture models
- Any setup files required by the module instances declared in the configuration files

In order to build a simulator executable, the user begins in the architecture's directory and types make. This command produces an executable file called MPSAS. To start the simulator, the user simply types its name at the operating system prompt.

Simple Architecture

The simple architecture contains one computer system simulation. The simple system simulates no specific computer; it contains the minimum module instances to create a SPARC computer and to run useful programs. The simple architecture is typically chosen for simple SPARC programs that do not need the facilities of an MMU or any special devices. The simple system is the fastest of all computer systems included with MPSAS.

Figure 6-15 shows the system. The boxes are module instances. The lines between the boxes represent one or more interfaces.

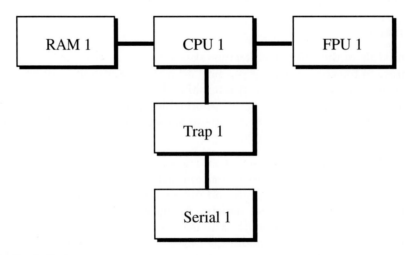

Figure 6-15 Simple System

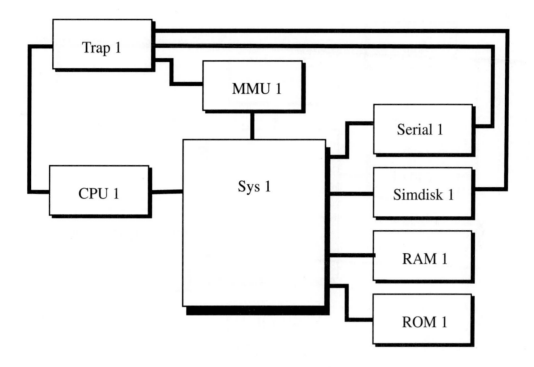

Figure 6-16   Sun4c System

Sun4c Architecture

The Sun4c architecture contains one computer system simulation. There is no simulation for the Sun4c cache and many of the I/O devices. Figure 6-16 shows the system.

Sun4e Architecture

The Sun4e architecture contains one computer system simulation. There is no simulation for the Sun4e cache and many of the I/O devices. Figure 6-17 shows the system.

MBus Architecture

The MBus architecture contains three computer system simulations: SP (single processor), DP (dual processor), and 600 MP. The SP and DP MBus systems simulate no specific computer; they contain simulations of MBus, SPARC Reference MMU, and a virtual cache. The 600 MP MBus system simulates a subset of the Sun 4/600 MP (600 MP) computer system (see "Multiprocessor System Implementation" in Chapter 9.)

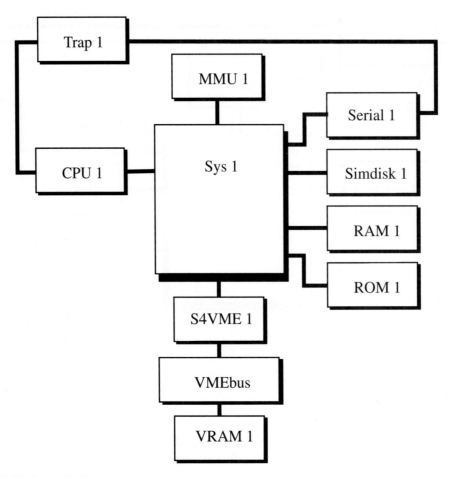

Figure 6-17   Sun4e System

Figure 6-18 shows the MBus DP system. The dotted lines in the MBus module instance are not paths in the MBus; they are just lines that pass under it.

The Sun 600 MP system contains the module instances shown in Figure 6-19.

MPSAS Modules

For designers interested in simulating SPARC MBus systems with devices that are available, MPSAS provides various modules. Listed below are all modules included with MPSAS. All modules simulate at the instruction level. A brief description of each module follows the list. For situations where designers need to write new modules, refer to the MPSAS Module Programmer's Guide, document number 800-6941-02.

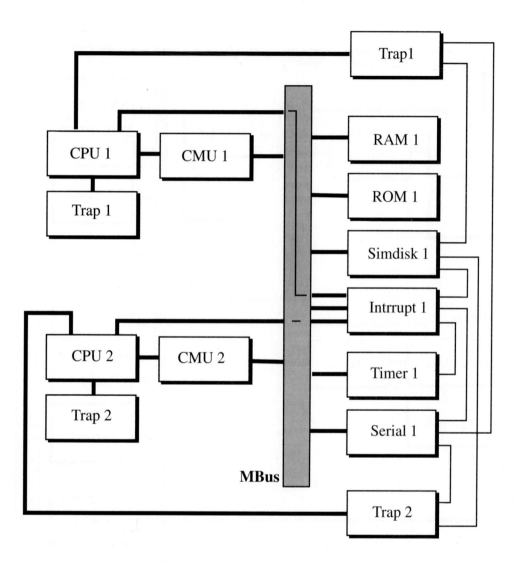

Figure 6-18 MBus Dual Processor System

- CMU: Cypress 604/605 Cache and MMU Module

- CPU: SPARC Processor Module

- Fcpu: Fast SPARC Processor Module

- Fpu: SPARC Floating-Point Unit Module

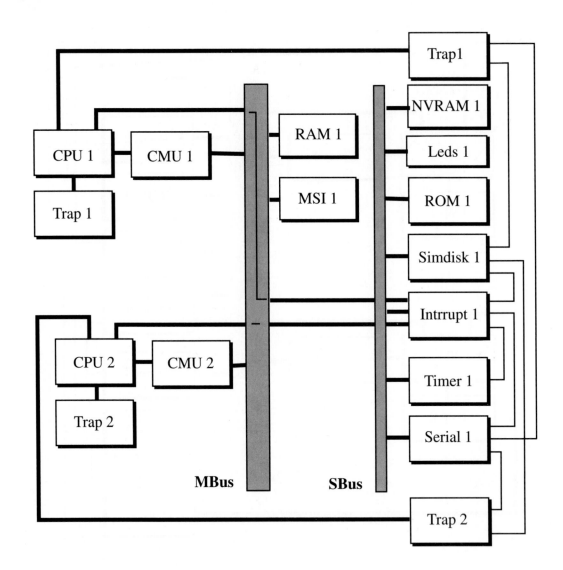

Figure 6-19 MBus-based Series 600MP System

- Gintr: SUN4m Interrupt Controller Module

- Gtimer: SUN4m Timer Module

- Intr: Interrupt Controller Module

- MBus: MBus Module

- MMU: Sun 4c/4e MemoryManagement Unit Module

- MSI: MBus to SBus Module

- RAM and ROM: Memory Modules

- S4VME: Sun4e SBus to VMEbus Controller Module

- SBus: SBus Module

- Serial: Dual Serial Port Module

- Sigio: Simulator Input/Output Module

- Simdisk: Simulated Disk Module

- Socket: Message to UNIX Socket Module

- Sys4c and Sys4e: Sun4c and Sun4e System Modules

- Timer: Simple Timer Module

- Trap: External Trap Module

- Ui: User Interface Module

- Vmebus: Primitive VMEbus Module

CMU: Cypress 604/605 Cache and MMU Module

The CMU (cache/MMU) module simulates the Cypress CY604 and CY605, as described by the SPARC RISC User's Guide, second edition, February 1990.

The CMU accepts memory access requests from a processor module. Depending on the request and the state of the CMU, the CMU may interrogate its cache for the data, pass the request to the Mbus, or handle the request itself. The CMU faithfully simulates the registers and functions of the CY604/CY605.

CPU: SPARC Processor Module

The cpu module simulates a SPARC Integer Unit. It supports SPARC Architecture Version 7 or 8 operation.

Fcpu: Fast SPARC Processor Module

The fcpu module simulates a fast SPARC Integer Unit. It supports SPARC Architecture Version 7, 8, or 9 operation. The version 9 operation is not yet documented.

Fpu: SPARC Floating-point Unit Module

The fpu module simulates a generic SPARC floating-point unit.

Gintr: SUN4m Interrupt Controller Module

The gintr module simulates a SW4m interrupt controller.

Gtimer: SUN4m Timer Module

The gtimer module simulates the Sun 4m timer/counter chip. The timer/counters follow the structure of other Sun-4™ architectures. The resolution of the timers is 500 ns.

Intr: Interrupt Controller Module

The intr module simulates an interrupt controller. It does not simulate any particular hardware.

MBus: MBus Module

The MBus module simulates the Level-1 and Level-2 MBus as defined in the SPARC MBus Interface Specification (see Appendix A). The differences between the specification and the module are:

- the module uses a fair, round-robin arbitration mechanism

- the module does not support reflective memory systems

- interrupts and AERR are completely external to the module

- coherent write invalidate transactions of any size are snooped

- supports a maximum of eight masters and eight slaves.

MMU: Sun 4c/4eMemory Management Unit Module

The MMU module simulates the MMU of the Sun4c (SPARCstation 1/1+) and Sun4e (SPARCengine le) systems. This two-level MMU is very simple and does not contain a cache or hardware tablewalk.

The context register of the sun4c/4e MMU is not in the MMU module, but rather in the sys module.

MSI: MBus to SBus Module

The MSI module simulates the MSI chip of the SPARCserver 600MP system, as defined by revision 1.0 of the "MBus/SBus Interface (MSI) Specification," document number 950-1376-00.

RAM and ROM: Memory Modules

The RAM and ROM modules each simulate a contiguous chunk of byte addressable memory.

S4vme: Sun4e SBus to VMEbus Controller Module

The S4vme module simulates the Sun S4-VME chip that exists in the SPARCengine IE board. This chip connects the SPARCengine lE SBus to the VME bus.

SBus: SBus Module

The SBus module simulates a simplified SBus. The characteristics of the SBus module are:

- The module uses a fair, round-robin arbitration mechanism
- Interrupts are external to the Sbus
- It supports a maximum of eight masters and eight slaves
- It does not support SBus rerun or late errors
- Slave addresses can be up to 36 bits in length
- DVMA SBus masters cannot access SBus slaves

Serial: Dual Serial Port Module

The serial module is modeled after the Z85C30 Serial Communications Controller (Z-SCC). For details on the Z85C30 SCC, see the Z8030/Z8530 Serial Communications Controller Technical Manual, 1988, Advanced Micro Devices.

Sigio: Simulator Input/Output Module

The Sigio module provides file system input and output facilities to modules.

Simdisk: Simulated Disk Module

The Simdisk module simulates a disk controller. It does not simulate any particular hardware.

Socket: Message to UNIX Socket Module

The socket module provides a mechanism to transfer MPSAS messages over a UNIX socket. This capability allows the modules in a MPSAS simulation to communicate with programs external to the MPSAS simulation in which they exist.

Any program can connect to the socket as long as it follows the protocol expected by the MPSAS modules communicating with it. For example, a socket module may be used to connect to another MPSAS simulation possibly running on a different machine, or it may be used to connect to another type of simulator (e.g., Verilog).

The socket module is a socket client. Because of this, two socket modules cannot be used to connect two MPSAS simulations. It is possible to enhance the socket module to support this feature in the future.

Sys4c and Sys4e: Sun4c and Sun4e System Modules

The Sys4c and Sys4e modules are the central modules in the Sun4c and Sun4e architectures, respectively. These modules implement system registers and route memory requests to various devices, including the memory management unit.

Timer: Simple Timer Module

> The timer module simulates a timer chip with one, two, four, or eight timers. The timers are similar to those in the Sun4c/4e architectures, except that they have 31 bits of resolution.

Trap: External Trap Module

> The trap module handles trap packets from the CPU. These are generated by the CPU when it executes a trap instruction that it has designated as external. These external traps typically implement input/output operations in an architecturally independent manner.

Ui: User Interface Module

> The Ui module provides a command-line user interface to the simulator. It parses commands entered by the user and executes them. It also allows modules to send it commands.

Vmebus: Primitive VMEbus Module

> The Vmebus module connects VME masters and VME slaves together. It supports 16- and 32-bit VME address spaces. The address range to which a slave responds may be specified to the Vmebus. The Vmebus arbitration is very simple: The first master to request the bus receives it until the slave is done.

Trace Tools

The built-in simulator trace facilities (`trace`, `dump`, and `group` commands) allow any module variables and messages to be traced. Trace tools are provided that simplify tracing of the `cpu` module as it executes instructions. These trace tools include a simulator command file used to set up the built-in simulator trace facilities for the `cpu` module and a UNIX utility to convert this trace output into trace records that can be displayed and analyzed.

MPSAS Examples

In this section, two examples are presented to give you an idea of what MPSAS can do and how it works. The examples introduce a number of different commands, along with some other features of the user interface. This section does not go into detail about the syntax of each command. That information is found instead in the MPSAS User's Guide chapter on the User Interface.

The first example demonstrates how MPSAS is used to run a simple program. The first example uses the version of MPSAS and support files of the simple architecture. It assumes that installation procedures have been carried out, so that the simulator and the program used by the examples are ready to run.

The second example runs the same program, but this time with a few more commands and features demonstrated.

A few assumptions are made about the example: it contains a SPARC processor module called `cpu1`, a memory module called `ram1`, and user interface related modules.

Example 1: Getting Started

In this example you will see how to start the simulator, load and run a simple program, and examine and change the contents of memory.

A typical session begins with a shell tool running; the current directory should be wherever MPSAS was installed on the machine. If you were actually running these examples, you would begin by changing directories to the one containing the simple architecture (i.e., `sparctools/mpsas/simple`) and then type MPSAS to execute the simulator. The following represents the screen output (characters in boldface are typed input; the rest is simulator output). MPSAS takes a few seconds to initialize, displaying the messages shown below as it does so.

```
hostname% cd sparctools/mpsas/simple
hostname% mpsas
Simple architecture - Mpsas Release 1.1
Preprocessing configuration file "config file".
Parsing configuration file "config file".
Creating C module classes.
Creating module instances and interfaces.
Performing interface configurations.
Performing interface configuration verifications.
serial1: Serial Port A is /dev/ttyp9
serial1: Serial Port B is /dev/ttypa
Negative phase is inactive.
uil:
```

The first line identifies the architecture and the release number of the simulator. The second and third lines show that the simulator is preprocessing and reading configuration information from file `config_file` in the current directory. The simulator then internally builds the system described in the configuration file. The two lines which begin with `serial1:` are the result of the initialization of module instance `serial1`.

The `uil:` prompt is from the user interface module, which is waiting for the next command. This prompt indicates that the simulator is currently focused on module instance `uil`. When the user interface requires a module instance name, it can be omitted if it is the currently focused module instance.

Next, the program named `tutorial` is loaded; it is located in the `stand` directory, as shown in the following screen image.

```
uil: help load
load <load address> <instance> <file> [<symtable start> [<symtable end>]]
     This command loads data into a module instance. It is used to
     initialize modules that contain memory (e.g. RAM, ROM, etc.). It reads
     data from SPARC a.out and ELF files and loads it into a module instance
     at the specified load address. The load address is interpreted by ....
uil: load 0 ram1 ../stand/tutorial
```

The help command shows the usage of the load command. The load command then loads the tutorial program from the MPSAS stand directory into address 0 of module instance ram1. The simulator also loads the program symbol table.

MPSAS simulates a bare machine, with no operating system, monitor, or other code besides that which may be loaded by the user. Therefore, the tutorial program, like any program run on MPSAS, contains its own trap tables and processor initialization code.

In the following screen output, a number of commands are executed that are specific to the SPARC processor module, so the simulator must be focused on cpu1. Notice that the prompt changes to show the new focus. Just to be sure that the program is loaded properly, the read command displays five words of memory starting at address 0 as instructions. The start of the trap table becomes visible.

```
uil: focus cpu1
cpu1: read inst 0 5
_trap_table::ba _start
_trap_table+0x4::mov %psr,%l0
_trap_table+0x8::nop
_trap_table+0xc::nop
_trap_table+0x10::mov 0x1, %l3
cpu1:
```

In the next screen output, the sh command invokes a shell with a command to show the source code for the tutorial program, tutorial.c, in the stand directory. The source code for the trap table, trap handlers, and other support code is also in that directory, but in this walk-through we will not deal with the support code. The program computes a function of the number in global variable num, leaving the result in global variable result. In this section, a number is written into num, the program runs until it stops, and then reads result. The support code stops the simulation when the program finishes, by issuing a special SPARC trap instruction understood by the simulator to be a request to stop the simulation.

```
cpu1: sh moro ../stand/tutorial.c
/*
* tutorial.c -- A tiny program used in the tutorial.
* You set num to something, run the program, and result contains the answer.
*/
```

```
unsigned num;/* you set this before you start */
unsigned result; * the answer will be here */
/*
 * fact (u) returns the factorial of u.
 */

unsigned
fact(u)
        unsigned u;
{
        unsigned factorial = 1;
        while (u)
                factorial *= u--;
        return factorial;
}
/*
 * main() just computes some useless number using fact().
 */

int
main()
{
        result = fact(num+1) - fact(num);
}
```

cpu1: **write word &num 3**
cpu1: **run**
trap1: cpu connected to me stopped the simulation.
cpu1: **read word &result 1**

```
_result               0x00000012 ....
```

cpu 1:

In the preceding screen output, the line of output beginning with trap1: is the indicator that this special trap instruction was executed by the program, stopping the simulation. The four dots to the right of the hex value of _result returned by the read command are an ASCII display of the four characters making up that word. Because all four characters are unprintable, they print as periods.

Next, the list command shows what variables are defined by the currently focused module instance, in this case cpu1. An entry with an asterisk after it has "members" (variables within the variable). These members are displayed when the entry is printed. As shown below, the SPARC processor module pc and psr are printed by means of the print command. The quit command exits from the simulator and returns to the shell prompt.

```
cpu1: list
cpu1 Variables:
annul         annulled_count            bytes        cc            chars
doubles       exec*       executed_count             ext_trap_pending
external_count            floats        fp           fpu_ea        g0
g1            g2          g3            g4            g5            g6
g7            hwords      i0            i1            i2            i3
i4            i5          i6            i7            instructionsintr_count
ir1           l0          l1            l2            l3            l4
l5            l6          l7            latest_instr  latest_instr_addr
latest_mem_addr          latest_mem addr_valid       latest mem_data
latest_data_mem_size     latest_trap_instr           latest_trap_num
latest_trap_pc           lwords       master_rcv_routine           npc
nwins         o0          o1            o2            o3            o4
o5            o6          o7            pc            prefetch
prefetch_instr           prefetch_instr_pc           prefetch_valid
psr*          sanitychecksp             stop on reset               tbr*
trap_count watchexec     watchexternal               watchintr     watchtrap
wim           words       y

cpu1: print pc
0x00001aa4 & _ exit+0x4
cpu1: print psr
impl=0x1 n=0 z=1 v=0 c=0 ec=0 ef=1 pil=0x0 s=1 ps=0 et=1 cwp=0x0

cpu1: quit
hostname%
```

Example 2: Going Further

In this second example, the same program is run again, but with a few more commands and features demonstrated.

To restart a simulation, it is necessary to exit the simulator and restart it. While it might work in some cases to simply reset the SPARC processor's pc and npc variables, resetting does not work in general because the simulator does not reset all the module instances. Exiting and restarting the simulator is one sure way to set the simulator to a known state.

In order to set up the program, the script tutorial_cmds is run in the simple architecture directory. A script is simply a file containing MPSAS commands. We begin by creating a user interface alias for the command sh more; we then use the alias to display the script.

```
hostname% mpsas
Simple architecture - Mpsas Release 1.1
Preprocessing configuration file "config file".
Parsing configuration file "config file".
```

```
Creating C module classes.
Creating module instances and interfaces.
Performing interface configurations.
Performing interface configuration verifications.
serial1: Serial Port A is /dev/ttyp9
serial1: Serial Port B is /dev/ttypa
Negative phase is inactive.

uil: alias m sh more
```

uil: **m tutorial cmds**
```
# tutorial_cmds - mpsas script to load and set up tutorial program.
# usage: tutorial_cmds <value for "num" variable>
if ($argc !=1) {\
    echo Usage: $0 \\<value\\>; flush \
}

load 0 raml ../stand/tutorial
focus cpul
write word &num $1
echo Tutorial program has been loaded and "num" has been initialized to $1.
```
uil:

Lines of a script that begin with # are ignored, as are blank lines. The `if` command ensures that one argument is specified ($argc == 1). The `load` and `focus` commands are the same as before, but the `write` command sets the value of num to $ 1, which is a notation that is replaced by the first argument to the command that invokes the script. Finally, the `echo` command simply writes its arguments to the screen or window, giving scripts a way of displaying arbitrary messages.

Next, the script is invoked by the `file` command, providing the number 3 as an argument. Now that the program is loaded and variable num is set, the `fork` command creates a copy of the simulator.

uil: **file tutorial_cmds 3**
```
Tutorial program has been loaded and "num" has been initialized to 3.
```

cpu1: **fork**
```
mpsas process 2934 active
mpsas process 2932 waiting
```

cpu1 :

The interaction at this point is with the copy (a child process), and any change in state will not affect the original simulator. Later we will return to the original simulator and continue from this saved state without having to exit from and restart the simulator and redo the setup.

In the next run a breakpoint is set. To begin, the `help` command, used without arguments, displays the usage statement for each command. We pipe the result to the UNIX `grep` utility to show only those lines containing the word "break." The ability to pipe output to arbitrary shell commands is often useful.

A breakpoint is set on the tutorial program's fact function, which computes the factorial of a number. The program is run. When the breakpoint is hit, the `where` command initiates a stack backtrace.

```
cpu1: help | grep break
breakpoint [add <address> | delete <number>] - breakpoints
breakpoint [add <address> | delete <number>] - breakpoints

cpu1: breakpoint add &fact

cpu1: run
cpu1: breakpoint 1 at_fact (0x1000) encountered.

cpu1: where
_fact(0x3 0x0 0x0 0x0 0x0 0x0)
_main+0x14(0x10a0 0x0 0x0 0x0 0x0 0x0)
_start+0x40(0x0 0x0 0x0 0x0 0x0 0x0)

cpu1:
```

The simulator does not really know how many arguments each function has or what their types are, so it just displays the cpu1 registers in0 (%i0) through in5 (%i5) in hexadecimal.

With the `set` command, cpu1's `watchexec` variable is set to 1 as we step through a few instructions. When `watchexec` is true (nonzero), the `cpu1` module instance prints instructions in disassembled form after it executes them. As we step through the program, note that displayed instructions have been completely executed.

```
cpu1: set watchexc=1

cpu1: step 4
cpu1.watchexec(31): _fact : sethi%hi (_end+0xffffbb70), %g1
cpu1.watchexec(32): _fact+0x4  : add%g1, 0x398, %g1

cpu1.watchexec(33): _fact+0x8  : save%sp, %g1, %sp
cpu1.watchexec(35): _fact+0xc  : st%i0, [%fp + 0x44]

cpu1:
```

In the next screen output the `watchexec` flag is off. The `when` command instructs the simulator to print the current window pointer in the cpu1's `psr` register whenever it changes, along with the `pc`. Execution continues.

```
cpu1: set watchexe=0
cpu1: when psr.cwp changes {print -v cpu1.psr.cwp,cpu1.pc}
```

```
cpu1: run
cpu1.psr.cwp: 0x6
cpu1.pc:        0x00001084        &_main+0x1c
cpu1: breakpoint 1 at_fact (0xl000) encountered.

cpu1:
```

Notice above that cpu1.psr.cwp changed before reaching the breakpoint. This change was due to the simulator performing the print. Next, cpu1's registers are displayed with the regs command.

```
cpu1: regs
Wlndow: 6
INS                 LOCALS          OUTS            GLOBALS

0: 0x000010a0       0x00000000      0x00000004      0x00000000
1: 0x00000000       0x00000000      0x00000000      0xFFFFFF98
2: 0x00000000       0x00000000      0x00000000      0x00000002
3: 0x00000000       0x00000000      0x00000000      0x00000000
4: 0x00000000       0x00000000      0x00000000      0x00000000
5: 0x00000006       0x00000000      0x00000000      0x00000000
6: 0x0000af80       0x00000000      0x0000af20      0x00000000
7: 0x00001a98       0x00000000      0x00001094      0x00000000

Y:      0x00600000
pc :    0x00001000_fact
npc:    0x00001004_fact+0x4
sp :    0x0000af20_end+0x6e90
fp:     0x0000af80_end+0x6ef0

psr:    0x114010a6
impl ver n z v c ec ef pil s ps et cwp
  1    1   - z - -  0  1   0 1 0  1   6
wim: 0x00000002  (.......X.)  ['.' is valid, 'X' is invalid]
tbr 0x00000000  (tba=0x0  tt=0x0)
cpu1 :
```

Execution continues when the run command is issued again.

```
cpu1: run
cpu1.psr.cwp:   0x5
cpu1.pc:0x00001 00c& fact+0xc
cpu1.psr.cwp:0x6
cpu1.pc:0x0000109c&_main+0x34
cpu1.psr.cwp:0x0
cpu1.pc:0x00001aa0&_ exit
trap1: cpu connected to me stopped the simulation.

cpu1:
```

In the final screen output, the simulator's expr command evaluates the result and compares it with the value of the program's result variable. Notice that the expr command prints the result in hexadecimal, decimal, symbolic (in case the value is an address), and character formats for convenience.

Finally, the quit command quits out of the simulator and returns to the original simulator. The simulator's state is now identical to its state just before the fork. There are several options at this point; for example, run the program again, fork and do so in yet another copy of the simulator.

```
cpu1: expr 4 * 3 * 2 - 3 * 2
0x1218  &_trap_table+0x12'\022'

cpu1: read word &result 1
_result 0x00000012 ....

cpu1: quit
Child exiting
mpsas process 2934 terminated
mpsas process 2932 active
No more children running. Next quit terminates the simulation.

cpu1: quit
hostname%
```

For more information about MPSAS, refer to the *MPSAS Module Programmer's Guide*, document number 800-6941-02 and the *MPSAS User's Guide*, document number 800-6795-02, available from Sun Microsystems Computer Corporation.

SunOS Multithreading Architecture 7⬛

The previous chapters focused primarily on the hardware components and considerations in designing multiprocessor systems. Inevitably one must focus on the software that must run on these systems. Considering that these systems support multiple simultaneous points of execution, multiple threads provide an efficient way for software developers to utilize the parallelism of the hardware. This chapter describes the SunOS multithreading architecture.

Introduction

In addition to having all the functionality and interfaces provided by SVR4, the Solaris operating environment, versions 2.2 and 2.3, also has several value-added features above and below the standard interfaces. The most important feature is the SunOS multithreaded architecture. The SunOS kernel is the first component in providing a complete multithreaded architecture. The kernel provides the foundation on which the multithreaded environment is built.

A thread, formally defined, is a sequence of instructions or a flow of control within a program or process. Traditional UNIX processes have only one sequence of instructions that can execute at any given time and are called single-threaded processes.

In contrast to single-threaded processes, a multithreaded process can execute several instruction streams concurrently (see Figure 7-1). This concurrence allows a multithreaded process to carry on more than one activity at a time. It is important to understand that multithreading benefits applications running on uniprocessor systems as well as multiprocessor systems.

Threads should be thought of as independent activities within a process, which can execute in parallel on multiprocessors.

The benefits of incorporating threads in SunOS include:

- Increased application throughput by concurrency of operations
- Increased application responsiveness—the entire application need not block, waiting for some event to happen
- Enhanced process-to-process communications -- handled implicitly by multithreaded applications

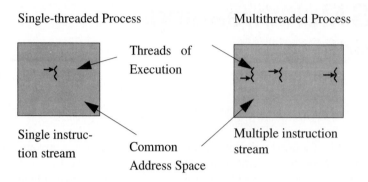

Figure 7-1   Single and Multithreaded Processes

- Creation of efficiently structured programs that carry on more than one activity at a time
- Programming gains from multiprocessing hardware,
- Efficient use of system resources

The following paragraphs elaborate further on these benefits.

Throughput

A single-threaded program must wait each time it requests a service from the operating system. On a uniprocessor, multithreading allows a process to overlap processing with one or more I/O requests as though it were doing asynchronous I/O. Threads provide this overlap of I/O requests although each request is coded in the usual synchronous style. The thread making a request waits, but another thread in the process can continue. Thus a process can have many I/O requests outstanding.

Availability

Availability is related to concurrency. The blocking of one part of a process should not block the whole process. For example, single-threaded applications that do something that takes awhile when a button is pressed typically display a "please wait" cursor and freeze while the operation is in progress. If such applications were multithreaded, long operations could be done by independent threads, allowing the application to remain active and making the application more responsive to the user.

Communications

A multiprocess application that communicates large amounts of data among its processes through traditional IPC (Interprocess Communications), facilities (for example, pipes or sockets) can benefit from multithreading through synchronization of shared data. Much of the communication among processes that requires extensive use of system resources is done implicitly in a multithreaded application because all threads within a process share the same address space.

Program Structure

Many programs are more efficiently structured with threads because they are not constrained by doing one activity at a time. Multithreaded programs can be more adaptive to variations in user demands than are single-threaded programs.

An application can create hundreds or even thousands of threads, one for each asynchronous task, with only minor impact on system resources. Threads use system resources only in proportion to the number of threads actually running.

Multiple Processors

Computers with more than one processor provide multiple simultaneous points of execution. Multiple threads are an efficient way for application developers to use the parallelism of the hardware.

A good example of this multiuse is a process that does a matrix multiplication. A thread can be created for each available processor. The threads each repeatedly compute a unique element of the result matrix by repeatedly doing the appropriate vector multiplication.

System Resources

Programs that use two or more processes that access common data through shared memory apply more than one thread of control. However, each process has a full address space and operating systems state. The cost of creating and maintaining this large amount of state makes each process much more expensive, in both time and space, than a thread. In addition, the inherent separation between processes may require a major effort by the programmer to communicate among the threads in different processes or to synchronize their actions.

SunOS Symmetric Multiprocessing (SMP)

SunOS 5.x contains some core modules and other modules, such as device drivers, file systems, and individual system calls which are dynamically loaded into the kernel as needed. The core of SunOS 5.x is a real-time nucleus that supports kernel threads of control. Kernel threads are also used to support multiple threads of control, called lightweight processes (LWPs) within a single UNIX process. Kernel threads are dispatched in priority order on the pool of available processors. The kernel also provides preemptive scheduling with very few nonpreemption points.

SunOS 5.x is intended to run on uniprocessor systems and tightly coupled shared-memory multiprocessors. The kernel assumes all processors are equivalent. Processors select kernel threads from the queue of runnable kernel threads. If a particular multiprocessor implementation places an asymmetric load on the processors (e.g., interrupts), the kernel will nonetheless schedule threads to processors as if they were equivalent.

In general, all processors see the same data in memory. This model is relaxed somewhat, in that memory operations issued by a processor can be delayed or reordered when viewed by other processors. In this environment, shared access to memory must be protected by synchronization primitives.

The shared memory is assumed to be symmetrical. Thus, the kernel currently does not ensure that processes scheduled on a particular processor are placed in a particular piece of memory that is faster to access from that processor.

SunOS 5.x provides a relatively "fine grained" locking strategy to take advantage of as many processors as possible. Each kernel subsystem has a locking strategy designed to allow a high degree of concurrency for frequent operations. In general, access to data items are protected by locks as opposed to entire routines. Infrequent operations are usually coarsely locked with simple mutual exclusion.

In order to protect and arbitrate access to critical data structures, synchronization locks use the indivisible test-and-set instructions (`swap` and `ldstub`), provided by the SPARC architecture. Unlike traditional UNIX implementations, interrupt levels are not used to provide mutual exclusion (see "Implementing Interrupts as Threads").

In a multiprocessor machine, the multithreaded kernel provides high concurrency within the system, thus making maximum use of each processor. Even environments running a mix of kernel-intensive applications, such as NFS servers, will see throughput increases proportional to the number of processors in the system.

Increases in performance on single-processor systems can also be obtained because the kernel takes advantage of multiple threads to asynchronously perform I/O. The synchronization locks used in the kernel have also been optimized to execute quickly and to consume little memory.

In summary, the important characteristics that make multithreaded SunOS particularly attractive include:

- A fully symmetric kernel. The SunOS kernel is a highly symmetric kernel that maximizes multiprocessor performance.

- The multithreaded kernel runs efficiently on single processor machines and exploits parallelism wherever possible, such as when performing I/O.

- The multithreading technology has made the kernel completely preemptive, thus improving its real-time responsiveness.

- SunOS provides a user-level model of multithreading.

- Traditional (single-threaded) applications will run unchanged in this new environment. Therefore, SunOS provides all benefits of UNIX SVR4—portability across hardware, interoperability across different vendor platforms, and scalability.

SunOS Multithreaded Model

Figure 7-2 illustrates the SunOS two-level multithreaded model. In this two-level model, threads are the portable application-level interface. Programmers write applications using threads and the runtime environment, as implemented by a threads library, schedules runnable threads onto execution resources, specifically LWPs.

Each LWP can be thought of as a virtual CPU that is available for executing code or system calls. Each LWP is separately dispatched by the kernel, can perform independent system calls, can incur independent page faults, and can run in parallel on multiple processors. All the LWPs in the system are scheduled by the kernel onto the available CPU resources according to their scheduling class and priority, as illustrated in Figure 7-3.

The importance of the two-level model lies in its ability to meet the demands of different programming requirements. Some programs have large amounts of logical parallelism, such as a window system that provides each widget with one input handler and one output handler. Other programs need to map their parallel computation onto the actual number of processors available. In both cases, programs want to easily have complete access to the system services.

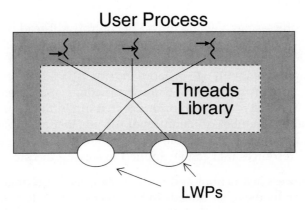

Figure 7-2   SunOS Two-Level Thread Model

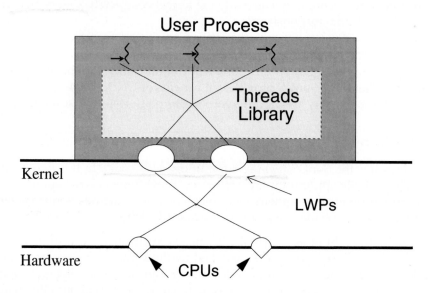

Figure 7-3   SunOS Kernel Thread Architecture

In addition, the two-level model uses system resources only as they are needed. Applications can have thousands of threads without needlessly wasting system-wide resources. In cases where an application needs a thread to be more like a processor, the application can create a bound thread, which is equivalent to an LWP.

The following section describes the user-level thread interface level. LWPs are discussed in further detail later in this chapter.

Threads Exposed

A traditional UNIX process has a single thread of control. A thread of control, or, more simply, a thread, has a program counter (PC) and a stack to keep track of local variables and return addresses. A multithreaded UNIX process is no longer a thread of control in itself; instead, it is associated with one or more threads. Threads execute independently. There is, in general, no way to predict how the instructions of different threads are interleaved, though they have execution priorities that can influence the relative speed of execution. In general, the number or identities of threads that an application process chooses to apply to a problem are invisible from outside the process. Threads can be viewed as execution resources that can be applied to solving the problem at hand.

Threads share the process instructions and most of their data. A change in shared data by one thread can be seen by the other threads in the process. Threads also share most of the operating system state of a process. Each thread sees the same open files. For example, if one thread opens a file, another thread can read it. Because threads share so much of the process state, threads can affect each other in sometimes surprising ways. Programming with threads requires more care and discipline than ordinary programming because there is no system-enforced protection between threads. (see Chapter 8 "Multithread Programming Facilities for Implementing Multithreaded Applications." The chapter also guides the programmer in the use of these facilities.)

Each thread can make arbitrary system calls and interact with other processes in the usual ways. Some operations affect all the threads in a process. For example, if one thread calls **exit**(), all threads are destroyed. Other system services have new interpretations; for example, a floating-point overflow trap applies to a particular thread, not to the whole program.

The architecture also provides a variety of synchronization facilities (see "Synchronization Architecture") to allow threads to cooperate in accessing shared data. The synchronization facilities include mutual-exclusion (mutex) locks, condition variables, reader/writer locks, and semaphores (see "Synchronization" in Chapter 8). For example, a thread that wants to update a variable might block waiting for a mutex lock held by another thread that is already updating it. To support different frequencies of interaction and different degrees of concurrency, several synchronization mechanisms with different semantics are provided.

It is important to note that threads in different processes can synchronize with each other via synchronization variables placed in shared memory, even though the threads in different processes are generally invisible to each other, as shown in Figure 7-4.

Synchronization variables can also be placed in files and have lifetimes beyond that of the creating process. For example, a file can be created that contains database records. Each record can contain a mutex lock variable that controls access to the associated record. A process can map the file into its address space. A thread within this process can directly acquire the lock that is associated with a particular record that is to be modified. If any thread within any process mapping the file attempts to acquire this lock, that thread will block until the lock is released.

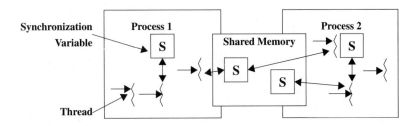

Figure 7-4   Synchronization Variables in Shared Memory

Lightweight Processes (LWPs)

When a thread needs to access a system service by performing a kernel call or by taking a page fault, it does so using the LWP that is executing it. The thread needing the system service remains attached to the LWP executing it until the system call is completed.

An LWP may also have some capabilities that are not exported directly to threads, such as a special scheduling class (see "Scheduling" later in the chapter). A programmer can take advantage of these capabilities while still retaining use of all the thread interfaces and capabilities (e.g., synchronization) by specifying that the thread is to remain permanently bound to an LWP (discussed further in the next section).

Threads are the interface for application parallelism. LWPs are an implementation technique for implementing threads. Few multithreaded programs, if any, will ever use the LWP interface directly.

Threads and LWPs

Since threads are implemented by a threads library and are not known to the kernel, threads can be created, destroyed, blocked, activated, and so forth without involving the kernel. The threads library manages the relationship of threads to LWPs. Additional LWPs are created automatically by the special SIGWAITING signal so that threads library can satisfy the application's, true concurrency requirements (see Figure 7-5).

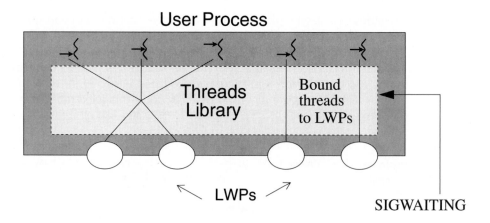

Figure 7-5   Thread Implementation via Threads Library

If each thread were really a kernel-level entity, the kernel would have to allocate kernel data structures for each one and be involved in context-switching threads, even though most thread interactions involve threads in the same process. In other words, kernel-supported parallelism (with LWPs) is relatively expensive compared to threads. Having all threads supported directly by the kernel would cause applications such as the window system to be much less efficient. Although the window system may be best expressed as a large number of threads, only a few of the threads ever need to be active (i.e., require kernel resources other than virtual memory) at the same instant.

Sometimes the number of threads should be the same as the number of LWPs. For example, a parallel array computation divides the rows of its arrays among different threads. If there is one LWP per processor, but multiple threads per LWP, each processor would spend overhead switching between threads. It would be better to know that there is one thread per LWP, divide the rows among a smaller number of threads, and reduce the number of thread switches. By specifying that each thread is permanently bound to its own LWP (as Figure 7-5 also illustrates), a programmer can write thread code that is really LWP code, much like locking down pages turns virtual memory into real memory.

A mixture of threads that are permanently bound to LWPs and unbound threads is also appropriate for some applications. An example of this would be some real-time applications that want some threads to have a global priority and real-time scheduling, while other threads can attend to background computations.

Because both levels of interface in the architecture are defined, a clear distinction is made between what the programmer sees and what the kernel provides. When it is appropriate to optimize the behavior of the program, the programmer has the ability to tune the relationship between threads and LWPs. This ability allows programmers to structure their application, assuming extremely lightweight threads, while bringing the appropriate degree of kernel-supported concurrency to bear on the computation. To some degree, a threads programmer can think of LWPs used by the application as the degree of real concurrency that the application requires.

Figure 7-6 will help visualize how this concept works.

The assignment of threads to LWPs is either controlled by the threads library or is specified by the programmer. The kernel sees LWPs and may schedule these on the available processors. In Figure 7-6, Process 1 (Proc 1) is the traditional UNIX process with a single thread attached to a single LWP. Process 2 has threads multiplexed on a single LWP as in typical co-routine packages, such as SunOS 4.0 `liblwp`. Processes 3 through 5 depict capabilities of the SunOS 5.x multithreaded architecture. Process 3 has several threads multiplexed on a fewer number of LWPs. Process 4 has its threads permanently bound to LWPs. Process 5 shows all the possibilities: a group of threads multiplexed on a group of LWPs, while having threads bound to LWPs. In addition, the process has asked the system to bind one of its LWPs to a CPU. Note that the bound and unbound threads can still synchronize with each other, both within the same process and between processes in the usual way.

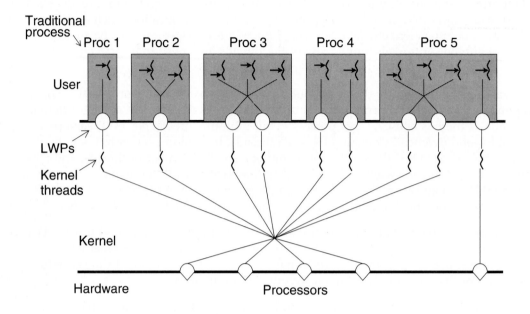

Figure 7-6   SunOS Multithreaded Architecture Example

Threads Library Architecture

It should be understood that threads are the programmer's interface for multithreading. Threads are implemented by a dynamically linked library that uses LWPs as kernel-supported threads of control (refer to Figure 7-5). Threads are lightweight enough so that they can be created quickly, thousands can be present, and synchronization can be accomplished rapidly. The threads library schedules threads on kernel-supported threads of control—LWPs.

Threads Library Implementation

Within the SunOS 5.x multithreaded architecture, each thread is represented by a thread structure that contains the thread ID, a set of registers including a PC, the thread signal mask, the thread priority, and a pointer to the thread stack. The storage for the stack is either automatically allocated by the library or it is passed in by the application on thread creation. Library-allocated stacks are obtained by mapping in pages of anonymous memory. The threads library ensures that the page following the stack is invalid. This represents a "red zone," so that the process will be signalled if a thread overflows its stack. If the application passed in its own stack storage, it can provide a red zone or pack the stacks in its own way.

Thread Scheduling

The threads library implements a thread scheduler that multiplexes thread execution across a pool of LWPs. The LWPs in the pool are set up to be nearly identical. This setup allows any thread to execute on any of the LWPs in this pool. When a thread executes, it is associated with an LWP and has all the attributes of being a kernel-supported thread. The threads library automatically adjusts the number of LWPs in the pool of LWPs that are used to run unbound threads.

All runnable, unbound threads are on a user-level, prioritized dispatch queue. Thread priorities range from 0 to the maximum capability of the architecture (for current SPARC implementations, this number is represented by 32-bits). A thread's priority is fixed in the sense that the threads library does not change it dynamically as in a timeshared scheduling discipline. It can be changed only by the thread itself or by another thread in the same process. The unbound thread's priority is used only by the user-level thread scheduler and is not known to the kernel.

Figure 7-7 illustrates the multiplexed scheduling mechanism.

An LWP in the pool is either idling or running a thread. When an LWP is idle, it waits on a synchronization variable (actually it can use one of two,) for work to do.

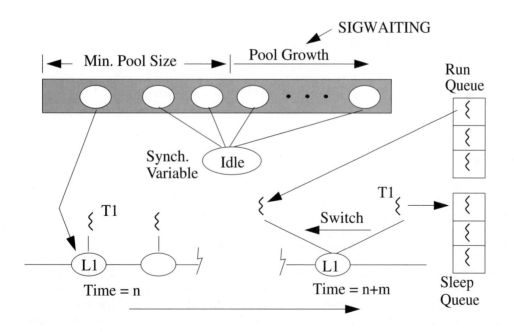

Figure 7-7   Thread Scheduling in the Pool

As Figure 7-7 illustrates, when a thread, T1, is made runnable, it is added to the dispatch queue, and an idle LWP L1 (if one exists) in the pool is awakened by signalling the idle synchronization variable. At Time = n, LWP L1 wakes up and switches to the highest priority thread on the dispatch queue. If T1 blocks on a local synchronization object (i.e., one that is not shared between processes), at Time = n + m, L1 puts T1 on a sleep queue and then switches to the highest priority thread on the dispatch queue. If the dispatch queue is empty, the LWP goes back to idling. If all LWPs in the pool are busy when T1 becomes runnable, T1 simply stays on the dispatch queue, waiting for an LWP to become available. An LWP becomes available either when a new one is added to the pool or when one of the running threads blocks on a process-local synchronization variable, exits or stops, freeing its LWP.

An unbound thread can be in one of four different states: Runnable, Active, Sleeping, or Stopped (see Figure 7-8). Note that while a thread is in the Active state, its underlying LWP can be (a) running on a processor, (b) sleeping in the kernel, (c) stopped, or (d) waiting for a processor on the kernel's dispatch queue. The four LWP states and the transitions between them can be looked upon as a detailed description of the thread Active state.

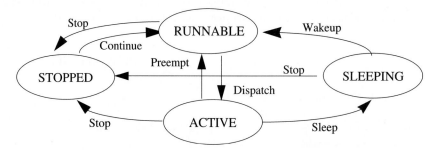

Figure 7-8   Simplified View of Thread State Transitions

This relationship between LWP states and thread states is shown in Figure 7-9.

When an unbound thread exits and there are no more `runnable` threads, the LWP that was running the thread switches to a small idle stack associated with each LWP and `idles` by waiting on a global LWP condition variable. When another thread becomes `runnable` the global condition variable is signaled, and an idling LWP wakes up and attempts to run any `runnable` threads.

When a bound thread blocks on a process-local synchronization variable, its LWP must also stop running. It does so by waiting on an LWP semaphore associated with the thread. The LWP is now `parked`. When the bound thread unblocks, the parking semaphore is signalled so that the LWP can continue executing the thread. When an unbound thread becomes blocked and there are no more `runnable` threads, the LWP that was running the thread also `parks` itself on the thread's semaphore, rather than `idling` on the idle stack and the global condition variable. This practice optimizes the case where the blocked thread becomes runnable quickly, since it avoids the context switch to the idle stack and back to the thread.

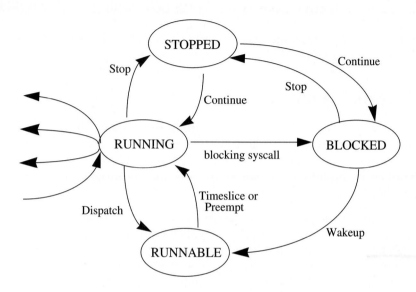

Figure 7-9   LWP States

Preemption

User threads compete for LWPs based on their priorities just as kernel threads compete for CPUs. A queue of active threads is maintained. If there is a possibility that a runnable thread has a higher priority than that of some active thread, the active queue is searched to find such a thread. If such a thread is found, then this thread is removed from the queue and preempted from its LWP. This LWP then schedules another thread, which is typically the higher priority runnable thread that caused the preemption.

SIGWAITING Signal

The current threads library implementation starts by guaranteeing that the application does not deadlock. It does so by using the SIGWAITING signal that is sent by the kernel when all the LWPs in the process block in indefinite waits (refer to Figure 7-7). The threads library ignores SIGWAITING by default. When the number of threads exceeds the number of LWPs in the pool, the threads library installs a handler for SIGWAITING. If the threads library receives a SIGWAITING and there are runnable threads, it creates a new LWP and adds it to the pool. If there are no runnable threads at the time the signal is received and the number of threads is less than the number of LWPS in the pool, then it disables SIGWAITING.

The number of LWPs in the pool can grow to be greater than the number of threads currently in the process because of previous receptions of SIGWAITING or uses of thr_setconcurrency command (see "Thread Creation and Scheduling" in Chapter 8). This condition can result in an excessive number of LWPs in the pool. The threads library therefore "ages" LWPs; they are terminated if they are unused for a "long" time, currently 5 minutes. Termination is implemented by setting a per-LWP timer whenever the LWP starts idling; if the timer goes off, the LWP is terminated.

SunOS Kernel Architecture

Each kernel thread is a single flow of control within the kernel's address space. The kernel threads are fully preemptible and can be scheduled by any of the scheduling classes in the system, including the real-time (fixed priority) class. Since all other execution entities are built by using kernel threads, they represent a fully preemptive, real-time "nucleus" within the kernel.

Another key feature of the SunOS kernel architecture is that kernel threads employ synchronization primitives that support protocols for preventing priority inversion. Priority inversion is a condition which occurs when a higher priority thread is blocked by one or more lower priority threads for a prolonged period of time. Priority inversion is discussed in further detail in "Realtime Scheduling" in this chapter.

SunOS also uses kernel threads to provide asynchronous kernel activity, such as asynchronous writes to disk, servicing STREAMS queues, and callouts. This removes various diversions in the idle loop and trap code and replaces them with independently scheduled threads. Not only does this process increase potential concurrency (these activities can be handled by other CPUs), but it also gives each asynchronous activity a priority so that it can be appropriately scheduled.

Interrupts are also handled by kernel threads. The kernel synchronizes with interrupt handlers via normal thread synchronization primitives. For example, if an interrupt thread encounters a locked mutex, it blocks until the mutex is unlocked. In SunOS, synchronization variables, rather than processor priority levels are used to control access to all shared kernel data.

Data Structures

In the traditional UNIX kernel, the user and proc structures contained all kernel data for the process. Processor data was held in global variables and data structures. The per-process data was divided among non-swappable data in the proc structure and swappable data in the user structure. The kernel stack of the process, which is also swappable, was allocated with the user structure in the user area, usually one or two pages long.

The SunOS kernel separates this data into data associated with each LWP and its kernel thread, the data associated with each process, and the data associated with each processor. Figure 7-10 shows the relationship of these data structures in the SunOS kernel.

The per-process data is contained in the proc structure. The proc structure contains a list of kernel threads associated with the process, a pointer to the process address space, user credentials, and the list of signal handlers. The proc structure also contains the vestigial user structure, which is much smaller than a page and is not practical to swap.

The LWP structure contains the per-LWP data such as the process-control block (pcb) for storing user-level processor registers, system call arguments, signal handling masks, resource usage information, and profiling pointers. It also contains pointers to the associated kernel thread and process structures. The kernel stack of the thread is allocated with the LWP structure inside a swappable area.

The kernel thread structure contains the kernel program counter and stack registers, scheduling class, dispatch queue links, and pointers to the stack and the associated LWP, process, and CPU structures. The thread structure is not swapped, so it also contains some data associated with the LWP that is needed even when the LWP structure is swapped out. Thread structures are linked on a list of threads for the process and on a list of all existing threads in the system.

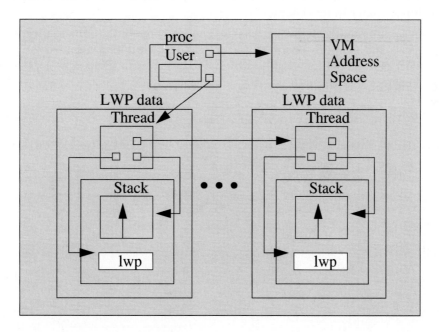

Figure 7-10 MT Data Structures for a Process

Per-processor data is kept in the CPU structure, which has pointers to the currently executing thread, the idle thread for that CPU, current run queues, and interrupt handling information. There is a substructure of the CPU structure that can be architecture-dependent, but the main body is intended to be applicable to most multiprocessing architectures.

To speed access to the thread, LWP, process, and CPU structures, the SPARC implementation uses a global register, **%g7**, to point to the current thread structure. A C preprocessor macro, **curthread**, allows access to fields in the current thread structure with a single instruction. The current LWP, process, and CPU structures are quickly accessible through pointers in the thread structure.

Scheduling

SunOS 5.x provides several scheduling classes. Every kernel thread is associated with a scheduling class. The scheduling class determines how kernel-level threads are dispatched with respect to each other.

The scheduling classes currently supported are sys (system), timesharing, and realtime (fixed-priority). The scheduler chooses the thread with the greatest global priority to run on the CPU. If more than one thread has the same priority, they are dispatched in round-robin order. SunOS real-time scheduling is discussed further in "Real Time Scheduling" later in this chapter.

SunOS 5.x is fully preemptible, which enables the implementation of a real-time scheduling class and support for interrupt threads. Preemption is disabled only in a few places for short periods of time; that is, a runnable thread runs as soon as is possible after its priority becomes high enough.

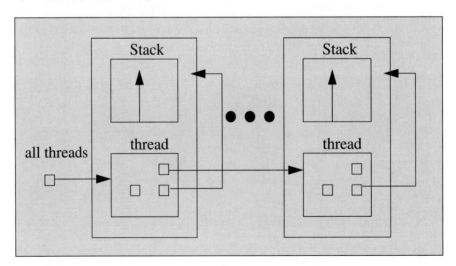

Figure 7-11 System Threads

System threads can be created for short or long-term activities. They are scheduled like any other thread, but usually belong to the system scheduling class. These threads have no need for LWP structures, so the thread structure and stack for these threads can be allocated together in a non-swappable area, as shown in Figure 7-11.

Stack allocations are handled by a segment driver, **seg_kp**. It handles virtual memory allocations for the kernel that can be paged or swapped out; it also provides the red zones to detect stack overflow. System threads use the segment driver for the stack and the thread structure in a non-swappable region. LWPs use it to allocate the LWP structure and kernel stack in a swappable region.

Synchronization Architecture

The kernel implements the same synchronization objects for internal use as are provided by the user-level libraries for use in multithreaded application programs. These objects are mutual exclusion locks, condition variables, semaphores, and multiple readers, single writer (readers/writer) locks. These interfaces are described in detail in Chapter 8.

Synchronization objects are all implemented such that the behavior of the synchronization object is specified when it is initialized. Synchronization operations, such as acquiring a mutex lock, take a pointer to the object as an argument and may behave somewhat differently, depending on the type and optional type-specific argument specified when the object was initialized. Most of the synchronization objects have types that enable collecting statistics, such as blocking counts or times. A patchable kernel variable can also set the default types to enable statistics gathering. This technique allows the selection of statistics gathering on particular synchronization objects or on the kernel as a whole.

The semantics of most of the synchronization primitives cause the calling thread to be prevented from progressing past the primitive until some condition is satisfied. The way in which further progress is impeded (e.g., sleep, spin, or other) is a function of the initialization. By default, the kernel thread synchronization primitives that can logically block, can potentially sleep.

A variant of the condition variable wait primitive and the semaphore inherent primitive are provided for situations where a kernel thread may block for long or indeterminate periods, but still be interruptible when signalled. There is no nonlocal jump to the head of the system call, as a traditional sleep routine might contain. When a signal is pending, the primitive returns with a value indicating that the blocking was interrupted by a signal and the caller must release any resources and return.

Implementing Interrupts as Threads

Since interrupts in SunOS are kernel threads, the kernel synchronizes with interrupt handlers via normal thread synchronization primitives. Most other implementations use processor priority levels.

This scheme has several drawbacks. First, the raising and lowering of interrupt priority can be an expensive operation, especially on architectures that require external interrupt controllers (remember that mutexes are heavily used). Second, in a modular kernel, such as SunOS, many subsystems are interdependent. In several cases (e.g., mapping in kernel memory or memory allocation) these requests can come from interrupt handlers and can involve many kernel subsystems. In turn, the mutexes used in many kernel subsystems must protect themselves at a relatively high interrupt priority from the possibility that they may be required by an interrupt handler. This need tends to keep interrupt priority high for relatively long periods, and the cost of raising and lowering interrupt priority must be paid for every mutex acquisition and release. Lastly, interrupt handlers must live in a constrained environment that avoids any use of kernel functions that can potentially sleep, even for short periods.

To avoid these drawbacks, the SunOS kernel treats most interrupts as asynchronously created and dispatched high-priority threads. This treatment enables these interrupt handlers to sleep, if required, and to use the standard synchronization primitives.

Interrupts must be efficient, so a full thread creation for each interrupt is impractical. Instead, SunOS 5.x preallocates interrupt threads, already partly initialized. When an interrupt occurs, a minimum amount of work is needed to move onto the stack of an interrupt thread and set it as the current thread. At this point, the interrupt thread and the interrupted thread are not completely separated. The interrupt thread is not yet a full-fledged thread (it cannot be descheduled); the interrupted thread is pinned until the interrupt thread returns or blocks and cannot proceed on another CPU. When the interrupt returns, the state of the interrupted thread is restored.

Interrupts can nest. An interrupt thread can itself be interrupted and be pinned by another interrupt thread. If an interrupt thread blocks on a synchronization variable (e.g., mutex or condition variable), it saves state (passivates) to make it a full-fledged thread, capable of being run by any CPU, and then returns to the pinned thread. Thus, most of the overhead of creating a full thread is only done when the interrupt must block, because of contention. On SPARC, this overhead involves copying the currently valid register window to the stack. Copying is done only if the interrupt handler sleeps, not during interrupt handling without contention.

While an interrupt thread is in progress, the interrupt level it is handling and all lower-priority interrupts must be blocked. This requirement is handled by the normal interrupt priority mechanism unless the thread blocks. If it blocks, these interrupts must remain disabled in case the interrupt handler is not reenterable at the point that it blocked or it is still doing high-priority processing (i.e., should not be interrupted by lower-priority work). While it is blocked, the interrupt thread is bound to the processor it started on as an implementation convenience and to guarantee that an interrupt thread will always be available when an interrupt occurs (though this guarantee may change in the future). A flag is set in the CPU structure, indicating that an interrupt at that level has blocked, and the minimum interrupt level is noted. Whenever the interrupt level changes, the CPU's base interrupt level is checked, and the actual interrupt priority level is never allowed to be below that level.

An interrupt can become a normal thread; the pinned thread is released and the CPU's interrupt priority level is lowered, allowing an interrupt thread to continue executing up into the kernel without blocking interrupts.

An alternative approach is to have the interrupt thread capture the device state and then wake up another thread that is waiting to do the remainder of the servicing with interrupts enabled. This approach has the disadvantages of requiring device drivers to be restructured and always requiring a full context switch to another thread.

The approach used in SunOS 5.x allows interrupt threads to become normal threads when required, thus, avoiding the disadvantages.

Interrupt Thread Cost

The additional overhead in taking an interrupt is about 40 SPARC instructions. The savings in the mutex acquire/release path is about 12 instructions. However, mutex operations are much more frequent than interrupts, so there is a net gain in time cost, as long as interrupts do not block too frequently. The work to convert an interrupt into a "real" thread is performed only when there is lock contention.

There is a cost in terms of memory usage also. Currently, an interrupt thread is preallocated for each potentially active interrupt level below the thread level for each CPU. Nine interrupt levels on the Sun SPARC implementation can potentially use threads. An additional interrupt thread is preallocated for the clock (one per system). Each kernel thread requires at least 8 Kbytes of memory for a stack. The memory cost can be higher if there are many interrupt threads.

However, it is unlikely that all interrupt levels are active at any one time, so it is possible to have a small pool of interrupt threads on each CPU and block all subsequent interrupts below the thread level when the pool is empty, essentially limiting how many interrupts can be simultaneously active.

Clock Interrupt

The clock interrupt is worth noting because it is handled specially. A clock interrupt occurs every 10 ms, or 100 times a second. There is only one clock interrupt thread in the system (not one per CPU); the clock interrupt handler invokes the clock thread only if it is not already active.

The clock thread could possibly be delayed for more than one clock tick by blocking on a mutex or by higher-priority level interrupts. When a clock tick occurs and the clock thread is already active, the interrupt is cleared and a counter is incremented. If the clock thread finds the counter nonzero before it returns, it will decrement the counter and repeat the clock processing. This situation occurs very rarely in practice. When it occurs, it is usually due to heavy activity at higher interrupt levels. It can also occur during debugging.

Real-time Scheduling

Having described the overall thread environment and how threads interact through the use of shared memory and synchronization objects, we describe in further detail the real-time scheduling features of SunOS.

Priority Model

Each kernel thread has an assigned priority (or user priority) and an inherited priority. The assigned priority determines the thread's global priority. The inherited priority, derived through priority inheritance as described below, and the global priority determine the dispatch priority, the actual value used in queuing and selecting a kernel thread for execution.

The dispatcher uses an array of dispatch queues, indexed by dispatch priority. When a kernel thread is made runnable, it is placed on a dispatch queue, typically at the end, corresponding to its dispatch priority. When a processor switches to a new kernel thread, it always selects the thread at the beginning of the highest priority non-empty dispatch queue. Kernel threads cannot change dispatch priority while on a dispatch queue; the thread must be first removed, its dispatch priority adjusted, and then the thread can be placed on a different dispatch queue.

When a kernel thread needs to wait on a synchronization object, it is placed on a sleep queue associated with the synchronization object. The sleep queue is maintained in dispatch priority order, so that when the synchronization object is released, the highest priority thread waiting for the object is at the head of the sleep queue.

Scheduling Attributes

A scheduling class associated with every kernel level thread unit determines its scheduling policy. The kernel scheduler dispatches threads based on priority. A kernel thread's priority is kept as a relative class that is compared by the kernel scheduling code to a global, system-wide priority map. The kernel checks the global priority to choose a kernel thread to run. Figure 7-12 illustrates how class-based priorities are mapped to global priorities.

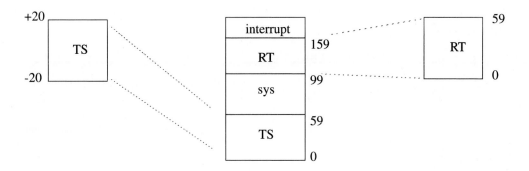

Figure 7-12 The Global Priority Model

A new thread inherits the scheduling class of its parent. The class consists of a class ID and a pointer to class-specific data. The class-specific data contains class-specific priority, a time quantum, and some other class-related data. A thread can change its scheduling class by using the **priocntl**(2) system call. The **priocntl**(2) system call can also be used to change other parameters associated with thread processor usage.

Scheduling class attributes are unique to each class; the timesharing class supports a time-slicing technique for threads using the processor. Timesharing class threads are scheduled dynamically, with a few hundred milliseconds per time slice. The timesharing scheduler switches context in round-robin fashion often enough to give every thread an equal opportunity to run. The sys class schedules the execution of special system threads and interrupt threads. Threads in the sys class have fixed priorities established by the kernel when they are started. A user thread cannot change its class to sys class. The real-time class supports a fixed priority technique of processor access. Real-time threads are scheduled strictly on the basis of their priority and the time quantum associated with them. A real-time thread with infinite time quantum runs until it terminates, blocks or is preempted. Figure 7-12 also shows the default configuration of scheduling classes in SunOS 5.0.

Note that interrupt thread priorities are computed such that they are always the highest priority threads in the system. If a scheduling class is dynamically loaded, the priorities of the interrupt threads are recomputed to ensure that they remain the highest priority threads in the system.

Scheduling

SunOS 5.0 is optimized to run on a shared-memory multiprocessor system; kernel threads, their data, and synchronization objects are shared by all processors. It can be assumed that each processor can send an interrupt to any other processor. Except for specially configured threads bound to a single processor, threads can be selected for dispatch on any processor.

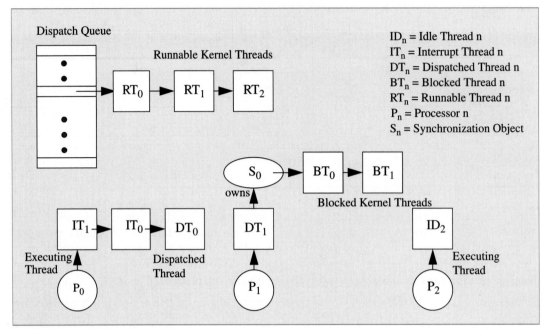

Figure 7-13 Scheduling Example

As far as scheduling is concerned, kernel threads can be in one of three states: blocked, runnable, or executing. Figure 7-13 shows examples of each of these cases.

Blocked kernel threads are those waiting on some synchronization object, such as BT_n. When the object is released, the highest priority or all waiting kernel threads in the sleep queue are made runnable. Unblocked kernel threads are placed at the end of the dispatch queue for their dispatch priority, such as RT_n. A kernel thread enters the executing state when a processor selects it for execution, such as DT_n. An executing thread can become blocked by waiting on a synchronization object, or can be preempted by a higher priority thread and placed back on the dispatch queue as a runnable thread. When an executing thread blocks, the system dispatches another kernel thread.

In a uniprocessor system, real-time scheduling is defined to mean that the highest-priority kernel thread is dispatched, within a bounded time of its becoming runnable. The obvious extension to an *n*-processor environment is that the *n* highest-priority kernel threads should be dispatched. Unfortunately, this state is not achievable in a system in which some threads are restricted to or from certain processors. Therefore, because of more local generalization, scheduling operations are emphasized in terms of a single thread or single processor at a time. As a result, a runnable thread will be dispatched if it has higher priority than some thread currently executing on a processor for which this thread has affinity. Stated from the processor point of view: Every processor is executing a thread with at least as high dispatch priority as the highest among the runnable threads having affinity for this processor. This objective can guarantee the dispatch latency for a thread only if it remains the highest-priority thread on the dispatch queue until dispatched.

Priority Inversion

Priority inversion is the condition that occurs when the execution of a high priority thread is blocked by a lower priority thread. If the duration of priority inversion in a system is unbounded, it is said to be uncontrolled. Uncontrolled priority inversion can cause unbounded delays during blocking, resulting in missed deadlines even under very low levels of processor utilization. Priority inversion occurs because of hidden scheduling and thread synchronization.

Hidden Scheduling

Hidden scheduling is defined as that work done asynchronously in the kernel on behalf of kernel threads without regard to their priority. One example is the traditional model of streams processing. In this traditional model, whenever a process is about to return from the kernel to user mode, the kernel checks to see if any requests are pending in the streams queues; if so, these requests are processed before the thread returns to user mode. In effect, these requests are being handled at the wrong priority.

To address the problem of hidden scheduling, kernel threads are used to do the processing, so that work done by these kernel threads will not preempt or run at the expense of real-time work. The processing of the streams queues has been dealt with in this fashion and similarly for the delayed processing scheduled via a time-out.

The Priority Inversion Problem

By way of illustration, consider the case where a high-priority thread attempts to acquire a `mutex`, which is held by a lower-priority thread, and is blocked. The amount of time can potentially be very long—in fact, it can be unbounded, since the amount of time a high-priority thread must wait for a `mutex` to become unlocked can depend not only on the duration of some critical sections, but on the duration of the complete execution of some threads. Figure 7-14 illustrates this situation: a low-priority thread T_2 blocks a high-priority thread T_1 because T_2 holds the synchronization object So which T1 wants to acquire. A medium-priority thread T_3 preempts the execution of T_2. T_1's blocking time is now dependent on the duration of T_3's execution.

To solve the priority inversion problem, SunOS implements a basic *priority inheritance protocol*. Simply stated, when a higher-priority thread is being blocked, its priority is given (or willed) to the lower-priority thread that is blocking its progress. When the lower-priority threads cease to block a high-priority thread, the lower-priority threads revert to their original priority.

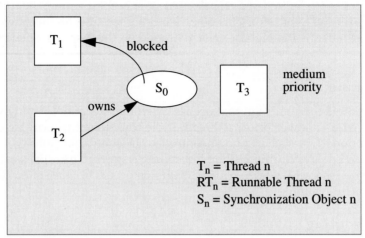

Figure 7-14   Priority Inversion

Having described the overall thread environment and the real-time scheduling mechanisms of SunOS, we describe in the next chapter the facilities for implementing multithreaded applications. The chapter also guides the programmer in the use of these facilities.

Further Reading

For readers interested in obtaining additional information on application migration or to simply increase their understanding of Solaris, the following reference is recommended for further reading:

Solaris Porting Guide, by M. Goodman, M. Goyal, and M. Massoudi; Prentice Hall, Englewood Cliffs, N.J. 07632, ISBN 0-13-030396-8.

Multithread Programming Facilities for Implementing Multithreaded Applications 8

This chapter on multithread programming describes the primary facilities for implementing multithreaded applications. It also guides the programmer in the use of these facilities. For further information, consult the SunOS 5.x Reference Manual available from SunSoft, Inc.

This chapter uses a number of typographic conventions:

- *This font* is used for emphasis, command arguments, variables in a command or code sequence. For example:

  thr_keycreate (3T)

- `This font` is used for program listings, command names, file names, and system names. For example:

  `#include <stdio.h>`

  It is also used for text that the system displays on the screen.

- **`This font`** indicates text that you type in a screen example sequence. For example:

  $ cc printmsg.c -o printmsg

Thread Creation and Scheduling

Thread Control Functions

This section introduces the Solaris Threads functions that create threads and control their execution.

`thr_create(3T)`

Creates and starts a new thread. The new thread executes the function specified in the call. The identity of the new thread is returned in a location provided by the caller. The thread identifiers are valid only within the process. Optional flags provide some control of the thread's behavior.

When the new thread is started, its execution begins by a procedure call to the specified function. The thread executes on a stack created by the threads library or one specified by the caller. The initial thread priority and signal mask are set to the same values as its creator. If the function returns, the thread exits.

Specifying a NULL stack base and a stack size of zero causes the threads library to allocate a default sized stack. Stack allocation is further discussed later on in the chapter.

The following scheduling options can be specified when creating a thread:

`THR_SUSPENDED`	The thread is immediately suspended after it is created. Use this option to operate on the thread (such as changing its priority) before you run it.
`THR_DETACHED`	The new thread is detached. Set this option when you do not want to wait for the thread to terminate. The termination of a detached thread is ignored.
`THR_BOUND`	The thread is created "bound." See the section entitled Lightweight Processes.
`THR_NEW_LWP`	The degree of concurrency is incremented. No binding is implied. See `thr_setconcurrency(3T)`.

`thr_exit(3T)`

Terminates the invoking thread and sets the exit status to the specified value. If the thread was not detached, its identifier and status are retained until `thr_join()` is executed by another thread. If the thread is the only one in the process, calling `thr_exit()` destroys the process with a zero exit status.

`thr_self(3T)`

Returns the thread identifier structure of the caller.

`thr_join(3T)`

Blocks until the specified thread exits. If no thread identifier is specified, any undetached thread that exits causes `thr_join()` to return. If a stack was specified when the thread was created, it can be reclaimed when `thr_join()` returns. A successful `thr_join()` returns the identifier of the thread that exited if the wait is successful. After `thr_join()` returns successfully, the returned `thread_id` is unusable in any subsequent thread operation.

Waiting for a detached thread, waiting for the current thread, or multiple `thr_join()`s on the same thread are all errors.

Thread Library Scheduling

Scheduling of threads is influenced by the Solaris Threads library function(s), `thr_setconcurrency()` and `thr_setprio()`. Normally, threads are scheduled only with respect to other threads in the process by means of simple priority levels with no adjustments and no kernel involvement. (Bound threads are treated differently.) Their system priority is usually uniform and is inherited from the creating process. (An application with multiple compute-bound threads can fail to schedule all of the runnable threads if `thr_setconcurrency`(3T) has not been called to adjust the level of execution resources. See `thr_setconcurrency(3T)` and "Thread Library Scheduling.")

`thr_setconcurrency(3T)`

Indicates the desired level of concurrency required by threads in the application. View this as the number of threads that can be simultaneously active (executing user code or system calls). If zero is specified (the default), Solaris Threads ensures that the process continues to progress without threads waiting indefinitely for execution resources. This scheme uses system resources efficiently, but it may not produce the most effective concurrency level. The actual number of simultaneously active threads may be more or less than the number specified. (Threads created with `THR_NEW_LWP` simply increment the degree of concurrency, see Lightweight Processes later on this chapter.)

`thr_setprio(3T)`

Sets the priority of the specified thread. The priority must be greater than or equal to zero. A greater value specifies an increased thread-scheduling priority.

`thr_getprio(3T)`

Gets the thread priority of the specified thread.

`thr_yield(3T)`

Yields the caller's executing status to any thread with the same or a higher priority.

Synchronization

The thread synchronization facilities synchronize threads both within a process and between processes.

Synchronization Variables

Any synchronization variable can be statically or dynamically allocated and must be allocated in memory that is globally accessible. Initializing the synchronization variable to zero specifies the default implementation variant in the default initial state. You can usually specify variations on the synchronization operation such as interprocess.

Threads in two or more processes can use a single synchronization variable jointly. Such use requires that the variable be allocated in memory that is shared by the processes through mapping files or System V shared memory. Refer to mmap(2) and shmop(2). Sharing the synchronization variable must also be specified when it is initialized by specifying USYNC_PROCESS. (For a local synchronization variable, specify USYNC_THREAD.) The variable can be initialized only by the process that first uses it.

Interprocess synchronization variables can also be placed in files. Once initialized, subsequent processes can then map the file in and use the synchronization variable. For example, an initialized interprocess mutual-exclusion (mutex), lock-synchronization variable (see below) can be stored in a file. Processes can map the file into their address space, acquire the mutex lock when they need to access it, access the file, release the lock, and unmap the file. The interprocess mutex lock ensures that other processes doing the same thing concurrently do not access or modify the data in the file while the process that has acquired the mutex lock holds it.

Mutex Lock

Mutex locks let one thread at a time hold the lock. They are typically used to ensure that only one thread at a time executes a section of code (called a critical section) that accesses or modifies some shared data. They use little memory and are fast. Use mutex locks to limit access to a resource to one thread at a time. Mutex locks can also be used to preserve code that is single threaded. Mutex locks let only the thread that sets a lock release it.

mutex_init(3T)

Initializes the mutex lock to unlocked. Arguments specify the mutex variable and its type. Mutexes can also be initialized to the default variant type (with USYNC_THREAD) by allocating them in zeroed memory.

mutex_destroy(3T)

Destroys the specified mutex initialized by mutex_init().

mutex_lock(3T)

Acquires the lock or blocks the calling thread if the lock is already held. Blocked threads wait on a prioritized queue.

mutex_trylock(3T)

Allows asynchronous polling of the specified lock. Acquires the lock if it is free and does not block (returns an error) if the lock is held. mutex_trylock() can be used to avoid deadlock in operations that would normally violate the lock hierarchy.

`mutex_unlock(3T)`

Unlocks the mutex. `mutex_unlock()` must be called by the thread that holds the mutex, which must be locked. If other threads are waiting for the lock, the thread at the head of the queue is unblocked.

Mutexes can be used to synchronize access to data and to ensure that changes to data are seen atomically in all threads (an atomic memory access preserves sequentiality), as shown in Code Example 8-1.

```
mutex_t count_mutex;
int count;

increment_count()
{
    mutex_lock(&count_mutex);
    count = count + 1;
    mutex_unlock(&count_mutex);
}

int
get_count()
{
    int c;

    mutex_lock(&count_mutex);
    c = count;
    mutex_unlock(&count_mutex);
    return (c);
}
```

Code Example 8-1   Mutex Example

The two functions in the example use the mutex for different purposes. `increment_count()` uses the mutex simply to ensure an atomic update of the shared variable. `get_count()` uses the mutex to guarantee that memory is synchronized when it refers to `count`.

Condition Variable

Condition variables are used to cause a wait until a particular condition is true. A condition variable must be used in conjunction with a mutex.

`cond_init(3T)`

Initializes the condition variable. Arguments specify the condition variable and its type. Condition variables can also be initialized to the default type (with `USYNC_THREAD`) by allocating them in zeroed memory.

`cond_destroy(3T)`

Destroys the state of the specified condition variable initialized by `cond_init()`.

`cond_wait(3T)`

Blocks until the condition is signalled. It atomically releases the associated mutex lock before blocking and atomically reacquires the mutex before returning. In typical use, a condition expression is evaluated under the protection of a mutex. If the condition expression is false, then the thread blocks on the condition variable. The condition variable is then signalled by another thread when it changes the condition value. This causes one (or all) of the threads waiting on the condition to unblock and (try to) reacquire the mutex. Since reacquiring the mutex can be blocked by other threads waiting for the mutex, the condition that caused the wait must be retested after the mutex has been acquired.

Since it is protected by the mutex, the condition can be a nontrivial expression. No order of acquisition is guaranteed if more than one thread blocks on the condition variable.

`cond_signal(3T)`

Signals one of the threads blocked in `cond_wait()` as shown in Code Example 8-2.

```
mutex_t count_lock;
cond_t count_nonzero;
unsigned int count;

decrement_count()
{
    mutex_lock(&count_lock);
    while (count == 0)
        cond_wait(&count_nonzero, &count_lock);
    count = count - 1;
    mutex_unlock(&count_lock);
}
increment_count()
{
    mutex_lock(&count_lock);
    if (count == 0)
        cond_signal(&count_nonzero);
    count = count + 1;
    mutex_unlock(&count_lock);
}
```

Code Example 8-2   Conditional Variable Use

`cond_broadcast(3T)`

Wakes all of the threads blocked in `cond_wait()`. Since `cond_broadcast()` causes all threads blocked on the condition to re-contend for the mutex, it should be used with care.

For example, you can use `cond_broadcast()` to allow threads to contend for variable amounts of resources when the resources are freed.

```
mutex_t rsrc_lock;
cond_t rsrc_add;
unsigned int resources, waiting;

get_resources(int amount)
{
    mutex_lock(&rsrc_lock);
    while (resources < amount) {
        waiting++;
        cond_wait(&rsrc_add, &rsrc_lock);
    }
    resources -= amount;
    mutex_unlock(&rsrc_lock);
}

add_resources(int amount)
{
    mutex_lock(&rsrc_lock);
    resources += amount;
    if (waiting > 0) {
        waiting = 0;
        cond_broadcast(&rsrc_add);
    }
    mutex_unlock(&rsrc_lock);
}
```

Code Example 8-3   Conditional Variable Broadcast

Note that in `add_resources()`, it does not matter whether `resources` is updated first or `cond_broadcast` is called first inside the mutex.

Calling `cond_signal()` or `cond_broadcast()` when the thread does not hold the mutex associated with the condition can lead to "lost wake-up" bugs. A lost wake-up occurs when a signal or broadcast has been sent, but a thread is waiting on the condition variable even though the condition is true. This situation occurs when the thread that calls `cond_signal()` does not hold the mutex. If the thread calls `cond_signal()` when another thread is between the test of the condition and the call to `cond_wait()`, then no threads are waiting, and the signal has no effect.

`cond_timedwait(3T)`

Blocks until the condition is signalled or until the time of day specified by the last argument has passed. The time-out is specified as a time of day so that the condition can be retested efficiently without recomputing the time-out value, as shown in Code Example 8-4.

```
timestruc_t to;
mutex_t m;
cond_t c;
...
mutex_lock(&m);
to.tv_sec = time(NULL) + TIMEOUT;
to.tv_nsec = 0;
while (cond == FALSE) {
    err = cond_timedwait(&c, &m, &to);
    if (err == ETIME) {
        /* timeout do something */
        break;
    }
}
mutex_unlock(&m);
```

Code Example 8-4   Timed Condition Wait Example

Semaphores

Solaris Threads provides conventional counting semaphores. Semaphores are nonnegative integer counts that are incremented and decremented. They are not as efficient as mutex. They need not be acquired and released by the same thread, so they can be used for asynchronous event notification (such as in signal handlers). Since they contain state, they can be used asynchronously without acquiring a mutex, as required by condition variables.

`sema_init(3T)`

Initializes the semaphore variable. Arguments specify the semaphore variable, its initial state, and its type.

`sema_destroy(3T)`

Destroys the state of the specified semaphore; initialized by `sema_init()`.

`sema_wait(3T)`

Blocks the thread until the semaphore becomes greater than zero, then decrements it.

`sema_trywait(3T)`

Decrements the semaphore if its count is greater than zero. Otherwise it returns an error.

`sema_post(3T)`

Increments the semaphore, potentially unblocking a waiting thread.

Code Example 8-5 is an example of a producer thread and a consumer thread that synchronize through a semaphore:

```
int rdptr = 0;
int wrptr = 0
data_t buf[BUFSIZE];
sema_t sem;
```

Thread 1	Thread 2

`while (work_to_do) {`
`    buf[wrptr] = produce();`
`    wrptr = (wrptr + 1) % BUFSIZE;`
`    sema_post(&sem);`
`}`
	`while (work_to_do) {`
	`    sema_wait(&sem);`
	`    consume(buf[rdptr]);`
	`    rdptr = (rdptr + 1) % BUFSIZE;`
	`}`

Code Example 8-5   Producer/Consumer Example with Semaphore

Read/Write Locks

Multiple readers, single writer locks allow many threads simultaneous read-only access to a protected object. They also allow a single thread write access to the object while excluding any readers. This type of lock is also called a read/write lock and is usually used to protect data that is read more often than it is written. Like mutexes, read/write locks must bracket.

`rwlock_init(3T)`

Initializes the read/write lock and sets its state to unlocked. Arguments specify the lock variable and type. Read/write locks can also be initialized to the default type (with `USYNC_THREAD`) by allocating them in zeroed memory.

`rwlock_destroy(3T)`

Destroys the state of the specified read/write lock; initialized by `rwlock_init()`.

`rw_rdlock(3T)`

Acquires a read lock. Blocks if a writer holds the lock.

`rw_tryrdlock(3T)`

Acquires a read lock or returns an error.

`rw_wrlock(3T)`

Acquires a write lock. Blocks if a writer or any readers hold the lock.

`rw_trywrlock(3T)`

Acquires a write lock or returns an error.

`rw_unlock(3T)`

Unlocks a read/write lock if the caller holds either the read or write lock.

Code Example 8-6 is a bank account. While it is possible to allow multiple threads to have concurrent read-only access to the account balance, only a single writer is allowed. Note that the `get_balance()` function needs the lock to ensure that the addition of the checking and saving balances occurs atomically:

```
rwlock_t account_lock;
float checking_balance = 100.0;
float saving_balance = 100.0;
...
rwlock_init(&account_lock, 0, NULL);
...
float
get_balance() {
    float bal;

    rw_rdlock(&account_lock);
    bal = checking_balance + saving_balance;
    rw_unlock(&account_lock);
    return(bal);
}

void
transfer_checking_to_savings(float amount) {
    rw_wrlock(&account_lock);
    checking_balance = checking_balance - amount;
    savings_balance = savings_balance + amount;
    rw_unlock(&account_lock);
}
```

Code Example 8-6   Read/Write: Bank Account

Comparing Primitives

The most basic synchronization primitive in Solaris Threads is the mutex lock. So, it is the most efficient mechanism in both memory use and execution time. The basic use of a mutex lock is to serialize access to a resource.

The next most efficient primitive in Solaris Threads is the condition variable. The basic use of a condition variable is to block on a change of state. Remember that a mutex lock must be acquired before blocking on a condition variable and must be unlocked after returning from `cond_wait()` and after changing the state of the variable.

The semaphore uses more memory than the condition variable. It is easier to use in some circumstances because a semaphore variable functions on state rather than on control. Semaphores do not require that the caller that set a state is the one that changes the state.

The multiple readers, single writer lock is the most complex Solaris Threads synchronization mechanism. The read/write lock is most efficiently used with a much coarser granularity than is effective with the other synchronization primitives. The basic use of a read/write lock is a resource whose contents are searched more often than they are changed.

Signals

Each thread has its own signal mask. Thus, a thread can block some signals while it uses memory or other state that is also used by a signal handler. All threads in a process share the set of signal handlers set up by signal(2) and its variants, as usual.

Signal Handling

If a signal handler is marked SIG_DFL or SIG_IGN, the action on receipt of the signal (exit, core dump, stop, continue, or ignore) is performed on the entire receiving process. So, the signal affects all the threads in the process.

Signals are divided into two categories: traps and interrupts.

Traps (such as SIGILL, SIGFPE, SIGSEGV) result from execution of a specific thread and are handled only by the thread that caused them. Several threads in a process could generate and handle the same type of trap simultaneously.

Interrupts (such as SIGINT, SIGIO) are asynchronous with any thread and result from some action outside the process. An interrupt can be handled by any thread whose signal mask has it enabled. If more than one thread is able to receive the interrupt, only one is chosen. One result is that several threads can be in the process of handling the same kind of signal simultaneously. If all threads mask a signal, it will remain pending on the process until some thread enables the signal. As in single-threaded processes, the number of signals received by the process is less than or equal to the number sent. For example, an application can enable several threads to handle a particular I/O interrupt. As each new interrupt comes in, another thread is chosen to handle the signal until all the enabled threads are active. Any additional signals remain pending until a thread completes processing and reenables the signal.

Threads can send signals to other threads in the process through thr_kill(3T). A signal initiated through thr_kill() behaves like a trap and is handled only by the specified thread. As usual, a signal is sent to another process by kill(2) or sigsend(2). There is no direct way for a thread in one process to send a signal to a specific thread in another process.

Unbound threads are not allowed to use alternate signal stacks. A thread that is bound can use an alternate stack because the state is associated with the execution resource.

(Bound threads are described later in the chapter.) An alternate stack must be enabled for the signal through sigaction(2) and declared and enabled through sigaltstack(2).

An application can have per-thread signal handlers based on the per-process signal handlers. One way is for the process-wide signal handler to use the identifier of the thread handling the signal as an index into a table of per-thread handlers. (Note that there is no thread 0.)

Non-local Goto

The scope of setjmp() and longjmp() is limited to one thread. In most threads, this limitation is not an issue. However, a thread that handles a signal can only perform a longjmp() if the setjmp() was performed in the same thread.

Async-safe Functions

Functions that can be called from signal handlers are said to be *async-safe*. In the threads library the following functions are async-safe in addition to those defined by POSIX (IEEE Std 1003.1-1990, 3.3.1.3 (3)(f), refer to The Threads Environment later on this chapter.

- sema_post()
- thr_sigsetmask()
- thr_kill()

Thread Signal Interface

A thread's signal mask applies equally to intra-process signals (signals sent between threads) and to interprocess signals.

thr_sigsetmask(3T)

Sets the thread's signal mask. A thread's initial signal mask is inherited from the parent thread.

thr_kill(3T)

Causes the specified signal to be sent to a specified thread.

Waiting for Signals

A new way to handle asynchronous signals is to wait for them in a separate thread. This method is safer and easier than installing a signal handler and processing them there.

sigwait(2)

Waits for a pending signal from the set specified by the argument, regardless of the signal mask. sigwait() clears the pending signal and returns its number. If more than one thread is waiting for the same signal, then one thread is chosen and it returns from sigwait().

sigwait() is typically used by creating one or more threads to wait for signals. Since sigwait() can retrieve even masked signals, the signals of interest are usually blocked in all other threads so they are not accidentally delivered. When the signals arrive, a thread returns from sigwait(), handles the signal, and waits for more signals. The signal handling thread is not restricted to using async-safe functions and can synchronize with other threads in the usual way.

```
mutex_t m;
int hup = 0;

main()
{
    thread_t t;
    int finishup = 0;
    sigset_t set;
    ...
    sigemptyset(&set);
    sigaddset(&set, SIG_hup );
    thr_sigsetmask(SIG_BLOCK, &set, NULL);
    thr_create(NULL, 0, handle_hup, NULL, THR_DETACHED, &t);
    do {
        stuff();
        } while (hup == 0);
}

handle_hup()
{
    sigset_t set;

    sigemptyset(&set);
    sigaddset(&set, SIGHUP);
    sigwait(&set);
    mutex_lock(&m);
    hup = 1;
    mutex_unlock(&m);
}
```

Code Example 8-7   Waiting for Signals with sigwait()

Threads and Process Resources

This section discusses how threads affect process creation and destruction. Then it discusses how threads interact with other process resources, such as timers and resource limits.

Process Creation and Destruction

When a process executes the fork(2) system call, it creates an exact duplicate of the process. The address space and all the threads (and LWPs, see "Lightweight Processes") are duplicated in the child. When one thread in a process calls fork(), it can cause interruptible system calls in the other threads to return EINTR.

A new system call, fork1(2), forks the complete address space but only the invoking thread. All other threads and LWPs in the original process are not duplicated in the new process.

Both the exit(2) and exec(2) system calls work as they do in single-threaded processes, except that they destroy all the threads in the address space. Both calls block until all the execution resources (hence all active threads) are destroyed. When exec() rebuilds the process, it creates a single LWP. The process startup code builds the initial thread. As usual, if the initial thread returns, it calls exit() and the process is destroyed.

If all the threads in a process exit, then the process itself exits with a status of zero.

Uses of **fork()** and **fork1()**

fork() has two basic uses. It duplicates the entire process (the BSD dump program uses this technique). And it creates a new process before calling exec(). For the latter purpose, fork1() is much more efficient than fork() because only one LWP and thread are duplicated.

Having fork() completely duplicate the process is most similar to the single-threaded fork(). It allows both basic uses and presents fewer pitfalls. Having fork1() fork only one thread provides an optimized fork that can be immediately followed by exec().

Hazards of **forking**

Call vfork(2) in a multithreaded application only when the main thread is running so that no other thread is run between the vfork() call and the exec() call. Any execution by other threads between the vfork() and exec() calls can result in all memory of the parent process being changed unexpectedly.

There is a hazard to using fork1(). It is critical to call only functions that do not require locks held by threads that no longer exist in the new process. This case can be difficult to determine because libraries can create hidden threads.

Alternatively, special attention should be given when using global state with fork(). For example, if a thread is reading a file serially when another thread in the process calls fork(), two threads will be reading the files after the fork() completes. Since the seek pointer for a file descriptor is shared after a fork(), the thread in the parent will receive some data while the thread in the child will get the rest.

There is another hazard when either fork() or fork1() is called. Locks that are allocated in memory that is sharable (i.e., mmaped with the MAP_SHARED flag) can be held by a thread in both processes, unless care is taken to avoid this situation.

Note, too, that system(3S) always calls vfork() and is unsafe. popen(3S) and dup2(3C) both call fork(), whose behavior must be accounted for.

Thread-specific Data

Thread-specific data (TSD) is maintained on a per-thread basis. TSD is the only way to define and refer to data that is private to a thread. Each thread-specific data item is associated with a key that is global to all threads in the process. Using the key, a thread can access a pointer (void *) that is maintained per-thread.

thr_keycreate(3T)

Allocates a global key value. The caller can optionally specify a function to be called when a thread that has a non-NULL value associated with the allocated key exits. The function is called with the current value bound to the key for the exiting thread as an argument. The function, called a destructor function, typically frees data pointed to by the bound value.

thr_setspecific(3T)

Binds a value to the key for the calling thread.

thr_getspecific(3T)

Retrieves the current value bound to the key for the calling thread.

Use of Thread-specific Data

When thread-specific data is used in a function that can be called at any time, the function must detect the first call to initialize the key, as shown in Code Example 8-8.

```
thread_key_t my_key;
int once = 0;
mutex_t keylock;

my_func()
{
    my_data_t *ptr;

    mutex_lock(&keylock);
    if (!once) {
        once = 1;
        thr_keycreate(&my_key, free);
    }
```

```
        mutex_unlock(&keylock);
        /* no locking beyond here since data is per-thread */
        thr_getspecific(my_key, &ptr);
        if (ptr == NULL) {
            /* first time called in this thread */
            ptr = (my_data_t *)malloc(sizeof(my_data_t));
            thr_setspecific(my_key, ptr);
        }
        my_use_it(ptr);
    }
```

Code Example 8-8   Self-initializing Thread-specific Data

Note that the key allocation and storage must be protected by a lock so that if two threads call the same function simultaneously, they do not both allocate keys.

Resource Limits

The resource limits are set on the entire process (in other words, the sum of the resource use of all the LWPs in the process). When a soft resource limit is exceeded, the offending LWP is sent the appropriate signal. The sum of the resource use (including CPU use) for all LWPs (and thus threads) in the process is available through getrusage().

Lightweight Processes

The threads library is the programmer's interface for multithreading. As stated in previous chapters, threads are scheduled onto lightweight processes (LWPs). Only programmers who need to design and implement a threads library of their own will use the LWP interface directly. For all others, the Solaris Threads library performs all needed uses of the LWP interface.

This section describes LWPs, how threads relate to them, and scheduling. Most of the details in this section are implementation-dependent.

Solaris Threads Implementation

As stated earlier in Chapter 7, the Solaris Threads library schedules threads onto lightweight processes (LWP) to execute program code and system calls. Solaris Threads provides two ways for LWPs to execute *ubound* and *bound* threads.

Unbound Threads

Threads that are scheduled on the pool of LWPs are called *unbound threads*. The library invokes LWPs as needed, and assigns them to execute runnable threads. After assuming the state of the thread, the LWP executes its instructions. If the thread becomes blocked on a synchronization mechanism, or if another thread should be run, the state of the thread is saved in process memory. The threads library then assigns another thread to the LWP to run.

Bound Threads

In some cases, a thread may require a special capability. For example, a thread may need to be scheduled on a real-time basis in strict priority with respect to all the other active threads in the system. Since unbound threads are only scheduled within a process, they are not scheduled with respect to threads outside the process. A programmer can take advantage of the extra capabilities while retaining use of all the thread interfaces and capabilities by specifying that the thread is to be permanently bound to an LWP when it is created. Such threads are called *bound threads*.

Thread Library Scheduling

The threads library automatically adjusts the number of LWPs in the pool used to run unbound threads. Its objectives are:

- To prevent the program from being blocked by lack of unblocked LWPs. For example, if there are more runnable unbound threads than LWPs and all the active threads block in the kernel in indefinite waits (e.g., read a tty), the process cannot progress until a waiting thread returns.

- To make efficient use of LWPs. For example, if the library creates one LWP for each thread, many LWPs are usually idle and the operating system is overloaded by the resource requirements of the unused LWPs.

The library usually ensures that there are enough LWPs in its pool for a program to proceed. If all of the LWPs in the process are blocked in indefinite waits (e.g., blocked reading from a tty or network), the operating system sends the new signal, SIGWAITING, to the process. This signal is handled by the threads library. If the process contains a thread that is waiting to run, a new LWP is created and the appropriate waiting thread is assigned to it for execution.

The SIGWAITING mechanism does not ensure that an additional LWP is created when one or more threads are compute-bound and another thread becomes runnable. A compute-bound thread can prevent multiple runnable threads from being started because of a shortage of LWPs. This situation can be prevented by a call to thr_setconcurrency() or by the use of the THR_NEW_LWP in calls to thr_create().

A contraction in the number of active threads can cause an excessive number of LWPs in the pool of a process. If LWPs in the pool remain idle for a certain period (i.e., there are more LWPs than active threads), the threads library destroys the unneeded ones. The library "ages" LWPs. They are deleted if they are unused for a "long" time, currently 5 minutes.

Scheduling Interface

Scheduling of threads is controlled through the Solaris Threads library functions, thr_setconcurrency(), thr_setprio(), and the THR_NEW_LWP option of `thr_create()`. The default number of LWPs created by the library is not always the optimum number for performance. The library may create too few or too many LWPs. You can influence the number of LWPs by creating them with the `THR_NEW_LWP` flag or with `thr_setconcurrency()`.

Unbound-thread scheduling uses simple priority levels with no adjustments and no kernel involvement. Thread scheduling regulates only how threads are assigned to LWPs. It has no effect on scheduling of LWPs by the kernel. The LWP's system priority is usually uniform and is inherited from the creating process.

`thr_create(3T)`

Creates and starts a new thread as described in "Thread Creation and Scheduling." There is a range of options between purely Solaris Threads library-based scheduling and purely kernel based scheduling. The options are selected by the `THR_BOUND` and `THR_NEW_LWP` flags.

Any combination of the options shown can be specified in the `flags` argument:

`THR_SUSPENDED`	The thread is immediately suspended after it is created. The thread does not execute the specified function until another thread executes `thr_continue()` to start it. If `THR_SUSPENDED` is not specified, the thread is runnable immediately.
`THR_DETACHED`	The new thread is detached. When a detached thread exits, its identifier, status, and other resources can be immediately reused. Other threads cannot wait for this thread to exit. A detached runnable thread can run and exit before `thr_create()` returns, unless other synchronization prevents it.
`THR_BOUND`	The new thread is permanently bound to a dedicated LWP.
`THR_NEW_LWP`	A new LWP is created along with the thread. The new LWP is added to the pool of LWPs used to execute threads. This option is the same as incrementing the concurrency level by calling `thr_setconcurrency()`.

When to Bind

Bind a thread to obtain one of the following properties of an LWP:

- Have the thread scheduled globally (on a system-wide basis instead of on a process basis); for example real-time
- Give the thread an alternate signal stack
- Give the thread a unique alarm or timer

```
thr_suspend(3T)
```

Immediately suspends execution of the specified thread. `thr_suspend()` returns when the specified thread is stopped. A thread that specifies itself to `thr_suspend()` must be restarted by some other thread.

```
thr_continue(3T)
```

Restarts a thread that has been suspended via `thr_suspend()` or that was created suspended.

LWP Scheduling

As stated in Chapter 7, the Solaris 2.2 kernel has three classes of process scheduling. Scheduling class is maintained for each LWP. Each scheduling class maps the priority of the LWP it is scheduling to an overall dispatching priority according to the configurable priority of the scheduling class. The highest priority scheduling class is real-time (RT). The middle priority scheduling class is system. The system scheduling class cannot be applied to a user process. The lowest and default priority scheduling class is timeshare (TS).

When a process is created, its one initial LWP inherits the scheduling class and priority of the parent process. As more LWPs are created to run unbound threads, they also inherit this scheduling class and priority. All unbound threads in a process have the same scheduling class and priority.

Bound threads have the scheduling class and priority of their underlying LWPs. Each bound thread in a process can have a unique scheduling class and priority that is visible to the kernel. Bound threads are scheduled with respect to all other LWPs in the system.

The scheduling class is set by the `priocntl(2)` system call. It can affect just the calling LWP or all the LWPs of one or more processes, as specified by the first two arguments. The third argument of `priocntl()` is the command, which may be one of:

PC_GETCID	Ignores the first and second arguments. The fourth argument points to a `pcinfo_t` structure, defined in `<sys/priocntl.h>`. If the name field of the structure contains a recognizable class name (RT or TS), the class ID and an array of class attribute data are returned.
PC_GETCLINFO	Ignores the first and second arguments. The fourth argument points to a `pcinfo_t` structure, defined in `<sys/priocntl.h>`. If the ID field of the structure contains a recognizable class identifier (RT or TS), the class name and an array of class attribute data are returned.

| PC_GETPARMS | Returns the class identifier and/or the class-specific scheduling parameters of the process(es) specified by the first two arguments. The results are returned in the `pcparms_t` structure pointed to by the fourth argument. |
| PC_SETPARMS | Sets the class identifier and/or the class-specific scheduling parameters of the process(es) specified by the first two arguments. The results are returned in the `pcparms_t` structure pointed to by the fourth argument. |

Timeshare Scheduling

Timeshare scheduling is designed to provide a "fair" distribution of the processing resource to the set of processes. Other parts of the kernel can monopolize the processor for an interval commensurate with human reaction times, without degrading response time as seen by the user.

The dispatch priority of timeshared LWPs is calculated from the instantaneous CPU use rate of the LWP, and from its nice1 level. The `nice(1)` level indicates the relative priority of the processes to the timeshare scheduler. LWPs with a greater `nice` value get a smaller, but nonzero, share of the total processing. An LWP that has received a larger amount of processing is given lower priority than one that has received little or no processing. In general, this arrangement biases priority in favor of I/O bound-processes, since they need few CPU cycles to keep going.

The `priocntl(2)` system call sets the `nice` level of one or more processes. `priocntl()` affects the `nice` level of all the timesharing class LWPs in the process. The `nice` level ranges from -19 to +20. The lower the value, the higher the priority.

Real-time Scheduling

The real-time class (`RT`) can be applied to a whole process or to one or more LWPs in a process. Unlike the `nice()` level of the timeshare class, LWPs that are classified real-time LWPs can be assigned priorities individually or jointly.

The scheduler always dispatches the highest priority real-time process or LWP. It preempts a lower priority process or LWP when a higher priority process or LWP becomes runnable. A preempted LWP is placed at the head of its level queue. A real-time LWP retains control of a processor until it is preempted, it suspends, or its real-time priority is changed. Processes and LWPs in the `RT` class have absolute priority over processes in the `TS` class. Given the latency of the system in recognizing interrupts and dispatching the highest priority process, the worst case behavior of the processes can be calculated.

A new LWP inherits the scheduling class of the parent process or LWP. An RT class LWP inherits the parent's time slice, whether finite or infinite. An LWP with a finite time slice runs until it terminates, blocks (e.g., to wait for an I/O event), is preempted by a higher priority runnable real-time process, or the time slice expires. An LWP with an infinite time slice ceases execution only when it terminates, blocks, or is preempted.

The `priocntl()` system call sets the real-time priority and time quantum of one or more processes. A `priocntl()` call affects the attributes of all the real-time LWPs in the process.

Alarms, Interval Timers, and Profiling

Solaris Threads provides a unique real-time interval timer and alarm per LWP, resulting in an interval timer for each bound thread. The timer or alarm delivers one signal to the thread when the timer or alarm expires.

Unbound threads do not have virtual time or profile interval timers (which can be expensive to maintain for threads). If timers are required, threads can be bound to an LWP and can use the underlying LWPs virtual time or profile interval timer. When these interval timers expire, either `SIGVTALRM` or `SIGPROF`, as appropriate, is sent to the LWP that owns the interval timer.

Profiling is enabled for each LWP individually [see `profil(2)`]. Each LWP can have a separate profiling buffer. A profiling buffer can be shared by two or more LWPs if accumulated data is desired. Profiling data is updated at each clock tick in LWP user time. The state of profiling is inherited from the creating LWP.

Stacks

Each thread requires swap space for its stack. The total amount of swap space limits the number of threads that can exist simultaneously and the size(s) of their stacks. Caution is advised in specifying thread stack size if many threads are required and your system has limited swap space. Alternatively, increase the swap space on your system.

When specifying the size of a thread stack, take into account the allocations needed by the invoked function and by each function called. The accounting should include calling sequence needs, local variables, and information structures.

Each thread stack created by the threads library has a red zone. A stack red zone is made by rounding the stack size to the next page boundary and appending an invalid page. Red zones are appended to all automatically allocated stacks whether the size is specified by the application or whether the default size is used.

`thr_minstack(3T)`

Specifies the minimum stack size for all threads. The size of any specified stack must be greater than or equal to the minimum. This requirement is equally true for stacks passed to the threads library and for stacks allocated by the threads library.

8

Using Threads

This section provides some guidelines on how to use threads.

Concurrency Strategies

Applications must cooperate and synchronize when sharing the data and the resources of the process.

Single-lock Strategy

One strategy is to have a single, application-wide mutex that is acquired whenever any thread in the application is running and is released before it must block. Since only one thread can be accessing shared data at any one time, each thread has a consistent view of memory. This strategy can be quite effective on a uniprocessor, provided care is taken to ensure that shared memory is put into a consistent state before the lock is released and that the lock is released often enough so that more than one thread can run. In fact, many operating system implementations have taken this approach.

Unfortunately, this approach cannot take advantage of more than one processor and will reduce uniprocessor concurrency if the lock is not dropped during most I/O. It also requires cooperation from all the modules and libraries in the system to synchronize on the single lock.

Reentrance

An alternate approach is to let each module or library independently synchronize itself. This scheme allows module synchronization to be hidden beneath the module interface. In other words, several threads can call functions in a module simultaneously and it is up to the function code to handle this situation. Such functions are said to be reentrant (also referred to as mt-safe). The assumption is that data shared between threads is only accessed by module functions. If mutable global data is available to clients of a module, then appropriate locks must also be made visible in the interface, and the module function cannot be made reentrant unless the clients are assumed to use the locks at the appropriate times.

Functions, such as `sin()`, that access no global data or access only read-only data and use no other global state (e.g., files) are trivially reentrant. Trivially reentrant functions can be entered by any number of threads simultaneously.

Functions that do access global state must be made reentrant by restricting potential concurrency.

The greatest performance benefit in multithreaded programs is obtained when asynchronous processing is maximized. In other words, minimizing synchronization of threads produces the greatest benefit to throughput. Code that is executed asynchronously must be reentrant. For purposes of multithreaded programming with Solaris Threads, reentrant code has the following characteristics:

- Never changes any element of global memory

- Never changes the state of a file or device

- Refers to an element of global memory only in special circumstances

Any point in a multithreaded program that performs an action counter to any of these rules must be protected by one of the synchronizing mechanisms provided by Solaris Threads.

Locking strategies

There are two basic strategies for making functions in modules reentrant: code locking and data locking.

Code Locking

Code locking guarantees that at most one thread is in module code at any one time. The code covered by the lock (usually a mutex) is called the *critical section* for the lock. There is one lock in the process for the module code. Multiple threads can be active in the process when they are executing different module's code. This is sometimes called a monitor.

Data Locking

Data locking guarantees that access to a *collection* of data that must be maintained consistently is synchronized. For data locking, the concept of a critical section for the lock still obtains, but now several threads can be in the critical section concurrently. For a mutual-exclusion locking protocol, only one thread can be in the critical section per collection of data. Alternatively, multiple readers, single writer protocol, several readers or one writer may be allowed per collection of data. Multiple threads can execute in a single module, provided they operate on different data collections or do not conflict on a single collection for the multiple readers, single writer protocol. So, data locking typically allows more concurrency than does code locking.

The collection of data associated with a lock can be any collection of data items that must be maintained consistently as a group. An extreme application of this principle would always lock the minimum consistent collection. While this may appear to maximize concurrency, it can cause severe performance degradation. The locking primitives are relatively cheap to use when there is no contention, but they are not free. Too fine a grain of data locking can cause locks to be acquired and released every few instructions.

Invariants

For both code locking and data locking it is important to understand invariants as a means for controlling locking complexity. An invariant is a condition or relation that is always true. The definition is modified somewhat for concurrent execution: an invariant is a condition or relation that is true when the associated lock is not set. When the lock is set, the invariant can be false. However, the code holding the lock must reestablish the invariant before releasing the lock.

For example, in a module that manages a doubly linked list of elements, a good invariant is, for each item on the list, the forward pointer to the next item on the list and the backward pointer to the previous item. Assume the module uses code-based locking and therefore is protected by a single, global mutex. When an item is deleted or added the mutex is acquired, the correct manipulation of the pointers is made, and the mutex is released. Obviously, at some point in the manipulation of the pointers, the invariant is false. However, the invariant is reestablished before the mutex is released.

In both code-based and data-based locking, you must still be careful not to hold locks across long operations. For example, if the client RPC code was locked with a single global mutex that was held for the duration of the call, the client application could only have one RPC in progress no matter how many threads it used. The usual technique is to drop all module locks before starting the long operation or the I/O. When the operation completes, the lock(s) can be reacquired. If everything is working, the invariant will be true after the lock(s) are reacquired, but the *state* of the module may have changed. For example, the item that the function was about to delete from a list may have already been deleted. After the lock(s) are reacquired, the state must be reverified to be sure the intended operation is still valid.

This example illustrates another reason why excessive attempts at increasing concurrency can actually degrade performance. Every time the lock(s) are dropped, the module state must potentially be reevaluated.

Deadlock

Deadlock is a permanent blocking of a set of threads that are competing for a set of resources. Just because some thread can make progress does not mean that there is not a deadlock somewhere else. The most common error causing deadlock is *self-deadlock* or *recursive deadlock*: a thread tries to acquire a lock it is already holding. Recursive deadlock is unbelievably easy to program by mistake. For example, if you write a code monitor in which every module function grabs the mutex for the duration of the call, then any call between functions protected by the mutex will immediately deadlock. If a function calls some code outside the module which, through some devious path, calls back into any method protected by the same mutex, then it too will deadlock.

The solution for this kind of deadlock is to avoid calling functions outside the module where it is unknown whether or not they will call back into the module without reestablishing invariants and dropping all module locks before making the call. Of course, after the call completes and the lock(s) are reacquired, the state must be reverified to be sure the intended operation is still valid.

An example of another kind of deadlock is when two threads, thread 1 and thread 2, each acquire a mutex, A and B, respectively. Then suppose that thread 1 tries to acquire mutex B and thread 2 tries to acquire mutex A. Thread 1 cannot proceed and it will be blocked waiting for mutex B. Thread 2 cannot proceed and it will be blocked waiting for mutex A. Nothing will ever change, so this case is a permanent blocking of the threads, and hence a deadlock.

This kind of deadlock is avoided by establishing an order in which locks are acquired (called a *lock hierarchy*). If all threads always acquire locks in the specified order, then this deadlock is avoided.

It is not always desirable to adhere to a strict order of lock acquisition. If thread 2 has built up a considerable number of assumptions about the state of the module while holding mutex B, giving up mutex B in order to acquire mutex A then reacquiring mutex B in order would cause it to discard its assumptions and to reevaluate the state of the module. The blocking synchronization primitives usually have variants that attempt to get a lock and fail if they cannot, for example, mutex_trylock(). This variant allows threads to violate the lock hierarchy in cases where there is no contention. Where there is contention, the held locks must usually be discarded and the locks reacquired in order.

Locking Guidelines:

- Try not to hold locks across long duration operations like I/O where doing so can impact performance.
- Don't hold locks when calling functions outside the module that may reenter the module.
- Don't try for excessive processor concurrency. Without intervening system calls or I/O operation, locks are usually held for short durations and contention is rare. Only attach those locks that actually have measured contention. In data-based locking, first try a lock for each "object," if the code is structured that way. This is usually sufficient.
- When using multiple locks, be sure that all threads acquire the locks in the same order to avoid deadlocks.

Thread Creation

Solaris Threads caches threads data structure, stacks, and LWPs, so repetitive creation of unbound threads can be cheap. Unbound thread creation is very inexpensive when compared to process creation or even to bound thread creation. It is roughly the same order of magnitude as is unbound thread synchronization, when you include the context switches to stop one thread and start another. The upshot of this is that it is usually better to create and destroy threads as required than to attempt to manage a pool of threads that wait for independent things to do. In other words, create a thread to do an asynchronous job that must maintain an execution history for the duration of the job being processed. A good example is an RPC server that creates a thread for each request and destroys it when the reply is delivered, instead of trying to maintain a pool of threads to service requests.

While thread creation is relatively cheap when compared to process creation, it is not cheap when compared to the cost of a few instructions. Threads should be created for processing that last at least a couple of thousand machine instructions.

Thread Concurrency

By default, Solaris Threads attempts to adjust the system execution resources (i.e., LWPs) used to run unbound threads to match the real number of active threads. It cannot make perfect decisions, but it at least ensures that the process continues to make progress. If the application has some idea of the number of (unbound) threads that should be simultaneously active (executing code or system calls), it should tell the library via `thr_setconcurrency()`. For example, a database server that has a thread per-user should tell Solaris Threads the expected number of simultaneously active users. A window server that has one thread per-client should tell Solaris Threads the expected number of simultaneously active clients. A file copy program that has one reader thread and one writer thread should tell Solaris Threads that the desired concurrency level is two. Alternatively, the concurrency level can be incremented once, via the `THR_NEW_LWP` flag, as each thread is created.

For the purpose of computing concurrency, unbound threads blocked on interprocess (`USYNC_PROCESS`) synchronization variables are considered active. Active bound threads should not be counted.

Bound Threads

Bound threads are more expensive than unbound threads. Since bound threads can change the attributes of the underlying LWP, Solaris Threads does not cache the LWPs when the bound threads exit. Solaris Threads asks the operating system for a new LWP when a bound thread is created and destroys it when the bound thread exits. Bound threads should be used only when a thread needs resources that are only available through the underlying LWP, such as a virtual time-interval timer or an alternate stack, or the thread must be visible to the kernel to be scheduled with respect to all other active threads in the system, as in real-time scheduling.

Unbound threads should be used even when it is expected that all threads are simultaneously active. This use allows Solaris Threads to cache LWP and thread resources efficiently to make thread creation and destruction fast.

Thread Creation Guidelines

Some simple guidelines for using threads are:

- Use threads for independent jobs that must maintain state for the life of the job.

- Don't use threads for very short jobs.

- Use threads to take advantage of CPU concurrency.

- Only use bound threads when absolutely necessary, that is, when some facility of the underlying LWP is required.

- Use `thr_setconcurrency`() to tell Solaris Threads how many threads you expect to be simultaneously active.

Guidelines for Threaded Programs and Libraries

These guidelines have been found important in developing threaded function libraries at Sun. Many of them apply also to developing threaded programs, in general.

- You must know what you import and whether or not it is safe.
  A threaded program can not arbitrarily enter nonthreaded code.

- Threaded code can refer to unsafe code only from the main thread.
  The practical consequence of this rule is to ensure that the static storage associated with the main thread is used only by that thread. See "Compatibility Issues With Global Error Variables" in this chapter.

- Sun-supplied libraries are defined to be *safe* unless explicitly documented unsafe.
  If a Reference Manual entry does not say whether a function is mt-safe, it is safe. All mt-unsafe functions are identified explicitly in the SunOS 5.x Reference Manual.

- The initial thread must protect shared data structures referred to by unsafe code.
  Having only the initial thread call unsafe code is not enough to protect shared data structures. An example of this is the `stdio` buffers in the C library. The initial thread must either ensure that no concurrent access to `stdio` buffers occurs when unsafe code is active or it must explicitly lock those buffers [via `flockfile()`] while unsafe code is active.

- Compilation flags must be used to manage binary-incompatible source changes.
  To enable programs that meet the portability constraints inherent in current ABIs, explicitly enable new facilities exhibiting a different binary behavior. Always either specify `-D _REENTRANT` when compiling or be sure that _REENTRANT is defined before any header file is included.

- To maintain binary compatibility in libraries, use old static storage with per-thread semantics for the main thread.

  Where a pre-thread static storage cell requires per-thread use, the main thread must use the preexisting storage cell. This use allows linking of both threaded and nonthreaded object files (subject to the other use rules defined here). A good convention is to provide a function of the name __*<cell>()* where *<cell>* is the name of the previous instance. Header files declaring *<cell>* must be protected by a flag, such as _REENTRANT, as described above. When the flag is set, the expression *<cell>* should expand to an expression that results in an *lvalue*. An example of this is the definition of errno:

  ```
  #ifdef _REENTRANT
  #define errno *(int *)__errno()
  #else
  extern int errno;
  #endif
  ```

  TSD is used to implement per-thread static storage.

- When making a library safe for multithreaded use, do not thread global process operations.

  Do not change global operations (or actions with global side effects) to behave in a threaded manner. For example, if file I/O had been changed to per-thread operation, threads would not be able to cooperate in accessing files.

  For thread-specific behavior, or "thread-cognizant" behavior, use thread facilities. For example, if the termination of main() should terminate only the thread exiting main(), the end of main() should be:

  ```
  thr_exit();
  /*NOTREACHED*/
  ```

Libraries

This section describes considerations for mt-safe programs and SunOS library facilities.

mt-safe Libraries

All routines that can potentially be called by a thread from an MT program must be mt-safe. This requirement means that two, or more, activations of a single routine must be able to *correctly* execute concurrently. (In other words, each of at least two threads must be able to correctly execute the same library function in parallel.) So, every library that an MT program links (i.e., uses) must provide interfaces that are all mt-safe.

Not all libraries are now mt-safe. Some of the more commonly used libraries have been made mt-safe. These are:

- `libc`

- `libm`

- `libw`

- `libintl`

- `libmalloc`

- `libmapmalloc`

- `libnsl` (only the TLI interface)

Consult the SunOS 5.x Reference Manual for additional libraries that are mt-safe.

mt-safe Interfaces

Functions in the mt-safe libraries fall into four groups:

- Functions that have an mt-safe interface that have always been mt-safe or have been modified to be completely mt-safe

- Functions that are not mt-safe because their size would have been unduly increased by being made mt-safe

- Functions that have an mt-unsafe interface; for example, returning a pointer to a buffer in the stack

- Functions that are the equivalent of the third group with interfaces that have been modified to make them mt-safe; functions in this group are identified by the suffix "_r"

Fully mt-safe functions are not changed in the mt-safe libraries. Use of these functions is transparent. Most functions with mt-safe interfaces and an mt-unsafe implementation have been modified to make them fully mt-safe. Use of these functions is also transparent.

Some small, mt-unsafe library functions are still left unchanged. The reference manual entry of each such function identifies it.

 Caution – There is no way to be certain that a function whose name does not end in "_r" is mt-safe other than checking its reference manual page. Use of a function identified to be mt-unsafe must be protected by a synchronizing device or restricted to the initial thread.

For most functions with mt-unsafe interfaces, an mt-safe version of the routine has been developed for use in the multithread context. The name of the new mt-safe routine is always the name of the old mt-unsafe routine with "_r" appended. Any time you find an "..._r" version of a familiar routine, use it in any multithreaded program.

8

Compatibility Issues with Global Error Variables

In nonthreaded applications, the variable errno has been used to return error codes from libc function library calls and is traditionally allocated in static, global storage. The same is true for t_errno for TLI functions. A global, shared-error variable will not work in a multithread environment. So, one error variable is allocated and managed in per-thread storage for each thread via the thread-specific data (TSD) facilities of libthread. You must include errno.h for the libc global error variable and tiuser.h for the TLI global error variable.

At a binary level, this inclusion results in a situation in which:

- Old object files (nonthreaded), or new object files generated without the _REENTRANT flag, reference the static storage labelled errno.

- New object files generated with _REENTRANT reference a new binary entry point, _errno, a function that returns the address of the storage cell for that thread's definition of errno.

- Programs using TLI in libnsl must also be compiled with the _REENTRANT flag and similarly reference a new entry point, _t_errno, a function that returns the address of the thread's definition of t_errno.

The main point is that new threaded object modules should be linked with old object modules only with great caution.

Unsafe Libraries

Routines in libraries that are not guaranteed mt-safe can be safely called by multithreaded programs if such calls are made only from the initial thread.

Another method of using routines that are not mt-safe is by synchronizing the threads' access to these routines. The synchronized protection must include access to implicit elements of the interface, such as error code globals. This method may have some cost in performance.

Not 4.0 LWP

SunOS Release 4.0 introduced a lightweight process library. The 4.0 LWP library supports a form of multithreaded programming with no kernel support. While Solaris Threads is generically similar to 4.0 LWP, the interface is completely different. There are other significant differences in implementation.

Solaris 2.2 contains no support for nor emulation of the 4.0 LWP library. Any application that uses the 4.0 LWP library must be ported to Solaris Threads before it can be run under Solaris 2.2

The Threads Environment

This section describes the environmental requirements and compilation and linkage options required to use threads successfully.

To compile and link a multithreaded program requires:

- Include files
  - thread.h
  - synch.h
  - errno.h
- The standard SunPro™ C compiler
- The standard Solaris linker
- The threads library (libthread)
- mt-safe libraries (libc, libm, libw, libintl, libmalloc, libmapmalloc, libnsl, etc.)

Multithreaded programs must be compiled with the -D _REENTRANT flag. This requirement applies to every module of a new application. If the -D_REENTRANT flag is omitted, the old definitions for errno, stdio, etc. are used. The default is to create single threaded programs compatible with previous releases.

In some cases the flag is turned on by header files like thread.h and synch.h for multithreaded programs.

All calls to libthread instances are effectively no-ops if the application does not link libthread. libc has defined a set of libthread stubs that are null procedures. True procedures are interposed by libthread when the application links both libc and libthread. A threaded program must be constructed to ensure that libthread physically interposes on the C library. The behavior of the C library is undefined if a program is constructed with an ld command line that includes the fragment:

```
.o' s ... -lc -lthread ...
```

A correct result is obtained when the command line contains only -lthread and does not contain -lc.

Do not link a single-threaded program with -lthread. Doing so causes some mechanisms that are required by multithreaded programs to be established at link time and initiated at runtime. This process wastes resources and produces misleading results during debugging.

8

Example Applications

Although the following applications along with accompanying code examples have been tried and tested, they are presented here only as guidelines.

File Copy

It is often advantageous to generate several I/O requests at once so that the I/O access time can be overlapped. A simple example of this is file copying. If the input file and the output file are on different devices the read access for the next block can be overlapped with the write access for the last block. Code Example 8-9 shows some of the code, and Figure 8-1 illustrates the operation. The main routine creates two threads: one to read the input, one to write the output.

Each `thr_create()` also adds an LWP to the pool on which threads are scheduled (`THREAD_NEW_LWP`), since the application requires full system resources for each thread. The LWPs are not permanently bound to the thread, so the threads package can destroy any unused LWPs.

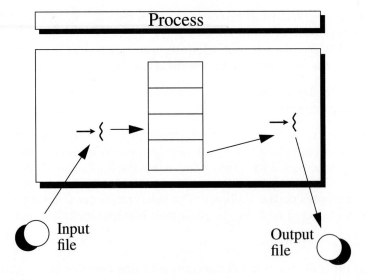

Figure 8-1   File Copy Illustration

The reader thread reads from the input and places the data in a double buffer. The writer thread gets the data from the buffer and continuously writes it out. The threads synchronize by using two counting semaphores: one that counts the number of buffers emptied by the writer and one that counts the number of buffers filled by the reader.

```
sema_t emptybuf_sem, fullbuf_sem;
/* double buffer */
struct {
  char data[BSIZE];
  int size;
} buf[2];
reader()
{
  int i = 0;
  sema_init(&emptybuf_sem, 2, 0, NULL);
  while (1) {
      sema_wait(&emptybuf_sem);
      buf[i].size = read(0, buf[i].data, BSIZE);
      sema_post(&fullbuf_sem);
      if (buf[i].size <= 0)
        break;
      i ^= 1;
  }
}

writer()
{
  int i = 0;
  sema_init(&fulbuf_sem, 0, 0, NULL);
  while (1) {
      sema_wait(&fullbuf_sem);
      if (buf[i].size <= 0)
        break;

      write(1, buf[i].data, buf[i].size);
      sema_post(&emptybuf_sem);
      i ^= 1;
  }
}

main()
{
  thread_t twriter;

  thr_setconcurrency(2);
  (void)thr_create( NULL, NULL, reader, NULL, THR_DETACHED, NULL;
  (void)thr_create( NULL, NULL, writer, NULL, , &twriter );
  thr_join(twriter, NULL, NULL);
}
```

Code Example 8-9   File Copy Example with Semaphore

The example is somewhat contrived since the system already generates asynchronous read-ahead and write-behind requests when accessing regular files. The example is still useful if the files to be copied are raw devices, since raw device access is synchronous.

Matrix Multiply

Computationally intensive applications benefit from the use of all available processors. Matrix multiplication is a good example of this (see Code Example 8-10).

When the matrix multiply is called, it acquires a mutex lock to ensure that only one matrix multiply is in progress. This scheme relies on mutex locks that are statically initialized to zero. The requesting thread then checks whether its worker threads have been created (see Figure 8-2). If not, it creates one for each CPU. Once the worker threads are created, the requesting thread sets up a counter of work to do and signals the workers via a condition variable. Each worker picks off a row and column from the input matrices, then updates the counter of work so that the next worker will get the next item. The MATRIX mul then releases the mutex lock so that computing the vector product can proceed in parallel. When the results are ready, the worker reacquires the mutex lock and updates the counter of work completed. The worker that completes the last bit of work signals the requesting thread.

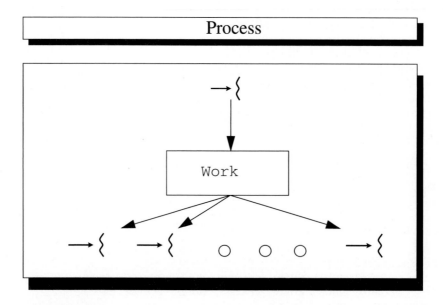

Figure 8-2   Matrix Multiply Illustration

```
struct {
  mutex_t lock;
  condvar_t start_cond, done_cond;
  int (*m1)[SZ][SZ], (*m2)[SZ][SZ], (*m3)[SZ][SZ];
  int row, col;
  int todo, notdone, workers;
} work;
mutex_t mul_lock;

matmul(int (*m1)[SZ][SZ], int (*m2)[SZ][SZ], int (*m3)[SZ][SZ]);
{
  int i;

  mutex_lock(&mul_lock);
  mutex_lock(&work.lock);
  if (work.workers == 0) {
      for (i = 0; i < NCPU; i++) {
        thread_create(NULL, NULL, worker, (void *)NULL,
                    THREAD_NEW_LWP);
      }
      work.workers = NCPU;
  }

  work.m1=m1; work.m2=m2; work.m3=m3;
  work.row = work.col = 0;
  work.todo = work.notdone = SZ*SZ;
  cv_broadcast(&work.start_cond);
  while (work.notdone)
      cv_wait(&work.done_cond, &work.lock);
  mutex_unlock(&work.lock);
  mutex_unlock(&mul_lock);
}
worker()
{
  int (*m1)[SZ][SZ], (*m2)[SZ][SZ], (*m3)[SZ][SZ];
  int row, col, i, result;

  while (1) {
      mutex_lock(&work.lock);
      while (work.todo == 0)
        cv_wait(&work.start_cond, &work.lock);
      work.todo--;
      m1=work.m1; m2=work.m2; m3=work.m3;
        row = work.row; col = work.col;
      work.col++;
      if (work.col == SZ) {
```

```
      work.col = 0;
      work.row++;
      if (work.row == SZ)
          work.row = 0;
   }
   mutex_unlock(&work.lock);
   result = 0;
   for (i = 0; i < SZ; i++)
     result += (*m1)[row][i] * (*m2)[i][col];
   (*m3)[row][col] = result;
   mutex_lock(&work.lock);
   work.notdone--;
   if (work.notdone == 0)
     cv_signal(&work.done_cond);
   mutex_unlock(&work.lock);
 }
}
```

Code Example 8-10   Matrix Multiply

Note that each iteration computed the results of one entry in the result matrix. In some cases this amount of work is not sufficient to justify the overhead of synchronizing. In these cases it is better to give each worker more work per synchronization. For example, each worker could compute an entire row of the output matrix.

Window System Server

A networked window system server tries to handle each client application as independently as possible. Each application should get a fair share of the machine resources, and any blocking on I/O should affect only the connection that caused it. This can be done by allocating a bound thread for each client application. While this scheme would work, it is wasteful in that it is rare that more than a small subset of the clients are active at any one time. Allocating an LWP for each connection ties up large amounts of kernel resources, basically for waiting. On a busy desktop, this amount can be several dozen LWPs. (A window system server that is designed to run with a single-level threads model would have different considerations about kernel resources, and could be designed quite differently.)

The code shown in Code Example 8-11 takes a different approach. It allocates two unbound threads for each client connection, one to process display requests and one to write out results. This allocation allows further input to be processed while the results are being sent, yet it maintains strict serialization within the connection. A single control thread looks for requests on the network. The relationship among threads is shown in Figure 8-3.

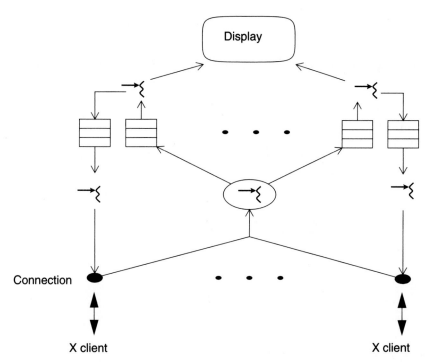

Figure 8-3   Window Server Threads

With this arrangement, an LWP is used for the control thread and for whatever number of threads happen to be active concurrently. The threads synchronize via queues. Each queue has its own mutex to maintain serialization and has a condition variable to inform waiting threads when something is placed on the queue.

```
main()
{
  /* set up server and listen port */
  for(;;) {
      poll(&fds, nfds, 0);
      for (i = 0; i < nfds; i++) {
        if (fds[i].revents & POLLIN)
            checkfd(fds[i].fd)
      }
  }
}

checkfd(int fd)
{
  struct connection *connp;
```

```
    if (fd == listenfd) {
        /* new connection request */
        connp = create_new_connection();
        thread_create(NULL, NULL, svc_requests, connp, 0);
        thread_create(NULL, NULL, send_replies, connp, 0);
    } else {
        requestp = new_msg();
        requestp->len =
          t_rcv(fd, requestp->data, BUFSZ, &flags);
        connp = find_connection(fd);
        put_q(connp->input_q, requestp);
    }
}

send_replies(struct connection *connp)
{
  struct msg *replyp;

  while (1) {
      replyp = get_q(connp->output_q);
      t_snd(connp->fd, replyp->data, replyp->len, &flags);
  }
}

svc_requests(struct connection *connp)
{
  struct msg *requestp, *replyp;

  while (1) {
      requestp = get_q(connp->input_q);
      replyp = do_request(requestp);
      if (replyp)
        put_q(connp->output_q, replyp);
  }
}

put_q(struct queue *qp, struct msg *msgp)
{
  mutex_lock(&qp->lock);
  if (list_empty(qp->list))
      cv_signal(&qp->notempty_cond);
  add_to_tail(msgp, &qp->list);
  mutex_unlock(&qp->lock);
}

struct msg *
get_q(struct queue *qp)
{
```

```
struct msg *msgp;

mutex_lock(&qp->lock);
while (list_empty(qp->list))
    cv_wait(&qp->notempty_cond, &qp->lock);
msgp = get_from_head(&qp->list);
mutex_unlock(&qp->lock);
return (msgp);
}
```

Code Example 8-11   Window Server

Debugging MT Programs

Multithreaded programming differs enough from conventional synchronous programming that it is worthwhile to identify some of the most common oversights that can result in a bug:

- Accessing global memory without the protection of a synchronous mechanism.

- Deadlocks caused by two threads trying to acquire rights to the same pair of global resources in alternate order; one thread controls the first resource, the other controls the second resource, and neither can proceed until the other gives up.

- Hidden gaps in synchronization protection. This is caused when a segment of code that is protected by a synchronous mechanism contains a call to a function that frees and then reacquires the synchronization mechanism before it returns to the caller. The result that appears to the caller is that the global data has been protected when it actually has not been protected.

Using adb

The commands that have been added to `adb` (adb is an interactive, general purpose debugger) for use with multithreaded programs are shown in table that follows.

Command	Function
`pid:A`	Attach to process # `pid`. This stops the process and all its LWPs.
`:R`	Detach from process. This resumes the process and all its LWPs.
`$L`	List all active LWPs in the stopped process.
`n:l`	Switch focus to LWP # n.
`$l`	Show the LWP currently focused on.
`num:i`	Ignore signal number num.

An example of the use of these commands is:

1. Determine the process identifier of the multithreaded program you want to debug.

2. Invoke `adb` on the program.

3. Type `pid:A` to attach to the hung process.

4. Type `$L` to list all the LWPs.

5. If there is more than one LWP, type `n:l` to switch to each LWP, and determine its state at the time the process stopped using standard `adb` commands such as `$c` and `$r`. For example, typing `3:l` switches focus to LWP #3. Type `$c` to see the stack trace for LWP #3, and type `$r` to see its registers.

You can have `adb` ignore signals by typing `num:i`. If the signal number `num` is received, the signal is passed to the process being debugged but is ignored by `adb`.

You can bind all the threads in a multithreaded program so a thread and an LWP are synonymous. Then when you use `adb`, each thread is accessible using the preceding commands.

Multiprocessor System Implementations 9≣

This chapter describes the system implementations that are setting the standard for a new generation of symmetric, high-performance, highly configurable SPARC multiprocessor systems available from Sun Microsystems Computer Corporation. The systems discussed are the Sun SPARCserver 600MP series, the SPARCcenter™ 2000, and the SPARCserver 1000.

Sun SPARCserver 600MP Series of SPARC/MBus-based MP Systems

Sun Microsystems initially offered a multiprocessor system in 1991. At that time Sun introduced the SPARC 600MP series of multiprocessor servers including models 630MP, 670MP, and 690MP. The 600MP series (also referred to as SPARCserver 600MP) enabled Sun to provide multiprocessing capabilities to its family of midrange database, file, and compute servers. In addition to the MP capabilities, the 600MP series provides flexible I/O, disk and memory expansion, and network connectivity. The 600MP serves as the foundation on which Sun will expand its multiprocessing architectures for the next generation of systems.

600MP System Architecture

The SPARCserver 600MP series is based on a modular MBus system architecture that ensures a unique balance of CPU and I/O scalability. By utilizing a modular MBus-based architecture on a single board, Sun reduced system cost, while also providing an easy upgrade path to future technology for its customers.

The 600MP series provides a tightly coupled, shared-memory model architecture. Processors are tightly coupled via the MBus and share the same image of memory, although each processor has a high-speed cache where recently accessed data and instructions are stored. A single copy of Solaris/SunOS coordinates the activities of all processors, scheduling jobs and coordinating access to common resources. All CPUs have equal access to system services, such as I/O and networking, unlike some designs where specific resources are attached to a specific CPU. Figure 9-1 illustrates the overall 600MP system architecture.

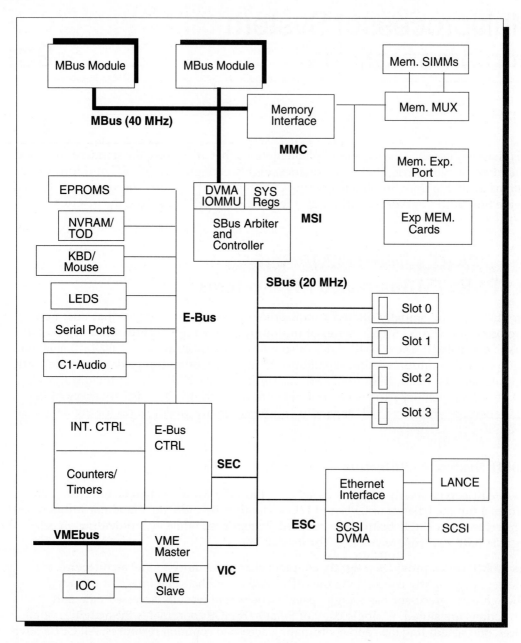

Figure 9-1   600MP System Architecture (block diagram)

The 600MP series satisfied one of Sun's primary implementation goals for its line of multiprocessing systems; that is, to separate CPU technology from the remainder of the product design. In the 600MP series, the standard MBus connector provides the interface between two separate boards. The main system functions and I/O are on the system board, while CPUs are located on modular daughtercards, the SPARC modules.

600MP System Description

The 600MP CPU supports up to four Level-2 MBus processors on two MBus module connectors. All processor modules on the same CPU must be of the same type.

Additional 600MP system features are as follows:

- SBus interface at 20 MHz to low-cost graphics and peripheral devices
- Three SBus expansion slots and one shared SBus/MBus slot (second processor module occupies same space as fourth SBus card)
- On-board memory of 16 or 32 SIMMS, ECC-protected, interleaved, using 80 ns fast page-mode SIMMS of 1- or 4-Mbit DRAM; up to 128 Mbytes on-board with 4-Mbyte SIMMs.
- ECC expansion memory up to 256 Mbytes on each of two boards using 4 Mbyte x 9 SIMMs (system total 640 Mbytes with 4-Mbyte SIMMS; future 2.4 Gbytes with 16-Mbyte SIMMs)
- VMEbus master and slave ports with I/O cache for the slave port
- LANCE Ethernet with local buffering and Emulex ESP236 SCSI interface
- TOD/NVRAM, EPROM, keyboard/mouse, counter/timers, diagnostic LEDs
- Two standard 25-pin serial ports, synchronous-capable
- ISDN audio interface

CPU Board Partitions

In addition to the 600MP modular MBus provisions, another architectural feature in the 600MP design is that the majority of the board is comprised of just a handful of devices that control all 600MP functions. As shown in Figure 9-1, the 600MP has five Application Specific Integrated Circuit (ASIC) partitions:

- MSI (MBus/SBus interface)
- MMC (Main Memory controller)
- SEC (SBus/EBus controller)
- ESC (Ethernet and SCSI controller)
- VIC (VMEbus and I/O cache controller)

The following paragraphs provide a brief overview of each ASIC.

MBus/SBus Interface

The MSI implements MBus-to-SBus and SBus-to-MBus functions such as:

- I/O memory management unit (IOMMU)
- Write buffers in both directions
- SBus arbiter
- MBus arbiter

The M-to-S asynchronous error registers and the arbiter enable register reside in this component, along with all SBus-related and IOMMU-related registers.

Main Memory Controller

The MMC interfaces the MBus to main memory both on- and off-board. It contains ping-pong write buffers, ECC generation and check logic, and the ECC error registers. The MMC also generates controls to the memory system. The MUX ASIC provides two-bank interleave access and address buffering for the memory system in 9-bit slices. It is used both on-board and on the memory expansion board.

SBus/EBus Controller

The SEC implements the multiprocessor interrupt logic, and interfaces the system to the 8-bit slave I/O on the E-bus ("E" stands for "eight-bit"). The SEC is accessed through the SBus, although it is not an SBus device. The SEC uses a special, multiplexed mode to receive address information from the MSI. The SEC also contains the system status and control register.

Ethernet and SCSI Controller

The ESC is an SBus device that interfaces the SBus to an on-board LANCE Ethernet and to an Emulex ESP236 SCSI interface.

The SCSI device is a DVMA master. The LANCE has a private 128-Kbyte buffer memory with DMA access into it; the processor must transfer data to and from main memory and the buffer. This procedure prevents dropping of Ethernet packets because of high memory latency.

VMElus and I/O Cache Controller

The VIC provides both master and slave interface to a VMEbus. The slave port supports up to 8 Mbytes of VME address space, and has an I/O cache for accelerating sequential activity. As a VME slave, the VIC behaves as a normal SBus DVMA master. The VME master port is accessed over the SBus by means of the same special multiplexing the SEC uses. It also receives some additional non-SBus information such as the LOCK instruction.

SPARC MBus Modules

SPARC MBus modules are the size of an SBus card (3.3 inches x 5.8 inches) and attach to the MBus connectors on the system board. By incorporating SPARC MBus modules, system manufacturers can easily build in upgradeability while enhancing the reliability and manufacturability of their products. At the same time they can bypass engineering effort that would otherwise be invested in turning a set of chips into a functioning CPU core.

A typical MBus module (or processor core) consists of an integer unit (IU), a floating-point unit (FPU), a memory management unit (MMU), a cache controller and MBus interface unit (CC/IU), and cache memory. This functionality can be integrated into varying numbers of chips. A single SPARC module can support up to two processor cores for a maximum of four CPUs on a single system board.

Two versions of SPARC modules can be installed into the SPARCserver 600MP series: the CYM6000 Cypress/Ross module and the SuperSPARC with SuperCache™ (external cache) module. A third module (not in production as of this writing) is the Cypress HyperSPARC module (see "SPARC Implementations" in Chapter 3). The Cypress CYM6000 series is discussed first, the HyperSPARC and SuperSPARC modules follow.

The Cypres CYM6000 Series

The Cypress CYM6000 series includes the CYM6001K, 6002K, and 6003K and the HyperSPARC-based CYM6221K, 6222K and 6226K modules. They each represent one of a range of modules from Cypress that provide a complete SPARC CPU for central CPU applications. These modules perform all the required SPARC CPU functions, including integer and floating-point computations, cache control, and memory management. They provide complete Level-1 and Level-2 MBus interfaces. The features of the 6001 through 6003 modules are summarized in Table 9-1.

As shown in the table, these three modules offer both single- and multiprocessor SPARCore™ modules to help customers extend their product lifetimes. In other words, a customer's uniprocessor offering can later be upgraded to a multiprocessor product with a daughterboard swap and an operating system upgrade.

Table 9-1   Features of the Cypress CYM6000 SPARCore Modules

Module	# Processors	Single/ Multiprocessing	Comprise
CYM6001K	1	Single	CY7C601, 602, 604, 157 (2x)
CYM6002K	2	Multiprocessing	CY7C601 (2x), 602 (2x), 605 (2x) 157 (4x)
CYM6003K	1	Multiprocessing	CY7C601, 602, 157 (2x)

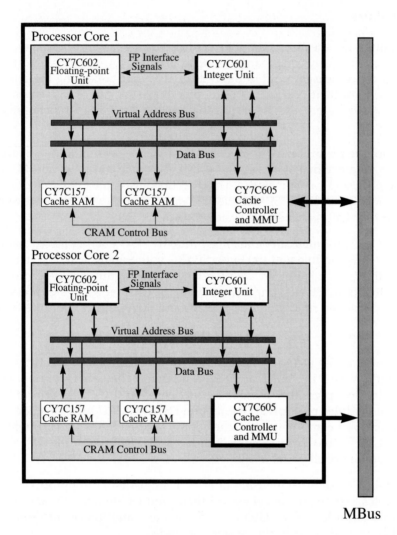

MBus

Figure 9-2   Cypress CYM6002 Dual-CPU MBus Module

The SPARCore module interfaces via the standard SPARC MBus connector. The CYM6001K module for uniprocessor systems contains a single SPARC CPU. The 40 MHz version is rated at 26.5 SPECmarks. Of the multiprocessing members of the family, CYM6002K multiprocessor modules each have two SPARC processors and can be used in multiples for additional processing power. Each 40 MHz CYM6002K module is rated at 49 SPEC throughput. An alternative approach to multiprocessing is to use multiple CYM6003K modules, which have single SPARC processors (26.5 SPECmarks at 40 MHz), but which incorporate the Cypress CY7C605 multiprocessing cache controller/MMU.

The Cypress SPARCore module incorporated in the initial 600MP system was the two processors' CYM6002 SPARC module. This module consists of complete dual-CPU core, including: dual memory management and cache controller with 64-Kbyte, direct-mapped, virtually addressed instruction/data cache; SPARC reference MMU with 64-entry, fully associative translation look-aside buffer (TLB); a 32-byte store buffer; and 32-byte read buffer. The module provides support for SMP, direct data intervention, and reflective memory support. Module performance is rated at 59 MIPS (sustained) and 51 SPECmark throughput. The CYM6002 Dual-CPU MBus Module is shown in Figure 9.2.

The Cypress HyperSPARC Modules

The Cypress HyperSPARC modules, including the CYM6221K, 6222K, and 6226K, provide MP system designers a range of high-performance MBus modules aimed at migrating existing 600MP system to higher performance levels or for use in the design of new MP system platforms. The HyperSPARC-based series of MBus modules provides designers with a choice of three different configurations of modules, allowing migration to different performance ranges from 52 to 156 SPECmarks throughput.

The Cypress CYM6221K, 6222K, and 6226K differ only in the number of CPU units and cache data units (CDU). Significant features are summarized in Table 9-2. The HyperSPARC CYM6226K module is shown in Figure 9-3.

The 6226K comprises two high performance CY7C620 integer/floating point unit, a CY7C625 cache controller, MMU and tag unit (CMTU), and four CY7C627 cache data units (CDU) for dual-level cache support. The HyperSPARC module also provides hardware support for symmetric, shared-memory multiprocessing as well as Level-2 MBus support for cache consistency and support for direct data intervention and reflective memory. The four CY7C627 CDUs provide support for a 256-Kbyte cache for the CY7C620 CPU. The CY7C620 is scalable from 55.5 to 80 MHz. It achieves a SPEC throughput of 107 at 55.5 MHz, 129 at 66 MHz, and 156 at 80 MHz.

The 600MP series is now available from Sun with a SuperSPARC (TMS390Z50) MBus module (see Chapter 3, "SPARC Implementations"). The SuperSPARC module (see Figure 9-4) combines the SuperSPARC microprocessor and the SuperCache controller (MXCC) onto a single module.

Table 9-2   Features of the Cypress CYM6221K, 6222K and 6226K Modules

Module	# Processors	Single/Multiprocessing	Comprise
CYM6221K	1	Single	CY7C620, 625, 627 (CDU) (2x)
CYM6222K	2	Multiprocessing	CY7C620 (2x), 625 (2x), 627 (2x)
CYM6226K	2	Multiprocessing	CY7C620 (2x), 625 (2x), 627 (4x)

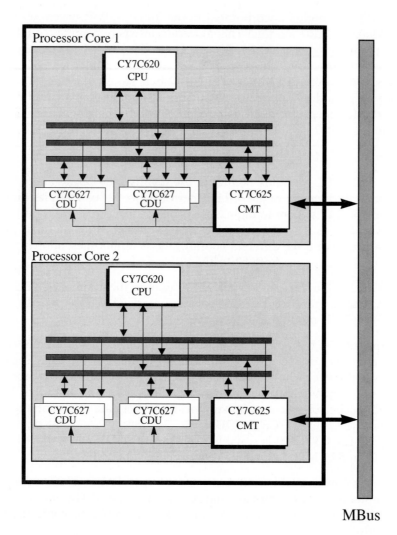

Figure 9-3   HyperSPARC CY7C620 MBus Module

The SuperSPARC module offers the following features:

- A SuperSPARC processor with integer, floating point, memory management, and cache

- Superscalar pipeline with up to three instructions per clock cycle

- Internal 20-Kbyte 5-way set-associative, physically addressed instruction cache

- Internal 16-Kbyte 4-way set-associative, physically addressed data cache

- Internal 64-byte Store Buffer

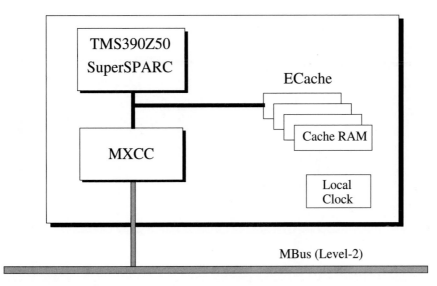

Figure 9-4   SuperSPARC Module

- SPARC Reference MMU with 64-entry, fully associative translation look-aside buffer (TLB) for hardware page-table-walking SuperSPARC module; support for 65,536 contexts

- Single/double precision on-chip FPU (which also does integer multiply and divide)

The Texas Instrument SuperSPARC MBus Module

The TI SuperSPARC MBus module consists of a single CPU chip on a standard MBus plug-in board. Included as well is a single multi-cache controller (MXCC) chip and 1 Mbyte of SRAM cache memory. All "glue logic" for multiprocessor interfacing is incorporated on-chip in SuperSPARC and the MXCC.

In addition to running on the MBus, the TI SuperSPARC modules can operate on the XBus packet-switched mode developed for very-large-scale multiprocessing (discussed later in this chapter). The XBus interface is contained in the MXCC and can support up to four system buses via bus watchers (see Figure 9-5). Where MBus can handle up to four CPU modules, XBus designs can be implemented with up to 64 modules, approaching 10 billion instructions per second at 50 MHz.

As the configuration in Figure 9-5 illustrates, each bus watcher (BW) can interface with a different system bus increasing available bandwidth between processors and memory. The choice of bus interface must be made statically in the system. The SuperSPARC module configures itself for operation in a particular mode, based on the condition of a signal pin. If the bit is a one, the MBus mode is enabled; otherwise XBus bus is selected.

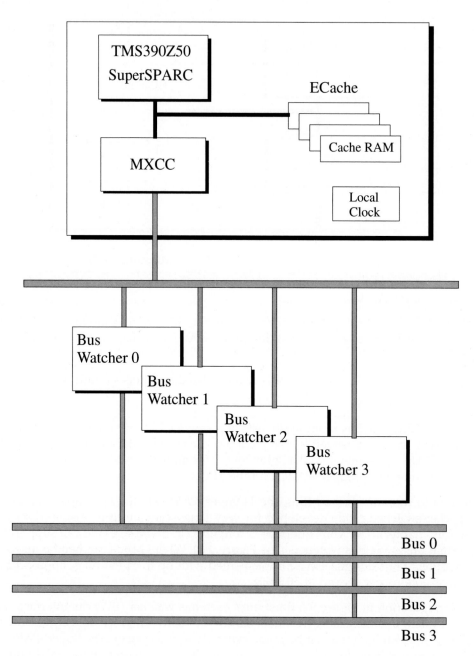

Figure 9-5   SuperSPARC MXCC Bus Interface

The SuperSPARC module's ability to handle both MBus and XBus protocols (see sections on XBus and XDBus in Chapter 5) differentiate it from the other MBus modules. The MXCC can be configured for either MBus or XBus operation with the MBSEL pin. The module can also sense what kind of system (MBus- or XBus-based) it is plugged into, and can then adjust (or alter) the voltage levels used to control the I/O lines. The module provides easy interchangeability and reduces the number of unique implementations needed to be built and inventoried.

In an MBus-based 600MP system, the SuperSPARC processor and the MXCC run asynchronously with the MBus. So, as faster SPARC chips become available, an upgrade is as simple as swapping modules. The SuperSPARC module provides a minimum of twice the performance on CPU test suites and application throughput as does the CY6002 module.

The SuperSPARC module in an XBus-based system implementation is discussed later in this chapter.

Maintenance of Cache Coherency

When there are multiple local caches in a multiprocessing system, as is the case in the 600MP systems, some mechanism must ensure that local copies of data remain consistent. To maintain data consistency, all caches in the system must participate in a multiprocessor cache coherence (consistency) protocol (see "Cache Coherency Considerations" in Chapter 6). The SPARC MBus provides transactions that make it possible to implement such coherence in a simple way. DVMA (Direct Virtual Memory Access) also participates in the coherence protocols, eliminating the need for processor cache-flushing around I/O operations.

Because cache coherency is supported both in the MBus specification and in the cache control logic, there is little overhead and impact on the performance of individual CPUs is minimal. With module caches snooping the MBus for coherent transactions and intervening to maintain consistency, copy-back (or write-back) operation is possible. The copy-back cache issues stores to memory only when flushing or reallocating a modified cache line, reducing MBus occupancy significantly compared to a write-through cache. This practice causes writes to main memory each time writes to the cache occur, putting substantial and unnecessary loads on the bus. All CPU-to-CPU and CPU-to-memory transactions occur on the MBus, which is less expensive and complex than the specialized synchronization buses used on older MP implementations.

Memory Management and DVMA

Some system facilities can be shared with multiple processors in a system, while others need to be replicated per processor. An example of replication is the memory management unit (MMU). Older Sun systems contained a single MMU consisting of several levels of static RAM tables indexed by a contexts number and by some bits of the virtual address. This older MMU was shared between the processor and DVMA.

Multiprocessor servers place different requirements on memory management. More contexts are necessary than the traditional 8-64 context supported in previous designs. More pages must be mapped at any time in order to reduce the frequency of page faults. Moreover, for speed the MMUs should be close to the processor and cache and thus must be on the module. Therefore, the MMUs must be physically small and lower in cost than an array of fast, expensive static RAM chips.

These needs are met by the SPARC Reference MMU (SRMMU) located within each module. SRMMU is based on tables in memory that contain the multiple-level mappings (see "SPARC Reference MMU" in Chapter 4). Each cache/MMU controller contains a context register and a base address register that points to the first level of tables in memory. A set of translation look-aside buffers (TLBs) that contain the set of recently used translations is also integrated. TLB misses are serviced by hardware, meaning that fewer traps into the operating system are needed to manage mappings once a page has been faulted in by the memory management code. Stale mappings are purged from the TLBs through use of MMU flush commands from the operating system.

The SPARC Reference MMU implementations used on the SPARC modules allow up to a maximum of 4096 contexts for the CY6002 and up to 65,535 contexts for the SuperSPARC design.

The SRMMU in each processor is not accessible from DVMA, so another memory management unit is implemented to translate DVMA addresses to system physical addresses. This unit is the I/O memory management unit (IOMMU). The IOMMU is similar to an SRMMU, except that there are no contexts, only one level of table, and no "referenced" or "modified" status per page. The IOMMU contains 16 TLB entries with least-recently used (LRU) replacement. It provides up to 2 Gbytes of virtual address space to device drivers, extending the limit of 1 Mbyte that was imposed in the older, shared-MMU systems.

DVMA through the IOMMU participates in system coherence with hardware support, so no processor cache-flushing is needed around I/O. DVMA activity can come from SBus devices (including on-board SBus devices such as SCSI and Ethernet) and also from VME on the SPARCserver 600MP systems. A DVMA address can come from an SBus master or a VMEbus master. DVMA can access main memory or any slave devices on the SBus. The only limitation is that DVMA cannot access devices on the VMEbus (although VMEbus masters can access VMEbus slaves, since the CPU does not participate in those accesses).

Interrupts from I/O devices can be steered to any processor in the system, meaning that the same hardware can support either a symmetric or an asymmetric multiprocessing operating system.

Write Buffers

The 600MP system incorporates a set of write buffers used to accelerate writes and to reduce bus occupancy for better overall system performance. While write buffers are not new to computer designs, some write buffers in implementations are by necessity visible to the software. Write buffers allow writes to complete concurrently with the processor, doing useful work; the implication is that error reports are not synchronous to instruction flow. Errors are considered to be rare events and should never be used for flow control.

600MP write buffers adhere to the following rules:

1. Once a write buffer has accepted a write, it must either guarantee that the write can occur without error, or the write buffer is responsible for reporting those errors.

2. Write buffers are read-stall. That is, after a write buffer has accepted a write, any subsequent access to that device must wait for the write operation to complete, thus ensuring that order is maintained. System write buffers are strongly ordered.

3. If a write buffer is visible to the software, it must have a synchronization mechanism; that is, software has a way of determining if a write is still pending or if it has completed.

Rule (2) does not apply to module write buffers, which are allowed to snoop cacheable items, but they must drain on atomic SPARC instructions or on read access to noncacheable data. Module write buffers follow the TSO model defined in SPARC Architecture V. 8 and described in Chapter 4.

Write buffers exist in many places in implementations of this architecture, but only two are visible to software. Invisible write buffers are in the memory controller, the SCSI/Ethernet interfaces, and the EBus interface; those write buffers will not acknowledge until they have determined that the address and size are a valid transaction; then they will accept the write. (If invalid, they will acknowledge with an eror; but the location of these buffers keeps that error-acknowledge from reaching the modules. Instead, the previous write buffer on the path receives the error and posts an interrupt.)

Visible write buffers exist in the MBus-to-SBus interface and the VME Master port. DVMA write buffers also exist between SBus or VME/IOC and the MBus.

Interrupt Architecture

The 600MP interrupt architecture employs 15 external interrupt levels that can be accepted by the MBus modules. The levels are encoded in a 4-bit code, IRL(3:0), with the code of "0" indicating that no interrupts are pending. In an MP environment, the capability to steer individual interrupts to any of the four processors is required. The ability to post interrupts via software ("soft" interrupts) to any of the processors at various levels is also necessary.

With both a VMEbus and an SBus supported in the system, interrupt levels can be shared by many devices in different environments. SunOS can select one or more sources to dispatch to a processor (or to an interrupt-handling thread) and can isolate sources so that different drivers can migrate easily from processor to processor.

Recall that in SunOS 5.x interrupts behave like asynchronously created threads. SunOS 5.x preallocates interrupt threads, already partly initialized. When an interrupt occurs, a minimum amount of work is needed to move onto the stack of an interrupt thread and set it as the current thread.

The 600MP hardware provides the flexibility that allows software to choose the best algorithms for servicing the interrupts. The interrupt hardware implementation is discussed in the following section.

Processor-to-Processor Interrupts

Interrupts in SPARC are defined in 15 interrupt priority levels, with level 15 as the highest priority. The interrupts pending to a particular processor are priority encoded and sent to the SPARC processor as a 4-bit code, IRL(3:0), as shown in Figure 9-6.

A code of "0" indicates that no interrupts are pending. Asynchronous interrupt sources should be properly synchronized prior to encoding to prevent spurious codes.

Associated with each processor is a register set that posts soft interrupts at any level. The register can have any bit asserted by writing to the associated set register with that bit asserted, and it can have any bit cleared by writing to the associated clear register with that bit asserted.

Deasserted bits in the data written have no effect. This mechanism eliminates the need for mutex locks around accesses to these registers.

Hardware has no information about the source of the `soft_interrupt`. The kernel must establish message areas in shared memory that can be polled by the recipient of the `soft_interrupt` to find the pending source(s). Any queueing of multiple soft interrupts must also be treated in the message areas.

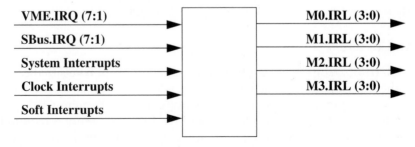

Figure 9-6   600MP Interrupt Servicing

Directed Interrupts

A directed interrupt is an interrupt that is always posted to the same target processor. Directed interrupts can come from specific devices, from error conditions, and from `soft_interrupts` posted from any processor.

Certain interrupts must always be sent to a particular processor. For example, the level-14 high-resolution timer interrupts are directed; one timer/counter is dedicated to each processor. Note that the level-10 time-tick interrupt is undirected, and one level-10 timer/counter serves the entire system.

Some device drivers are not reentrant, and therefore some interrupts may not be distributed to multiple processors.

Undirected Interrupts

An undirected interrupt comes from a system device, and the interrupt steering logic selects a target processor based upon some distribution scheme.

For a smaller MP system, for example, one with four or fewer processors, the expected interrupt traffic is small enough that a single processor can handle identifying sources and scheduling different processors to service those interrupts, via memory descriptors and directed interrupts.

In a large MP system, the allocation can be handled in hardware. The hardware/software distribution criterion is this: If a single processor receives all undirected interrupts and schedules them for service on the different processors in the system, then the time spent should be small enough that a process running on that processor will not be significantly slower than a process running on any other processor in the system. A maximum "scheduling" load of 5% is recommended.

In order to support more flexible allocation algorithms, the "current target" is programmable; that is, one of the processors in the system can be selected to receive all undirected interrupts.

Broadcast Interrupts

A broadcast interrupt is an interrupt that is posted to all processors in the system, including the processor that initiates the posting (if the interrupt is from a processor). A broadcast interrupt can be issued at any interrupt level.

Implementation of broadcast is system-dependent; in a small MP system, it may be implemented with a series of processor-to-processor interrupts, while in larger systems it may be issued as a single message.

The effect of a broadcast interrupt is to set the same level `soft_interrupt` for all processors. The issue of a broadcast interrupts should be done in a single kernel routine that hides the differences in implementation. The acknowledgment of broadcast interrupts must be handled in the shared-memory message area used for `soft_interrupts`.

600MP Interrupt Structure

Within the 600MP interrupt structure, each processor receives directed interrupts for level-14 profiling.

Each processor can receive a directed interrupt on any level; the interrupt is asserted by writes to a register associated with that processor.

All undirected system interrupts go to the processor indicated by the interrupt target register. That processor (referred to hereafter as the current interrupt target, or CIT) can schedule the interrupt to any processor via the directed interrupt mechanism and shared memory communication, or the processor can service the interrupt. All hard level-15 interrupts are broadcast to all processors; the assertion of any level-15 source sets the level-15 bit in each processor interrupt pending register. Each processor can acknowledge by clearing its own copy of that bit. Only one processor can service the interrupt source, but each processor can clear its own pending bit.

A read-only register shows the interrupts that are asserted at any time. When the current interrupt target processor has scheduled an interrupt to a processor for service, it writes a mask bit in a corresponding register, so that the presence of that interrupt no longer causes the CIT to trap for that interrupt source.

When the then-current scheduled processor has serviced the interrupt, it must also deassert that mask bit so subsequent interrupts from that source are again routed to the CIT.

The registers associated with interrupts are:

- Processor interrupt registers

- System interrupt registers

- Tlmer/counter registers

- Interrupt target register

I/O Architecture

This section describes elements of the I/O architecture.

- SBus

- VME and I/O cache

- I/O cache

- VMEbus interface

- VMEbus master port

SBus

An on-board SBus enables the user to take advantage of high-performance and low-cost peripherals from Sun and from third parties. A total of four SBus slots are present on the SPARCserver 600MP. Three SBus slots are available in the absence of a second MBus module. With 32-byte activity, the SBus provides sustained performance, assuming an ideal master, of 53-Mbyte/sec writes to memory, and 30-Mbytes/sec reads from memory. Each is capable of being accessed as a slave. Slave capabilities are established in the SBus slot configuration register for that slot.

The SBus card implementation must be compliant at least with SBus revision A.2; some implementations may be compliant with a more recent version of the SBus specification.

Depending on slave device capabilities, the SBus slot configuration register can be programmed to resize bursts into smaller transfers.

VME and I/O Cache

VMEbus support provides a bridge to older configurations and to widely available VME peripherals. Up to 11 VMEbus slots are present, depending on the model of the 600MP system. The VMEbus channel provides a 32-Kbyte I/O cache (IOC) to accelerate sequential activity between VMEbus masters and system memory. This IOC provides VME masters with an 8-Mbyte window of virtual address space with which to read and write memory and enough buffers to support up to 1024 simultaneous transfers in progress. The I/O system is tuned to provide optimal performance for masters that do 32-byte burst accesses. IOC activity matches that burst size by buffering VME writes into 32-byte packets and doing 32-byte reads on behalf of multiple sequential VME reads. VMEbus activity through the IOC will provide a sustained 16-Mbyte/sec writes and 13-Mbyte/sec reads. Both numbers assume an ideal master.

I/O Cache (IOC)

The I/O cache provides accelerated sequential VME slave port activity. Unlike previous IOC designs used at Sun, this IOC is not shared with SCSI or Ethernet traffic. IOC accesses to memory are always 32-byte bursts. On VME reads from main memory, leading fragments can be discarded. On VME writes to main memory that use the IOC, the writes will always start and end on 32-byte boundaries, independent of the addresses used.

Write-backs and flushes always trigger a 32-byte burst access. The IOC is not cycle-by-cycle coherent with main memory, but is coherent on a 32-byte burst basis. In SunOS this is known as the "Streaming I/O" model.

The IOC is a write-back cache with a no-write-allocate policy. It is required that descriptors shared between the IUs and VME devices be non-IOC cacheable.

Each 32-byte line in the IOC maps to an 8-Kbyte section of VME address space. A total of 8 Mbyte of VME address space is allocated to the slave port. Because of the 8 Kbyte mapping, IOMMU entries for VME must be made identically on a pair of sequential 4-Kbyte pages; that is, the write-allowed, cacheable, and valid bits must be the same, although the physical pages do not have to be physically contiguous.

VME slave port accesses can use or bypass the IOC on an 8-Kbyte page basis. The IOC does not participate in general SBus activity. SBus masters will achieve maximum bandwidth by issuing accesses that are system cache line-sized (32 bytes).

VMEbus Interface

The SPARCsystem 600MP system board VMEbus interface is designed to be as similar as possible to previous Sun VME interfaces. The VIC provides a single chip interface between the MBus and VMEbus (see Figure 9-7) with a minimum amount of glue logic. The VIC provides both master and slave interface to the VMEbus.

The 600MP VMEbus has the following attributes:

- Uses VME C.1 specification base (same as Sun 4/300 family)

- Allows any processor to access the VMEbus as a master and talk to any slave device

- The SPARCsystem 600MP acts as a slave device for VMEbus masters to perform DVMA accesses to system main memory

- Allows any VMEbus master to access any SBus card through DVMA; however, an SBus DVMA master cannot access the VMEbus

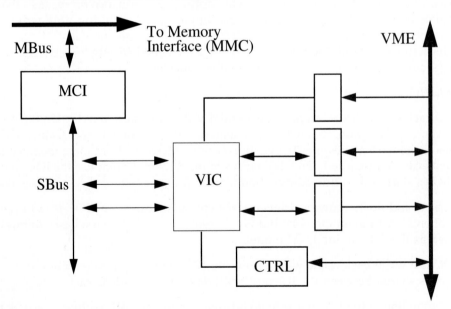

Figure 9-7   VMS Subsystem Partition (simplified block diagram)

- Provides the same, or improved, basic master/slave address and data capabilities as previous Sun VMEbus implementations

- I/O cache provides acceleration of sequential VME slave port activity, similar to the Sun-4/400 and 3/400 Series products

VMEbus Master Port

The VME Master Port has 8-, 16-, and 32-bit access, with 32-bit access not allowed in 16-bit space. The port is accessed in one of four system address spaces.

Atomic bus cycles are guaranteed atomic on the VMEbus; other activity can occur on the system buses during this time. In keeping with previous Sun VME implementations, atomic cycles are implemented by holding VME BBSY between a load and a store, rather than by the VME atomic transaction protocol.

SPARCcenter 2000 MP System[1]

Following on the footsteps of the 600MP, Sun Microsystems Computer Corporation introduced the SPARCcenter 2000 in 1992. In development just under two years, the SPARCcenter 2000 is the first implementation of a second generation of symmetric, high-performance, highly configurable SPARC multiprocessor systems. With up to 20 processors, two interleaved XDBuses for the system interconnect, extensive main memory, expansibility and large I/O capacity, the SPARCcenter 2000 meets the computing needs of large department to medium-scale enterprises.

The SPARCcenter 2000 defines a new standard for shared-memory multiprocessor computers. In keeping with a modular architecture approach, the SPARCcenter 2000 is composed of three types of units: the processor unit, the memory unit and the I/O unit. All these units are interconnected through two XDBuses. Much like the MBus provides the interconnect for MBus modules in the 600MP series, the XDBus provides the interconnect between processor boards. The XDBus is flexible enough and fast enough to deliver outstanding performance (see SPARC System Performance) and to maintain scalability to levels which are unheard of in today's marketplace. This arrangement again provides the ability to separate CPU technology from the remainder of the product design.

System Architecture

Figure 9-8 illustrates the SPARCcenter 2000 system architecture.

---

1. Portions reprinted with permission from IEEE from SPARCcenter 2000: Multiprocessing for the 90s, COMPCON, San Francisco, Feb. 1993 © IEEE.

As illustrated, the XDBuses provide a high-speed packet-switched interconnect between processor, memory, and I/O units. The XDBus backplanes provide 320 Mbyte/sec of data throughput at a 40 MHz clock rate. The XDBuses operate in parallel, and the system can be rebooted with a single XDBus in case of a permanent failure of one of them. The system's functional units are connected to both XDBuses. Memory banks are attached to individual XDBuses, and a memory unit is composed of two interleaved memory banks.

The processor modules are identical to those used in the 600MP system, and consist of a SuperSPARC processor and multicache controller. The system can use up to 20 SuperSPARC processors on 10 individual system boards (see Figure 9-9).

The main memory is configured in multiple memory units. All these units have the same access time from every processor and I/O device, regardless of their physical locations in the system. Physical memory addresses are interleaved between the two XDBuses on a 256-byte boundary, and memory banks attached to the same bus can also be interleaved to avoid bottlenecks. A memory unit can have a memory capacity between 64 Mbytes with 4-Mbit DRAM chips and 512 Mbytes with 16-Mbit DRAM chips. A fully configured system can support 5 Gbytes of main memory.

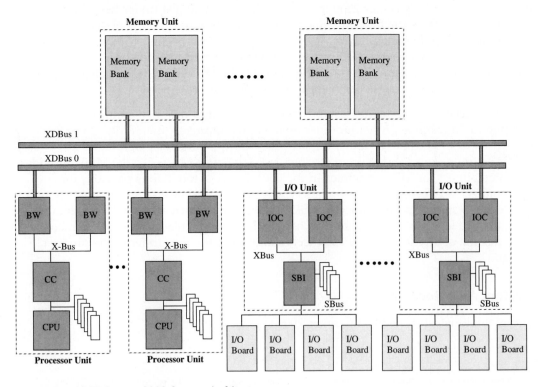

Figure 9-8   SPARCcenter 2000 System Architecture

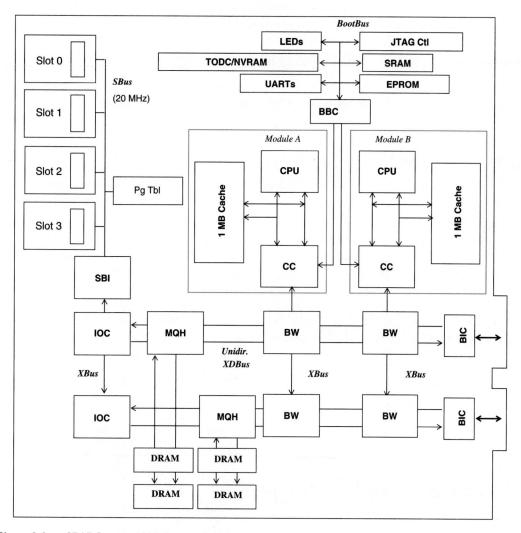

Figure 9-9   SPARCcenter 2000 System Board

The SPARCcenter 2000 offers incrementally expandable I/O with up to ten SBus channels, one per system board. Each SBus channel supports four SBus slots for a maximum configuration of 40 SBus peripheral boards. Each SBus is connected to the XDBuses through an I/O unit. Like memory, all SBus channels are accessed with the same latency from every processor. Each SBus delivers 50 Mbytes/sec of sustainable data throughput.

A system may contain up to ten system boards. Each board contains a backplane interface connection to dual XDBuses, two sockets for the SuperSPARC modules, sockets for 16

SIMMs, an SBus with four slots, the local XDBus segments, and a JTAG interface for diagnostics and configuration. Each system board contains two processor units, a memory unit and an I/O unit. The actual implementation is highly integrated. The system board consists primarily of nine large 100-Kbyte gate CMOS ASICs—four bus watchers (BW), two memory queue handlers (MQH), an SBI interface (SBI) and two I/O caches (IOC)—and ten smaller ASICs. Two board bus arbiters (BARB) and eight bit-sliced pipeline registers connect the on-board XDBus segments to the backplane via bus interface chips (BIC).

XDBus Backplane

The XDBus backplane consists of two bidirectional segments of the XDBuses.The system board supports unidirectional segments for each XDBus. Figure 9-10 illustrates the architecture of the XDBus interface.

The XDBus segments consists of 64 bits for address and data and 8 bits for parity. The BICs separate the unidirectional on-board XDBuses and the bidirectional backplane XDBuses. The BIC is composed of two pipeline registers, one between the outbound on-board segment and the backplane segment and the other between the backplane segment and the inbound on-board segment. Each BIC has an 18-bit-wide data path, including 16 bits of data/address and 2 bits of parity. Four BICs are necessary to provide the interface between the on-board and backplane segments of a single XDBus.

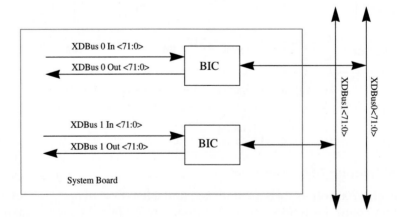

Figure 9-10   Unidirectional XDBus Interfaces

The XDBus uses a packet-switched protocol to transfer data. In a packet-switched protocol, the requestor arbitrates for the control of the bus and, as soon as it is granted, sends a request packet and immediately releases the bus. The bus is free to be used by other clients while the request is being processed. When the requested data is available, a reply packet is issued. Reply packets are tagged so that they can be matched with the corresponding request. A packet-switched protocol permits optimal utilization of the raw bandwidth.

The XDBus runs at 40 MHz and uses low voltage-swing technology called GTL (Gunning Transceiver Logic[2]). GTL uses a 0.8V voltage swing between 0.4 and 1.2V. This technology is specially designed for high-speed, high density CMOS gate arrays. GTL permits CMOS to be used in a terminated transmission line environment. Because the power dissipation is low, a wide bus like the XDBus can be driven directly from an ASIC without the need for costly external drivers.

The XDBus backplane also provides identifiers (Board IDs) to uniquely identify each system board. A system board can be plugged into any slot of the cardcage, and the Board ID can be accessed at system configuration time through a pseudo-register. No jumper or switch settings are required for any configuration, thus avoiding the possibility of installation errors.

A minimum system consists of at least one system board with a single processor and one memory unit. Because all units are equally accessible, the specific locations of the memory, processors, and I/O devices are not fixed. If an application requires only four processors but three Gbytes of memory, the system can be configured with six system boards with fully populated memory units but only two SPARCmodules. The boards can be plugged in any slot.

Processor Unit Architecture

The processor unit consists of a SuperSPARC processor, an external cache, and system support devices connected to the BootBus. Figure 9-11 illustrates the main components of the processor unit and their interconnections.

The external cache includes the CC, two BW ASICs, and 1 Mbyte of parity-protected SRAM. The SuperSPARC processor, the CC, and the SRAM are located on the SuperSPARC module. The module is a small daughtercard that plugs through a 100-pin connector onto the system board. The BWs are located directly on the system board.

The SuperSPARC processor, the CC, and cache make up each module. Recall that the SuperSPARC module can provide both MBus and XBus/XDBus functionality. The CC and the two BWs implement the cache consistency protocol. The BW chips contain a copy of the cache tags to minimize contention between the processor and the XDBus accesses. The cache consistency protocol relies on snooping the XDBus traffic. The BW basically filters out almost all bus transactions, leaving the processor free to access the cache most of the time. When sharing is detected, the BW updates some state bits or retrieves the requested data from the cache. Each BW contains half of the duplicated tags; they are interleaved on a 256 byte boundary.

---

2. Inquires concerning GTL should be directed to the Xerox Corporation's Palo Alto Research Center

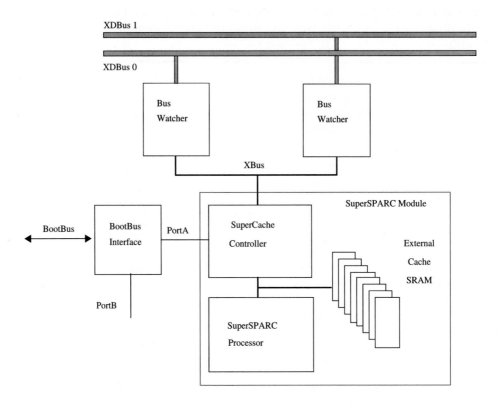

Figure 9-11   Processor Unit and System Interconnects

The BWs and the CC are interconnected by the local packet-switched bus, XBus. XBus and XDBus transactions are similar except in the use of dedicated commands to maintain the two copies of cache tags consistently. The use of a packet-switched protocol on the XBus is also key to the performance of the processor in a multiprocessor environment. Although the external cache handles only a single miss at a time, multiple requests may be outstanding. For instance, multiple requests for block invalidation or update can be issued from the same processor unit, guaranteeing that the processor does not stall, even when much data is shared with other processors.

The processor module and the XBus are clocked at 40 MHz. Most of the CC operates synchronously to the processor clock. The XBus interface operates synchronously to the system clock, and there is an asynchronous boundary inside the CC. The CC is also connected to a local bus called the BootBus. Support devices like a time-of-day clock, UART, scratchpad memory, and an EPROM are attached to the BootBus. The BootBus is shared by the two processors on the same system board.

I/O Architecture Subsystem

This section discusses elements of the I/O architecture.

- I/O Unit

- BootBus

- Control Board

- Arbitration

- Interrupt Management

I/O Unit

The SPARCcenter 2000 system board supports a complete SBus that is used as an I/O bus. This SBus has four slots and is clocked at 20 MHz. All peripheral devices are connected to the SBus.

The I/O unit provides the bridge between the SBus and the XDBus complex. The I/O unit is composed of two I/O cache chip (IOC), an SBus interface chip, and an external page table (XPT). The IOCs and the SBI are interconnected with an XBus. Figure 9-12 depicts the architecture of the I/O unit.

The I/O Unit provides three different I/O models:

- Programmed I/O. The processor directly reads and writes the I/O devices.

- Consistent direct virtual memory access (DVMA) I/O. In this mode, the data is moved directly between the SBus and the XDBus complex, and the SBus address is translated into a physical XDBus address by the XPT. This mode is called consistent because the data is moved into the "shared memory image" in the I/O cache. In this mode, there can be only one pending transaction between an SBus board and the memory system.

- Stream Mode DVMA. As for the previous mode, SBus addresses are translated by the XPT, but the data is not moved directly between the SBus and the memory system. Instead, it goes through pairs of buffers. These double buffers are not part of the shared memory image and are not kept consistent until they are flushed or invalidated by software.

The IOC contains a small, fully associative write-back cache which is kept consistent. Data is read from this cache or written into this cache when I/O transfers are done in consistent DVMA mode. The IOC also provides simultaneous I/O accesses to the XDBus for each SBus slot. Even if an SBus board has an XDBus transaction pending, the other SBus boards can still access the XDBus. The IOC provides the interface between XDBus and the local XBus.

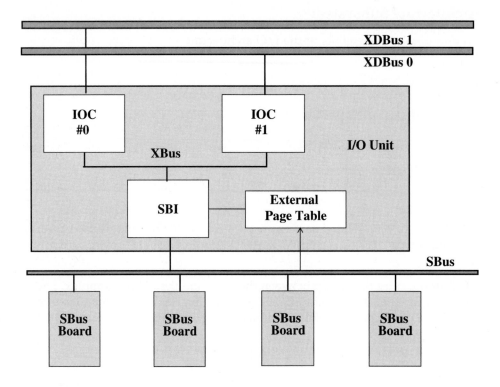

Figure 9-12   I/O Unit Architecture

The SBI contains the read and write buffers used in stream mode DVMA. Each SBus slot has its own pair of double buffers, which are managed under software. The stream mode is the more efficient of the two DVMA modes. In stream mode, each SBus can sustain 50 Mbytes/sec when using 64-byte bursts and 30 Mbytes/sec when using 16-byte bursts. The peak bandwidth is 80 Mbytes/sec. The transfer mode is selected on a slot basis.

The external page table implements a single-level page table through a set of SRAM chips. It can map up to 64 Mbytes of DVMA address space. Each entry maps a 4-Kbyte page. The XPT is controlled by the SBI and is maintained as consistent by the kernel.

The SPARCcenter 2000 supports the Revision B.0 of SBus. All SBus transfer sizes (2, 4, 8, 16, 32, and 64 bytes) are supported in both DVMA I/O modes. All SPARC addressable quantities are supported in programmed I/O mode. Each slot supports the full 28-bit address space. The SBus clock is independent of the system clock. An asynchronous boundary is implemented inside the SBI. An important feature of the SPARCcenter 2000 implementation of SBus is the parity extension support for data integrity. Parity can be enabled on a slot basis, so that devices that are not supporting parity can still be used.

BootBus

Each SPARCcenter 2000 system board supports an 8-bit local bus, called the BootBus. This bus is shared by the two processor units and is used to access system support devices. The BootBus is controlled by the BootBus controller chip (BBC). The cache controllers are connected to the BBC through a 12-signal interface.

Two types of devices are connected to the BootBus: fast and slow devices. The SuperSPARC processors can access the fast devices simultaneously. However, the slow bus can be accessed by only one processor at a time. Figure 9-13 illustrates the connection between the processor units and the BootBus devices.

Connected to the fast bus are 512 Kbytes of EPROM, 16 Kbytes of SRAM, three status registers, two semaphore registers, the system software reset register, and the system board version register. The EPROM contains the boot code and the SRAM is used as a scratchpad and for the stack.

Connected to the slow bus are the LED diagnostic register, a control register, a UART that provides two RS232 ports, a UART for a keyboard/mouse interface, the JTAG master interface register, and a time-of-day/nonvolatile RAM chip. The slow devices are shared through one of the semaphore registers.

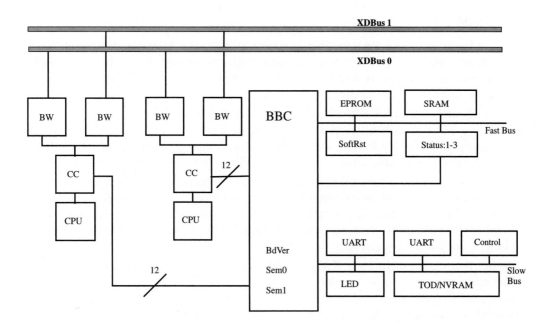

Figure 9-13 Processor and BootBus Interface

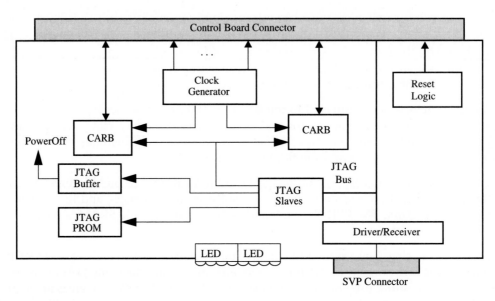

Figure 9-14 Control Board Block Diagram

Control Board

The control board provides system clock generation, central arbitration, power-on reset generation, and the JTAG port for a service processor connection. It also has some LEDs to indicate the status of power and some system signals. Figure 9-14 details the major functional units of the control board.

The control board supports the clock generation logic. The 40 MHz system clock is generated as a PECL signal. All clock traces on the distribution path have the same length and an equal number of loads to minimize the skew. The clock received by the central arbiters (CARB) has the same clock path as the XDBus client chips on the system board.

The reset logic generates a general system reset signal which is forwarded to all system boards. A reset is generated when either the reset switch on the front panel is activated, a power-on condition is detected, the optional service processor requests a system reset, a fatal error is detected in the system, or one of the processor requests a reset by setting a bit in one of the BootBus registers.

The control Board also includes a JTAG PROM, which contains the system ID and the Ethernet address.

Arbitration

The SPARCcenter 2000 uses a two-level arbitration scheme to grant access to the XDBus. Because the two XDBuses operate in parallel, the arbitration logic is duplicated for each of them. The arbitration is implemented with two types of ASIC: the board arbiter (BARB) and the central arbiter (CARB). Arbitration requests generated by XDBus client devices are collected by BARBs and forwarded to the CARB. The CARB then selects a client device as XDBus master by issuing a grant signal to that client's BARB. This selection is made according to specific requirements of priority and fairness. Finally, the BARB forwards the grant signal to the device. Figure 9-15 illustrates the architecture of this hierarchical arbitration scheme.

The BARB and the CARB also participate in the data consistency protocol by merging the "Shared" and "Owner" signals issued by the BWs when they respectively detect that a block is present in the cache and modified.

The arbitration algorithm uses multiple levels of priorities to provide an implicit flow control mechanism. It also supports an explicit flow control mechanism, which is activated when one of the XDBus client detects that one of its incoming queues is becoming congested.

Interrupt Management

XDBus provides a generic interrupt transport mechanism that indicates a target unit for the interrupt (possibly broadcast), an interrupt level, and an interrupt source identification. When a processor unit receives an interrupt packet, it sets the corresponding interrupt source bit and interrupt level in internal registers. This source identification allows the amount of interrupt polling performed by the processor to be reduced.

Individual processors can issue arbitrary interrupt packets, providing a general mechanism for interprocessor interrupts.

The I/O unit transforms the level-sensitive interrupt scheme of SBus to the packet-oriented transport provided by XDBus. It also provides a mutual-exclusion mechanism which prevents interrupt service race conditions by multiple processors and identifies exactly which SBus device asserted a given interrupt level. This mechanism further reduces the amount of SBus device polling.

I/O units can be individually programmed at any time to direct interrupts to a specific processor. This capability allows static or dynamic interrupt load balancing by the kernel.

Memory Unit Architecture

The SPARCcenter 2000 memory unit consists of two memory banks, one per XDBus (see Figure 9-16). A memory bank is defined as a memory array controlled by a memory queue handler (MQH) ASIC. The MQH interfaces directly to the XDBus and controls the memory array. The MQH supports read and write operations on 64-byte blocks only (unit of block transfer on the XDBus). The MQH does not support writes on smaller quantities, and the main memory in the SPARCcenter 2000 is always cached.

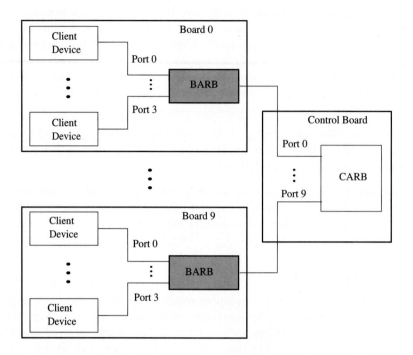

Figure 9-15 Arbitration Hierarchy

A memory bank is the unit of interleaving. A memory bank consists of one or two groups of four custom SIMMs. These are the two possible configurations (in addition, of course, to the case where the bank is not populated at all).

The MQH can handle DRAM densities from 1 Mbit to 256 Mbits. The first generation of SPARCcenter 2000 uses 4-Mbit and 16-Mbit DRAMs.

The MQH is connected to the SIMM through a memory bus, a 72-bit-wide TTL bus also clocked at 40 MHz. However, the timing access to the SIMM is fully programmable, allowing DRAM with different timing to be used.

The memory is protected by an error correcting code, which detects and corrects single-bit errors and detects all double-bit errors. It can also detect triple- and quadruple-bit errors if the erroneous bits are in the same nibble. The MQH is implemented as a 100-Kbyte CMOS gate array.

Because of XDBus interleaving, for each memory group on a given XDBus there must be an identical group on the other XDBus. The memory size increment is the memory capacity of two groups of four SIMMs.

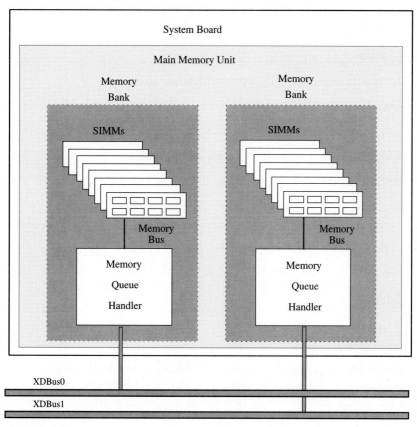

Figure 9-16 Memory Units

The physical memory address space is entirely programmable, and each memory group is controlled by a distinct address decode register. The memory bank on the same XDBus can be configured for no interleave, 2-way interleave, or 4-way interleave, by programming the address decoding registers of the MQHs.

In a shared-memory symmetric multiprocessor system, the motivation for an interleaved main memory is to allow multiple, independent accesses. With the XDBus packet-switched protocol, multiple memory transactions issued by different processors and I/O devices can be pending at the same time. In large configurations, memory bank interleaving reduces the probability of "hot spots" developing on a given MQH.

Sun SPARCserver 1000

Like the SPARCcenter 2000, the SPARCserver 1000 systems use processor modules that are user-upgradeable and are designed to accommodate several generations of processor modules. The SPARCserver 1000 incorporates up to eight 50-MHz SuperSPARC CPUs. Much like the SPARCcenter 2000, the throughput of the SPARCserver 1000 comes from the use of processors interconnected via XDBuses to multiple independent memory banks and multiple SBuses.

To summarize, features of the SPARCserver 1000 include:

- One to eight SuperSPARC CPUs, each with 1 Mbyte of SuperCache

- 32 Mbytes to 2 Gbytes RAM, with NVRAM support

- Up to 8.5 Gbytes internal disk, 100 Gbytes external disk

- One to four SBuses, three to twelve SBus slots

- Up to four on-board SCSI-2 and TP Ethernet interfaces

System Bus Architecture

The XDBus connects the SuperSPARC modules to the memory subsystem, the I/O subsystem, and each other. The logical organization of the SPARCserver 1000 system board is shown in Figure 9-17.

Memory Subsystem

The SPARCserver 1000 has many features that eliminate memory contention. Each of these features speeds up the processing by reducing the likelihood that a processor will need to wait for one of its supporting functional components. Figure 9-18 illustrates the SPARCserver 1000 s memory subsystem.

A SPARCserver 1000 can be configured with up to 2Gbytes of main memory, using 16-Mbit DRAM chips. High performance is ensured by offering extensive interleaving and a high-performance SIMM organization. The memory system also transparently includes nonvolatile SIMMs to effectively accelerate synchronous disk transfers.

The SPARCserver 1000 supports up to 4-way interleaving; 4 separate banks of memory can supply data in parallel. The memory system is organized so that each bit of a 64 bit word is on a different DRAM, thus with ECC the system can tolerate the loss of an entire DRAM.

I/O Subsystem

The SPARCserver 1000 provides up to four independent, high-performance I/O units. The units provide for high throughput as well as low latency by using optimized block transfer modes, a nonblocking I/O cache, and a low-contention SBus mechanism. Each of the four units provides a complete SBus peripheral expansion bus with three slots.

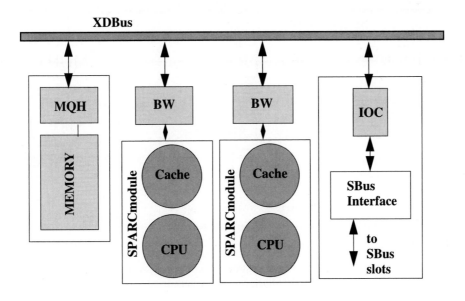

Figure 9-17   SPARCserver 1000 Logical Organization

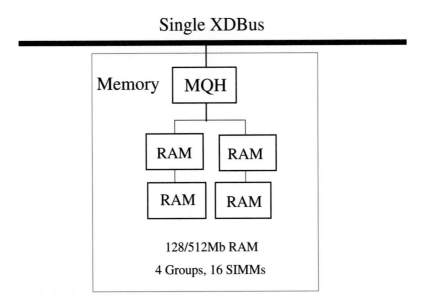

Figure 9-18   SPARCserver 1000 Memory Subsystem

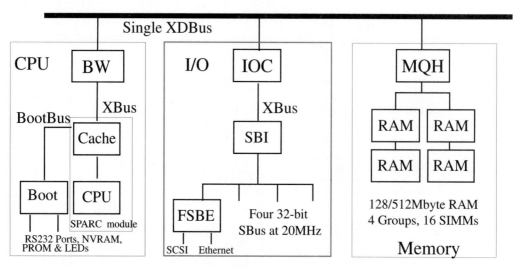

SPARCserver 1000 CPU, I/O and Memory building blocks of the SPARCserver 1000 include: BW, Bus Watcher, IOC, Input Output Cache, MQH, Memory Queue handler, SBI, SBus Interface, and FSBE, Fast SCSI Buffered Ethernet.

Figure 9-19   SPARCserver 1000 XDBus System Interconnect

Included on each unit is an on-board Ethernet and Fast SCSI port. Each SBus is connected to the backplane by an SBus interface (SBI) ASIC and includes an MMU dedicated to I/O processing and an I/O cache (see Figure 9-19). The basic building blocks shown in the figure include: BW (bus watcher), IOC (input/output cache), MQH (memory queue handler), SBI (SBus interface), and FSBE (fast SCSI buffered ethernet).

The SBus complies with the SBus Specification Revision B.0, including all burst sizes (including 64-byte) and parity support. Each SBus can sustain 55-Mbyte/sec write and 49-Mbyte/sec read rates.

Along with the basic building blocks, the SPARCserver 1000 system boards (Figure 9-20) consists of twin CPU blocks sharing a single BootBus, a single SBus I/O block that includes an integrated FSBE/S interface, and a single memory bank on one XDBus. The backplane accepts up to four system boards for a total of 8 CPUs, 16 SBus slots, and 2048 Mbytes of RAM.

If you compare the SPARCserver 1000 subsystems shown in Figure 9-19 with those shown in Figure 9-8, you will note the similarity between the two systems, the SPARCserver 1000 being a scaled-down implementation of the SPARCcenter 2000.

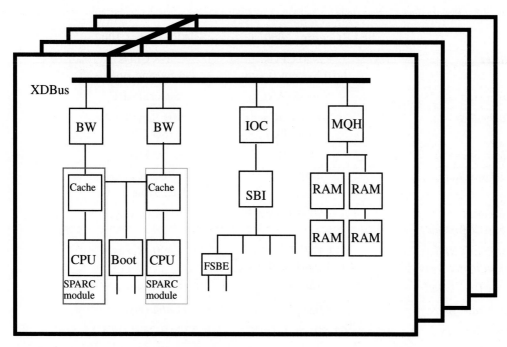

Figure 9-20   SPARCserver 1000 System Boards

Sun provides a comprehensive system solution for a wide range of computational needs. From the hardware design emphasizing modularity and performance to the multithreaded Solaris 2 kernel, the SPARCserver 1000, SPARCcenter 2000, and SPARCserver 600MP series provide solutions to a wide range of computationally intensive problems previously provided only by specialized and costly systems.

SPARC System Performance

In summary this section presents SPARC system performance comparisons. Tables 9.3 and 9.4 show feature and performance comparisons between the SPARCserver 600MP, SPARCcenter 2000 and SPARCserver 1000 systems.

The modularity of these systems lend themselves well to the definition of new functional units for more specialized purposes, such as high-speed compute servers, network servers, and graphics host. A compute server for example, must deliver cost effective compute power and high throughput at lower cost. The delivery of cost effective compute power, however, entails much more than just fast CPUs. It requires careful attention to modularity and system balance. A balanced compute server goes beyond raw compute power. As more processors are added, other aspects of the system must also be able to expand to accommodate the additions and avoid bottlenecks.

Table 9-3   Performance Comparisons

	SPARCcenter 2000	SPARCserver 1000
Model	2-20 CPUs 1-10 System Boards	1-8 CPUs 1-4 System Boards
Processor	SuperSPARC	SuperSPARC
Cache Size	1 MB SuperCache (per CPU)	1 MB SuperCache (per CPU)
Clock Speed	40 MHz	50 MHz
Package Slots	4-40 SBus	1-4 SBus Channels (3-12 SBus Slots)
Estimated transactions/sec[1]	~500 (8-way)	~400 (8-way)
Estimated NFS operations/second	2,422 (8-way)[4] 408.4 AIMs (20-way)[5]	1,400 (8-way)
SPECrate_int92[2]	21,196 (16-way)	10,113 (8-way)[6]
SPECrate_fp92[3]	28,064 (16-way)	11,864 (8-way)[7]
Main Memory	64 MB-5GB (ECC)	32 MB-2GB (ECC)

1. SMCC estimated transactions per second

2. Based on the SPECrate92 benchmark. SMCC results are based on enhanced versions of SPARCompiler products, from SunPro, which included optimization with a Kuck & Associates preprocessor.

3. Based on the SPECrate 92 benchmark. SMCC results are based on Apogee compilers from Apogee Software with a Kuck & Associates preprocessor.

4. LADDIS (NFS file server performance) results, SPECnfs_A93 ops/sec.

5. AIM III Multi-user throughput results, 4,002 jobs/min.

6. OS = Solaris version 2.2.

7. SPECrate_fp92 = 12,710 with Apogee 1.059.

The modularity offered by the 600MP the SPARCcenter 2000 and SPARCserver 1000 demonstrates that by separating CPU technology from the remaining subsystems designers can reduce system cost, while also providing easy and cost saving upgrade paths to future technology. The multi-level bus architectures also provide modular approaches for implementing highly configurable, balanced, SPARC multiprocessor systems. In addition, the combination of logical subsystem organization, large scale multiprocessing, packet-switched backplane interconnects, extensive main memory and I/O capacity, reliability and availability make these systems unique. In conjunction with the Solaris/SunOS Multithreaded operating environment, these systems are designed to meet both the high capacity I/O and computationally intensive demands of a very wide range of applications.

Table 9-4   SPARCserver 600 MP Series Comparisons

	SPARCserver 630MP			SPARCserver 670MP			SPARCserver 690MP		
Model	41 1 CPU	52 2 CPU	54 4 CPU	41 1 CPU	52 1 CPU	54 4 CPU	41 1 CPU	52 2 CPU	54 4 CPU
Processor	SuperSPARC			SuperSPARC			SuperSPARC		
Cache Size	1 MB SuperCache (perCPU)			1 MB SuperCache (perCPU)			1 MB SuperCache (perCPU)		
Clock Speed (Mhz)	40	45		40	45		40	45	
Package Slots	3 VMEBus slots 4 SBus slots			7 VMEbus slots 4 SBus slots			11 VMEbus slots 4 SBus slots		
Estimated transactions/sec[1]	120	180	220	120	180	220	130	200	250+
Estimated NFS operations/second	1000+	n/a	n/a	1000	n/a	n/a	1000+	n/a	n/a
SPECrate_int92[2]	1263	2812[4]	5624[4]	1263	2812[4]	5624[4]	1263	2812[4]	5624[4]
SPECrate_fp92[3]	1503	3346[4]	6692[4]	1503	3346[4]	6692[4]	1503	3346[4]	6692[4]
Main Memory	64 MB -1 GB (ECC)			64 MB -1 GB (ECC)			64 MB -1 GB (ECC)		

1. SMCC estimated transactions per second.

2. Based on the SPECrate92 benchmark. SMCC results are based on enhanced versions of SPARCompiler products, from SunPro, which include optimization with a Kuck & Associates preprocessor.

3. Based on the SPECrate 92 benchmark. SMCC results are based on Apogee compilers from Apogee Software with a Kuck & Associates preprocessor.

4. Estimates.

9

The Next Decade of Innovation 10 ≡

While advances in computer architectures have provided significant improvements in today's computing environments, during the next decade these systems still must solve many problems that users have: Users want to leverage their existing investments in technology when new technologies arrive; users want to easily turn data into useful information; and users want the new enabling technology and efficient operating environments to break through the productivity ceiling that characterizes earlier computing environments. The next generation of systems will need to provide a more flexible paradigm for the development and maintenance of new, efficient operating environments.

Enter Distributed Object-based Computing.

Development is already underway to enhance the Solaris operating environment to include a new set of technologies that will enable cooperating, distributed, object-oriented applications to share and exchange data transparently. These technologies include:

- The ToolTalk service for object- and process-oriented messaging—this mechanism passes messages and commands between applications and is largely context-free. ToolTalk is currently available with Solaris.

- Project DOE for distributed, object-oriented application building—this key set of technologies for building the next generation of interoperating applications is being developed at SunSoft. The ToolTalk service provides a migration path to Project DOE.

These object-oriented technologies establish the foundation upon which the next generation of object-based environments will be built—environments that will take computing beyond the limits of today's information-processing bottlenecks. SunSoft is committed to focusing its established expertise on building a technology foundation for future object-based environments.

The following sections describe the ToolTalk service and Project DOE.

ToolTalk and Project DOE: Introduction and Overview

ToolTalk is an interapplication communication mechanism. It allows applications to talk to each other and update each other. Other, similar, products require that these features be hardwired into the applications. Thus, participating software vendors need to agree in advance how their products will work together. ToolTalk operates like an open bulletin board, instead. Software vendors can publish their formats, and other software vendors can subscribe to find out how to work with that package.

ToolTalk uses the drag-and-drop metaphor to allow independent applications to interoperate across a network. It is a major step toward distributed objects, linking the present Solaris with the future.

ToolTalk is the first piece of SunSoft's object-oriented technology. To be effective to users across a network, object-oriented technology must be distributed.

Project DOE, which means Distributed Objects Everywhere, is SunSoft's vision of distributed object-based computing, the next phase of SunSoft's object-oriented technology following on the footsteps of ToolTalk.

As an extension of the existing Solaris environment, Project DOE provides interoperability without added complexity. Development time is decreased with standard mix-and-match objects. And, objects simplify system administration, too.

DOE-enabled applications will allow scenarios such as the following:

- You can establish links between data objects in two or more applications. When data in the originating application changes, the link is refreshed and updated in the linked-to applications. The data is stored and managed by the linked-from application.

- You can embed objects from one application inside another application. You are presented with a single "compound" document, and the applications that work with pieces of the document are automatically invoked as various objects are referenced. For example, a spreadsheet could embed a graph object inside a presentation table. The data to generate the graph would come from ranges in the spreadsheet and the graphing application would be invoked when the graph is selected by the user. The embedded graph object is stored along with the other pieces of the compound document, but the spreadsheet has no knowledge of data format and may have the graphing application assist it in storing the data.

- You can work with collections of objects, some supplied by SunSoft, others supplied by outside vendors. The object handlers understand only their own objects and depend on well-defined interfaces to communicate with other object handlers. Communication is completely transparent to the end-user, who does not have to be concerned about details such as file systems, database formats, or concurrency control.

The ToolTalk Service

The ToolTalk service is a network-spanning, interapplication communication service that allows your application to communicate with other autonomous applications in a process-oriented or object-oriented manner. The ToolTalk service is used by independent applications to communicate with each other without having direct knowledge of each other. Applications communicate by creating and sending ToolTalk messages. The ToolTalk service receives these messages, determines the recipients, and then delivers the messages to the appropriate applications. Figure 10-1 illustrates how applications use the ToolTalk service.

The ToolTalk service provides *multicast* messaging. That is, an application sends a message that is delivered by the ToolTalk service to multiple receivers. Multicast messaging, with the concept of one-to-many communications, falls between broadcast messaging (one-to-all) and point-to-point messaging (one-to-one). The ToolTalk service also provides point-to-point messaging between applications.

The ToolTalk service supports two types of messaging, *process-oriented* and *object-oriented* messaging. Process-oriented messages are addressed to other processes; object-oriented messages are addressed to objects managed by processes.

Before an application is modified to use the ToolTalk service, a *message protocol*—a set of ToolTalk messages that describes operations applications agree to perform—must be defined. The message protocol specification includes the set of messages and how applications should behave when they receive the messages.

Applications can send two classes of ToolTalk messages, *notices* and *requests.* A notice is informational, a way for an application to announce an event. Applications that receive a notice absorb the message without returning results to the sender. A request is a call for an action, with the results of the action recorded in the message, and the message returned to the sender as a reply.

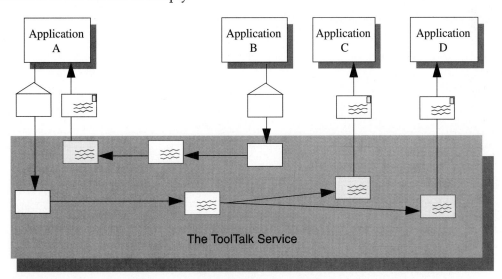

Figure 10-1   Applications Using The ToolTalk Service To Communicate

Applications using the ToolTalk service to communicate usually have something in common—the applications are running in the same session or they are interested in the same file or data. Applications register this interest by joining sessions or files (or both) with the ToolTalk service. This file and session information is used by the ToolTalk service in conjunction with the message patterns to determine the applications that should receive a message.

The ToolTalk Architecture

Figure 10-2 illustrates the ToolTalk service architecture.

The following ToolTalk service components work together to provide interapplication communication and object information management:

- `ttsession` is the ToolTalk communication process. One `ttsession` runs in an *X* server session or process tree session and communicates with other `ttsessions` when a message needs to be delivered to an application in another session.

- `rpc.ttdbserverd` is the ToolTalk database server process. One `rpc.ttdbserverd` is installed on each machine that contains a disk partition that stores files of interest to ToolTalk clients or files that contain ToolTalk objects.

  File and ToolTalk object information is stored in a records database managed by `rpc.ttdbserverd`.

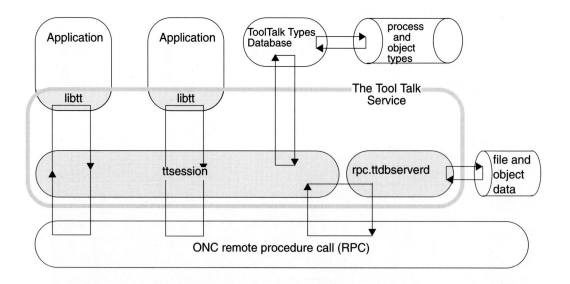

Figure 10-2   ToolTalk Service Architecture

- `libtt` is the ToolTalk application programming interface (API) library. Applications include the API library in their program and call the ToolTalk functions in the library.

The ToolTalk service uses the SunSoft ONC Remote Procedure Call (RPC) to communicate among these ToolTalk components.

Applications provide the ToolTalk service with process and object type information. This information is stored in the ToolTalk Types database.

CASE Interoperability Message Sets

The ToolTalk service also provides a set of CASE (Computer Aided Software Engineering) interoperability messages. These message sets, developed jointly by Digital Equipment Corporation, Silicon Graphics Inc., and SunSoft, provide CASE tools vendors with a protocol that encourages development of "plug-and-play" CASE tools.

To achieve control flow integration in an integrated CASE environment, applications need to support messages that enable interapplication control. This control integration allows applications to interchange state information and to provide services to each other in a controlled and well-behaved manner.

The CASE interoperability message sets define a standard set of CASE functionality available through control integration services. Each message set describes an area of functionality in the CASE environment. The message sets are:

- Analysis and Design Message Set—Defines messages for functions that deal with the software architecture of an application. Typical functions for manipulation include structure chart editors, data flow diagrams, and flow charts.

- Browsing Message Set—Defines messages for functions that process queries on source code.

- Building Message Set—Defines an interface to build utilities. This message set includes the initiation of build processes at different granularities, error notifications, and recording of dependencies.

- Debugging Message Set—Defines a standard interface for a debug utility. This message set includes the common functions associated with debug utilities.

- Editing Message Set—Defines a detailed collection of messages for text editing tools. These messages focus on the definition and manipulation of buffers and views and on text editing functions.

- Version Management Message Set—Defines messages for tools that manage version histories of software artifacts. This message set includes check-in, check-out, and other related version control functions.

ToolTalk service provides a migration path to Project DOE. Thus, adoption of ToolTalk now is important for developers who wish to be in position to participate in Project DOE and also to protect their development investment.

ToolTalk References

The documents listed in Table 10-1 contain further information on the ToolTalk service. These references facilitate the process of adopting ToolTalk message sets. Note that you can use only the message sets that meet the specific functional integration needs. Your applications can then interoperate with any other application with the same message set.

Table 10-1 ToolTalk Reference Documents and Services

Documents	Topics	Audience
The ToolTalk Service: An Interoperability Solution	How to integrate with the ToolTalk service; ToolTalk API reference	Application developer, system administrator
Solaris 2.2 Desktop Integration Guide	Information on the Classing Engine, a desktop-style database used by the ToolTalk service and the ToolTalk message protocol used by the DeskSet	Application developer
OpenWindows Version 3.2 Reference Manual	Manual pages for ToolTalk binary files and utilities	Advanced user, system administrator, application developer
Solaris 2.2 System Configuration and Installation Guide	Installation of the Solaris 2.x operating environment including the OpenWindows software	System administrator, application developer

Project DOE

Project DOE (Distributed Objects Everywhere) is SunSoft's vision for distributed computing. Project DOE is SunSoft's enhanced implementation of the Object Management Group (OMG) specification for object-oriented applications development and use in heterogeneous distributed environments. In contributing to the development of a standard for object-oriented applications, SunSoft has also laid the groundwork for migration from its ToolTalk service to the future Distributed Object Management Facility (DOMF).

Project DOE provides the basis for complete interoperability of all applications and their data, regardless of where they are on the network. Object-orientation further provides a new and important paradigm for improving software construction, maintenance, and use. Object-orientation will alter the way in which programmers work, as well as increase the rate which they produce next generation applications. Through greater code reuse, more flexible coding, greater interapplication integration, and more automated tools, programmers will see greater productivity, even as applications continue to grow more complex.

The Benefits of Distributed Objects

The DOE environment will enable SunSoft—as well as other Object Request Broker (ORB) implementors—to bridge the existing gap between operating systems and applications. (In the object management architecture, the ORB provides the means for defining interfaces to and invoking operations on objects.) In time, operating systems will cease to have the relevance they do today; instead, the Object Management Group standards, together with network and user interface APIs, will ensure application portability and interoperability.

Among the benefits of object-based applications and the DOE environment are:

- Greater functionality—Applications can be built from existing components or by leveraging the extensible capabilities of objects to extend existing objects with the addition of more functionality.

- Interoperability—Because all objects have standardized interfaces, their internal logic is hidden from other objects thus promoting stability in interfaces and ensuring that objects and applications are interoperable.

- Extensibility—Dependencies are limited with objects because they have no knowledge of the internal workings of other objects; only their interfaces are defined. Objects can evolve without changing their relationship to the rest of the system.

- Supportability—Object technology reduces software maintenance effort through the production of better quality systems. Where errors do appear, they are likely to be highly localized and hence easier to fix.

- Reduced development cost—Assembling new applications out of reusable components reduces the cost of new development. Rapid prototyping can reduce design efforts as well as ease administrative requirements. Finally, reduced maintenance costs (often the largest expense in software development) result from higher software quality and easier modification.

- Transportable—Object applications will span the network easily, thanks to powerful framework services that manage global naming, location, and communication of objects. Both intra- and interapplication communication with objects becomes possible, providing better integration and network independence.

- Higher quality—Object-orientation goes further than any other software implementation methodology in encouraging modularity. The benefits of modular programming, when implemented well, manifest themselves in better defined interfaces and greater code reuse. Because preexisting components are already proven, the likelihood they will be robust is great.

- Scalability—Large systems are easier to build and maintain when their subsystems can be developed and tested independently of one another. Object-oriented development encourages decomposition, making it especially well-suited to large systems. Because software systems also tend to grow and evolve, object-oriented technology offers an additional benefit in enabling easier modification and enhancement without the intricate intermodule dependencies of conventional software design.

Features of DOE

DOE provides a broad set of features for the support and integration of object-based applications in a client-server computing environment. Among those capabilities and services are:

- A distributed, object-oriented computation model—Affords the flexibility to provide object-oriented facilities across heterogeneous distributed networks

- Location independence—Enables complete freedom for object location because of complete protocol and network transport transparency

- Scalability—Scales across computing platforms and networks ranging from stand-alone machines to large area networks

- Support for full interoperability between applications—Complies fully with the OMG standard for complete object and application interoperability

- Standard interfaces which allow interchangeability—Leverages the object-oriented benefit of information hiding and extensibility to permit graceful evolution of objects and applications

- Full range of services—Includes security, licensing, and distribution

- Framework—Provides a sound architecture based upon the OMG ORB standard for distributed object management

- Tools—Facilitate migration, application development, and system management

Figure 10-3 illustrates how DOE services are layered.

DOE Services

DOE is a feature-rich environment that incorporates a suite of core services designed to provide facilities to simplify the manipulation and interaction of objects. DOE services include:

- Naming—Provides a basic way of mapping a compound string name to a particular object reference

- Persistent Storage Manager—Performs mapping and persistent storage management automatically

- Associations—Define well-formed, formal relationships between objects; associations tie objects together, making them easier to manipulate and invoke

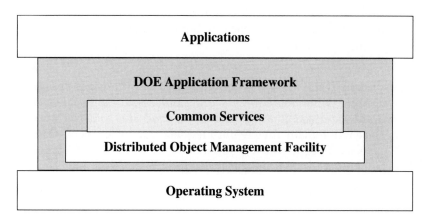

Figure 10-3 DOE Architecture

- Properties—Are both state and metastate for objects

- Events—Provide a way of structuring computations; that is, events provide a mechanism for one object to signal a change in state to other interested objects

- Life-cycle Set of Services—Provide a set of protocols to make full life-cycle object management easier. Objects that are moved or copied between systems have to be externalized as they are moved from the origin system and internalized in the destination system.

Preparation for DOE

Migration to DOE requires a conscious planning effort. The suggestions that follow will help prepare the application developer for DOE. While DOE is not currently a product, some things can be done to position application development to ease the transition to DOE when it becomes available.

DOE and Threads

Threads is an important structuring concept guiding how software can be built. Although important for concurrency, threads is also a natural way to do things. The DOE environment, particularly the object server, relies upon multiple threads. An understanding of the problems and use of threads and the thread package can help prepare conceptually for this part of DOE.

Architecting for Concurrency

One of the key issues in migrating a program to DOE is deciding how to handle concurrency. Concurrency is critical because it affects both clients and servers. Concurrency is generally achieved through the use of threads. Even though synchronous calls are possible, in many cases clients will be multithreaded, which circumstance effectively provides for the concurrency. A default will be a server where all incoming calls are dispatched concurrently.

Clients are concerned about concurrency because requests can take a long time to complete, especially if the request is going across a network. It is desirable for a client to do some computing while the request is being processed, the usual case if the program implements a user interface. It is also probably a good idea to use multiple threads so that the user interface will remain alive while a request to an object is outstanding. Even when a request is expected to be handled quickly, one may want to be prepared for the unusual case where something goes wrong and the request hangs for a long time.

Servers are concerned about concurrency because servers can receive multiple concurrent requests. When designing a server (example follows), it is important to consider how to handle concurrent requests. At a minimum, ensure that concurrent requests do not conflict with each other and corrupt the server's internal state.

If the application is both a client and a server, then it must be concerned with the possibility of deadlock. Deadlock can easily occur if the application blocks when it makes a request. If that request causes a synchronous request to be sent back to the application, that request will block, and the result is deadlock.

This situation could easily arise if another object is used that talks back to the application by means of a callback object. Consider the following scenario: A client issues a request to the object. All other requests are blocked while this request is serviced. A request is issued to another object, providing it a callback object that the program implements. That other object issues a request to the callback object, blocking on that request. That request is blocked because the application is not servicing new requests. Both programs are now blocked waiting for the other to proceed and, hence, deadlock.

When designing a new program, often the best approach is to use multiple threads. Using multiple threads allows a server to process multiple requests concurrently. It allows a client to keep its user interface alive while another request is pending. However, most existing applications are single-threaded. It may not be possible to invest the engineering effort to convert all of the code to use multiple threads. Fortunately, techniques that minimize the amount of old code that must be changed can be used to address concurrency issues.

Object Server Example

Object servers are usually a multithreaded process that provides concurrent access. Consider an example illustrating an object server, where a spreadsheet cell has value to many people in a corporation. The content of the spreadsheet cell reflects the profit and loss for a quarter, and it is desirable to incorporate this information into a large number of reports. It may also be desirable to access this cell from remote sites. But most importantly, it would be desirable to access it concurrently. Thread support and concurrency within the object server will achieve the desired level of functionality.

An object server is usually a multithreaded process. It is particularly important to have object servers be multithreaded if they will be used recursively. For example, a particular object server implements a particular object and provides all the functionality for that object. It is layered so that this particular object server can clearly make use of other objects. In this fashion, an object system works with one object implemented and others used, and those objects can recursively use features of this particular object server.

If only a single thread is utilized, it becomes difficult for recursion to work properly. It is still possible, just harder to do. Most object servers that are written for DOE will likely be multithreaded processes; new code written for DOE will almost certainly be multithreaded processes. Software that is not originally written for DOE but is ported to it may use threads only in a limited fashion.

Object servers are Solaris processes and can have implementations of multiple instances of objects. A particular process can supply the execution for many different objects of the same type. A particular process can also have multiple interfaces to different objects within it. Every interface can have multiple implementations internal to it. Nothing is a "one," everything is in multiples. There may be multiple server processes per host in order to insulate a particular process from other processes for performance, resource management, or security reasons. There can be multiple processes supporting multiple objects on the host, and there can be multiple objects within a host. Each object can have different interfaces with different implementations.

Using ToolTalk

ToolTalk, SunSoft's interapplication communication mechanism, will also aid in the transition to DOE. SunSoft is committed to supporting the ToolTalk APIs in the DOE environment, enabling applications that use ToolTalk today to be transparently supported under DOE tomorrow. It is also beneficial to use ToolTalk because many of the concepts in DOE and ToolTalk are similar. Using ToolTalk will help programmers to understand the conceptual shift involved in moving to a system like DOE.

Compatibility with Interface Definition Language (IDL)

Developers can also write their interfaces in an Interface Definition Language (IDL)-compatible manner. IDL is the standard language for defining interfaces. IDL is officially sanctioned by OMG and contrasts with other non-OMG interface languages. IDL is currently available from SunSoft.

Interfaces written in IDL provide a method of defining the requirements between two parts of the system in a way that promotes system longevity. Different parts of the system can be constructed and plugged together much later because the interfaces were well-defined and understood from the beginning. Software can be written and put into the system even though only the interfaces are known—a requirement when creating a large distributed system.

IDL is not a complete programming language. It is meant to be independent of any programming language. IDL defines interfaces, not the implementation. IDL interfaces are generic and contain no implementation details. Neither the language nor the operating system is important in defining IDL, thus enabling multiple implementations of the same interface. Performance requirements may dictate different interface implementations which have different performance characteristics. The interface is the same, but performance may be different for different clients.

IDL also provides a flexible way to deal with evolution and extension. It ensures robustness within the system by virtue of defining interfaces. When the system evolves, the interfaces may need to evolve as well. By using the inheritance mechanisms of IDL, one can build a server that can support both old and new interfaces. Software can be constructed that will support multiple interfaces. This approach also eases evolution, since a system may support the multiple versions of an interface while simultaneously providing for all of the interfaces within the same process. As with C++, extension through IDL is provided through subclassing. Straight subclassing of an interface allows more specialization, as would be done in a normal object-oriented system.

The Future of Objects

Through Project DOE, SunSoft and Sun Microsystems Computer Corporation have defined a path to a future of objects. Project DOE provides a foundation for object-oriented environments, permitting real-world modeling of applications for CASE, greater interoperability between systems, and simplified and more powerful representation of and communication between applications and users. Project DOE represents a significantly more powerful paradigm for all phases of computing—application integration will become de facto—across the entire enterprise computing environment.

ToolTalk provides the migration path to Project DOE through compatible services and capabilities. Application developers can begin their journey toward complete object-orientation through ToolTalk now knowing their migration to Project DOE will be smoothed.

MBus Interface Specification[1]

Introduction

The SPARC™ MBus is a private, high-speed interface which connects SPARC™ processor **modules** to physical memory **modules** and I/O **modules**. The specification could be thought of as a generic integrated circuit pin interface specification. The interface is not intended for use as a general expansion bus on a system backplane spanning numerous boards. Rather, it is intended to operate in a carefully controlled geographical area with the interconnect and associated circuitry located on only one printed wiring board. Modules consist of one or more integrated circuits, one (or more) of which contain the MBus interface.

The two major goals of MBus are that it be simple and that it be compatible with CMOS technology. Simplicity is achieved by having only a few well-specified transactions with a minimum of options using a small set of signals. CMOS compatibility is covered by the electrical specifications and protocols.

Features

- fully synchronous, nominally 40 Mhz
- circuit switched
- 64-bit, multiplexed address and data
- 64 gigabytes of physical address space
- multiple-master
- centralized arbitration, reset, interrupt distribution, and clock distribution
- overlapped arbitration with "parking"
- shared memory multiprocessor(MP) signals and transactions
- supports a write-invalidate type of cache consistency protocol

[1] A SPARCInternational Inc. and Sun Microsystems Computer Corporation publication. Reprinted with permission from SPARC International Inc., and Sun MicroSystems Computer Corporation. ©Sun Microsystems Inc.

A

MBus Levels

The complete MBus Specification has two levels of compliance, Level 1 and Level 2. Level 1 includes the basic MBus signals and transactions needed to design a complete uniprocessor system. Level 2 introduces additional signals and transactions needed to design a cache coherent, shared-memory multiprocessor.

A device which conforms to Level 1 of the Specification will be classified as a level 1 device while those devices conforming to Level 2 of the Specification shall be referred to as level 2 devices. Level 1 devices will function properly in a level 2 system. Since one of the intents of MBus is to allow for modular SPARC solutions, care has been taken to ensure all modules in an MBus system can be compatible.

Level 1 Overview

The Level 1 MBus supports two transactions, Read and Write. These transactions simply read or write a specified SIZE of bytes from a specified physical address. These transactions are supported using a subset of the MBus signals, namely a 64-bit multiplexed address/data bus (MAD[63:0]), an address strobe signal (MAS/), and an encoded acknowledge on three signals (MRDY/, MRTY/, MERR/). Additional Level 1 signals support arbitration for modules (MBR/, MBG/, MBB/) as well as interrupt inputs (IRL[3:0]), interrupt output (INTOUT/), reset (RSTIN/), asynchronous errors (AERR/), scan (SCANDI, SCANDO, SCANCLK, SCANTMS1, SCANTMS2) and module identification (ID[3:0]). The MBus reference clock (CLK) completes the signal requirements for a Level 1 system.

It is assumed that there are **central** functional elements to perform reset, arbitration, interrupt distribution, time-out, and MBus clock generation as shown in Figure A-1. All modules with the exception of processor and Time-out modules accept an ID[3:0] input which is used as an aid to system configuration. Also the binary value input to a module on ID[3:0] is output as part of MAD[63:0] during the address phase of every transaction.

Level 2 Overview

The Level 2 MBus includes all Level 1 transactions and signals and adds four transactions and two signals to support cache coherency. This is to facilitate the design of shared-memory multiprocessor systems. In Level 1, details of the caches inside modules are not visible to the MBus transactions. This changes with Level 2, where many aspects of the caches are assumed as part of the new MBus transactions. To participate in sharing between processor caches on an MBus using Level 2 transactions, a cache must minimally support a "write-back" policy, an "allocate" policy on write misses, and have a block or sub-block size of 32 bytes. Cache lines are assumed to have at least five states (invalid, exclusive clean, exclusive dirty, shared clean, and shared dirty).

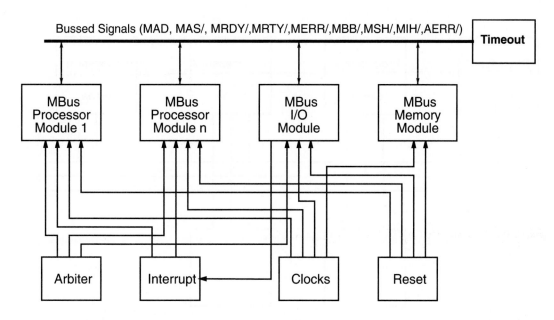

Figure A-1   MBus System Elements and Their Connectivity.

The additional transactions present in Level 2 systems are Coherent Read, Coherent Invalidate, Coherent Read and Invalidate, and Coherent Write and Invalidate. The two additional signals are Shared (MSH/) and Inhibit (MIH/). Coherent transactions, with one rare exception (Coherent Write and Invalidate used with write-through caches) have SIZE=32 bytes. The cache coherency protocol is a "write invalidate" protocol, where the cache being written issues a Coherent Invalidate transaction if the line is not exclusive. This indicates to all caches that they should immediately invalidate the line since it will contain "stale data" after the write completes. All caches "snoop" Coherent Read transactions and assert MSH/ if the address of the transaction is present in their cache. By observing MSH/, caches can update the state of the lines they hold. If a cache is the "owner," it asserts the signal MIH/ to tell memory not to send data and then supplies the data to the requesting cache. Coherent Read and Invalidate, and Coherent Write and Invalidate are simply the combination of a Coherent Invalidate with either a Coherent Read or a Write. Their purpose is to reduce the quantity of MBus transactions needed and thus conserve bandwidth. Figure A-2 shows a simplified MBus MP system.

Definitions

0x—0x as a prefix to a number, indicates that the number is hexadecimal.

MASTER—A module is an MBus master when it "owns" the MBus. Masters assert the signal MAS/ to initiate transactions.

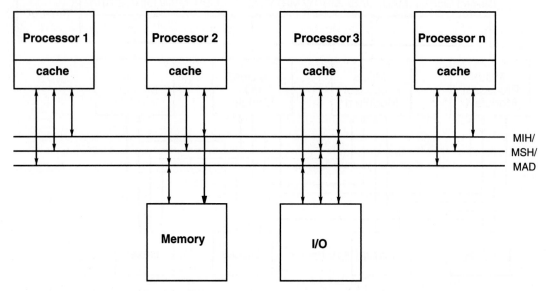

Figure A-2   Standard Level-2 Shared Memory MP

SLAVE—A module is an MBus slave when it responds to transactions directed at it. Slaves assert the signals MRDY/, MRTY/ and MERR/ as an acknowledgment to an MBus master.

BLOCK—A 32 byte data burst transfer size, this quantity is equal to the block (or sub-block) size of the system caches.

TRANSACTION—A transaction is a complete MBus operation such as a Read or Write. It is made up of one address cycle and one or more data acknowledgment cycles. Due to RETRY and RELINQUISH and RETRY acknowledgments a transaction may be repeated many times.

BURST TRANSFER—A multidata-cycle MBus data transfer. MBus allows 16-byte, 32-byte, 64-byte, and 128-byte burst transfers.

BLOCK TRANSFER—A special case of MBus burst transfer, where the data transfer size is equal to the block size (32 bytes).

OWNED—A block of data is said to be owned when there is one (and only one) cache in the system which is responsible for writing it back to memory as well as supplying the block when requested by other caches. If no cache is the owner, memory is considered the owner.

SHARED—A block of data is said to be shared when more than one cache in the system currently possesses a valid copy of it.

EXCLUSIVE—A block of data is said to be exclusive when there is only one cache in the system which contains a valid copy of it.

DIRTY—A block of data is said to be dirty when it has been written to in a write-back cache. Dirty blocks must be written back to main memory if displaced (victimized). A dirty block is "OWNED" by that cache block.

VALID—A block of data is said to be valid when it is present within a processor's cache and can be supplied to that processor upon request. Valid means the cache line is in one of four states: exclusive clean, exclusive dirty, shared clean, or shared dirty.

WRAPPING—This concerns the order in which data will be delivered for multicycle transfers. For MBus, Read transfers larger than 8 bytes require multiple cycles. Wrapping implies that the data to be delivered first is specified by the low order address bits. That is, the transfer address may not be burst size aligned.

Compliance and Additional Features

Full compliance with either Level 1 or Level 2 implies a certain minimal functionality within the MBus modules, particularly Level 2 modules where details of the module caches are exposed. Modules may contain more than this level of functionality either to enhance performance, or to enable building a broader range of systems from MBus components. This is at the discretion of module designers and is implementation-specific. An example of a performance enhancement is reflective memory support where memory is updated by observing the data being transferred from cache to cache. An example of functionality enhancement is support for simple second level caches. It is not within the scope of the MBus specification to cover details of these enhancements. MBus is merely a defined set of transactions operating on a defined set of signals. Module enhancements will be covered as "application notes" by module designers and vendors. See Appendix B, "MBus Module Design Guide", for some insight into the nature of the two enhancements mentioned above.

Basic Assumptions for Level 2

Consistency Quantity	The data quantity upon which consistency will be maintained will be a cache block or, when implemented, a cache sub-block. It is also assumed that the same (sub-) block size will be used throughout the system and corresponds to the MBus Block size of 32 bytes.
Cache Write Policy	While playing the Level 2 consistency game, all caches in the system will follow a write-back policy with write allocate.
Cache Consistency Protocol	An ownership-based protocol will be employed. Figure A-3 shows a simplified state transition diagram.

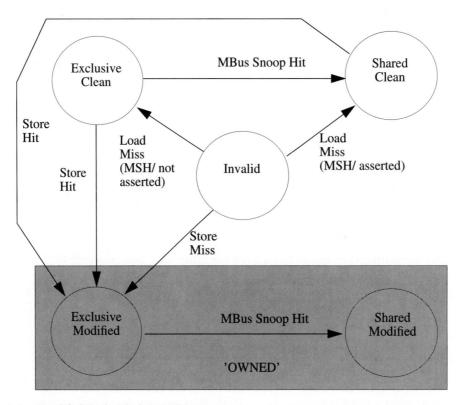

Figure A-3   Simplified Cache Block State Diagram

Homogeneous Modules	All modules using the same MBus will play the same consistency game. The modules will appear identical as far as the MBus is concerned, yet they may differ internally.
Second-Level Caches	It is assumed that all second-level caches will be physically addressed.

Signal Definition

Physical Signal Summary

Table A-1 summarizes all the MBus Module physical signals. A slash (/) following the signal name indicates that the signal is active low (true when '0').

Table A-1   Physical Signal Summary

Physical Signals					
Signal Name	**Signal Description**	**Output**	**Input**	**Line Type**	**Sig Type[1]**
MCLK	MBus clock	clock buffer	Mast./Slv/Arb.	dedicated	BS
MAD[63:0]	Address/Control/Data	Master/Slave	Master/Slave	bussed	TS
MAS/	Address strobe	Mater	Slave	bussed	TS
MRDY/	Data ready indicator	SLAVE	Master	bussed	TS
MRTY/	Xaction retry indicator	Slave	Master	bussed	TS
MERR/	Error indicator	Slave	Master	bussed	TS
MSH/	Shared (level-2only)	Bus Watcher	Master	bussed	OD
MIH/	Inhibit (level-2 only)	Bus Watcher	Master/Memory	bussed	TS
MBR/	Bus request	Master	Arbiter	dedicated	BS
MBG/	Bus grant	Arbiter	Master	dedicated	BS
MBB/	Bus busy indicator	Master	Arbiter/Master	bussed	TS
IRL[3:0]	Interrupt Level	Interrupt Logic	CPU Modules	dedicated	BS
ID[3:0]	Module Identifier	System	MBus Modules	dedicated	BS
AERR/	Asynchronous error out	Module	Interrupt Logic	bussed	OD
RSTIN/	Module reset in signal	Reset Logic	Master/Slave	impl depen	BS
INTOUT/	Interrupt Out	I/O Modules	Interrupt Logic	dedicated	BS
SCANDI	Scan Data In	System	Modules	dedicated	BS
SCANDO	Scan Data Out	Modules	System	dedicated	BS
SCANCLK	Scan Clock	System	Modules	dedicated	BS

1. BS = bi-state, TS = tri-state, OD = open drain

Physical Signal Descriptions

MCLKMBus master clock—The distribution of the MCLK signal in a system is implementation-dependent. For example, depending on the connector, each module on the MBus may be given one or more identical MCLK lines which could originate from a single clock generator.

MAD[63:0]—Memory Address and Data. During the address phase, MAD[35:0] contains the physical address (PA[35:0]). The remaining signals (MAD[63:36]) on the bus contain the transaction-specific information which is described in "Multiplexed Signal Descriptions". During the data phase, MAD[63:0] contains the data of the transfer. The bytes are organized as shown in Figure A-4. For transactions involving less than a double word (8-bytes), the data must be aligned. For example, all even-addressed words will be aligned on MAD[63:32] whereas all odd-addressed words will be aligned on MAD[31:0]. As another example, byte address 2 of an odd-addressed word will be carried on MAD[15:8] i.e. byte 6 on the MBus. Unused data lines during the data phase are undefined.

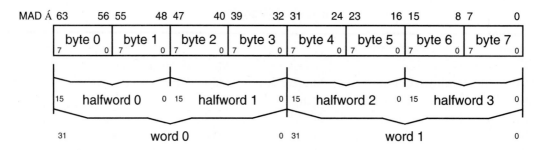

Figure A-4   Byte Organization

MAS/—Memory Address Strobe. This signal is asserted by the bus master during the very first cycle of a bus transaction. The cycle in which it is asserted is referred to as the "address cycle" or "address phase" of the transaction. For transactions that receive a Relinquish and Retry or a Retry acknowledgment, MAS/ will be asserted again until the transaction gets a normal or error acknowledgment. Other cycle timing is discussed with respect to MAS/. For example, A+2 indicates the second cycle after MAS/ assertion; i.e., MAS/ assertion is A+0.

MRDY/—MBus ready transaction status bit. This bit is one of the three bits used to encode the transaction status as shown in Table A-2. The encoding with MRDY/ asserted alone indicates that valid data has been transferred. The three status bits (MRDY/, MRTY/, and MERR/) are normally asserted by the addressed slave. The ERROR2 (Time-out) acknowledgment will be asserted by the bus monitor.

Table A-2   Transaction Status Bit Encoding

MERR/	MRDY/	MRTY/	Meaning
H	H	H	idle cycle
H	H	L	Relinquish and Retry
H	L	H	Valid Data Transfer
H	L	L	reserved
L	H	H	ERROR1=> Bus Error
L	H	L	ERROR2=> Time-out

MRTY/—MBus retry transaction status bit. This bit is one of the three bits used to encode the transaction status as shown in Table A-2. The encoding with MRTY/ asserted alone indicates that the slave wants the master to abort the current transaction immediately and start over. The master will *relinquish* bus ownership upon this type of a retry acknowledgment. Note that if any type of acknowledgment other than "Valid Data

Transfer" is issued, the cycle it is issued is the last cycle, regardless of how many further acknowledgment cycles would normally occur. The three status bits (MRDY/, MRTY/, and MERR/) are normally asserted by the addressed slave.

MERR/—MBus error transaction status bit. This bit is one of the three bits used to encode the transaction status as shown in Table A-2. The encoding with MERR/ asserted alone indicates that a bus error (or other system implementation specific error) has occurred. Note that if any type of acknowledgment other than "Valid Data Transfer" is issued, the cycle it is issued is the last cycle, regardless of how many further acknowledgment cycles would normally occur.The three status bits (MRDY/, MRTY/, and MERR/) are normally asserted by the addressed slave.

MBR/—MBus Request signal. This signal is asserted by an MBus master to acquire bus ownership. There is one unique MBR/ signal per master.

MBG/—MBus Grant signal. This signal is asserted by the external arbiter when the particular MBus master is granted the bus. There is one unique MBG/ signal per master.

MBB/—MBus busy signal. This signal is asserted as an output during the entire transaction, from and including the assertion of MAS/ to the assertion of the last MRDY/ or first other acknowledgment which terminates the transaction (such as an error acknowledgment). If a master wishes to keep the bus and perform several transactions without releasing the bus between them, it keeps MBB/ asserted until the last MRDY/ of the last transaction of the group. The potential master device samples this signal in order to obtain the bus ownership as soon as the current master releases the bus. MBB/ locks *arbitration* on a particular MBus. A master is allowed to assert MBB/ prior to the assertion of MAS/ (to hold the bus). It is also allowed to keep MBB/ asserted after the assertion of the last acknowledgment in a few special cases for performance reasons. This continued assertion of MBB/ should only occur while MBG/ is still parked on the current master. The MAS/ of the transaction prompting the continued assertion of MBB/ should be generated quickly (2 cycles is the recommended maximum delay). For more details on arbitration see "Arbitration Protocol" in Chapter 4.

MIH/—Memory InHibit signal. This signal is only present in level-2 MBus modules. It is asserted by the owner of a cache block at the beginning of the second cycle after it receives the address (its A+2 cycle)[2] to inform the Main Memory that the current Coherent Read or Coherent Read and Invalidate request should be ignored. This is because the owner, not the Memory, will be responsible for delivering the cache data block. If no device asserts MIH/ during its A+2 cycle, main memory will be responsible for delivering the data. If main memory starts delivering data and MIH/ is asserted, the memory delivery shall be aborted immediately. Any data which was received from main

---

2. See Appendix B for notes to designers who wish to avoid the A+2 requirement.

memory in this case should be ignored. It should be noted that because of the restriction on MIH/ either occurring simultaneously with or before MRDY/, there will be at most two cycles worth of data to ignore. While MIH/ is sourced by a module (for one cycle) two cycles after receiving MAS/ it may be observed by a cache in the interval from its A+2 until it observes an acknowledgment. This variation in where MIH/ can be observed is due to the possibility for MBus repeaters and modules that do not meet the A+2 timing.

MSH/—Cache block SHared signal (wired-or, open-drain). This signal is only present in level-2 MBus modules. Whenever a Coherent Read transaction appears on the bus, the bus monitor of each processor module should immediately search its cache directory. If a valid copy is found, the MSH/ signal should be asserted in the second cycle after the address is received (its A+2 cycle). The MSH/ signal is also sampled (observed) by external caches. It is asserted as an output (for a single cycle) if there is a cache hit in the snooping directory. While MSH/ is sourced by a module two cycles after receiving MAS/ it may be observed by a cache from its A+2 until it observes an acknowledgment. This variation in where MSH/ may be observed is due to the possibility for MBus repeaters and modules that do not meet the A+2 timing. Signals are sourced at the beginning and observed or sampled at the end of a cycle. Due to the open drain nature of MSH/ and the associated slow rise time, while the signal is driven active low for one cycle, it can be observed active low for up to two cycles, and the trailing or rising edge of the signal is considered asynchronous.

RSTIN/—Module reset input signal. This signal should reset all logic on a module to its initial state, and ensure that all MBus signals are inactive or tri-state as appropriate. The minimum assertion time of RSTIN/ will be system implementation dependent, although the default assertion time will be 1024 MBus clock (MCLK) periods (25.6 microseconds). RSTIN/ should be treated as asynchronous.

AERR/—Module asynchronous error detect out signal. This signal is asserted by the module as a level to indicate that an asynchronous error was detected by the module. It remains asserted until a software-initiated action resets a bit that is maintaining the signal assertion. AERR/ is open drain because several modules could assert it simultaneously. AERR/ may be asynchronous.

INTOUT/—Module Interrupt out signal. This signal is asserted by an I/O module as a level to indicate an interrupt request to the system. It remains asserted until a software initiated action resets a bit that is maintaining the signal assertion. INTOUT/ may be asynchronous. This signal is **optional**.

IRL[3:0]—These pins carry the Interrupt Request level inputs to a SPARC Integer Unit. They are only used by processor modules. IRL[3:0] may be asynchronous. Each processor module receives a dedicated set of IRL[3:0].

ID[3:0]—These pins carry the Module Identifier. These signals are not needed by Level 1 processor modules, which have a default ID of 0xF, and are **optional** for other modules who may obtain this information by other means. ID[3:0] is reflected as MID[3:0] during the address phase of every transaction, and is also used to identify a unique address range for Module identification, initialization and configuration.

If modules do not have ID[3:0] input pins, the system must provide a function that allows each module to obtain a unique ID[3:0] value in an internal ID[3:0] register. One way this can be accomplished is to have a logic function with a known MBus address attached to the MBus arbiter. There are unique MBR/ and MBG/ lines per module and so this function when addressed, would return a unique ID[3:0] value on MAD, based on which module's MBG/ was asserted just prior to the beginning of the ID Read transaction when MBB/ was de-asserted.

SCANDI—This signal corresponds to the signal TDI as described in IEEE P1149.1 (hereafter referred to as P1149). It is an input to the module and is used for receiving scan data from the system. This is the input of the scan ring and should not be inverted or gated. This signal changes on the falling edge of SCANCLK and should be sampled on the rising edge of SCANCLK. Scan is **optional**.

SCANDO—This signal corresponds to the signal TDO as described in P1149. It is an output of the module and is used for sending the scan data to the system. This is the output of the scan ring and should not be inverted or gated. **SCANDO** should be driven on the falling edge of SCANCLK and will be sampled on the rising edge of SCANCLK. Scan is **optional**.

SCANCLK—This signal is used to supply the clock to the scan ring on the module. (Typically 5 MHz) Scan is **optional**.

SCANTMS1—This signal is an input to the module. It is used to control the TAP controller state machine. It corresponds to the TMS signal as described in P1149. Scan is **optional**.

SCANTMS2—This signal is an input to the module. It is used to reset the TAP controller state machine. It corresponds to the TRST/ signal as described in P1149. Scan is **optional**.

A

Multiplexed Signal Summary

Table A-3 summarizes the multiplexed MBus signals. All multiplexed signals are active high (true when '1').

Table A-3   Multiplexed Signal Summary (valid during address phase)

Multiplexed Signals (valid during address phase)		
Signal Name	**Physical Signal**	**Signal Description**
PA[35:0]	MAD[35:0]	Physical address for current transaction
TYPE[3:0]	MAD[39:36]	Transaction type
SIZE[2:0]	MAD[42:40]	Transaction data size
C	MAD[43]	Data cacheable (advisory)
LOCK	MAD[44]	Bus lock indicator (advisory)
MBL	MAD[45]	Boot mode/local bus (advisory)(optional)
VA[19:12]	MAD[53:46]	Virtual address (optional)(level-2)
reserved	MAD[58:54]	reserved for future expansion
SUP	MAD[59]	Supervisor Access Indicator (advisory)(optional)

Multiplexed Signal Descriptions

PA[35:0]—Physical address of current transaction which is multiplexed on MAD[35:0].

TYPE[3:0]—The transaction types are encoded in bits MAD[39:36] as shown in Table A-4. Most of the transaction types are reserved.

Table A-4   TYPE Encoding (as defined by the SIZE signals in Table A-5)

TYPE[3]	TYPE[2]	TYPE[1]	TYPE[0]	Data Size	Transaction Type
H	H	H	H	-	reserved
H	H	H	L	-	reserved
H	H	L	H	-	reserved
H	H	L	L	-	reserved
H	L	H	H	-	reserved
H	L	H	L	-	reserved
H	L	L	H	-	reserved
H	L	L	L	-	reserved
L	H	H	H	-	reserved
L	H	H	L	-	reserved
L	H	L	H	32B	Coherent Read & Invalidate(CRI)

Table A-4   TYPE Encoding (as defined by the SIZE signals in Table A-5) (Continued)

TYPE[3]	TYPE[2]	TYPE[1]	TYPE[0]	Data Size	Transaction Type
L	H	L	L	any	CoherentWrite & Invalidate (CWI)
L	L	H	H	32B	Coherent Read(CR)
L	L	H	L	32B	Coherent Invalidate(CI)

SIZE[2:0]—The transaction data SIZE information is encoded in bits MAD[42:40]. The size field is encoded as $\log_2$ [number of data bytes transferred]. The encoding of the SIZE bits is shown in Table A-5.

For transactions with SIZE greater than 8 bytes, more than one MRDY/ will be needed. For read transactions, MBus supports a feature called "wrapping." During the address phase, MAD[2:0] are don't care, and MAD[35:3] defines the 8 bytes to be returned with the first MRDY/. This means that the address defines which data to return first, and this will vary. Data returned on subsequent MRDYs will be for the address associated with incrementing MAD[n:3] where n = 3 for SIZE = 16-bytes, n = 4 for SIZE = 32-bytes, up to n = 6 for SIZE = 128-bytes. As the address is (conceptually) incremented, the MAD[n:3] field will wrap around without incrementing MAD[35:n+1], which is static for the duration of transaction.

Wrapping affects all modules that have to deliver data with SIZE greater than 8 bytes. An exception is Level 2 cache controllers, which may choose not to support wrapping for snoop read hits, when they supply the data. This means that Level 2 processor modules that don't support wrapping on the snoop port cannot share an MBus with Level 2 MBus processors that issue "wrapped" requests. To ensure maximum compatibility, Memory and I/O modules should all support wrapped requests to their slave ports, but should only issue aligned requests from their master ports.

The wrapping feature is not supported for writes. Write transactions with SIZE greater than 8 bytes should have address bits MAD[n:3] be zero, and MAD[2:0] are undefined as for reads.

For transactions with SIZE less than or equal to 8 bytes, unneeded address lines are undefined. e.g. for SIZE = 8 bytes, MAD[2:0] are undefined.

Table A-5   SIZE Encoding

SIZE[2]	SIZE[1]	SIZE[0]	Transaction Size
L	L	L	Byte
L	L	H	Half-word (2 bytes)
L	H	L	Word (4 bytes)
L	H	H	Double-word (8 bytes)
H	L	L	16-byte Burst
H	L	H	32-byte Burst

VA[19:12]—Virtual Address 19 through 12 (multiplexed on MAD[53:46]). This field only applies to MBus level-2 Coherent transactions. It is used to carry the virtual address bits 19 through 12 associated with the physical address of a Coherent Read transaction. These bits are used by virtually indexed caches that desire to index into the dual directories via the virtual "superset" bits to avoid synonym problems. This assumes a minimum page size of 4K in the system and maximum cache size of 1MB. Modules that choose not to provide this function nor to support non-coherent transactions (such as a level-1 device) should drive these lines *high*.

MID[3:0]—Module identifier signals (multiplexed on MAD[63:60]). This field is sourced by all MBus modules and reflects the value input into the module on the ID[3:0] input signals. For level-1 processor modules this field is driven *high(0xF)*. This field is observed by slave ports that wish to issue a Relinquish and Retry acknowledgment, so that they can identify the master with which to reconnect in a multimaster system configuration.

C—Cacheable indicator (multiplexed on MAD[43]). When this signal is asserted, it indicates the state of the cacheable bit for the address of the transaction in the module MMU (if there is one). If a module has insufficient information to determine the level of this bit for a transaction, it should leave the bit de-asserted. This is an **advisory** bit, not used by MBus transactions, but possibly of use to the slave device.

An example use of C would be to inform a second level cache of the cacheability state of the address of a transaction with SIZE less than 32 bytes.

LOCK—Lock indicator signal (multiplexed on MAD[44]). If the MBus master intends to lock access to a device residing on MBus (main memory is one MBus device) or some other bus connected to MBus, and perform N indivisible MBus transactions to the device, this bit needs to be asserted during the address cycles of all N MBus transactions. The locking master must keep MBB/ asserted during each locked cycle and not de-assert it until the end of the final locked transaction (however MBB/ may be suspended for a time by an R&R acknowledgment). The de-assertion of MBB/ signals the MBus arbiter to release the MBus. It is the final de-assertion of MBB/ after possible intervening R&R acknowledgments which tells the device to release its lock. LOCK is an **advisory** bit, not used by MBus transactions directly, but possibly of use to the slave device or bus interface.

An example use of LOCK would be to "lock" an MBus master to a particular slave. If an MBus processor performed an atomic operation to a resource arbitrated externally to MBus, such as a dual-ported memory device or another bus, then the external arbiter could prevent any other (non MBus) device from accessing that resource by locking arbitration. The referenced slave device in a LOCKed transaction could be, in essence, dedicated to the requesting master. The MBus slave port interface interprets an assertion of the MBus LOCK bit as saying "become locked" and a final de-assertion of MBB/ at the end of the locked sequence as saying "become unlocked", and reports this information to the arbiter for the "locked" device (or bus). If the slave port supports R&R acknowledgments, it must know not to clear the locked state when MBB/ is removed due to an R&R.

MBL—MBus boot mode / local bus indicator (multiplexed on MAD[45]). This signal is asserted by processor modules during the address phase of boot mode transactions, or during local bus transactions (SPARC processor accesses with ASI = 0x1). It is system implementation-dependent whether or not local bus transactions are employed in a system. This is an **advisory** bit, not used by MBus transactions, but possibly of use to the slave device. This bit is **optional**. If unused by an implementation it should remain de-asserted.

SUP—Supervisor access indicator (multiplexed on MAD[59]). This signal is asserted by processor modules and indicates that the MBus transaction is a processor Supervisor access. This is an **advisory** bit, not used by MBus transactions, but possibly of use to the slave device. This bit is **optional**. If unused by an implementation, it should remain asserted.

An example use of SUP would be to enable more state to be captured on processor asynchronous write errors.

reserved—This 5-bit field (multiplexed on MAD[58:54]), is reserved for future MBus expansion. The lines should be driven *high* if not used.

MBus Transactions

Semantics

1. Basic cycle is read/write (size), where size is from 1 to 128 bytes.

2. Bus cycles greater than 8 bytes are performed as bursts.

3. Data rate is controlled by the slave. Master must be able to accept a burst read, or source a burst write, of requested size, at maximum transfer rate.

4. Master starts bus cycle with MAS/ (address transfer phase). Master also asserts MBB/ at (or before) this time.

5. In the case of burst mode, multiple acknowledgments are used and the bus cycle ends with the acknowledgment of the last data transfer. The master de-asserts MBB/ at end of the last cycle (except for locked bus cycles).

6. Locked bus cycles are an indivisible sequence of basic bus cycles. Locked cycles are also terminated immediately by error acknowledge and individual transactions in the sequence may be suspended by retry or relinquish and retry acknowledgments.

Note – In the transaction semantic diagrams that follow, optional wait states are indicated as x, y, or z cycles. x, y, and z can be zero.

Level 1 Transaction Types

Read

A Read operation can be performed on any size of data transfer which is specified by the SIZE bits in Figure A-5. Read transactions support wrapping as defined in section 2.4. Read transactions involving less than 8 bytes will have undefined driven data on the unused bytes. The minimum MBus Read transaction will take 2 cycles. This minimum time is for the cases when no data is returned on MAD, such as during R&R or error acknowledgments. If data is being returned, an extra cycle is required to avoid bus contention. The arbitration protocol creates a dead cycle between transactions which ensures there will be no bus contention between back-to-back reads from different masters. If a module locks the bus and performs back-to-back reads, it is its responsibility to ensure a dead cycle to avoid contention   Note that the protocol means that a master *must* be able to receive data at the maximum rate of the MBus for the duration of the transaction, i.e. 8 bytes on every consecutive clock. Figure A-5 depicts the semantics of a Read operation. Refer to Chapter 8 for details pertaining to cycle waveforms.

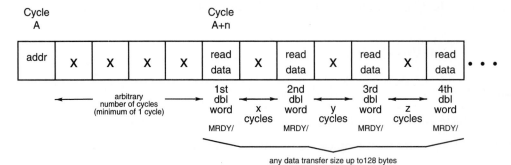

Figure A-5   Read Semantics

Write

A Write operation can be performed on any size of data transfer which is specified by the SIZE bits in Figure A-6. Write transactions involving less than 8 bytes will have undefined data on the unused bytes. The writing master will immediately drive the data in the period after the address phase of the transaction, and immediately after receipt of each MRDY/ in transactions with SIZE greater than 8 bytes. Note that the protocol means that a master *must* be able to source data at the maximum rate of the MBus for the duration of the transaction, i.e., 8 bytes on every consecutive clock. The minimum MBus Write operation will take 2 cycles (minimum is actually 3 cycles if different masters are performing back-to-back writes). Figure A-6 shows the basic semantics of a Write operation.

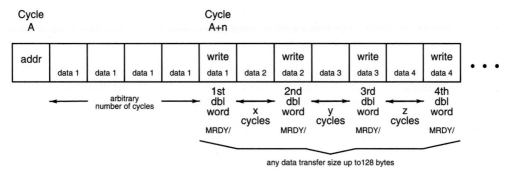

Figure A-6   Write Semantics

Due to the nature of the cache-consistency protocol, the Write transaction works equally well in Level 1 and Level 2 MBus implementations. Writes can be used for non-cacheable accesses as well as for write-backs of dirty (sub-)blocks. Write transactions do not need to be snooped and the MIH/ and MSH/ signals must not be asserted during the operation.

R&R acknowledgments issued to Block Write transactions to cacheable locations introduce a detailed design problem, in that the write-back buffer in this case may be the only source of the most up to date data. This introduces the prospect of having to snoop the write back buffer. To simplify the design of processor modules, the MBus specification eliminates the need for processor modules to snoop write-back buffers and places the burden of handling this case of R&R acknowledgment on the module that issues the R&R. Modules that issue R&R acknowledgments to cacheable block write transactions must capture the address(es) of the cache line(s) until they complete the transaction to which they issued R&R. Should other modules attempt to read the line(s) during this interval the R&R issuing module must detect this and issue R&R to the intervening Coherent Read(CR) or Coherent Read and Invalidate(CRI) transaction(s). In general it should be possible for most modules to avoid the need to issue R&R to cacheable block write operations and hence avoid this complexity. The only likely exception is a coherent bus adaptor.

Additional Transaction Types for Level 2

Coherent Read

A Coherent Read operation is a block read transaction that maintains cache consistency. The participants in the transaction are the requesting cache, the other caches which snoop, and memory (or a second level cache). There are three possible read scenarios which the caches that snoop can experience:

1. For a snooping cache which does not have a copy of the requested block, it simply ignores this transaction.

2. For a snooping cache which does have a copy of the requested block but does not *own* it, it simply asserts MSH/ for one cycle during its cycle A+2[3]. It will mark its copy as shared (if not already marked as such).

3. For a snooping cache which owns the requested block, it will assert both the MSH/ and MIH/ signals for one cycle during bus cycle A+2 and start shipping the requested data no sooner than its cycle A+6, (4 cycles after it issued MIH/). If its own copy of the block was labeled exclusive, it will be changed to shared, else no status change will take place for its own copy.

Upon receiving the data block, the requesting master shall label the block *exclusive* if no one asserts MSH/ during its cycle A+2 and *shared* if the signal MSH/ is asserted during its cycle A+2. Figure A-7 depicts the semantics of a Coherent Read operation where memory latency is long.

Case (c) above needs further elaboration. This is the only case where MIH/ is asserted. This signal affects three parties. It is sourced by the snooping (intervening) cache and observed by both memory (or a second level cache) and the requesting cache. It tells the requesting cache that it may have received stale data from memory, and to ignore that data and data it may receive on the next clock and wait until the fourth or later clock for the correct data. It tells memory to stop sending data *immediately*, which means memory may send one more MRDY/ before it can stop. The delay of 4 clocks at the requesting cache and the snooping (intervening) cache serve two related purposes. The first is to allow time for MRDY/ and MAD from the memory to be turned off before the snooping cache asserts MRDY/ and MAD, and so avoid bus contention. The second is to allow for implementations that buffer the MBus.

The earliest that memory (or a second level cache) is allowed to issue MRDY/ (or any acknowledgment) is its cycle A+2. This ensures that acknowledgments never occur before MIH/. Figure A-7 shows the semantics of a Coherent Read transaction.

Coherent Invalidate

An Invalidate operation can only be performed on a block basis. All Invalidate operations will be snooped. If an Invalidate operation hits in a cache, then that copy will be invalidated immediately, regardless of its state. **One module (normally a memory controller) is responsible for the acknowledgment of the Coherent Invalidate transaction.** This is accomplished on its cycle A+2 or later. All acknowledgment types

---

3. See Supplement B for notes to designers who wish to avoid the A=2 requirement.

are possible. Memory will only ever issue normal acknowledgments (MRDY/) to Coherent Invalidates, but coherent bus adaptors may issue other acknowledgments, particularly R&R. It should also be noted that a Coherent Invalidate transaction will have SIZE = 32B during the address phase, but it will only be expecting one MRDY/ for the acknowledgment. Also the address may not be 32-byte aligned. Memory (or coherent bus adaptor) designers should take note of this. If in a particular system, caches cannot guarantee to complete their invalidation before their A+2 cycle, the memory controller for that system should delay the acknowledgment as appropriate. This implies that memory controllers should have a feature that allows the time to acknowledge invalidates to be varied to some extent, either hardwired or through a programmable register. A recommended range for the programmable delay is A+2 to A+10. This programmable delay is the MBus flow control technique to guarantee that invalidates can be completed at any rate they are issued.

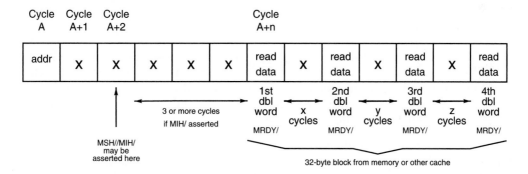

Figure A-7   Coherent Read Semantics

This Coherent Invalidate MBus transaction is issued when a write is being performed into a cache line that is Shared. Before the write can actually be performed, all the other systems caches must have their local copies invalidated (write-invalidate cache-consistency protocol). Snooping caches will not assert MSH/ during A+2. The MAD lines will contain undefined data during the data phase cycles. If a Coherent Invalidate transaction should receive an R&R acknowledgment there is a possibility that the line which is about to be written becomes invalidated by an intervening invalidation transaction on the bus. This means that when the cache regains the bus it should issue a Coherent Read and Invalidate transaction, not a Coherent Invalidate transaction, to once again allocate the (sub-)block. Figure A-8 shows the basic semantics of an Invalidate operation.

For any particular system, selecting which module will be responsible for acknowledging Coherent invalidates introduces some issues for memory controller designers. In most systems a single memory controller will be responsible. In systems with a coherent bus adaptor, the adaptor will be responsible. If it is desired to use a memory controller in a system that also has a coherent bus adaptor, it is then required to be able to tell the memory controller not to respond to invalidates. This should be accomplished during system initialization prior to enabling any caches, preferably by writing a bit in a register in a memory controller.

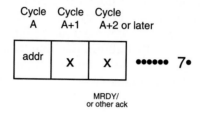

Figure A-8   Coherent Invalidate Semantics

Coherent Read and Invalidate

Since the MBus supports a write-invalidate type of cache-consistency protocol, a special Coherent Read and Invalidate transaction, which combines a Coherent Read transaction with a Coherent Invalidate transaction, was included to reduce the number of MBus transactions. Caches that are performing Coherent Reads with the knowledge that they intend to immediately modify the data can issue this transaction.

Each Coherent Read and Invalidate transaction will be snooped by all system caches. If the address hits and the cache does not own the block, then that cache will immediately invalidate its copy of this block, no matter what state the data was in. If the address hits and the cache owns the block, then it will assert MIH/ and supply the data. When the data has been successfully supplied, the cache will then invalidate its copy of this block. Figure A-9 shows the basic semantics of a Coherent Read and Invalidate operation. Note that it is identical to the Coherent Read operation, except that the system caches will invalidate the block. All of the detailed comments concerning MIH/ for the Coherent Read transaction apply equally to the Coherent Read and Invalidate transaction. MSH/ is not driven during the Coherent Read and Invalidate transaction.

Coherent Write and Invalidate

A Coherent Write and Invalidate transaction combines a Write transaction with a Coherent Invalidate transaction. The Coherent Write and Invalidate transaction is intended to reduce the number of MBus transactions. This transaction can be used by Level-2 modules that wish to support a write through cache, a degree of functionality beyond the requirements for level-2 MBus. (Supporting write through caches is useful for implementing simple 2nd level caches that support inclusion.) CWI is also of use to block copy and block fill mechanisms.

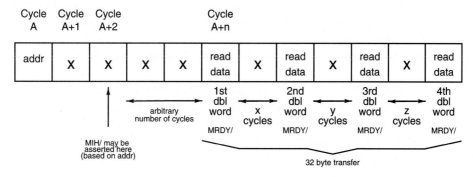

Figure A-9   Coherent Read and Invalidate Semantics

Each Coherent Write and Invalidate transaction will be snooped by all system caches. If the address hits, then caches will invalidate their copies of this block no matter what state the data was in. Figure A-10 shows the basic semantics of a Coherent Write and Invalidate operation. Note that it is identical to the Write operation, except that the system caches will invalidate the block. All SIZE values are allowed and a single 32-byte block is invalidated regardless of the value of SIZE. Due to the nature of the cache coherency protocol neither MIH/ nor MSH/ is asserted.

All SIZE values are allowed in order to better accommodate write through caches. Systems with only either write through or write back caches work naturally, but a system with both a write through and a write back cache are very unlikely to work in a way that preserves cache consistency. This mixed system is not anticipated or recommended as a real MBus configuration.

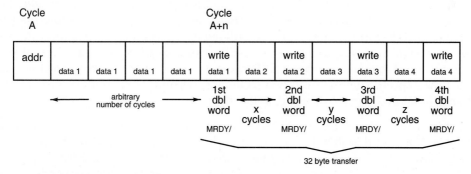

Figure A-10 Coherent Write and Invalidate Semantics

Acknowledgment Cycles

It is a requirement that any transaction once issued *must* correctly accept *any* acknowledgment type. This applies to all Level 1 and Level 2 transactions. The earliest that an acknowledgment can be issued is A+1 for Read and Write and A+2 for all

Coherent Transactions. Processor caches that are supplying data as part of a Coherent Read transaction may only issue either normal or error acknowledgments. They may not issue R&R or Retry acknowledgments.

Idle Cycles

When there is no bus activity or when it is necessary to insert wait states in between the address cycle and the data cycle or between consecutive data cycles, an addressed slave can simply refrain from asserting any transaction status bits (MERR/, MRDY/, and MRTY/). The number of wait cycles which can be inserted is arbitrary, as long as it does not exceed the system time-out interval (see "Acknowledgment Cycles" for time-out details).

Relinquish and Retry (R&R)

When a slave device cannot accept or supply data immediately, it can perform a *relinquish and retry* acknowledgment cycle by asserting MRTY/ for only one bus cycle. This will indicate to the requesting master that it should release the bus immediately so that the bus can be re-arbitrated and possibly used by another MBus master. This involves at least one dead cycle until the suspended transaction can be performed in the case when the bus is still granted to the re-trying master.   When the bus is no longer granted to the master in question, then the suspended transaction must wait until bus ownership is once again attained. When a transaction that receives an R&R acknowledgment regains bus mastership it must issue the same transaction over from the beginning. An exception to this is when a Coherent Invalidate turns into a Coherent Read and Invalidate (see "Coherent Invalidate"). For Level 1 **modules**, for all transactions with SIZE greater than 8 bytes, a relinquish and retry acknowledgment can be asserted on any data transfer. For Level 2 **modules,** for all transactions with SIZE greater than 8 bytes, (including the Level-1 READ and WRITE transactions) R&R can only be issued on the first acknowledgment. It is the responsibility of the slave port to time the duration of the transaction that is causing it to issue R&R, and return an ERROR2 acknowledgment to the correct master when its device specific time-out interval (200 micro-seconds is recommended) has passed **and** the master has reconnected to the slave.

There are two different cases that cause slaves to issue R&R acknowledgments. The first is slow devices. If a device is slow to respond, the slave interface should wait a short interval (around one microsecond is recommended), and then issue an R&R acknowledgment. It should also capture the ID of the master from the MAD lines during the address phase (MID[3:0] field) and enter a "port busy" state while waiting for the device attached to the slave to respond.   The master will eventually reconnect and the R&R process will be repeated until either the device responds or the slave time-out interval (which should be much greater than the short interval, 200 microseconds is recommended) is exceeded.   The slave will then issue the normal or error acknowledgment respectively and exit the "port busy" state.

In systems with multiple masters, the slave that issues R&R must capture the ID of the master whose transaction is being postponed in order to know which master should receive the normal or error acknowledgment when the slave can complete the transaction. If a master with an ID other than that captured by the slave port should access the slave port while it is in the "port busy" state, it should simply be given an R&R acknowledgment.

The second cause of R&R acknowledgments is the resolution of **deadlock** situations where there are a master and a slave port sharing an MBus interface and simultaneous transactions on both ports requires one transaction to back off. R&R requires the current owner of MBus to relinquish ownership in order to resolve the deadlock. R&Rs used to resolve deadlocks are inherently stateless and do not require a "port busy" state.

A detail of significance is that R&R can be issued to a transaction that is part of a locked sequence of transactions. By definition, all transactions in a locked sequence are addressed to the same device, e.g., main memory (or second-level cache) or an I/O adapter. There is only one "port busy" state per device, so there is only one source of R&R for a locked sequence.

Normally, main memory will not issue R&R. Multiple R&R sources from main memory would restrict locked sequences to addresses within one memory bank, Also, some aspects of coherent cache design are simplified by locking some MBus sequences such as fills and their associated write-back (if any). These sequences rely on either a memory system that does not issue R&R or an appropriately designed second level cache or coherent bus adaptor that does. For more details see "Level 1 Transaction Types".

It should be noted that processor caches which assert MIH/ and then supply data cannot issue R&R acknowledgments.

Valid Data Transfer

A valid or ready data transfer is indicated by a responding slave with the assertion of the MRDY/ transaction status bit for only one cycle. This signal needs to be asserted on reads to indicate to the requesting master that valid data has just arrived. On writes, MRDY/ indicates to the writing master that the data has been accepted and that the writing master shall stop driving the accepted data. The next double-word, if a write burst was being performed, will be driven onto the bus in the cycle immediately following the assertion of MRDY/.

ERROR1 => Bus Error

When the responding device asserts only the MERR/ transaction status bit, the requesting master will interpret this as an external bus error just having taken place. The meaning of "Bus Error" is implementation-dependent.

ERROR2 => Time-out

This acknowledgment is expected to be generated by some sort of watchdog timer logic in the system that primarily detects transactions that are not acknowledged. This is accomplished by timing the shorter of either the assertion of MBB/ or the time since the last MAS/ assertion, as follows.

A time-out counter should start on the assertion of MBB/ and count until the de-assertion of MBB/, or until the timer has counted the time-out interval. If the counter counts to the time-out limit, a time-out error acknowledgment should be generated by the time-out monitor circuitry. When counting ceases, the counter should be reinitialized to its initial condition. If MAS/ is asserted during the time that counting is enabled (MBB/ assertion) the counter should be reinitialized, but continue counting. The number of cycles for the time-out interval is system implementation-dependent. An interval of 200 microseconds is recommended. This error code can also be used to indicate a system implementation dependent error. Time-out is the suggested interpretation of an ERROR2 acknowledgment.

ERROR3 => Uncorrectable

This acknowledgment is mainly used by the addressed memory controller to inform the requester that in the process of accessing the data some sort of uncorrectable error has been encountered (like parity, uncorrectable ECC, etc.). This error code can also be used to indicate a system implementation-dependent error. Uncorrectable error is the suggested interpretation of an ERROR3 acknowledgment.

Retry

This acknowledgment differs from the *Relinquish and Retry* acknowledgment in that the master will not, in this case, release bus ownership if it is no longer granted the bus, but rather the transaction will immediately begin again with an address phase (MAS/, etc.) as soon as the retried master is ready to do so. Retry errors can occur on any acknowledgment of a transaction. This type of acknowledgment can be useful when a correctable ECC error has occurred in the main memory subsystem.

Should a Retry acknowledgment occur on other than the first acknowledgment cycle, the issue of "Data Correctness" arises. Modules that use delivered data prior to completion of the transaction may not be able to tolerate delivery of bad data. They may choose to treat Retry acknowledgments as equivalent to ERROR3 acknowledgments. This assumes that the Retry is "stateless" and the slave device issuing it will not hang or otherwise malfunction if the transaction is not retried. This is a detail at the discretion of system implementors.

Reserved

This acknowledgment is reserved for future use. Should a master receive a Reserved acknowledgment its behavior is undefined.

Arbitration

Arbitration Principles

- The Arbiter is a separate unit from both the slave(s) and master(s).

- Arbitration is overlapped with current bus cycle.

- Back-to-back transactions by different masters are not allowed. There must be at least one dead cycle in between each transaction during which MBB/ is de-asserted.

- Arbitration algorithm is implementation dependent. (Fair bandwidth allocation should be maintained.)

- Bus parking will be employed. (Current master keeps the bus until it is taken away by another request.)

- Locked cycles are accommodated to handle indivisible operations.

Arbitration Protocol

The MBus arbitration scheme assumes a central arbiter. The exact algorithm used by the arbiter (like round-robin, etc.) is implementation-dependent.

Bus Requestors

A requesting module requests the MBus by asserting its dedicated MBR/ signal and then waits for assertion of its dedicated grant signal MBG/ by the arbiter. Upon receiving its dedicated grant signal (MBG/), the requesting master can start using the bus by asserting MAS/ and MBB/ as soon as MBB/ is released (de-asserted) by the previous master. It is not necessary for the requesting master to assert MAS/ immediately, but it is necessary to assert MBB/ to acquire and hold the bus. A requesting master is not guaranteed to gain bus ownership if it does not immediately assert MBB/ upon detecting the condition of its MBG/ asserted and MBB/ de-asserted because if some other master is requesting the bus, the arbiter will then assert the grant to the new requestor.

The requestor, upon receiving its dedicated grant signal (MBG/) should immediately remove its dedicated request (MBR/) on the next clock edge. It is allowed to assert MBR/ in anticipation of needing the bus, and then de-assert it prior to receiving MBG/. However, this may waste bus cycles and should be avoided.

Bus Arbiter

The arbiter uses only the MBRn/, MBGn/, signals from each master and the common bussed MBB/ signal. The arbiter receives the requests (MBR/n) and resolves which grant (MBG/n) to assert. A grant remains asserted until at least one cycle after the current master has de-asserted MBB/ when it becomes "parked," and may be removed at any time after this in response to assertion of further requests. If no other requests (MBR/n) are asserted, the grant (MBG/n) remains asserted (parked). Only one grant (MBG/) is asserted at any time. A dead cycle between successive transactions of different masters will always occur with the MBus arbitration scheme. See "Timing Diagrams" for example transactions.

Figure A-11 shows a block diagram and a state diagram of an arbiter that resolves two requests and issues the two associated grants. In the state diagram, the state names are indicated in bold text within the state circles. The signal outputs associated with each state are indicated in normal text within the state circles. In the state transition equations, ! indicates NOT, & indicates AND and # indicates OR. The signals are represented in their positive logic form. The reset signal MRST is omitted from the state transition equations for clarity. For larger arbiters, the state transition diagram becomes more complex. There will always be two states per MBG signal, one for the case where a grant has been issued but not accepted, and the other for the case where the grant has been (potentially) accepted and the arbiter remains parked on that grant.

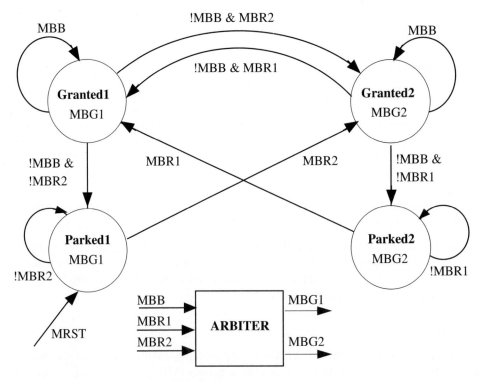

Figure A-11 Example of a Two-Grant MBus Arbiter

MBus Configuration Address Map

A small portion of the MBus memory space has been preallocated to each potential MBus module, to allow for a uniform method of system configuration. There is an individual space per MBus ID, 16 spaces in total. The ID of a module is determined by the value on the ID[3:0] pins. Level 1 processor modules do not have slave interfaces and so will not respond at the configuration address map locations. Table A-6 shows the configuration address spaces of MBus.

Table A-6 MBus Configuration Address Map

Configuration Spaces	MBus Identifier
0xFF0000000 to 0xFF0FFFFFF	Range for ID=0x0[1]
0xFF1000000 to 0xFF1FFFFFF	Range for ID=0x1
0xFF2000000 to 0xFF2FFFFFF	Range for ID=0x2
. .	.
. .	.
. .	.
0xFFF000000 to 0xFFFFFFFFF	Range for ID=0xF

1. reserved for "boot prom"

One 32-bit location in each space (0xFFnFFFFFC where n=ID) is fixed and should contain the Implementation Number and Version Number of the MBus module in an **MBus Port Register (MPR)** which is shown in Figure A-12. A processor accessing the 16 possible MPRs can determine what ID slots are present (through time-out) and what devices they contain from the contents of the MPR. Other than this one address, the use of the address range is implementation-specific and specified by module vendors. Examples of items located in these configuration address ranges are registers that determine the address ranges which memory and I/O modules respond to. Similarly, implementation-specific registers and memories necessary to configure and test modules would reside at locations within the device-specific configuration address space.

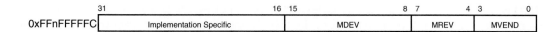

Figure A-12 MBus Port Register Format

MDEV—MBus Device number. This field contains a unique number which indicates the vendor-specific MBus device that is present at the referenced MBus port. Refer to Vendors for their MDEV assignments.

MREV—Device Revision number. This field contains a number that can be interpreted as a revision number or some other variable of a device. Refer to Vendors for their MREV assignments, if any.

MVEND—MBus vendor number. This field contains a unique number which indicates the vendor of the device present at the referenced MBus port. Refer to Supplement A for current MVEND assignments.

On coming out of reset, processor modules will fetch instructions from MBus address 0xFF000000 and subsequent memory locations. This means that the configuration address space for ID=0x0 is special and always needs to be present. MBus ID=0x0, then, can be considered as the "boot PROM" MBus module.

MBus Electrical Characteristics

MBus Electrical Principles

Bus Protocol—The MBus is a fully synchronous bus. The frequency of operation is 40 Mhz.

Sampling—All signals are changed and sampled on rising clock edges.

Driver Overlap—No bussed signal is driven in the same cycle by more than one source. All bussed control signals (except MSH/ and AERR/ which are open-drain) follow a sequence from tri-state to active low to driven high to tri-state, normally on successive rising clock edges. Since MBB/ can be driven by two sources with only one dead cycle in between, the drive high followed by tri-state must occur within a single cycle. The multiplexed address data bus signals (MAD) follow a sequence from tri-state, to active high or low, to tri-state. MAD lines should always be high or low before tri-stating to ensure MAD lines are always at a known logic level.

Noise—To avoid noise problems due to "floating" signals or very slow rise time signals, high impedance holding amplifiers are required on the MAD lines. Bussed control lines require high impedance pull-up resistors. These amplifiers and/or resistors are a centralized function, provided by the system.

Driver Turn On—There are many cases in the protocol where it is necessary to turn on and drive a signal in the same clock cycle. It is a general assumption that this is also done even for cases where it is not absolutely necessary. Care needs to be taken where a driver is turned on before the signal is driven as the protocol does not define the cases where this may be possible. This is particularly true for **CR** and **CRI** which are three party transactions.

Signal Grouping

For timing purposes, signals are divided into four groups, MAD[63:0], bussed control, point-to-point control and misc. (See Figure A-13) Bussed control includes MAS/, MRDY/, MERR/, MRTY/, MBB/,MSH/, and MIH/. Point-to-point control includes MBR/ and MBG/. Misc. includes RSTIN/, IRL[3:0], INT-OUT/, and AERR/.

SIGNAL CLASS	SIGNAL
BUSSED CONTROL:	MAS/, MRDY/, MRTY/, MERR/, MBB/, MSH/, MIH/
POINT-TO-POINT CONTROL:	MBR/, MBG/
MAD:	MAD[63:0]
MISC:	RSTIN/, AERR/, IRL[3:0], INT-OUT

Figure A-13 MBus Signal Grouping for Timing Purposes

Definitions

tcod—Clock to output delay time for the bussed control lines.

tocoh—Clock to output hold time for the bussed control lines.

tmod—Clock to output delay time for the MAD lines.

tmoh—Clock to output hold time for the MAD lines.

tpod—Clock to output delay time for the point to point control lines.

tpoh—Clock to output hold time for the point to point control lines.

tcis—Input setup time for bussed control lines.

tcih—Input hold time for bussed control lines.

tmis—Input setup time for MAD lines.

tmih—Input hold time for MAD lines.

tpis—Input setup time for point to point control lines.

tpih—Input hold time for bussed control lines.

Tcp—Clock period.

Tpwh—Clock High period.

Tpwl—Clock Low period.

Tskur—Rising edge clock skew.

Tskuf—Falling edge clock skew.

Timing Reference Diagram

Figure A-14 shows a Reference Timing Diagram.

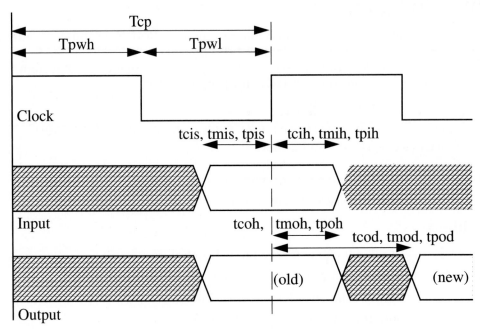

Figure A-14 Reference Timing Diagram

Clocks

The clocks provided to the module by the system will have the characteristics detailed in Figure A-15.

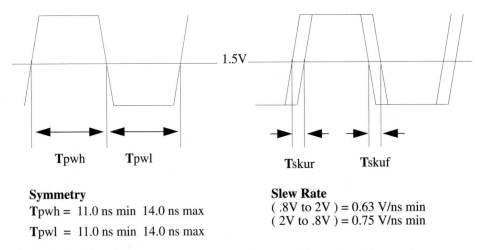

Symmetry
Tpwh = 11.0 ns min 14.0 ns max
Tpwl = 11.0 ns min 14.0 ns max

Slew Rate
(.8V to 2V) = 0.63 V/ns min
(2V to .8V) = 0.75 V/ns min

Figure A-15 CLOCK Specification

Level-1 and Level-2 Clock Characteristics (Ta = 0-70C)

Table A-7   Level-1 and Level-2 Clock Characteristics

Parameter	min	max	Unit
Tcp	25	25	ns
Tpwh	11	14	ns
Tpwl	11	14	ns
Tskur	0	1.5	ns
Tskuf	0	1.5	ns

Level-1 AC Characteristics (MAD and Control) (Ta = 0-70C)

Table A-8   Level-1 AC Characteristics[1]

Parameter	min	max	Unit
tmis		3	ns
tmih		2	ns
tmod	-	18	ns
tmoh	4	-	ns
tcis		3	ns
tcih		2	ns
tcod	-	16	ns
tcoh	4	-	ns

1. All times are for a capacitive load of 100pF

Level-2 AC Characteristics (MAD and Control) (Ta = 0-70C)

It should be noted that the timing specification listed here is for a reference load represented by the SPICE models System-max and System-min (available from SPARC International). Conformance with this Level-2 ac specification is achieved by chip vendors **guaranteeing** that these timing numbers have been achieved when performing a SPICE analysis using accurate models of chip internal circuitry driving the reference loads System-max and System-min. This gives a more complete degree of compatibility between modules from different vendors than the simple RC load usually used in IC specifications.

The reference loads, System-max and System-min, include elements of a typical MBus system, including IC packages, MBus connectors, and printed wiring board traces.

The specification listed is **not** to be used as the timing criteria a chip tester would be programmed with. It is expected that data sheets from different vendors will be quoted for different test environments and so will differ from the numbers in this table. These numbers also represent the minimum requirements. Chip vendors can exceed these specifications.

It is recommended that MBus systems designers perform SPICE or similar analysis on their particular printed wiring board layout. In order to facilitate this, it is recommended that MBus chip vendors provide accurate SPICE models of their I/O circuitry to their customers.

The timing listed in Table A-9 is for a 40 MHz MBus system. It is recommended that systems be designed with a TOTAL clock skew budget of less than or equal to 1.5 ns across all MBus devices. That is to say, the difference between the arrival time of the earliest and latest clocks (measured at 1.5V) to MBus modules should at most be 1.5 ns.

Table A-9   MBus Level-2 AC Characteristics (MAD and CNTRL)[1]

Parameter	SPEC	Load
tcod max	17.5	System-max
tcoh min	2.5	System-min
tmod max	18.5	System-max
tmoh min	2.5	System-min
tpod max	14.5	System-max
tpoh min	2.5	System-min
tcis max	6.0	
tcih max	1.0	
tmis max	5.0	
tmih max	1.0	
tpis max	9.0	
tpih max	1.0	

1. All times in nano-seconds

Note – All Level-2 timing values are relative to the pads on the DIE.

Level-1 and Level-2 AC Characteristics(Scan) (Ta = 0-70C)

Table A-10 MBus Level-1 and 2 AC Characteristics (Scan signals)

SCAN (SCANDI, SCANDO SCANTMS1, SCANTMS2)[1]		
Signal	**SPEC**	**Comments**
Clk to output max	25.0	Measured Relative to SCANCLK Falling Edge
Clk to output min	2.5	Measured Relative to SCANCLK Falling Edge
Input set up max	20.0	Measured Relative to SCANCLK Rising Edge
Input Hold max	20.0	Measured Relative to SCANCLK Rising Edge

1. All times in nanoseconds; timing values are relative to the pads on the DIE.

Level-1 and Level-2 DC Characteristics (Ta = 0-70C)

Table A-11 Level-1 and Level-2 DC Characteristics

Symbol	Signal Description	Conditions	min	max	unit
VCC	Supply Voltage		4.75	5.25	V
Vih	Input High Voltage level		2.0	VCC	V
Vil	Input Low Voltage level		VSS	.8	V
Iil	Input Leakage			+-1.0	mA
Iol	Output Leakage			+-1.0	mA
Iih	Input High Current			20	mA
Iilo	Input Low Current			-10	mA
Voh	Output high Voltage	Ioh = -2 mA	2.4	VCC	V
Vol	Output Low Voltage	Iol = 2 mA	0.0	0.4	V
Vol	Output Low Voltage(MSH/)	Iol = 8 mA	0.0	0.4	V
Vol	Output Low Voltage(AERR/)	Iol = 3 mA	0.0	0.4	V
Cin	Input Capacitance			10	pF
Cout	Output Capacitance			12	pF
Ci/o	Input/Output Capacitance			15	pF

The dc specification represents the minimum MBus requirements. MBus components may exceed the minimum requirements. It should not be inferred that meeting the dc specifications means that this will guarantee compliance with the ac specifications.

A

General Electrical Topics

A.C. Threshold Assumptions

Inside the chip—The threshold point used to evaluate timing inside of a chip will vary from vendor to vendor. Consult with your vendor to establish the threshold point of the MBus driver input.

Outside the chip (System level)—All MBus levels are TTL and should be measured as follows: Low=.8V; High=2.0v. For the clocks however, 1.5V should be used as the threshold for the purposes of making timing measurements and calculations.

Asynchronous signals

An IRL[3:0] level should be treated as an asynchronous input group by a processor module. All four IRL lines should transition between valid logic levels within 10 ns to avoid spurious interrupts on fast modules.

RSTIN/ should be treated by a module as an asynchronous input signal. It may be asserted for several reasons. When asserted for power-on reset it is recommended that it be asserted for a minimum of100ms. For other reset events it is recommended that it be asserted for a minimum of 25 us.

AERR/ should be treated as an asynchronous input signal to the interrupt logic. It must remain asserted until de-asserted by software action.

MID[3:0] are hard-wired stable signals.

Reset and Initialization

As explained under the signal description of RSTIN/, **modules** should tri-state all bussed lines and drive all point to point signals inactive high when RSTIN/ is asserted. This must be accomplished within the default assertion time of RSTIN/. It is the responsibility of the **system** to ensure that all bussed control signals (CNTRL) are high and all MAD lines are at stable logic levels before RSTIN/ is de-asserted to any module. After coming out of reset, processor modules may take some time to respond to transactions. System designers need to be aware of the characteristics of the processor modules they intend to support in order to ensure they do not time out when accessing modules coming out of reset. The SCANTMS2 signal must be asserted during power-up reset to modules that implement P1149 (JTAG).

Pull Ups and Holding Amplifiers

High impedance pull-up resistors are required on MAS/, MRDY/, MRTY/, MERR/, MBB/ and MIH/. 10K ohms is recommended. A 1.5K ohm pull-up resistor is recommended for AERR/. A 619 ohm pull-up resistor is recommended for MSH/. MAD[63:0] signals require holding amplifiers. An example of a holding amplifier is shown in Figure A-16. The recommended high output impedance driver Iol and Ioh max, at Vol and Voh respectively, is 100mA. It is the responsibility of the system to provide pull ups and holding amplifiers.

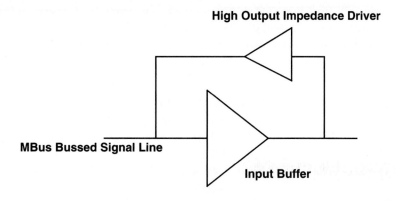

High Output Impedance Driver

MBus Bussed Signal Line

Input Buffer

Figure A-16 Holding amplifier

Mechanical Specifications

The mechanical specification consists of the connector and its associated pin-out and the mechanical drawings for the module printed wiring boards.

MBus Connector

The MBus Module concept of field-upgradeable performance requires a connector with high reliability, ease of installation, and a foolproof keying scheme. The aggressive MBus cycle time goal of 25ns requires a connector with excellent electrical performance, i.e., transmission line characteristics with low capacitance and inductance. Finally, promoting MBus as a physical, as well as logical standard requires a connector which is widely available in the marketplace. Based on the above requirements, the **AMP "Microstrip"** (part # 121354-4) has been selected. This is the module part (shrouded male pins) of a mating pair of connectors.

Caution – Make sure the system the module is being designed for provides standoffs on either side of the connector. This is required to help prevent breakage of the connector if by accident the module is "over rotated" while "walking" the module out. That is to say, if one end of the connector stays mated while the other is de-mated it is very likely that the end of the connector that stays mated will break once the module has swung up by 30 - 40 degrees.

MBus Connector Pin-out

For a description of the signals listed refer to "Signal Definition". It should be noted here that the signals provided at the connector are sufficient to support two processors per module. Therefore, you will find two sets of bus request, bus grant, and interrupt lines. The clock signals MCLK0-3 are identical clocks that must be provided by all systems. Four clocks are provided to allow for modules that have many clock loads.

Table A-12 MBus Pin-out

1. SCANDI	Blade1		2. SCAN TMS1
3. SCANDO			4. SCANTMS2
5. SCANCLK		GND	6. IRL0[1]
7. IRL0[0]			8. IRL0[3]
9. IRL0[2]		GND	10. INTOUT/
11. MAD[0]			12. MAD[1]
13. MAD[2]		GND	14. MAD[3]
15. MAD[4]			16. MAD[5]
17. MAD[6]		GND	18. MAD[7]
19. MAD[8]			20. MAD[9]
21. MAD[10]	Blade2		22. MAD[11]
23. MAD[12]			24. MAD[13]
25. MAD[14]		+5V	26. MAD[15]
27. MAD[16]			28. MAD[17]
29. MAD[18]		+5V	30. MAD[19]
31. MAD[20]			32. MAD[21]
33. MAD[22]		+5V	34. MAD[23]
35. MAD[24]			36. MAD[25]
37. MAD[26]		+5V	38. MAD[27]
39. MAD[28]			40. MAD[29]
41. MAD[30]	Blade3		42. MAD[31]
43. MBR0/			44. MSH/
45. MBG0/	GND		46. MIH/
47. MCLK0			48. MRTY/
49. MCLK1	GND		50. MRDY/
51. MCLK2			52. MERR/
53. MCLK3	GND		54. MAS/
55. MBR1/			56. MBB/

Table A-12 MBus Pin-out (Continued)

57. MBG1/	GND		58. RESERVED1
59. MAD[32]			60. MAD[33]
61. MAD[34]	Blade4		62. MAD[35]
63. MAD[36]			64. MAD[37]
65. MAD[38]		+5V	66. MAD[39]
67. MAD[40]			68. MAD[41]
69. MAD[42]		+5V	70. MAD[43]
71. MAD[44]			72. MAD[45]
73. MAD[46]		+5V	74. MAD[47]
75. MAD[48]			76. MAD[49]
77. MAD[50]		+5V	78. MAD[51]
79. MAD[52]			80. MAD[53]
81. MAD[54]	Blade5		82. MAD[55]
83. MAD[56]			84. MAD[57]
85. MAD[58]		GND	86. MAD[59]
87. MAD[60]			88. MAD[61]
89. MAD[62]		GND	90. MAD[63]
91. RESERVED2			92. IRL1[0]
93. IRL1[1]		GND	94. IRL1[2]
95. IRL1[3]			96. AERR/
97. RSTIN/		GND	98. ID[1]
99. ID[2]			100. ID[3]

Timing Diagram Examples

The following idealized wave-form diagrams are included in order to assist in understanding the operations of the MBus. In most of the waveforms, the bus is shown already granted to one of the masters. All waveforms also show MBB/ asserting with MAS/ and de-asserting immediately after the last acknowledgment is received. This is not a requirement of the MBus protocol. It should also be noted that only two masters are depicted using the MBus (MBR1/, MBR2/). However, this can be extended to as many masters as can be supported electrically (as discussed in "MBus Electrical Characteristics"). A line intermediate between high and low is shown on MAD[63:0]. This indicates the time that the MAD lines are driven by holding amplifiers and does not indicate that an indeterminate voltage level is permitted on MAD[63:0]. The crosshatched areas indicate the bus is being driven to valid logic levels but the data is indeterminate.

Word Read

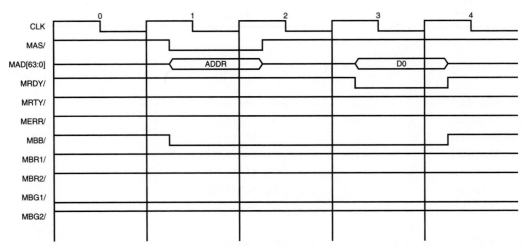

Waveform 1   Word Read

Waveform 1 depicts a simple word read transaction by a master who has already been granted the bus (master 1). The number of cycles between the address cycle and the data cycle(s) of all the waveforms in this section is implementation dependent. Waveform 1 shows a minimum memory latency of 2 cycles.

Word Write

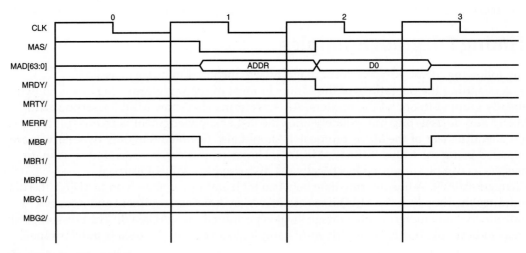

Waveform 2   Word Write

Waveform 2 depicts a simple word write transaction by a master who has already been granted the bus (master 1). Note how the data is immediately driven onto the MAD lines after the address cycle and that the bus has been granted to master 1 prior to the beginning of the transaction. The slave response time is implementation dependent. Waveform 2 depicts the minimum write time of 2 cycles.

Burst Read with No Delays

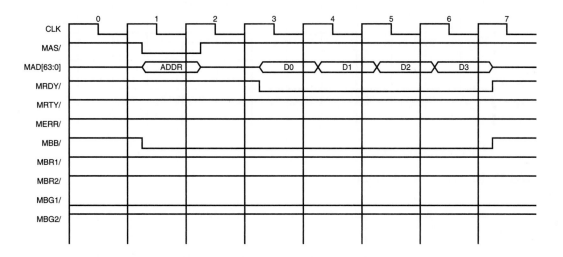

Waveform 3   Burst Read with No Delays

Waveform 3 depicts a burst read operation of 32 bytes where the slave device supplies the data at the maximum rate possible. Note again that the bus has been granted to master 1 prior to the beginning of the transaction.

Burst Read with Delays

Waveform 4 depicts a burst read operation of 32 bytes where the slave device cannot supply the data at the maximum rate possible. Wait states are inserted between each 8-byte quantity by simply de-asserting MRDY/ for an arbitrary number of cycles (shows 1 cycle of delay inserted between each 8-byte transfer as well as 3 wait states before the burst response begins). Note again that the bus has been granted to master 1 prior to the beginning of the transaction.

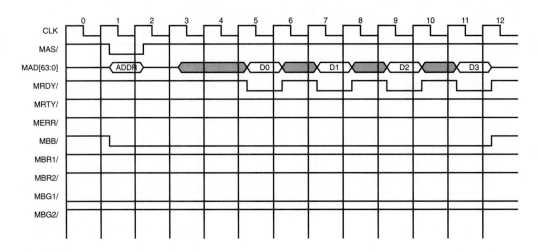

Waveform 4   Burst Read with Delays

Burst Write with No Delays

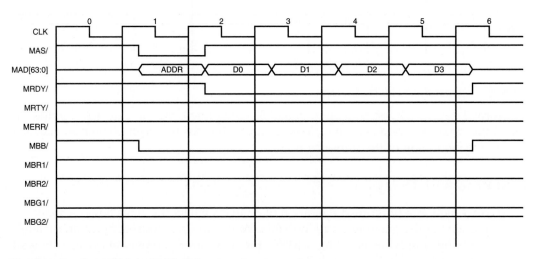

Waveform 5   Burst Write with No Delays

Waveform 5 depicts a burst write operation of 32 bytes where the slave device accepts the data at the maximum rate possible. Note again that the bus has been granted to master 1 prior to the beginning of the transaction. Note also how the next doubleword to be written is driven in the cycle immediately after MRDY/ asserts.

Burst Write with Delays

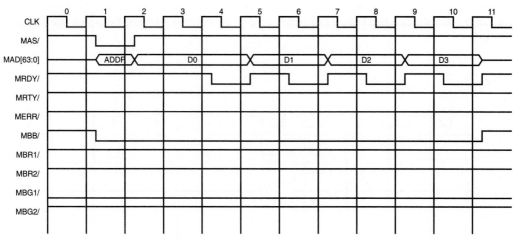

Waveform 6   Burst Write with Delays

Waveform 6 depicts a burst write operation of 32 bytes where the slave device cannot accept the data at the maximum rate possible. Wait states are inserted between each 8-byte quantity by simply de-asserting MRDY/ for an arbitrary number of cycles (This Waveform 6 shows 1 cycle of delay inserted between each 8-byte transfer as well as 2 wait states before the beginning of the burst). Note again that the bus has been granted to master 1 prior to the beginning of the transaction. Also note how the next double-word to be written is driven in the cycle immediately after MRDY/ asserts.

Relinquish and Retry

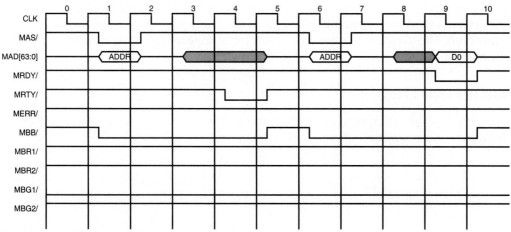

Waveform 7   Relinquish and Retry

Waveform 7 depicts a Read operation in which the addressed slave needed to inform the master that it should relinquish the bus and retry the operation again once bus ownership has been attained. In the case shown above, the master in question maintained ownership as no one else wanted the bus. Thus, only one dead cycle is present between the Read transactions.

Retry

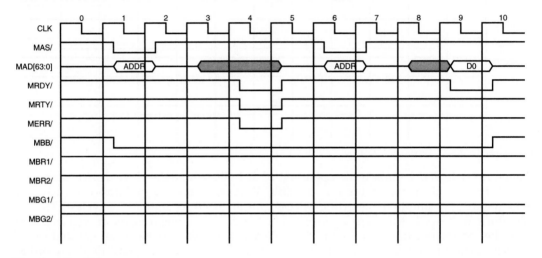

Waveform 8   Retry

Waveform 8 depicts a Read operation in which the addressed slave needed to inform the master that it should retry the operation immediately. The master must always keep MBB/ asserted upon a Retry acknowledgment. However, there must be at least one dead cycle between the Retry acknowledgment and the ensuing MAS/ as is shown in Waveform 8. This dead cycle must be present for both read and write operations which were Retried.

ERROR1 (Bus Error)

Waveform 9 depicts an operation in which the addressed slave detected some sort of a bus error or other system implementation dependent error.

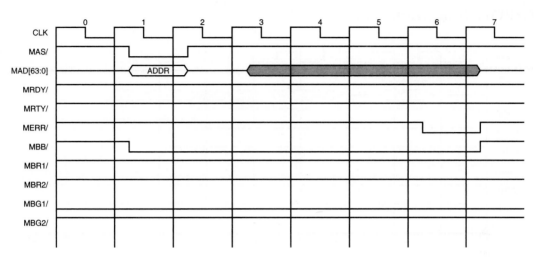

Waveform 9   ERROR1 (Bus Error)

ERROR2 (Time-out)

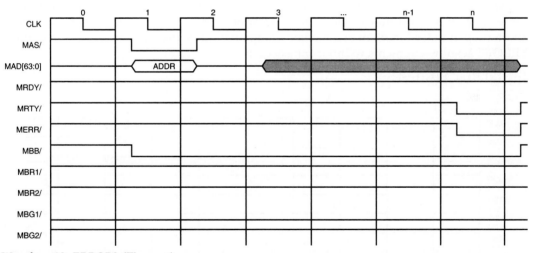

Waveform 10 ERROR2 (Time-out)

Waveform 10 depicts an operation in which a time-out or other system implementation dependent error occurred.

ERROR3 (Uncorrectable)

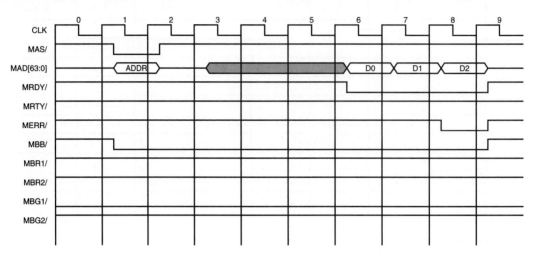

Waveform 11   ERROR3 (Uncorrectable)

Waveform 11 depicts an operation in which an uncorrectable or other system implementation dependent error occurred. Note how the Uncorrectable acknowledgment came on the third data transfer of a burst operation. The transaction must be immediately aborted upon detection of an error acknowledgment. This also applies to ERROR1 and ERROR2 acknowledgments to burst transactions.

Initial Bus Arbitration

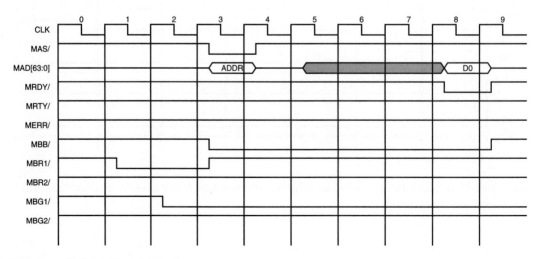

Waveform 12   Initial Bus Arbitration

Waveform 12 depicts a master requesting an idle bus in order to perform a word read. This actually depicts the first transaction after reset, as there is no grant initially, a condition that can only occur at that time.

Arbitration from Master 1 to Master 2

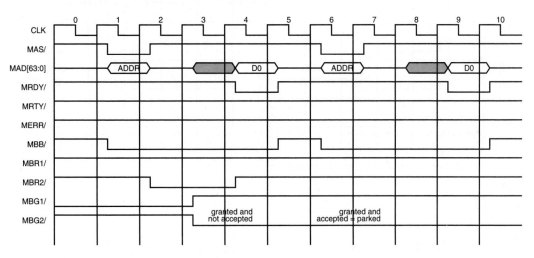

Waveform 13 Arbitration from Master 1 to Master 2

Waveform 13 depicts how the bus ownership is turned over to another master. It was assumed that the bus was already parked on master 1 and module 1 decides to start a cycle during cycle 1 by asserting MBB/ and MAS/. Later Master 2 requests and is granted the bus. After MBB/ is de-asserted Master 2 drives MAS/ and MBB/. At this time the grant is parked on master 2.

Arbitration with Multiple Requests

Waveform 14 depicts arbitration when two masters are continually requesting bus ownership. Initially the bus has been parked on master 1 who then performs a transaction by asserting MBB/ and MAS/. Master 2 then acquires the bus followed by master 1 again. Note how the requests must be de-asserted once the grants are obtained.

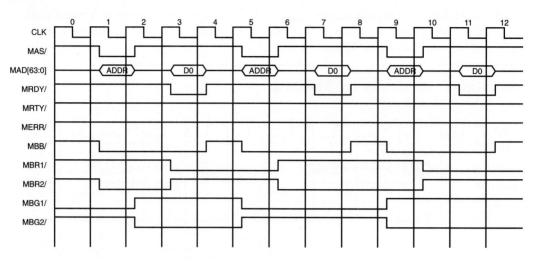

Waveform 14   Arbitration with Multiple Requests

Locked Cycles

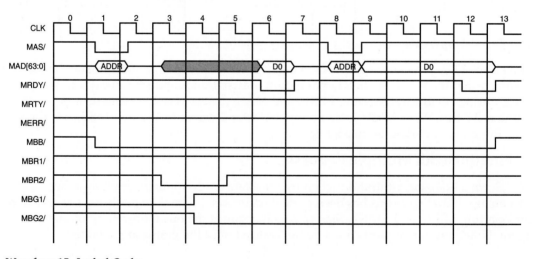

Waveform 15   Locked Cycles

Waveform 15 depicts a read cycle followed by a locked write cycle. Note how MBB/ does not de-assert until the completion of the write operation, despite re-arbitration of the bus as in the above case.

Coherent Read of Shared Data

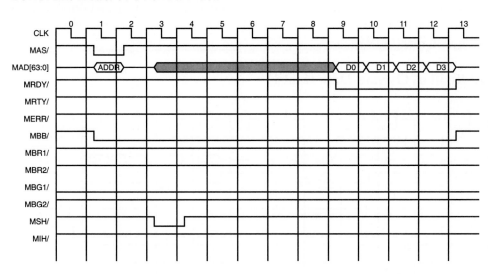

Waveform 16 Coherent Read of Shared Data

Waveform 16 depicts a Coherent Read in which the requested data actually exists in one (or more) other cache(s) in the system, but is not owned by any cache(s). These caches will assert MSH/ on cycle A+2 (or A+7 - refer to Supplement B) as shown.

Coherent Read of Owned Data (long-latency memory)

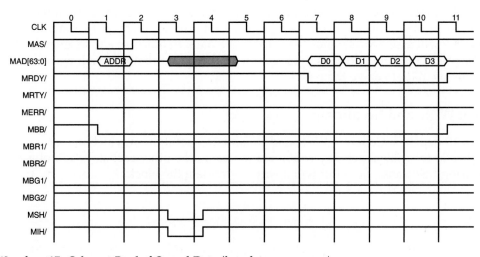

Waveform 17 Coherent Read of Owned Data (long-latency memory)

Waveform 17 depicts a Coherent Read operation in which the requested data is owned by another cache in the system. The owning cache (as well as any other cache with the same data) will assert MSH/ during cycle A+2 (or A+7 - refer to Supplement B). Only the owning cache will assert MIH/.

Coherent Read of Owned Data (fast 1)

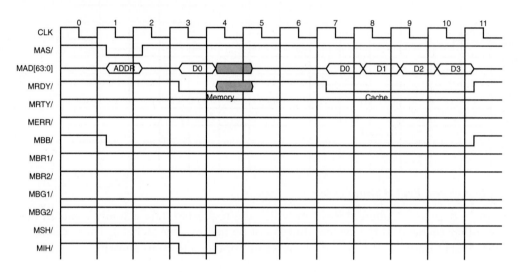

Waveform 18 Coherent Read of Owned Data (fast memory)

Waveform 18 depicts a Coherent Read operation in which the requested data is owned by another cache in the system. The owning cache (as well as any other cache with the same data) will assert MSH/ during cycle A+2 (or A+7 - refer to Supplement B). Only the owning cache will assert MIH/ and then supply the data. In this case above, memory has already begun to respond and thus must get off the bus immediately to allow the cache which owns the data to drive the bus.

Coherent Write and Invalidate

Waveform 19 depicts a Coherent Write and Invalidate operation in which one or more other caches in the system actually contained the data. The other cache(s) will not assert MSH/ during this transaction, but will always invalidate the block.

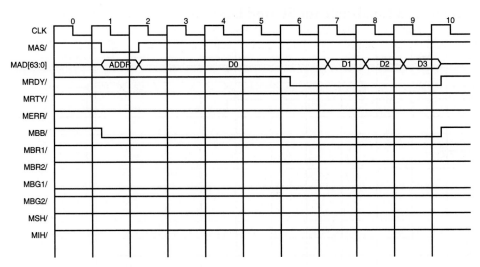

Waveform 19 Coherent Write and Invalidate

Coherent Invalidate

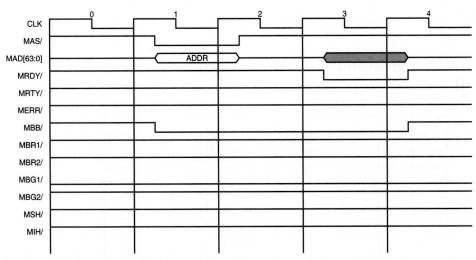

Waveform 20 Coherent Invalidate

Waveform 20 depicts a Coherent Invalidate operation. Memory (or second level cache), in this case, will assert MRDY/ during A+2 (or later - refer to Supplement B). System caches which contain the data being invalidated will not assert MSH/ during this transaction.

Coherent Read and Invalidate (of Shared Data)

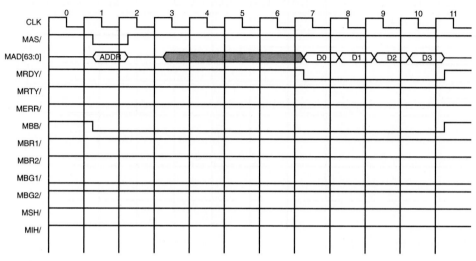

Waveform 21 Coherent Read and Invalidate (of Shared Data)

Waveform 21 depicts a Coherent Read and Invalidate operation in which no system cache owned the piece of data. All caches in the system will invalidate their copies of the block upon detection of a Coherent Read and Invalidate transaction. Note how the MSH/ line does not assert for CRI.

Coherent Read and Invalidate (of Owned Data)

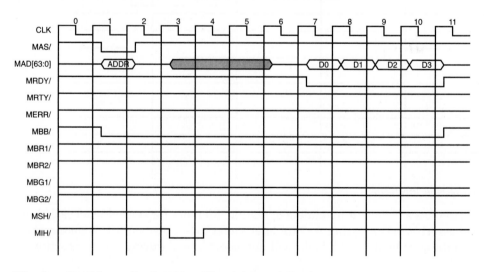

Waveform 22 Coherent Read and Invalidate (of Owned Data)

Waveform 22 depicts a Coherent Read and Invalidate operation in which a system cache owned the piece of data and so supplied it. It then invalidated its copy. Other caches also invalidated their copies.

Supplement A

MBus Port Register Assignments

Table A-13 MPR Vendor Assignment

MVEND	Vendor
0x0	Fujitsu
0x1	Cypress/Ross
0x2	Reserved
0x3	LSI Logic
0x4	TI
0xF	reserved for systems

A

Supplement B

Notes to Implementors

There are many things of significance to the design of MBus components scattered throughout the specification or implied by the specification. These notes are to help clarify some of these issues for implementors.

Memory Controllers

Memory controllers will probably only be slave devices and so should not need to connect MBR/, MBG/ or MBB/. Memory controllers will not issue R&R acknowledgments, although Retry acknowledgments may prove useful to ECC memory controllers. Memory controllers must accommodate wrapped requests and it is recommended that for compatibility they accommodate all transfer sizes allowed for by the specification. The only signals multiplexed on MAD during the address phase of interest to most controllers are TYPE and SIZE.

To enhance compatibility, it is recommended that memory controllers accommodate Level 2 functionality. This means they should recognize all Coherent transactions. Generally this does not add complexity beyond identifying the transaction, as most Coherent transactions are simple reads and writes from the memory controllers perspective. Beyond this, Level 2 compatibility involves two significant details. First, during Coherent Read and Coherent Read and Invalidate transactions the MIH/ signal may be asserted. Memory controllers interpret this signal as telling them to immediately abort the transaction. Secondly, the Coherent Invalidate Transaction must be acknowledged by memory. This means that if multiple memory controller configurations or systems with coherent bus adaptors and memory controllers are allowed, there must be a means to disable memory controllers as the source of acknowledgment. This might be through a pin or a bit in a configuration register. Also the acknowledgment should occur on A+2 or later. Memory controllers may choose to provide a programmable cycle count for the invalidate acknowledgments in order to accommodate a wider range of modules and system configurations. There is no need for memory controllers to observe MSH/. Write and Coherent Write and Invalidate transactions are identical to memory controllers, i.e., all sizes are supported. Also, to support modules with nonstandard MIH/ and MSH/ timing and coherent bus adapters, memory controllers should consider providing a programmable means to vary the minimum acknowledgment timing to Coherent Read and Coherent Read and Invalidate Transactions.

A detail of memory controller design is how errors are handled and how data is delivered in the presence of errors. MBus does not specify system details of this nature. A conservative memory design will always ensure that incorrect data is never transferred across the MBus. This may cost performance as generally it takes time to detect errors.

Less conservative designs may report errors after incorrect data is delivered, either synchronously with an error acknowledgment, or asynchronously via the AERR/ signal. This approach may not be acceptable to many computer vendors. Processor modules that are using the "wrapping" feature to restart the processor early will have no error recovery mechanism with either the late synchronous or asynchronous error reporting approach.

I/O Adapters

An MBus I/O adapter can be broken down into a Master section and a Slave section, the MBus I/O adapter slave port being the processor to I/O bus connection for programmed I/O, and the MBus I/O adapter master port being the I/O bus to memory connection for DMA. Most of the complexity is in the I/O adapter MBus master section. A generic MBus I/O master port requires an I/O MMU (probably a SPARC Reference MMU or a derivative) and, possibly an I/O cache.

A central issue in I/O adapter design is I/O consistency, i.e., ensuring that both I/O and processors do not obtain stale data. I/O consistency must be handled by software cache flushing in Level 1 MBus systems, as there is no Invalidate transaction for Level-1 MBus. For Level-2 systems, data consistency can be handled completely by hardware, or by a combination of hardware and software, depending on the sophistication of the I/O adapter MBus master interface. Complete hardware handling of data consistency can be accomplished in several ways, depending on the performance and complexity goals. The highest performance (and highest complexity) design uses an I/O cache that has control logic and dual directories similar to a Level-2 processor module. A simpler design does not use dual directories and implements consistency by using locked read modify write sequences for DMA write transfers with SIZE other than 32-bytes. This design provides efficient cache consistent transfer for 32-byte DMA transactions and less efficient cache consistent transfer for DMA transactions of less than 32-bytes.

The MBus I/O adapter slave port will generally turn MBus transactions into equivalent I/O bus transactions. A typical I/O bus might be VMEbus or SBus. I/O adapter slave ports will probably issue R&R acknowledgments to deal with slow devices and "deadlocks," and so will need the circuitry to handle R&R time-out and ID capture. I/O adapter slave ports will also probably need to observe the LOCK bit on MAD in conjunction with MBB/, and forward a LOCK indication to the "other" bus interface. MBus I/O adapter slave ports may also choose to buffer MBus write transactions (i.e., return an immediate acknowledgment to the MBus master before completing the write transaction). If they do, it is desirable that there be a means to turn off this feature and also a means to flush the write buffers.

Reflective Memory Support

Reflective Memory operations, where memory is updated with the new data that appears on MBus during Coherent Read transactions that assert MIH/ are permitted but not required. It is recommended that caches have the ability to perform their part of Reflective transactions as an option that can be enabled when they are installed in a system where the memory supports this feature. (This implies the ability of the cache asserting MIH/ during a Coherent Read transaction to ensure the cache line be marked as clean after it has supplied the data, because memory will be updated with the most recently modified data). Memory controllers, by observing MIH/ and waiting for the subsequent data, can obtain the most recent data and can update memory. The memory controller design will probably need a queue, and the system designer should ensure that this queue can never overflow. That is, the maximum rate at which reflected data is delivered to memory should not exceed the memory system's ability to absorb it. MBus has no mechanism for memory to control the arrival rate of data transactions when caches are supplying the data.

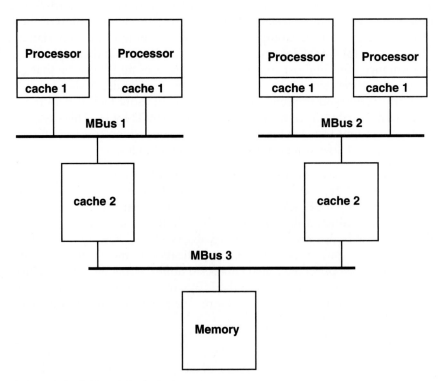

Figure A-17 Generic Multi-Level Cache System

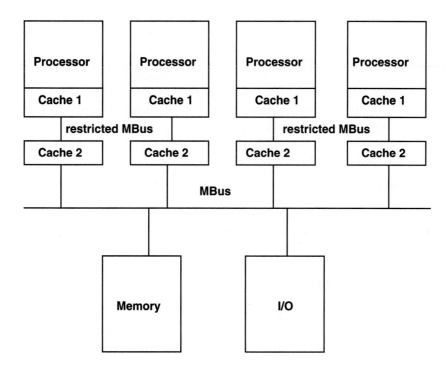

Figure A-18 Simple Second-Level Cache System

Second-Level Cache Issues

Second-level caches are implicitly supported by MBus transactions. There are several kinds of systems with second-level caches envisaged using MBus. The most generic system uses the Level-2 protocols and can support several CPU modules at the first level sharing a common second level cache as shown in Figure A-17. This requires a complex second level cache which has two competing ports and must resolve deadlock situations. There are several complexities that these designs must deal with. R&R on Write (write-back) and R&R on Coherent Invalidate both produce a similar problem, in that a temporary state is created where there is no "owner." Memory is assumed the default owner, which causes a failure of consistency. A uniform solution is for interfaces that issue R&R on Coherent transactions to assume temporary ownership of the line until the R&R is resolved. This circuitry would detect accesses to the line the R&R was outstanding against, and "relinquish and retry" those accesses. Another problem concerns Coherent Read and Invalidate. Should a Coherent Read and Invalidate transaction result in MIH/ being asserted from a cache on the same bus, the second-level cache must capture the Coherent Invalidate in a queue and forward it to other caches when appropriate.

A simpler use of second-level caches has one processor per second-level cache and does not use the complete Level-2 protocol. This type of system is shown in Figure A-18. It requires MBus CPU modules that can support a "write-through" cache mode and accept an Invalidate transaction. With this level of support it is possible to ensure that lines that are in the first-level cache are always present in the second-level cache (inclusion), and so all logic associated with coherence will be included at the second-level cache. The Invalidate exceeds Level-1 requirements and the write-through capability is additional to the minimum requirements of Level 2.This design point is useful where the size of the first-level cache is constrained and the system performance would otherwise be limited by the resulting miss rates and a saturated MBus.

Another simple use of a second-level cache is shown in Figure A-19. Because MBus is a circuit-switched bus, its ultimate performance is limited by memory latency. When designing large memory systems, it is difficult to achieve low latency. A solution is to use a large second-level cache in front of memory that essentially acts as a buffer to memory. This allows latencies close to the minimum MBus latency to be achieved.

Timing of MSH/ and MIH/

MBus timing is specified with MSH/ and or MIH/ assertion on A+2, i.e., 2 cycles after MAS/ is received. This assumes a "dual directory" structure where there are a dedicated duplicated set of tags as part of the MBus "snoop" logic, and they operate synchronous to the MBus clock. If it is desired **not** to have a dual directory or there is a need to synchronize from a clock other than the MBus clock, then the A+2 timing need not be met as long as some restrictions apply. The basic restriction is that memory acknowledgments should never occur before MIH/. This restriction limits the minimum latency of MBus memory systems to the MIH/ timing. Systems that wish to accommodate modules with nonstandard MIH/ timing need to guarantee minimum memory latencies relative to these modules via a programmable minimum memory CR or CRI latency mechanism implemented in the memory controller(s).

In general, modules with variable MSH//MIH/ timing will also need to restrict the maximum rate at which Coherent Invalidates might arrive. This is accomplished via a programmable delay on acknowledgments to CI transactions, implemented in the memory controller(s).

Supporting variable timing condenses to a few rules. If you are a cache performing a CR or CRI, then source MIH/ and MSH/ for a single cycle as soon as you can and at the same time. Specify the worst case MIH//MSH/ timing from MAS/ (e.g., A+7) in order that system designers know what minimum read latency to program memory controllers with. If you are a snooping cache (either intervening or nonintervening), then observe MIH//MSH/ in the interval from MAS/+2, to when you observe your first MRDY/. If you are memory, do not issue MRDY/ (or any acknowledgment) to CR and CRI transactions before you can observe MIH/ from the slowest module in a system.

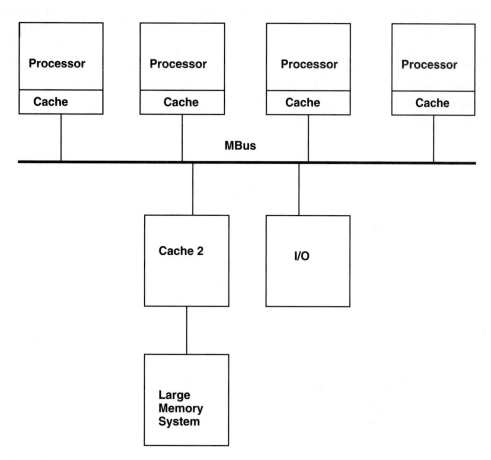

Figure A-19 Simple Second-Level Cache Example 2

Compatibility Issues

A number of compatibility issues are covered in the specification. Here are just a few compatibility issues which might easily be overlooked:

- **Wrapping**—Generally, compatibility on wrapping is an issue between a module and memory or I/O devices. Memory should support wrapped requests and this resolves most compatibility issues. An exception is Level-2 processor modules that do not issue wrapped requests and do not wish to deliver data to wrapped Coherent Read transactions when they assert MIH/. Modules that issue wrapped Coherent Read transactions will clearly not mix in a system with modules of this nature.

A

- **MSH/ and MIH/ timing**—For modules that generate MIH/ and MSH/ on other than A+2, memory must have a minimum latency greater than or equal to the MIH/ and MSH/ timing. Modules with A+2 timing should mix with modules with variable timing.

- **Virtual Address bits in MAD**—Modules that do not generate the Virtual Address "super-set" bits on Coherent transactions cannot mix with modules that use direct mapped virtual addressed caches.

MBus Module Design Guide   B

Introduction

Purpose

The purpose of this document is to convey the necessary information needed to build an MBus module that will work at 40 MHz in MBus-based system products.

Scope

This document attempts to describe some significant aspects of designing 40 MHz MBus modules. Items include:

- PCB construction and routing

- Mechanical specifications and connector pin-out

- Skew management for clocks

- Timing specifications and their derivation for an MBus chip

- Testability and scan

Where possible, recommendations are made that allow the designer to construct a module without engaging in time-consuming analysis of an implementation. In some cases, however, this will not be possible, particularly if a new chip is being used to drive the MBus that has not been already analyzed. In those cases, procedures are defined and examples given that try to walk the designer through what for many may be unfamiliar problems.

If a new module design uses one of the chips currently available (such as MBus interface chips used in MP systems from Sun Microsystems) or the same driver and package of one of the chips, significant analysis detailed in this document can be leveraged. What is meant by "the same driver" is the same vendor, same process technology, and same cell design. The dc specification of 8 mA is not sufficient, for example, to ensure that timing requirements will be met.

B

The MBus Interface specification allows MBus modules from different vendors to be plugged into various platforms from Sun Microsystems, creating a wide range of SPARC-based workstation processors with the shortest possible development cycles. The following subsections comprise a list of design references, MBus modules, and platforms so that electrical and mechanical compatibility can be attained to maximize the field-upgrade possibilities.

Reference Documents

It is recommended that the following reference documents be available as design aides:

- *MBus Interface Specification* (See Appendix A of this book)

- *IEEE P1149.1/Dxx JTAG Standard*

- *HSPICE™ User's Manual*; Meta-Software, Inc. Campbell Ca.

MBus Modules

- Cypress/Ross CYM6002—40 MHz Level-2 MBus, dual processor module, 2x (601 IU, 602 FPU, 605 CMU, and 2 16 K x 16 SRAMs)

- Texas Instruments SuperSPARC™—40 MHz Level 2 MBus, single Texas Instruments IU/FPU

- Texas Instruments SuperSPARC™ with external cache—40 MHz Level-2 MBus, 50 MHz single Texas Instruments IU/FPU with MXCC cache controller and 8x 128 K x 9 SRAMs

MBus Platforms

SPARCstation™ 10 Multiprocessor System accepts one or two MBus modules, system expansion through S Bus.

600MP Multiprocessor System-accepts one or two MBus modules, system I/O expansion through SBus, and VMEbus (one SBus slot is lost if an MBus module is placed in the second module position).

Electrical Specifications

This section deals with the analysis of the three classes of signals that comprise the MBus as implemented on Sun Microsystems MBus-based products; see Figure B-1 for signal grouping and Figure B-2 for the timing specifications. The timing requirements for the remainder of the signals are considerably looser, see Figure B-3, and hence do not need such analysis.

SIGNAL CLASS	SIGNAL
BUSSED CONTROL	MAS, MRDY, MRTY, MERR, MBB, MSH, MIH
POINT TO POINT CONTROL	MBR[3:0], MBG[3:0]
MAD	MAD[63:0]

Figure B-1   MBus Signal

The timing specifications found in Figure B-2 detail the requirements a chip must conform to if it is to be able to communicate over the MBus. For chips to be MBus-compliant, chip vendors must have performed the SPICE analysis on the reference load and complied with these numbers. Supplement B1 describes the process which should be used to generate the MBus propagation delay for each of the signal classes in order to guarantee compliance with MBus requirements.

It should be noted that the specifications listed in Figure B-2 are intended to be used along with the MBus system SPICE model in the design of the MBus interface portion of a chip/module. The specification is not to be used as a tester timing criterion. The differences in the loading would produce erroneous results.

Tester specifications are generated by constructing a SPICE model of the chip/module that meets the design timing specifications, as detailed in this section, and then simulating the resultant model against the tester load. Care must be taken to model accurately the topology between the chip/module-under-test and the tester electronics. Alternatively, empirical methods can be used to generate tester timing specifications.

Clocks

The clocks provided to the module by the system will have the characteristics detailed in the "MBus Interface Specification", Figures A-14, and A-15 (see Appendix A of this book). It should be noted, however, that these specifications can only be guaranteed if the module conforms to the guidelines for PCB construction and routing as defined in this document.

MBus Chip Timing Specifications

The timing values listed in Figure B-2 correspond to a 40 MHz MBus system with a TOTAL clock skew of less than or equal to 1.5 ns across all MBus devices. That is, the difference between the arrival time of the earliest and latest clocks (measured at 1.5V) on the MBus will at most be 1.5 nsec. The timing listed in Figure B-2 is for the MAD and control signals. The balance of the signals on the bus are specified in Figure B-3.

B

Timing Assumptions

Thresholds:

Inside the chip

The threshold point used to evaluate timing inside an ASIC will vary from vendor to vendor. Consult with the one you are working with to establish the MBus driver input threshold point.

Outside the chip (system-level)

All MBus levels are TTL and should be measured as follows: Low=.8V; High=2.0V. For the clocks, however, 1.5V should be used as the threshold for the purposes of making timing measurements and calculations.

OUTPUTS		
Signal	**SPEC**	**Load**
bused control		
tcod max	17.5	System-max
tcoh min	2.5	System-min
MAD		
tmod max	18.5	System-max
tmoh min	2.5	System-min
point to point control		
tpod max	14.5	System-max
tpoh min	2.5	System-min
INPUTS		
Signal	**SPEC**	
bused control		
tcis max	6.0	
tcih max	1.0	
MAD		
tmis max	5.0	
tmih max	1.0	
point to point control		
tpis max	9.0	
tpih max	1.0	
NOTE: All times in nano-seconds		

Figure B-2   MBus Chip Design Specifications: MAD and CNTRL

Multiprocessor System Architectures

OUTPUTS		
Signal	**SPEC**	**Comments**
Asynchronous		
MOD_IRQ,AERR	75	MIN time output Must be stable
SCAN (SCAN DI, SCAN DO, SCAN TMS1, SCAN TMS2)		
Clk to output max	25.0	Measured Relative to SCAN CLK
Clk to output min	2.5	Measured Relative to SCAN CLK
INPUTS		
Signal	**SPEC**	Comments
Asynchronous		
IRL[3:0]	75	The sample interval for these signals must not be any longer than this
MRST max	340	
SCAN		
tmis max	20.0	Measured Relative to SCAN CLK
tmih max	1.0	Measured Relative to SCAN CLK
NOTE: 1)All times in nano-seconds 2) MID[3:1] are static, therefore, no timing is specified.		

Figure B-3   MBus Chip Design Spec: MISC signals

Models and simulation conditions:

The models used in generating the specification were constructed to allow the following parameters to be varied:

- Printed Circuit Board impedance (45 - 71 ohms; see Supplement B1)

- IC package signal capacitance

- Effective inductance of the power paths due to the MBus output drivers switching simultaneously (see Supplement B1)

- Junction temperature (0 - 105 Deg. C)

- Power supply (5 V +/- 5%)

- Via and component hole capacitance

This allows a view of the circuits' behavior at the extremes addressed by worst case commercial design practice. The extremes modeled here were derived to facilitate the evaluation of clock-to-out delay and clock-to-out hold times for each of the three signal classes.

DC Specifications:

The following assumptions are used for dc drive capability of the drivers for each of the signal cases.

Table B-1   DC Drive Assumptions

SIGNAL	LEAKAGE (max) microamp	DC DRIVE (min) milliamp
MAD	14	1
Bused Control	50	1;8(MSH): 2.5(AERR)
Point-to-Point	50	1
All Others	50	1

Miscellaneous Timing Issues

Reset

All bused control signals are to be tri-stated asynchronously when reset is asserted (see Figure B-4). Furthermore, the system ensures that all bused control signals will be driven high while reset is asserted and for three clocks after RSTIN has been de-asserted. Therefore, all modules must not drive any of the shared control signals during a power-up cycle. This does not include request/grant lines, which are not shared.

There are several sources of reset in an MBus-based system. This section will touch on the relevant aspects that may be of concern to MBus module designers. These are Power-on Reset (POR), Software Reset (SWR), Reset Switch (RSTSW), and for the 600MP Systems (see Chapter 9), VME Reset IN (jumper selectable; used only when the board is not the VME slot-1 master). In addition, each module may detect a Watchdog Reset if it experiences an error condition, which is a trap with traps disabled. This condition resets only the one processor and generates a broadcast level-15 interrupt to the system. Each module may also receive a local software reset (SI) through that processor's control register; this facility is for diagnostic purposes only. Local software reset through the module control register will disable snooping for a long period of time, so it is not allowed during normal MP operations.

When a processor is reset, it needs to determine the source of the reset; the hierarchy it should search is local-watchdog, local SI, SWR, RSTSW, POR.

A reset is intended to put the processor or system into a known state. In order to allow for some robustness in bringing up the system, no state is reset in hardware unless it is absolutely necessary in order to ensure controllability. The contents of processor general registers, caches, tags, TLBs, and main memory are unaffected by RESET. All I/O devices and state machines will be reset; it is not possible to reset part of the system and leave the rest untouched.

A reset switch is provided on-board for bringing up the system. This switch generates the equivalent of a power-on reset, with cache and memory contents preserved. The switch is not user accessible. A reset initiated with the switch will leave status in the system control and status register.

Device, Bus, or Bit	State after POR or SWR or RSTSW	State after Watchdog
Caches	disabled	unchanged
Module MMUs	disabled	unchanged
"Dual" bit (cache snooping)	off	unchanged
Book-mode bit (1 = boot mode, 0 = translate)	1	1
SI bit	0	0
Module write buffers	empty	drain normal
Watchdog Bit	0	1

Figure B-4   Reset State

Generating MBus Chip-level Timing Specifications

This section contains sample calculations for a hypothetical MBus chip. These are provided to illustrate how the MBus chip timing is to be derived in order to verify compliance with the specification.

The method to be used combines simulations of the internal chip delays with HSPICE simulations of the output driver driving the appropriate reference model of the system and module. More specifically, HSPICE simulations modeling the heaviest load (drvd, driver delay) and the lightest load (drvh, driver hold) will be run for each of the three signal classes. Note that in the most heavily loaded cases there can be up to 4 bus masters in the model. Hence, to comprehensively model the system each bus master in turn driving the bus must be simulated. The worst performer of the bunch defines the driver delay for that signal class (see Figure B-5). The MBus propagation delay is then added to the simulated delay from the clock input of the die to the output signal be analyzed arriving at the INPUT to the output driver (see Figure B-6).

The MBus driver propagation delay (txdrvd, where x can be c, m, or p) extracted from the HSPICE output (see Figure B-5) is the propagation delay from the input of the MBus driver (Figure B-6 label A) to the signal being stable at every receiver, (Figure B-6 label B). Likewise the MBus driver hold time (txdrvh) is the time it takes the voltage at any receiver to leave its current logic level (output hold).

The simulation for this sample chip involved driving a lossy transmission line model of the system model with hypothetical but representative HSPICE driver models.

Note – All timing values are relative to the signals arriving at the DIE of the receiver.

OUTPUTS		
SIGNAL	OUTPUT DELAY	LOAD
bused control		
tcdrvd	10.7	Max
tcdrvh	1.7	Min
MAD		
tmdrvd	11.9	Max
tmdrvh	1.9	Min
point to point control		
tpdrvd	6.5	Max
tpdrvh	2.5	Min
NOTE: All times in nanoseconds		

Figure B-5   Sample MBus Propagation Delay Times

Clock to Output Delay

This is the time from the arrival of a rising edge (1.5V) on the clock at the die of the sourcing part until all receivers have reached the new logic level. The conditions listed in Figure B-8 represent the worst case conditions for determining clock-to-output delay.

When determining the MBus delay from HSPICE simulations, the value to use is the difference between the time the input to the MBus driver passes through threshold and the latest time that the signal at the die of any of the receivers (if the driving part listens to its own line, then the driver is also a receiver) passes through threshold and stays there.

Source@ slow process(WNWP), Temp=105°C, Vdd=4.75V

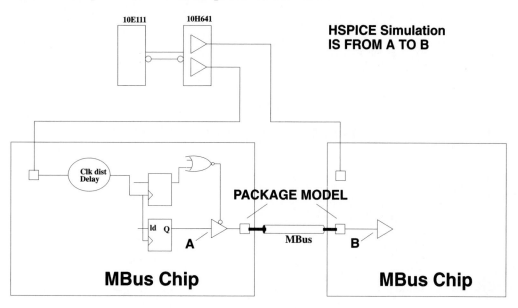

Figure B-6   MBus Clock-to-output Delay Circuit

Bused Control: MAS

$$\frac{\text{CK to Q}}{\text{Delay}} = \left[\left(2.5, \begin{smallmatrix}\text{On-chip clk}\\\text{distribution}\\\text{delay}\end{smallmatrix} \right) + \left(1.5, \begin{smallmatrix}\text{Clk to Q}\\\text{Flip-Flop}\end{smallmatrix} \right) + \left(1.0, \begin{smallmatrix}\text{NOR}\\\text{delay}\end{smallmatrix} \right) + \left(11.0, \begin{smallmatrix}\text{MBus prop}\\\text{delay}\end{smallmatrix} \right) \right]$$

$$\frac{\text{CK to Q}}{\text{Delay}} = 16.0 \text{ ns}$$

MAD: MAD60

$$\begin{array}{l}\text{CK to Q}\\ \text{Delay}\end{array} = \Big[\,(\,2.5,\ \substack{\text{On-chip clk}\\ \text{distribution}\\ \text{delay}})+(\,1.5,\ \substack{\text{Clk to Q}\\ \text{Flip-Flop}})+(\,1.0,\ \substack{\text{NOR}\\ \text{delay}})+(\,11.9,\ \substack{\text{MBus prop}\\ \text{delay}})\Big]$$

$$\begin{array}{l}\text{CK to Q}\\ \text{Delay}\end{array} = 16.9\ \text{ns}$$

Point to Point Control: MBG1

$$\begin{array}{l}\text{CK to Q}\\ \text{Delay}\end{array} = \Big[\,(\,2.5,\ \substack{\text{On-chip clk}\\ \text{distribution}\\ \text{delay}})+(\,1.5,\ \substack{\text{Clk to Q}\\ \text{Flip-Flop}})+(\,11.0,\ \substack{\text{MBus prop}\\ \text{delay}})\Big]$$

$$\begin{array}{l}\text{CK to Q}\\ \text{Delay}\end{array} = 10.5\ \text{ns}$$

Clock-to-Output Hold

This is the time from the arrival of a rising edge (1.5V) on the clock at the die of the sourcing part until the first receiver has left its current logic level. The conditions listed in Figure B-8 represent the conditions for determining clock-to-output hold time (see Figure B-7).

When determining the MBus delay from HSPICE simulations, the value to use is the difference between the time the input to the MBus driver passes through threshold and the earliest time that *any* of the receivers (if the driving part listens to its own line, then the driver is also a receiver) leaves the current logic level.

NOTE: The receiver logic and clock distribution delay are to be calculated as follows:

(2.17 ns internal delay nom) x (1.5 slow process multiplier) x (.9 0 C multiplier) x (.94 high voltage multiplier) = 2.76 ns.

Source@ fast process(SNSP), Temp= 0 °C, Vdd= 5.25 V

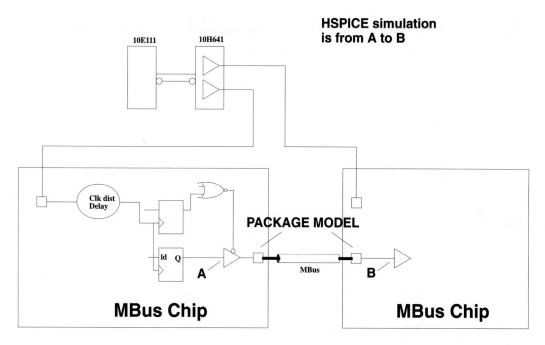

Figure B-7   MBus hold circuits

Bused Control: MBB

CK to Q
Delay $= \left[(0.7, \begin{smallmatrix}\text{On-chip clk}\\\text{distribution}\\\text{delay}\end{smallmatrix}) + (0.5, \begin{smallmatrix}\text{Clk to Q}\\\text{Flip-Flop}\end{smallmatrix}) + (0.25, \begin{smallmatrix}\text{NOR}\\\text{delay}\end{smallmatrix}) + (1.7, \begin{smallmatrix}\text{MBus prop}\\\text{delay}\end{smallmatrix}) \right]$

CK to Q
Delay $= $ **3.15 ns**

MAD: MAD34

CK to Q
Delay $= \left[(0.7, \begin{smallmatrix}\text{On-chip clk}\\\text{distribution}\\\text{delay}\end{smallmatrix}) + (0.5, \begin{smallmatrix}\text{Clk to Q}\\\text{Flip-Flop}\end{smallmatrix}) + (0.25, \begin{smallmatrix}\text{NOR}\\\text{delay}\end{smallmatrix}) + (1.9, \begin{smallmatrix}\text{MBus prop}\\\text{delay}\end{smallmatrix}) \right]$

CK to Q
Delay $= $ **3.35 ns**

POINT TO POINT CONTROL; MBG3

$$\text{CK to Q Delay} = \left[\,(0.7,\ \text{On-chip clk distribution delay}) + (0.5,\ \text{Clk to Q Flip-Flop}) + (2.5,\ \text{MBus prop delay})\,\right]$$

$$\text{CK to Q Delay} = 3.7\ \text{ns}$$

Note – Note: On some modules, the reset line is bidirectional. This section has only described the reset signal as an input to a module.

CONDITIONS	System MAX.	System MIN.
Trace		
MAD:	MAD60	MAD34
bused control:	MAS	MBB
POINT to POINT CONTROL:	MBR0	MBR3
Number of MBus drivers switching simultaneously	68	1
Printed Circuit Board impedance		
inner layers	45 ohms	71 ohms
outer layers	40 ohms	77 ohms
Via capacitance	1.0pF	0.1pF
Capacitance for component holes	1.0pF	0.75pF
Capacitance of IC package	See Supplement B2	
Junction temp	105 Deg C	0 Deg C
Process model	Slow N,P	Fast N,P
Power supply voltage	4.75 volt	5.25 volt
NOTE: The worst case temp shown above will depend on the power dissipation of your IC and the thermal impedance of its package.		

Figure B-8   Simulation Conditions

Mechanical Specifications

The mechanical specifications consists of the connector and its associated pin-out. Mechanical drawings for the module printed wiring boards are provided in Supplement B6.

MBus Connector

The MBus Module concept of field-upgradeable performance requires a connector with high reliability, ease of installation, and a foolproof keying scheme. The aggressive MBus cycle time goal of 25 ns requires a connector with excellent electrical performance, i.e., transmission line characteristics with low capacitance and inductance. Based on the above requirements, the "Microstrip" style connector (AMP part number 121354-4 and Fujitsu part number FCN-264P100-G/C) are recommended.

 Caution – Make sure that the system the module is being designed for provides standoffs on either side of the connector. This is required to help prevent breakage of the connector if by accident the module is "over rotated" while "walking" the module out. That is to say, if one end of the connector stays mated while the other is de-mated, it is very likely that the end of the connector that stays mated will break once the module has swung up by 30 - 40 degrees.

MBus Connector Pin Assignments

For a description of the signals listed in Figure B- 9 refer to the SPARC MBus Interface Specification (see Appendix A). It should be noted that the signals provided at the connector are sufficient to support two processors per module. Therefore, two sets of bus request, bus grant, and interrupt lines are provided. Also, provision has been made for four identical clock lines to allow modules with many clock loads.

The following five signals provide the scan hooks for debug, fault diagnosis, and fault isolation. These are detailed in "Testability Issues".

The SCAN signals are: SCAN DI, SCAN DO, SCAN CLK, SCAN TMS1, SCAN TMS2.

1.	SCAN DI	Blade	12	SCAN TMS1
3.	SCAN DO		4	SCANTMS2
5.	SCAN CLK	GND	6	MIRL0[1]
7.	MIRL0[0]		8	MIRL0[3]
9.	MIRL0[2]	GND	10	INT-OUT/

Figure B-9   MBus Pin-out

11.	MAD[0]		12	MAD[1]
13.	MAD[2]	GND	14.	MAD[3]
15.	MAD[4]		16.	MAD[5]
17.	MAD[6].	GND	18.	MAD[7]
19.	MAD[8]		20.	MAD[9]
21.	MAD[10]	Blade2	22.	MAD[11]
23.	MAD[12]		24.	MAD[13]
25.	MAD[14]	+5V	26.	MAD[15]
27.	MAD[16]		28.	MAD[17]
29.	MAD[18]	+5V	30.	MAD[19]
31.	MAD[20]		32.	MAD[21]
33.	MAD[22]	+5V	34.	MAD[23]
35.	MAD[24]		36.	MAD[25]
37.	MAD[26]	+5V	38.	MAD[27]
39.	MAD[28]			MAD[29]
41.	MAD[30]	Blade3	42.	MAD[31]
43.	MBR[0]/		44.	MSH/
45.	MBG[0]/	GND	46.	MIH/
47.	MCLK0		48.	MRTY/
49.	MCLK1	GND	50.	MRDY/
51.	MCLK2		52.	MERR/
53.	MCLK3	GND	54.	MAS/
55.	MBR[1]/		56.	MBB/
57.	MBG[1]/	GND	58.	SPARE1
59.	MAD[32]		60.	MAD[33]
61.	MAD[34]	Blade4	62.	MAD[35]
63.	MAD[36]		64.	MAD[37]
65.	MAD[38]	+5V	66.	MAD[39]
67.	MAD[40]		68.	MAD[41]
69.	MAD[42]	+5V	70.	MAD[43]
71.	MAD[44]		72.	MAD[45]
73.	MAD[46]	+5V	74.	MAD[47]
75.	MAD[48]		76.	MAD[49]
77.	MAD[50]	+5V	78.	MAD[51]

Figure B-9   MBus Pin-out   (Continued)

79.	MAD[52]		80.	MAD[53]
81.	MAD[54]	Blade5	82.	MAD[55]
83.	MAD[56]		84.	MAD[57]
85.	MAD[58]	GND	86.	MAD[59]
87.	MAD[60]		88.	MAD[61]
89.	MAD[62]	GND	90.	MAD[63]
91.	SPARE2		92.	MIRL1[0]
93.	MIRL1[1]	GND	94.	MIRL1[2]
95.	MIRL1[3]		96.	AERR/
97.	MRST/	GND	98.	MID[1]
99.	MID[2]		100.	MID[3]

Figure B-9   MBus Pin-out   (Continued)

PCB Board Construction and Routing

PCB Construction

Power and ground planes must be used in order to provide as low an impedance path for ground and power as possible. Figure B-10 details a recommended board stack up and the dielectric thickness for each of the layers. The resulting fab must have an impedance of 57 ohms +/- 20 %.

One of the hazards of using a high density connector with the power and ground pins enclosed by the signal pins is that the power and ground planes surrounding the power pins are significantly perforated. It is, therefore, strongly recommended that multiple power and ground planes be used to insure good quality power supplies to the module. Furthermore, the antipads used on the power and ground planes at the MBus connector must be kept to the absolute minimum size (58 mils, for example). This minimizes the amount of inductance in the power supply and return paths.

Supplement B contains a mechanical drawing specification. Two of the specified holes—referenced by note 3—require plating. These holes must be 170R_150D plated holes. In addition, 0.32 x 0.28 inch rectangular copper shapes must be provided (for chassis ground connections to reduce electromagnetic interference) over the mounting holes on top and bottom layers, located 20 mils from edges of the module. The shapes must be totally cleared on solder mask. The shapes must be capacitively connected to logic ground via 220 pF capacitor. One 220 pF capacitor per mounting hole. The trace connections from the capacitors must be 50 mils thick and kept to a minimum length. See Supplement B6 for details.

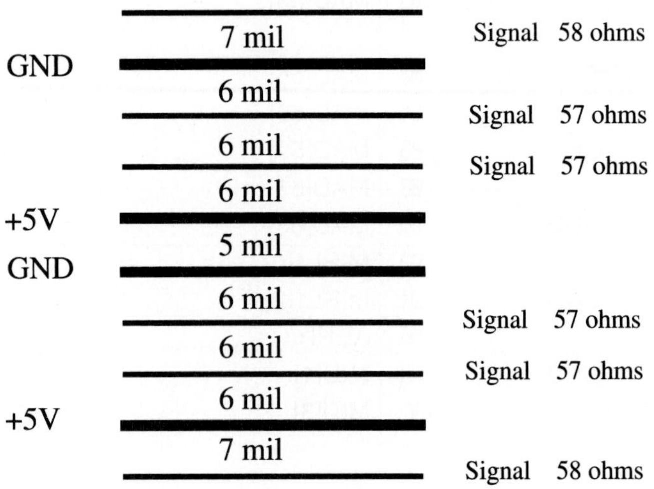

GND	7 mil	Signal	58 ohms
	6 mil	Signal	57 ohms
	6 mil	Signal	57 ohms
	6 mil		
+5V	5 mil		
GND	6 mil	Signal	57 ohms
	6 mil	Signal	57 ohms
	6 mil		
+5V	7 mil	Signal	58 ohms

NOTES:
1) All inner layers are 1oz outer are 1/2oz plated up to 1.5oz
2) Board thickness must be 0.062 +/- 0.008 inches
3) Signal ohms are +/- 20%

Figure B-10 Board Stackup

SPICE Model

The model used here for the printed circuit board is the U element introduced in versions of HSPICE labeled 9007, or later; see the HSPICE manual for more details. For reference, a discrete RLC model is provided in Figure B-11. See Supplement B2 for further details.

NOTE: ALL dimensions are in mils

1) Microstrip

Er = 4.1 - 5.2
d = 7 +/-1.5
t = 1.7 +/-.5
w = 7 +/-1

Micro strip parameters:
Nom Zo=57.97, Co=2.49 pF/in, Lo=8.37 nH, Tpd=0.14 nS/in
Min Zo=40.39, Co=3.72 pF/in, Lo=6.07 nH/in, Tpd=0.15 nS/in
Max Zo=77.19, Co=1.78 pF/in, Lo=10.58 nH/in Tpd=0.14 nS/in

2) Dual stripline

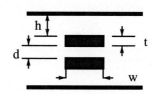

Er = 4.1 - 5.2
h = 6 +/-1
d = 6 +/-1.5
t = 1.3 +/-.1
w = 6 +/-1

Dual stripline parameters:
Nom Zo=57.46, Co=3.20 pF/in, Lo=10.56 nH, Tpd=0.18 nS/in
Min Zo=45.28, Co=4.27 pF/in, Lo=8.75 nH/in, Tpd=0.19 nS/in
Max Zo=71.49, Co=2.40 pF/in, Lo=12.27 nH/in Tpd=0.17 nS/in

$$Reff = Length * Resistivity / n$$
$$Ceff = Length * Cap / n$$
$$Leff = Length * Inductance / n$$

MAX LOADING	MIN LOADING
er = 5.2	er = 4.1
Resistivity = .097 W/in	Resistivity = .097 W/in
Zo min = 45.28 W	Zo min = 71.49 W
Cap = 4.27 pF/in	Cap = 2.40 pF/in
Inductance = 8.75 nH/ **in**	Inductance = 12.27 nH/ **in**

Figure B-11 RLC PCB Model

B

Routing

Clock Distribution

An essential requirement for the MBus to run at 40MHz is that system clock skew be kept to as small a value as is practical. This is primarily a result of a lack of available circuitry to control clock skew at the ASIC level. Therefore, each clock line that is used must have a load of 25 pF +/- 10% at the end of the line. Figure B-12 shows a clock line that has the maximum number of chips on it, clock 0, and one that has a single receiver, clock 3. Note that clock 3 has load balancing capacitors on it to minimize the variation in capacitive load from one clock to another. As can be seen, 4 clocks are provided to the module. If fewer than 4 clocks are required, simply do not hook up those not needed.

The following considerations should be adhered to:

- All loads must be equidistant from source.

- Clocks shall be routed on inner layers with an impedance of 57 ohms, tolerance +/- 20%

- Clocks shall be routed, from the MBus connector, as a star with 3 branches at the end of a 2.8 inch trace. The length of the branches shall be 1.7 inches each. The diode (HSMS-2822) termination shall be 0.7 inches past the IC (see Figure B-12).

- All clock lines used on the module must have the same number of vias, not to exceed 9 (2 between connector and hub of star, 1 at hub of star, 2 on each of the 3 branches).

- Load on each clock line used = 25 pF, tolerance +/- 10%

Note – This includes via capacitance (0.4 pF per via) and does not include the capacitance of the trace itself.

It is *strongly* recommended that the circuit description of the MBus module clock trace, pictured in Figure B-12, be adhered to. If that is not possible, an analysis *must* be done to insure that the resulting skew across *all* receivers (remember your module will be communicating with other modules as well) of the MBus clocks is less than or equal to 1.5 ns.

It should also be noted that the test clock, pin 5, is expected to be routed in a similar fashion. That is, if it goes to multiple loads on the module, it must be routed as a star and diode (HSMS 2822) terminated. However, load balancing capacitors are not required as the timing requirements are considerably looser. It is highly recommended that chips using this clock receive it with inputs having hysteresis.

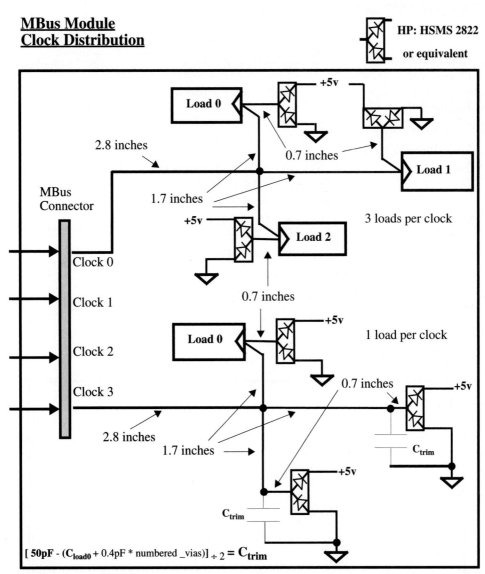

**MBus Module
Clock Distribution**

HP: HSMS 2822

or equivalent

$$[\ 50pF - (C_{load0} + 0.4pF * numbered\_vias)]\div 2 = C_{trim}$$

NOTE: Total load of devices (chip loads + trimming caps) at the end of each clock signal shall be 25 pF +/- 10%. Capacitance values are +/- 0.5 pF (C < 10 pF).

Figure B-12 Clock Topology and Termination

Routing of the MBus (Memory/address and Control)

These are guidelines to use in constructing your module. You may choose or need to vary from these based upon the results of your SPICE analysis of the MBus timing.

1. All modules with more than 1 load on the MBus signals must be routed with a star topology to minimize troublesome reflections (stubs must start at the connector pin, see Figure B-13).

2. Stub lengths shall be as follows:

   a. For a dual master module:

Control lines:	TOTAL STUB LENGTH (both stubs added together) NOT TO EXCEED 3.4 in. For a single stub: max stub length = 2.0 in.
Mad lines:	TOTAL STUB LENGTH (both stubs added together) NOT TO EXCEED 5.0 in. For a single stub: max stub length = 3.0 in.

   b. For a single master module:

   Control lines: max stub length = 2.0 in.
   Mad lines: max stub length = 3.0 in.

   c. For any module:

   Min line length: 0.7in.

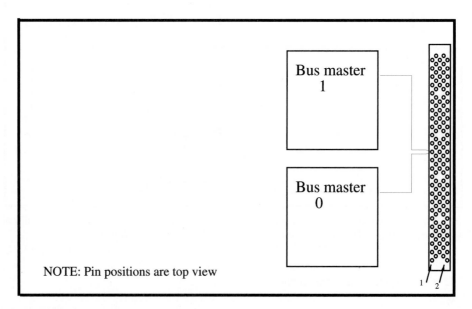

Figure B-13 Dual Master Module (Top View)

Power and Environment Considerations

Power

MBus modules must conform to the following power supply specifications per slot. It should be noted here that the max current specifications reflect the capabilities of the connector and the PCB into which it is mounted, which may in fact exceed the heat handling capacity of some systems. Care should be taken when designing modules that they do not exceed the thermal power budget of the target system.

Table B-2   Power Requirements

PARAMETER	CONDITIONS	SYMBOL	MIN	MAX	UNITS
Supply Voltage	Icc=10A, T=70 °C	+5V	4.75	5.25	V
Ripple +5V	Icc=10A, T=70 °C	Vr5	-0.1	0.1	V
dc current	+5V=5.0, T=70 °C	Icont5		10.0	A
Peak current	+5V=5.0, T=70 °C Tpeak=1 ms	Icont5		15.0	A

Heat Removal

An air flow rate of 300 linear feet per minute should be provided over components on the top and bottom sides.

Environmental

The following environmental restrictions for an operating MBus module apply:

• Ambient air temperature to be within the range of 0 to 50 degrees C

• Humidity not to exceed 85%, non-condensing.

• Altitude not to exceed 10,000 feet.

Testability Issues

The area around each module component which must be kept clear is defined by the bonding area required, access to test pads, and access for chip removal and replacement. Also, additional area may be required if the routability of the board is not adequate with respect to the density of the chips' I/O pads.

B

A desirable goal for the module design would be to include test circuits capable of locating defective devices. This is typically accomplished with scan test access paths at the module level. The preferred scan methodology for MBus modules is IEEE P1149.1/Dxx (here after referred to as P1149), however some limited support of non P1149 scan control will be provided.

Testability of Interconnects

Bare boards should be tested for opens, shorts, bad vias, and so forth.

MBus SCAN Pin Definitions

SCAN SIGNALS:

SCAN DI
This signal corresponds to the signal TDI as described in P1149. It is an input to the module and is used for receiving scan data from the system. This is the input of the scan ring and should not be inverted or gated. This signal changes on the falling edge of SCAN_CLK and should be sampled on the rising edge of SCAN_CLK.

SCAN DO
This signal corresponds to the signal TDO as described in P1149. It is an output of the module and is used for sending the scan data to the system. This is the output of the scan ring and should not be inverted or gated. SCAN DO should be driven on the falling edge of SCAN_CLK and will be sampled on the rising edge of SCAN_CLK.

SCAN CLK
This signal is used to supply the clock to the scan ring on the module, typically 5 MHz.

SCAN CLK could be operational in some MBus systems during normal chip operation, in addition to SCAN testing operations. Therefore, when designing MBus interface chips or modules, it is suggested that noise coupling analysis be done with regard to SCAN CLK switching.

SCAN TMS1
This signal is an input to the module. It is used to control the TAP controller state machine. It corresponds to the TMS signal as described in P1149.

SCAN TMS2
This signal is an input to the module. It is used to reset the TAP controller state machine. It corresponds to the TRST signal as described in P1149.

Supplement B1 - Evaluation of MBus Propagation Delay

You will be simulating the delay from the input of the MBus driver to the pad of the receiving ASIC where the signal arrives. If the value is within the limits calculated for setup and hold, then your module should work across the expected variations in temperature, process, and voltage.

This procedure assumes the user has access to a UNIX-based machine running HSPICE version 8907c or later.

A brief summary of the procedure is as follows:

1. Creation Of Pcb Model For Module

2. Creation Of Package Model For Ic

3. Creation Of Driver Subcircuit File

4. Update Path In `In.lib` Statement

5. Edit Pcb Parameters (see Supplements B2 and B3)

6. Run Hspice

7. Evaluate Results

The files needed/provided are as follows; collectively, they make up the target MBus system SPICE model. The names shown are for illustrative purposes only; for example, MAD34 may not be the lightest load MAD signal in the target system (see Figure B-8 for details).

1. **mad34**: The model used for the analysis of hold time for the MAD signals. This model represents the lightest load a MAD signal can experience.

2. **mad60busmstr0:** The model used for the analysis of clock-to-output delay time for bus master 0 driving the MAD signals. This model represents the heaviest load a MAD signal can experience.

3. **mad60busmstr1:** The model used for the analysis of clock-to-output delay time for bus master 1 driving the MAD signals. This model represents the heaviest load a MAD signal can experience.

4. **mad60busmstr2:** The model used for the analysis of clock-to-output delay time for bus master 2 driving the MAD signals. This model represents the heaviest load a MAD signal can experience.

5. **mad60busmstr3:** The model used for the analysis of clock-to-output delay time for bus master 3 driving the MAD signals. This model represents the heaviest load a MAD signal can experience.

6. **mbb:** The model used for the analysis of hold time for the bused control signals. This model represents the lightest load a bused control signal can experience.

7. **masbusmstr0:** The model used for the analysis of clock to output delay time for bus master 0 driving the bused control signals. This model represents the heaviest load a bused control signal can experience.

8. **masbusmstr1:** The model used for the analysis of clock to output delay time for bus master 1 driving the bused control signals. This model represents the heaviest load a bused control signal can experience.

9. **masbusmstr2:** The model used for the analysis of clock to output delay time for bus master 2 driving the bused control signals. This model represents the heaviest load a bused control signal can experience.

10. **masbusmstr3:** The model used for the analysis of clock to output delay time for bus master 3 driving the bused control signals. This model represents the heaviest load a bused control signal can experience.

11. **mbr3:** The model used for the analysis of hold time for the point-to-point control signals. This model represents the lightest load a point-to-point control signal can experience.

12. **mbr0:** The model used for the analysis of clock to output delay time for the point-to-point control signals. This model represents the heaviest load a point-to-point control signal can experience.

Creation of Pcb Model for Module

You will need to create six models for the module PCB, one for each of the following signals: 1) mad34, 2) mad60, 3) mbb, 4) mas, 5) mbr3, and 6) mbr1. These are used in the analysis of setup and hold times for control and data lines, see example in Supplement B5.

Creation of Package Model for Ic

Create model for I.C. package, see example in Supplement B4. In each of the 12 files replace the phrase "YOUR IC PACKAGE MODEL GOES HERE," with the name of your driver subcircuit.

Creation of Driver Subcircuit File

If the signal is bidirectional, be sure the model contains a subcircuit for the receiver.

Note – The pulse width statement for node 2 assumes that the tri-state enable for the driver is active low. If this is not the case then that statement needs to corrected.

In each of the 12 files replace the phrase "YOUR DRIVER SUBCIRCUIT GOES HERE," with the name of your driver subcircuit.

Update Path in .LIB STATEMENT

In each of the 12 files replace the phrase "YOUR PATH GOES HERE," with the path name to your transistor library.

Edit PCB Parameters

Edit the U element models for the PCB traces to reflect the characteristics of your module PCB. See the HSPICE manual from Meta-Software and Supplement B2 for formulas. In each of the 12 files replace the phrase "YOUR PCB MODEL GOES HERE," with your model statement.

Run HSPICE

Execute HSPICE for each of the 12 files. See below for an example.

    HSPICE mad34 > plot 1000000

Evaluate Results

You will be simulating the delay from the input of the MBus driver to the pad of the receiving ASIC where the signal arrives. If the value is within the limits calculated for setup and hold, see "Generating MBus Chip-Level Timing Specifications", then your module should work across the expected variations in temperature, process, and voltage.

MBus driver delay; MBus master 0 driving

Rising Edge:

(**34.3,** Last receiver passes thru 2V) - (**25.5,** Rising edge at driver input) = **8.8 ns**

Falling Edge:

(**61.6,** Last receiver passes thru .8V) - (**50.6,** Falling edge at driver input) = **11.0 ns**

B

Supplement B2 - HSPICE Parameters

This section describes the derivation of the parameters to be used for HSPICE simulations of the MBus.

Wherever available, the calculations for the parameters have been shown. If the values are engineering estimates, no calculations have been shown.

The scaling factors for the simulations are specific to the particular simulation configuration. The variables are (a) the driver or drivers being simulated and (b) the number and type of drivers on the chip that can switch simultaneously.

Note also that the mA ratings for the drivers represent its dc capabilities, and actual switching currents are much greater. For the purposes of calculating the scaling factors, it is assumed that the switching currents scale with the dc current capabilities. Hence, an 8 mA driver is assumed to produce twice the switching current of a 4 mA driver.

Equivalent Pin Grid Array Circuit

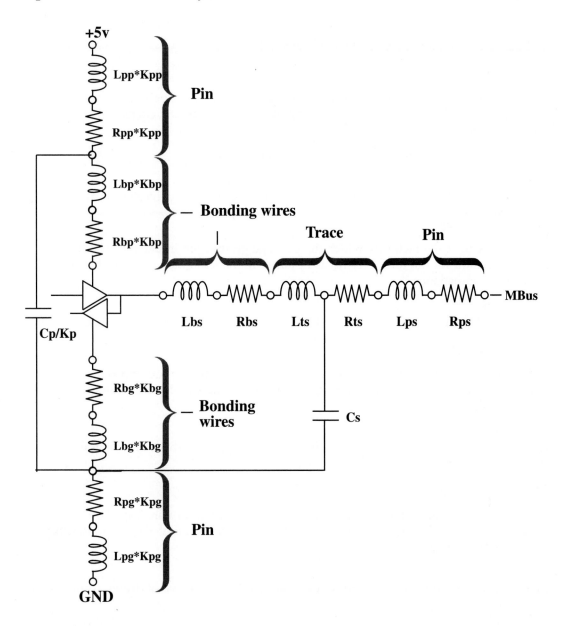

Figure B-14 *Equiv. Circuit for PGA package*

B

Sample Model Parameters

Package

Package: pin count and package type, for example, 223 CPGA

Scaling Factor Kpp

Definition: This is the factor by which the package power pin impedance is scaled in order to account for the total current, as opposed to the simulated current, that flows through the impedance.

Assumption: A 4 mA driver is considered a standard drive

Calculation:
Kpp = (Total current thru VDD pins in std drives / std drive of driver(s) simulated) / Np

Scaling Factor Kpg

Definition: This is the factor by which the package ground pin impedance is scaled in order to account for the total current, as opposed to the simulated current, that flows through the impedance.

Calculation:
Kpg = (Total current thru VSS pins in std drives / std drive of driver(s) simulated) / Ng

Scaling Factor Kbp

Definition: This is the factor by which the package power bond wire impedance is scaled in order to account for the total current, as opposed to the simulated current, that flows through the impedance.

Calculation:
Kbp = (Total current thru VDD bond wires in std drives / std drive of driver(s) simulated) / Npmsi

Scaling Factor Kbg

Definition: This is the factor by which the package ground bond wire impedance is scaled in order to account for the total current, as opposed to the simulated current, that flows through the impedance.

Calculation:
Kbg = (Total current thru VSS bond wires in std drives / std drive of driver(s) simulated) / Ngmsi

Scaling Factor Kp

Definition: This is the factor by which the package power-ground capacitance is scaled in order to account for the total current, as opposed to the simulated current, that shares the capacitance.

Assumption: A 4 mA driver is considered a standard drive.

Calculation:
Kp = (Total current thru VDD or VSS pins in std drives / std drive of driver(s) simulated)

Vdd Pins (Np)

Definition: This is the number of pins connected to the power plane of the package.

Vss Pins (Ng)

Definition: This is the number of pins connected to the ground plane of the package.

Package Ground Plane Capacitance (Cp)

Definition: This is the capacitance between the power and ground planes on the package.

Vdd/Vss Pin Resistance (Rpp) (Rpg)

Definition: This is the resistance of a Vdd or a Vss pin.

Vdd/Vss Pin Inductance (Lpp) (Lpg)

Definition: This is the inductance of a Vdd or a Vss pin.

Calculation:
Lpp = Lpg = ((m•X)/(2•p)) (ln(2•X/r) - 1 + (mc/4m))
m = mc = 4•p•10e-7 H/m   X = 0.15″   2•r = 0.008″

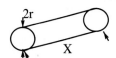

Sig Bond Wire Resistance (Rbs)

Definition: This is the resistance of a 1 mil diameter gold bond wire used for a signal.

Calculation:
Rbs = r•X
r = 1.2096 ohms/inX = 0.150″

Sig Bond Wire Inductance (Lbs)

Definition: This is the inductance of a bond wire used for a signal.

Sig Package Trace Resistance (Rts)

Definition: This is the resistance of a signal trace on the package.

Calculation: Value calculated assuming 750 mil of 1/2 oz Cu.

Sig Package Trace Inductance (Lts)

Definition: This is the inductance of a signal trace on the package.

Calculation: Total inductance per LSI is 17.5 nH. Of this, Lps is 2.9 nH and Lbs is 4 nH. This leaves 10.6 for the trace on the package.

Sig Capacitance (Cs)

Definition: This is the net capacitance of the package on a signal. It includes signal-to-signal capacitance.

Sig Pin Inductance (Lps)

Definition: This is the inductance of a signal pin.

Sig Pin Resistance (Rps)

Definition: This is the resistance of a signal pin.

Pcb Parameters

Stackup

The board is a 10-layer board with the following construction: (See Figure B-15)

Layers 3, 4, 7 and 8 are 6mil trace and space. Layers 1 and 10 are 7mil trace and space.

	7 mil	Signal 58 ohms
GND	6 mil	Signal 57 ohms
	6 mil	Signal 57 ohms
	6 mil	
+5V	5 mil	
GND	6 mil	Signal 57 ohms
	6 mil	Signal 57 ohms
	6 mil	
+5V	7 mil	Signal 58 ohms

Figure B-15 Board Stackup

Impedance Range for Inner Layers (3, 4, 7 And 8)

Dual strip line

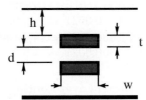

Er = 4.1 - 5.2
h = 6 +/-1
d = 6 +/-1.5
t = 1.3 +/-.1
w = 6 +/-1

Dual strip line parameters:
Nom Zo=57.46, Co=3.20 pF/in, Lo=10.56 nH, Tpd=0.18 ns/in
Min Zo=45.28, Co=4.27 pF/in, Lo=8.75 nH/in, Tpd=0.19 ns/in
Max Zo=71.49, Co=2.40 pF/in, Lo=12.27 nH/in Tpd=0.17 ns/in

Definition: This is the range of impedances that one should expect due to variation in all board construction parameters.

Calculation:
$Zo = Z1 + Z2$
$Z1 = ((87/(er + 1.41)^{1/2}) \cdot \ln((5.98 \cdot h)/(0.8w+t)) \cdot (1-(h/(d+t+h)))$
$Z2 = (60/(er)^{1/2}) \cdot \ln((5.98 \cdot (d+2t+2h))/(p \cdot (0.8w+t))) \cdot (h/(d+t+h))$

Nominal   w = 0.006 mils   d = 0.006 mils   t = 0.0014 mils   h = 0.006 mils   er = 4.65
Maximum   w = 0.006 mils   d = 0.007 mils   t = 0.0012 mils   h = 0.007 mils   er = 4.1
Minimum   w = 0.006 mils   d = 0.005 mils   t = 0.0014 mils   h = 0.005 mils   er = 5.2

Impedance Range for Outer Layers (1 And 10)

Microstrip

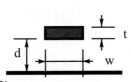

Er = 4.1 - 5.2
d = 7 +/-1.5
t = 1.7 +/-.5
w = 7 +/-1

Microstrip parameters:
Nom Zo=57.97, Co=2.49 pF/in, Lo=8.37 nH, Tpd=0.14 ns/in
Min Zo=40.39, Co=3.72 pF/in, Lo=6.07 nH/in, Tpd=0.15 ns/in
Max Zo=77.19, Co=1.78 pF/in, Lo=10.58 nH/in Tpd=0.14 ns/in

Definition: This is the range of impedances that one should expect due to variation in all board construction parameters.

Calculation :
Zo = ((87/((er+1.41)^1/2))•ln((5.98•h)/(0.8w+t)))-sm
Nominal   h = 0.006 w = 0.007 t = 0.0021 er = 4.65 sm = 2
Maximum   h = 0.007 w = 0.007 t = 0.0021 er = 4.1 sm = 1
Minimum   h = 0.005 w = 0.007 t = 0.0021 er = 5.2 sm = 3

Impedances for Setup Analysis (Inner Layer Routing)

Definition: This is the variation in the impedance to be used for setup analysis. It gives the maximum discontinuity that one can expect on the inner layers.

Calculation:
Maximum   w = 0.006 mils d = 0.007 mils t = 0.0012 mils h = 0.007 mils   er = 5.2
Minimum   w = 0.006 mils d = 0.005 mils t = 0.0014 mils h = 0.005 mils   er = 5.2

Values: Maximum   = 59.75 ohms
               Minimum   = 49.49 ohms

Impedances for Hold Analysis (Inner Layer Routing)

Definition: This is the variation in the impedance to be used for hold analysis. It gives the maximum discontinuity that one can expect on the inner layers.

Calculation:
Maximum   w = 0.006 mils d = 0.007 mils t = 0.0012 mils h = 0.007 mils   er = 4.1
Minimum   w = 0.006 mils d = 0.005 mils t = 0.0014 mils h = 0.005 mils   er = 4.1

Values: Maximum   = 66.20 ohms
               Minimum   = 54.8 ohms

Supplement B3 - Simulation Parameters

Temperature

Definition: This is the junction temperature to be used in the simulations.

Calculation:
Tj = Ta + qja•Pd
Ta = 45 °C qja = 20 Pd = 3

Input Rise Time

Definition: This is the rise time on the input to the driver.

Input Fall Time

Definition: This is the fall time on the input to the driver.

Vil

Definition: This is the point on the input waveform to the driver that a low going input is considered valid. This is used for propagation delay measurements as well.

Vih

Definition: This is the point on the input waveform to the driver that a high going input is considered valid. This is used for propagation delay measurements as well.

Voh

Definition: This is the point on the high going output waveform of the driver that the output is considered valid.

Vol

Definition: This is the point on the low going output waveform of the driver that the output is considered valid.

Supplement B4 - PACKAGE MODEL, FILE LISTING

EXAMPLE IC-PACKAGE MODEL:

```
*********************************************
*
*       Module IC package
*
*
.subckt MODIC-pkg      1              2              3
* NODES:      driver input  Tri-state enable  MBus I/O @ pin
*
*    Power pin
*
lPGApPN      99     500    6.94 nH
rPGApPN      500    501    .19
```

```
*
*    Power - Ground plane capacitance
*
cPGApC      501    504    19.2 pF
*
*    Bonding wire to power for 8 mA driver
*
lPGAp8BW      501    502    4.8 nH
rPGAp8BW      502    588    .272
*
*    8 mA driver and TLCHT receiver
*
x8DRVR   1 2 99  99  924 588 522   BT8-pkg
x8RCVR   924   4  588 522 TLCHT-pkg
c8load   4     522    1 pF
*
*    Bonding wire to ground for 8 mA driver
*
rPGAg8BW      522    503    .229
lPGAg8BW      503    504    4.8 nH
*
*    Ground pin
*
rPGAgPN      504    505    .14
lPGAgPN      505    0      5.2 nH
*
*    Bonding wire to MBus for 8 mA driver
*
lPGAmbBW      924    506    4.0 nH
rPGAmbBW      506    507    .181
*
*    Trace inside package to MBus for 8 mA driver
*
lPGAmbTR      507    508    10.6 nH
```

```
cPGAmbC        508    504    10.0 pF
rPGAmbTR       508    509    .1
*
*    MBus pin
*
lPGAmbPN       509    510    2.9 nH
rPGAmbPN       510    3      .06
*
.ends MODIC-pkg
```

Supplement B5 - MODEL FOR MODULE PCB

EXAMPLE MODULE MODEL ; SIGNAL : mad34

```
*************************************************
*
*      Module 0
*

c300 918 0 1pF

*************************************************
*
*      Module 1
*
x2mbconn  800  350 0 MBus-cn

U9_tr   350  0   351  0   umicro L = 17.78 mm

xMODIC0 1     2      351     MODIC-pkg
```

EXAMPLE MODULE MODEL ; SIGNAL : mad60

```
*************************************************
*
*       Module 0
*
x1mbconn 918  300 0 MBus-cn

u2_tr 300 0 301 0 udstrip L= 10.160 mm
u3_tr 301 0 302 0 udstrip L= 40.640 mm
u4_tr 302 0 303 0 udstrip L= 25.400 mm

u5_tr 300 0 304 0 udstrip L= 10.160 mm
u6_tr 304 0 305 0 udstrip L= 15.240 mm
u7_tr 305 0 306 0 udstrip L= 25.400 mm


xMODIC0 1    2          303    MODIC-pkg
xMODIC1 1    99         306    MODIC-pkg


*************************************************
*
*       Module 1
*
x2mbconn  800  350 0 MBus-cn

u8_tr 350 0 351 0 udstrip L= 10.160 mm
u9_tr 351 0 352 0 udstrip L= 40.640 mm
u10_tr 352 0 353 0 udstrip L= 25.400 mm

u11_tr 350 0 354 0 udstrip L= 10.160 mm
u12_tr 354 0 355 0 udstrip L= 15.240 mm
u13_tr 355 0 356 0 udstrip L= 25.400 mm

xMODIC2 1    99         353    MODIC-pkg
xMODIC3 1    99         356    MODIC-pkg
```

Supplement B6 - MBus Module Mechanical Drawings

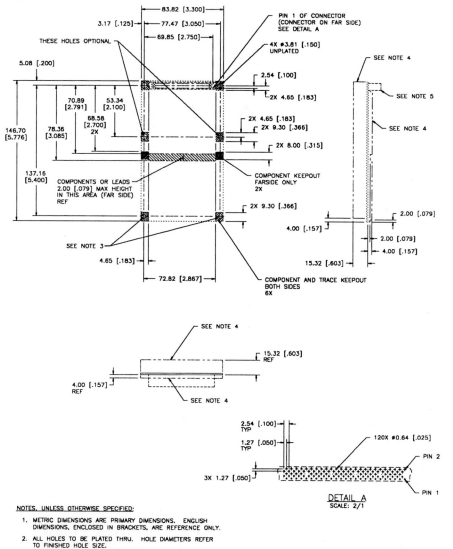

NOTES. UNLESS OTHERWISE SPECIFIED:

1. METRIC DIMENSIONS ARE PRIMARY DIMENSIONS. ENGLISH
   DIMENSIONS, ENCLOSED IN BRACKETS, ARE REFERENCE ONLY.

2. ALL HOLES TO BE PLATED THRU. HOLE DIAMETERS REFER
   TO FINISHED HOLE SIZE.

3. SEE SECTION 2.1 FOR HOLE SIZE AND PLATING DETAILS.

4. COMPONENETS OR LEADS ARE TO REMAIN WITHIN THE
   INDICATED ENVELOPE.

5. 100-PIN CONNECTOR, MALE. 16.45 [.647] HIGH.
   AMP PART NUMBER 121354-4

MBUS BOARD SPEC, 5.77IN

JIM AMMON 5-15-93

Figure B-16 MBus Module Mechanical Drawings

≡ *B*

Multiprocessor System Architectures

Glossary

A

abort

> To terminate, in a controlled manner, a processing activity in a computer system because it is impossible or undesirable for the activity to proceed.

absolute address

> (1) An address that identifies a storage location or a device without the use of any intermediate reference. (2) An address permanently assigned by the designer to a storage location. (3) Synonymous with explicit address, machine address, specific address.

absolute path name

> For a file or directory, the list of directories from the *root directory* through the tree structure to the desired file name or directory name, each name in the series separated by a slash character (/).

abstract syntax

> A description of a data structure that is independent of machine-oriented structures and encodings.

abstract syntax notation one (ASN.1)

> The International Organization for Standardization open systems interconnection (OSI) language for describing abstract syntax.

access

> To obtain entry to or to locate, read into memory, and make ready for some operation. Access is usually used with regard to disks, files, records, and network entry procedures.

access time

> Generally, the time required for information to be gathered from some remote source, such as data from a computer's memory or data from a hard disk.

address

(1) A number used by the system software to identify a storage location.
(2) In networking, a unique code that identifies a *node* to the *network*.

address space

The range of memory locations to which a CPU can refer; effectively, the amount of memory a CPU could use if all of the memory were available.

algorithm

A sequence of steps designed to solve a problem or to execute a process such as drawing a curve from a set of control points.

alias

(1) In electronic mail, an easy-to-remember name used in place of a full name and address. Also, a name used to identify a distribution list—several user names grouped under a single name. (2) An alternate label. For example, a label and one or more aliases can be used to refer to the same data element or point in a computer program. (3) A distortion or artifact in the digital reproduction of an audio waveform that results when the signal frequency is too high compared to the sampling frequency.

aliasing

(1) The jagged *artifact* in a line or in the silhouette of a curve that results from drawing on a *raster* grid. Aliasing occurs in all graphical images drawn on raster displays, but it is especially noticeable in low-resolution monitors. The *sampling* frequency is a major factor in aliasing. Synonymi *jaggies*. See also *antialiasing*. (2) See *command aliasing*.

allocate

To reserve memory for use by a program. Programs often need certain system resources such as memory or disk space, and they request them as needed from the operating system. The process of responding to a request for a resource is called allocation. The two basic types of allocation are *static allocation*, in which memory is set aside when the program starts and remains allocated while the program is running, and *dynamic allocation*, in which memory is allocated and deallocated while the program is running. See also *deallocate, pointer, dynamic allocation*, and *static allocation*.

ALU

See *arithmetic and logic unit (ALU)*.

American National Standards Institute (ANSI)

An organization that reviews and approves product standards in the United States. In the electronics industry, its work enables designers and manufacturers to create and support products that are compatible with other hardware *platform*s in the industry. Examples are *PHIGS* and *GKS*. See also *International Organization for Standardization (ISO)*.

American standard code for information interchange (ASCII)

The standard binary encoding of alphabetical characters, numbers, and other keyboard symbols.

antialiasing

An algorithm designed to reduce the stair-stepping *ASCII*s (sometimes called *jaggies*) that result from drawing graphic primitives on a *raster* grid. The solution usually relies on the *multi-bit raster*'s ability to display a number of *pixel* intensities. If the intensities of neighboring pixels lie between the background and line intensities, the line becomes slightly blurred, and the jagged appearance is thereby diffused.

API

See *application programmer's interface (API)*.

application

A software program specially designed for a particular task or the specific use of a software program. Graphics applications are usually designed to enable the user to manipulate data or images or to create images from data or from a library of shapes.

application developer

The person who creates an application to perform a particular task.

application layer

The layer of *network* standards concerned with providing services to network users at an application-based level. The seventh and highest layer in the *ISO/OSI model* developed for the *International Organization for Standardization (ISO)*, the application layer relies on services performed at lower levels, but is the layer least involved with the underlying network hardware. Tasks performed on the application layer vary with the uses of a network, but they might include login procedures, electronic mail, terminal emulation, database management, and the operation of file servers and print servers.

application programmer's interface (API)
> (1) The interface to a library of language-specific subroutines (called a *graphics library*) that implement higher level graphics functions. See also *binding*. (2) A set of calling conventions defining how a service is invoked through a software package.

arbiter
> Typically a VLSI device used to arbitrate, or resolve, equal access to memory and/or bus use.

architecture
> The specific components of a computer system and the way they interact with each other.

arg
> See *argument*.

arg list
> Argument list.

argument
> An item of information following a *command*. It may, for example, modify the command or identify a file to be affected.

arithmetic and logic unit (ALU)
> A part of a computer that performs arithmetic, logical, and related operations.

array
> An arrangement of elements in one or more dimensions.

ASCII
> (Pronounced "as-kee.") See *American standard code for information interchange (ASCII)*.

ASIC
> (Pronounced $\bar{a}$-*sic*).) Application-specific integrated circuit. A *gate array* or other nonstandard chip design for proprietary use.

ASMP
> Asymmetric multiprocessing: An arrangement where one of the processors is designated as the master and the other are slaves to that master. The master is the only processor that executes the operating system--to perform I/0 operations, to manage memory, and so on.

ASN.1

See abstract syntax notation one (ASN.1)

assembly language

A computer-oriented language with instructions that are usually in a one-to-one correspondence with computer instructions. It may provide facilities such as use of microinstructions.

asserted

The state of a signal used to initiate an action. Contrast with *unasserted*.

assertion

(1) A *conditional* statement in the operating system source code intended to prevent the kernel from going astray and damaging important data. (2) A Boolean statement in a program that tests a condition that should, if the program is operating correctly, evaluate as true. If the condition is false, an error has occurred, and the program typically terminates with an appropriate error message. Assertions are useful for debugging programs.

associative array

A collection of data (an *array*) where individual items may be indexed (accessed) by a string, rather than by an integer as is common in most programming languages.

asymmetric multiprocessing

A form of multiprocessing in which a single processor acts as a *master* to a series of *slave* processors. Contrast with *symmetric multiprocessing*.

asynchronous

(1) Without regular time relationship; unexpected and unpredictable with respect to the execution of a program's instructions. Contrast with *synchronous*. (2) A form of data transmission in which information is sent one character at a time, with variable time intervals between characters; generally used in communicating via modem. Asynchronous transmission does not use a separate clock signal to enable the sending and receiving units to separate characters by specific time periods. Instead, each transmitted character consists of a number of data bits (the character itself) preceded by a "begin character" signal, called a start bit, and ending with an optional parity bit followed by one or more "end character" signals, called stop bits.

atomic transaction

A sequence of bus cycles in which an SBus master retains control of the bus to prevent any other master from accessing the bus. Atomic transactions are used to implement *semaphores*.

attribute

(1) In databases, the name or structure of a field is considered to be an attribute of a record. For example, the files `lastname`, `firstname`, and `phone` would be attributes of each record in a `phonelist` database. The structure of each field, such as its size or the type of information it contains (alphabetic or numeric), would also be attributes of the record. (2) The form of information items provided by the X.500 directory service. The directory information base consists of entries, each containing one or more attributes. Each attribute consists of a type identifier together with one or more values. Each directory read operation can retrieve some or all attributes from a designated entry. (3) In screen displays, elements such as additional information stored with each character in the video buffer of a video adapter running in character mode: attributes control the background color and foreground color of the character, underlining, and blinking.

auto-configuration

The process by which the host fetches SBus IDs and *FCodes*, beginning at location 0 of each slave used to identify the device.

B

backbone

The primary connectivity mechanism of a hierarchical distributed system. All systems that have connectivity to an intermediate system on the backbone are assured of connectivity to each other. This does not prevent systems from setting up private arrangements with each other to bypass the backbone for reasons of cost, performance, or security.

background

(1) In the OPEN LOOK GUI, an underlying area on which objects, such as controls and windows, are displayed. (2) To run a system so that the terminal is left free for other uses. See *background process*.

background process

A command that a user has directed the system to work on while the user continues to type commands to the *command interpreter*.

backplane

Connector blocks and wiring units constituting most or all of the interconnection circuits of a system. Typically used to interconnect modular plug-in cards in a standardized connector. Provides a parallel communications medium.

Berkeley software distribution (BSD)
UNIX versions developed at the University of California, Berkeley. They bear names such as BSD 2.7 and BSD 4.2.

big-endian
A format for storage or transmission of binary data in which the most significant bit (or byte) comes first (the word is stored "big-end-first"). Contrast with *little-endian*.

binary
From bi-, meaning two; generally, a term describing a system, statement, or condition that has two components, alternatives, or outcomes. In mathematics, binary is the base-2 number system, in which values are expressed as combinations of two digits, 0 and 1.

binary-coded decimal (BCD)
A system for encoding decimal numbers in binary form to avoid rounding and conversion errors. In BCD coding, each digit of a decimal number is coded separately as a binary number. Each of the decimal digits 0 through 9 is coded in four bits, and for ease of reading, each group of four bits is separated by a space. This format, called 8-4-2-1 after the weights of the four bit positions, uses the following codes:

0000 = 00101 = 5
0001 = 10110 = 6
0010 = 20111 = 7
0011 = 31000 = 8
0100 = 41001 = 9

See also *extended binary-coded decimal interchange code (EBCDIC)*, and *packed decimal*.

binder
A tool or application that provides a user interface to the binding process. See *binding*.

binding
(1) Language-dependent code that allows a software library to be called from that computer language. (2) The process during which a client finds out where a server is so that the client can receive services. *NFS* binding is explicitly set up by the user and remains in effect until the user terminates the bind, for example, by modifying the /etc/fstab file. NIS binding occurs when a client's request is answered by a server and is terminated when the server no longer responds. (3) A logical relationship between any two elements, such as a file type, an application, a print script, a color, a filter, or another element that can be used for displaying

or operating on a file. Thus, an application can be bound to a print script so that files the user generates with that application always print in a particular way.

bipolar

Literally, having two opposite states, such as positive and negative. In information transfer and processing, a bipolar signal is one in which opposite voltage polarities represent on and off, as in a logic circuit.

bistable

A term describing a system or device that has two possible states, such as on and off. See also *flip-flop*.

bit

Short for "binary digit." Indicates the smallest unit of information stored in a digital memory. Binary digits indicate two possible values: on and off. A single bit is represented in memory as 0 (off) and 1 (on).

block

A unit of data that can be transferred by a device, usually 512 bytes long.

block-check character (BCC)

In longitudinal redundancy checking and cyclic redundancy checking, a character transmitted by the sender after each message block and compared with a block-check character computed by the receiver to determine if the transmission was successful.

block device

A device where block I/O transfers are possible, usually a magnetic or optical disk.

blocking

(1) In the OPEN LOOK GUI, a window that does not allow input to any other window of the application except itself. (2) In data storage, the process of breaking a file up into fixed-size blocks. (3) In communications, the process of preventing a signal from being transmitted. (4) In multithreading, a thread that wants to update a variable might block waiting for a mutex lock held by another thread that is already updating it.

blocking factor

The size of the chunk of data transferred to or from a *block device*. Common blocking factors are 128, 256, and 512 bytes. See also *block*.

boot

To load the system software into memory and start it running.

boot block

> An 8-Kbyte disk block that contains information used during booting; block numbers pointing to the location of the /boot program on the disk. The boot block directly follows the disk label.

bootbus

> An 8-bit bus used to access system support devices.

boot PROM

> In Sun workstations, contains the *PROM monitor* program, a command interpreter used for booting, resetting, low-level configuration, and simple test procedures. See also *ID PROM, EEPROM,* and *NVRAM.*

boot server

> A server system that provides client systems on the network with the programs and information they need to start up. The *master server* and *slave server*s can be boot servers.

Bourne shell

> The *shell* used by the standard Bell Labs UNIX.

breakpoint

> A point in a program as specified by an instruction, instruction digit, or other condition, where the program can be interrupted by external intervention or by a monitor routine.

BSD

> See Berkeley software distribution (BSD).

buffer

> (1) A storage device that holds data to be transmitted to another device. (2) A temporary work area or storage area set up within the system memory. Buffers are often used by programs, such as editors, that access and alter text or data frequently.

bug

> An error in the hardware or software of a computer system.

burst transfer

> A single bus cycle in which multiple words of data are transferred.

bus

> A circuit over which data or power is transmitted, one that often acts as a common connection among a number of locations.

bus cycle

On the SBus, a series of clock cycles beginning (in the case of a *DVMA master*) with a particular master receiving a grant and, in all cases, concluding with address strobe being unasserted by the SBus controller. For DVMA masters, a bus cycle is divided into two phases: a translation cycle and a slave cycle. However, in the case of a *CPU master*, the translation cycle does not occur as part of the bus cycle.

bus device

An external device that connects to the bus and has an assigned device address and/or priority level.

bus error

A system fault that occurs when a process has attempted to access an area of memory that is restricted or does not exist. Bus errors cause bus error traps that cause processor traps through a specific trap vector address. See also *segmentation fault, and trap.*

bus master

See *master.*

bus priority

A scheme for allocating preferential access to a *bus.*

bus request

A request from a device on the bus for control of the bus to become the *bus master* and to start an interrupt or perform a data transfer.

bus sizing

On the SBus, a transfer mode in which a slave requests the master to turn a word transfer into two half-words, or four byte transfers. Each transfer is performed using a separate bus cycle. The first bus cycle is called the original bus cycle; remaining bus cycles are called follow-on bus cycles.

byte

A group of adjacent binary digits (*bits*) operated on by the computer as a unit. The most common sized byte contains eight binary digits.

byte acknowledgment

On the SBus, an acknowledgment to indicate that the slave has read or written a byte from the most-significant byte of the data lines. If the transfer size is greater than a byte, the master initiating the transfer may perform *bus sizing.*

byte addressing

On the SBus, a determination that the smallest addressable unit of information is a byte.

C

cache

A buffer of high-speed memory filled at medium speed from main memory, often with instructions and programs. A cache increases effective memory transfer rates and processor speed.

CAD

See *computer-aided design (CAD)*.

call

To summon a program into action.

central processing unit (CPU)

The part of the computer in which calculations and manipulations take place. See also *arithmetic and logic unit (ALU)*.

checkpoint

A place in a computer program at which a check is made, or at which a recording of data is made for restart purposes.

checksum

The sum of a group of data items associated with the group for checking purposes. The data items are either numerals or other character strings regarded as numerals during the process of calculating the checksum.

chip

(1) A small chunk of silicon bearing the equivalent of a large number of electrical components. (2) An *integrated circuit (IC)*.

class

A grouping of data having similar characteristics.

client

(1) In the *client-server model* for file systems, the client is a machine that remotely accesses resources of a compute server, such as compute power and large memory capacity. (2) In the client-server model for window systems, the client is an *application* that accesses windowing services from a "server process." In this model, the client and the server can run on the same machine or on separate machines.

client-server model

A common way to describe network services and the model user processes (programs) of those services. Examples include the name-server/name-resolver paradigm of the *domain name system (DNS)* and file-server/file-client relationships such as *NFS* and diskless hosts. See also *client*.

client system

A system on a network that relies on another system, called a *server system*, for resources such as disk space.

closed architecture

Any computer design with specifications not freely available. Such proprietary specifications make it difficult or impossible for third-party vendors to create ancillary devices that work correctly with a closed-architecture machine; usually, only its original master can build peripherals for such a machine. Contrast with *open architecture*.

command aliasing

In the UNIX shell, the process of renaming or customizing the behavior of commands. For example, the user can *alias* the UNIX history command to h. In other words, to execute history, the user merely types h.

command interpreter

A program that accepts commands from the keyboard and causes the commands to be executed. The *C shell* is an example of a UNIX command interpreter.

command stream

A sequence of control information passed from one processor to another.

compiler

A *translation* program that converts a high-level computer language (such as FORTRAN) into *machine language*.

computer-aided design (CAD)

A system by means of which engineers create a design and can view the proposed product on a graphics terminal.

concatenate

(1) To string together two or more sequences, such as files, into one longer sequence. The UNIX cat command, for example, concatenates files. (2) The process of combining a sequence of *transformations* into one operation.

conditional

An action or operation that takes place based on whether or not a certain condition is true.

contention

(1) On a network, competition among stations to use a communications line or network resource. (2) A situation in which two or more devices attempt to transmit at the same time, thus causing a collision on the line.

(3) A free-for-all method of controlling access to a communications line, in which the right to transmit is awarded to the station that wins control of the line. In this type of contention, each station listens to the line and waits for it to become inactive. When the line is free, any station that wants to transmit bids for the line by sending a request-to-send message to its intended recipient. If the response is positive, the station is free to transmit, and all other nodes must wait until the line is free again before attempting any transmissions of their own.

context switching

A type of multitasking; the act of turning the central processor's attention from one task to another, rather than allocating increments of time to each task in turn. See also *multitasking*.

cooperative multitasking

See *multitasking*.

CPU

See *central processing unit (CPU)*.

CPU master

An SBus master that includes a central processing unit with a private means to perform virtual address translation (in contrast to a DVMA master which uses the SBus controller to perform virtual address translation). A bus cycle initiated by a CPU master consists only of a slave cycle. Typical SBus systems have one CPU master.

C shell

The standard shell provided with Berkeley standard versions of UNIX.

cycle

A circular reference. A chain of references that lead back to the start.

cyclic-redundancy check (CRC)

(1) An error check in which the check key is generated by a cyclic algorithm. (2) A system of error checking performed at both the send and receiving station after a *block-check character (BCC)* has been accumulated.

D

daemon

A process that runs in the background, handling commands delivered for remote command execution. Typical daemons are the mailer daemon and the printer daemon.

daisy chain

A specific method of propagating signals along a bus. This method is often used in applications in which devices not requesting a daisy-chained signal respond to a signal by passing it on. The daisy chain scheme permits assignment of device priorities based on the electrical position of the device on the bus.

database management system (DBMS)

A software system facilitating the creation and maintenance of a database and the execution of programs using the database.

data compression

Application of an algorithm to reduce the bit rate of a digital signal or the bandwidth of an analog signal while preserving as much as possible of the information—usually with the objective of meeting the constraints in subsequent portions of the system.

dataless client

A *client system* that relies on a *server system* for its home directory, and on a local disk for its root directory and swap space.

data source

(1) The originator of computer data. Frequently, a data source is an analog or digital data collection device. (2) In communications, the portion of a *data terminal equipment (DTE)* device that sends transmitted data.

data transfer bus (DTB)

Part of the *VMEbus* specification that contains data and address pathways and associated control signals. Functional modules called DTB masters and DTB slaves use the DTB to transfer data between each other.

daughterboard

A printed circuit board that attaches to another board, often the main system board (*motherboard*), to provide functionality or performance.

deadlock

A situation in which the software is not responding because of errors or because two or more processes are each waiting for one or more of the other processes to conclude before continuing.

deadly embrace

See *deadlock*.

deallocate

To reclaim or free previously allocated memory. See also *allocate* and *pointer*.

default

An alternative value, attribute, or option assumed when none has been specified.

delimiter

(1) A flag that separates and organizes items of data. (2) A character that logically separates words or arguments on a command line. Two frequently used delimiters in the UNIX system are the space and the tab.

demand paging

A protocol that allows a program's required area to be noncontiguous and partially nonresident. This arrangement permits the maximum use of a system's total available memory by allowing the computer system to execute programs that are larger than the allocated physical main memory within the processor.

DES

See *data encryption standard (DES)*.

descriptor

A data structure that uniquely identifies a hardware device or software function.

deskside

A system enclosure that stands next to the user's desk. Contrast with *desktop*.

desktop

An entire system that fits on the top of the desk. Contrast with *deskside*.

device-dependent

A term applied to software that has been written for a specific computer device; runs on that device exclusively. Software that can run only on a specific vendor's computer is known as vendor-dependent. Contrast with *device-independent*.

device driver

The software that converts *device-independent* graphics commands into device-specific (*device-dependent*) display.

device-independent

A term applied to software that has been written expressly for portability across dissimilar computer systems. An *industry standard* graphics library, such as *PHIGS*, is a device-independent interface. Contrast with *device-dependent*.

device name

The name that the system uses to identify a device. For example, `/dev/rst0` (or just `rst0`) is the device name for a 1/4-inch tape.

dhrystone

A general-performance benchmarking test, originally developed by Rheinhold Weicker in 1984 in the attempt to measure and compare the performance of computers. The test reports general system performance in dhrystones per second. It is intended to replace the older and less reliable whetstone benchmark. The dhrystone benchmark, like most benchmarks, consists of standard code and is revised periodically to minimize unfair advantages given to certain combinations of hardware, compiler, and environment. Contrast with *whetstone*.

direct memory access (DMA)

The transfer of data directly into memory without supervision of the processor. The data is passed on the bus directly between the memory and another device. Contrast with *direct virtual memory access (DVMA)*.

directory

A type of file that can contain other files and directories.

directory path name

The complete name by which the directory is known. The path name gives the sequence of directories by which the directory is linked to the *root directory*.

direct virtual memory access (DVMA)

A mechanism to enable a device on the SBus to initiate data transfers between it and other SBus devices, such as system memory. Contrast with *direct memory access (DMA)*.

dispatcher

In some multitasking operating systems, the set of routines responsible for allocating CPU time to various applications.

dispatch table

Also known as a jump table, a vector table, or an interrupt vector table. A table of identifiers and addresses for a certain class of routines such as interrupt handlers (routines carried out in response to certain signals or conditions). See also *interrupt handler*.

distributed file system

A file system that exists on more than one machine, enabling each user to access files on other machines.

DMA

See *direct memory access (DMA)*.

double-precision

An adjective that describes a number stored in twice the amount (two words) of computer memory required for storing a less precise (*single-precision*) number. Double-precision numbers are commonly handled by a computer in floating-point form.

double-word

A group of 64 signals or bits taken as a unit (eight bytes of data).

DRAM

Acronym for "dynamic random-access memory." See *dynamic RAM (DRAM)*. See also *static RAM (SRAM)* and *VRAM*.

driver

A software subsystem that controls either a hardware device (*device driver*) or another software subsystem.

dumb terminal

A terminal with no memory, processor, nor firmware that can perform only when connected to a host computer.

DVMA cycle

An SBus cycle initiated by a *DVMA master*. A DVMA cycle consists of a translation cycle and a slave cycle.

DVMA master

An SBus master able to initiate a bus cycle that uses the SBus controller to perform virtual address translation (in contrast to a CPU master which has a private means for virtual address translation). A bus cycle initiated by a DVMA master consists of a translation cycle and a slave cycle.

dyadic

A reference to a pair. A dyadic processor contains two processors controlled by the same operating system. In mathematics, a dyadic operation is one in which there are two operands. In Boolean algebra, a dyadic Boolean operation is one in which there are two operands, both of which are significant.

dynamic allocation

(1) An allocation technique in which the resources assigned to a system are determined by criteria applied at the moment of need. (2) Assignment of system resources to a program at the time the program is executed rather than at the time it is loaded into main storage. Dynamic allocation almost always implies that dynamic deallocation is possible too, so data structures can be created and destroyed as required. Compare with *static allocation*. See also *allocate* and *deallocate*.

dynamic linking

> A technique in which the resources assigned to a system, or the loading of program modules or routines into the main memory for execution, are made available during program execution.

dynamic RAM (DRAM)

> (Pronounced "dee-ram.") A type of semiconductor random-access memory that stores information in integrated circuits that contain capacitors. Because capacitors lose their charge over time, the dynamic RAM must be periodically "refreshed" or recharged. Contrast with *static RAM (SRAM)*.

E

EBCDIC

> Abbreviation for expanded binary coded decimal interchange code. An 8-bit code used to represent 256 unique letters, numbers, and special characters.

ECC

> See *error checking and correction (ECC)*.

EEPROM

> Electrically erasable PROM (programmable read-only memory). A non-volatile PROM that can be written to as well as read from. In Sun workstations, an EEPROM holds information about the current system configuration, alternate boot paths, and so on. See also *boot PROM, NVRAM*, and *ID PROM*.

element

> In computer terminology, any entity that can be defined as a standalone item within a broader context. For example, a data element is an item of data with the characteristics or properties of a larger set; a picture element (*pixel*) is a single dot on a computer screen or in a computer graphic.

e-mail

> Electronic mail.

embedded

> An adjective referring to items, such as program code or commands, that are built into their carriers rather than associated with or called by them when needed.

emulate

> To imitate one system with another, primarily by hardware, so that the imitating system accepts the same data, executes the same computer programs, and achieves the same results as the imitated system. Contrast with *simulate*.

emulation6 trap

> A trap used when the CPU is emulating a different CPU type. See also *emulate* and *trap*.

entry

> (1) A unit of information treated as a whole by a computer program. For example, a value in a spreadsheet cell or in one particular field of a database record. (2) The process of entering information, often in a predetermined form or format, for a computer program to act upon. For example, typing a number into a spreadsheet cell.

enumerated data type

> A data type that contains a set of values that is given a particular order. For example, an enumerated data type might be defined to include the set of colors red, green, blue, and yellow. The color red is defined as the first value of the type; yellow is the last value.

environment

> The conditions under which a user works while using the UNIX system. A user's environment includes those things that personalize the user's login and how the user is allowed to interact in specific ways with UNIX and the computer.

environment variable

> Instruction that determines certain characteristics of an *environment*. The UNIX C shell environment variables are similar to *shell variable*s, except that environment variables can be passed to every C shell that runs. Many applications use environment variables to set configuration directories, specify base directories for commands or data, and pass other information about the user environment to the program.

EPROM

> (Pronounced "ee-prom.") Acronym for erasable programmable read-only memory. A nonvolatile memory chip that is programmed after it is manufactured. EPROMS provide way for hardware vendors to put variable or constantly changing code into a prototype system when the cost of producing many PROM chips would be prohibitive. EPROMs differ from PROMs in that they can be erased (generally by removing a

protective cover from the top of the chip package and exposing the semiconductor material to the ultraviolet light) and can be reprogrammed after having been erased. See also *EEPROM, PROM,* and *ROM.*

error checking and correction (ECC)

The detection, in the processing unit, and correction of all single-bit errors, plus the detection of double-bit and some multiple-bit errors.

error recovery

The process of correcting or bypassing a fault to restore a computer system to a prescribed condition.

event processing

A program feature belonging to more advanced operating-system architectures such as UNIX. Programs used to be required to interrogate, and effectively anticipate, every device that was expected to interact with the program, such as the keyboard, mouse and printer. Unless sophisticated programming techniques were used, one or two events happening at the same instant would be lost. Event processing solves this problem through the creation and maintenance of an event queue.

exception

In CPU terminology, a computation error, usually resulting in a *trap.*

executable file

A file that can be processed or executed by the computer without any further translation. When a user types in the file name, the commands in the file are executed.

execute

(1) To run a file as a program. (2) To perform one or more instructions. In programming, execution implies loading the machine language code of the program into memory and then performing the instructions.

explicit address

See *absolute address.*

exponent

In a floating-point representation, the numeral that denotes the power to which the implicit floating-point base is raised before being multiplied by the fixed-point part to determine the real number represented.

exponential notation

See *floating-point representation.*

extended binary-coded decimal interchange code

See *EBCDIC.*

extended transfer

An extended SBus cycle protocol (also called a 64-bit transfer) in which 64-bits of data are transferred per clock cycle during the slave cycle. The upper 32 bits of data are multiplexed onto the Size<2:0>, Read, and PhysAddr<27:0> lines.

F

FCodes

Forth byte codes. See also *open boot*.

FDDI

See *fiber distributed data interface (FDDI)*.

fiber distributed data interface (FDDI)

An emerging high-speed networking standard. The underlying medium is fiber optics, and the topology is a dual-attached, counter-rotating token ring. FDDI networks can often be spotted by the orange fiber "cable."

field-programmable logic array (FPLA)

Also known as programmable logic array (PLA). An integrated circuit containing an array of logic circuits in which the connections between the individual circuits, and thus the logic functions of the array, can be programmed after manufacture, typically at the time of installation (in the field). The programming can be performed only once, and it is typically done by passing high current through fusible links on the chip.

FIFO

(Pronounced "fie-foe.") See *first-in, first-out (FIFO)*.

FIFO file

See *named pipe*.

file

A sequence of bytes constituting a unit of text, data, or program. A file can be stored in the system memory or on an external medium such as tape or disk.

file handle

In *NFS*, a data structure that allows systems to uniquely identify files over the network. A *stale NFS file handle* is one that contains data that is out of date with respect to the file it refers to.

file name

The name of a file as it is stored in a directory on a disk. See also *path name*.

file permissions

A set of permissions assigned to each file and directory that determines which users have access to read, write, and execute its contents.

file system

In the SunOS operating system, a tree-structured network of files and directories through which the user can move to access the files and directories contained there.

file system hierarchy

The structure of the *file system*, consisting of a tree of files and directories, with a root directory at the top and directories that act as parent directories and child directories throughout. See *parent directory* and *child directory*.

file table

The table containing references to all files being accessed by the current program.

first-in, first-out (FIFO)

A method of processing a queue in which items are removed in the same order in which they were added—the first in is the first out. Such an order is typical of a list of documents waiting to be printed.

fixed-point arithmetic

Arithmetic performed on fixed-point numbers.

fixed-point notation

A numeric format in which the decimal point has a specified position. Fixed-point numbers are a compromise between integral formats, which are compact and efficient, and floating-point numeric formats, which have a great range of values.

flag

An argument to a command indicating a particular option or modification. UNIX flags usually are indicated by a leading hyphen (-).

flash PROM

A type of programmable read-only memory (PROM) that can be reprogrammed by a voltage pulse or a flash of light. See also *PROM*.

flip-flop

A bistable device (a device capable of assuming two states) which can assume a given stable state depending upon the pulse history of one or more input points and having one or more output points.

floating-point accelerator (FPA)

A device (board or *integrated circuit (IC)*) that speeds up floating-point calculations.

floating-point coprocessor

See *floating-point accelerator (FPA)*.

floating-point representation

A representation of a real number in a floating-point representation system. For example, a floating-point representation of the number 0.0001234 is 0.1234–3, where 0.1234 is the fixed-point part and –3 is the *exponent*.

FLOPS

Acronym for floating-point operations per second, a measure of the speed at which a computer can operate. See also *MFLOPS*.

follow-on bus cycle

On the SBus, one of up to three bus cycles during a bus sizing operation that follows the original bus cycle.

foreground

(1) In UNIX, running under direct control of the terminal; the terminal cannot be used for anything else until a foreground task finishes or is halted. Contrast with *background*. (2) In the OPEN LOOK GUI, the controls and the *pane* of a window.

fork

A system call to create a new process. The new process is called a *child process*. The original process is called a *parent process*.

Forth

A programming language originated by Charles Moore in the late 1960s. Moore chose the language's name, a shortened version of the word "fourth" because he believed it was a fourth-generation language. Forth is an interpreted, structured language that uses threading, which lets programmers easily extend the language and enables Forth to fit a great deal of the functionality into limited space.

Forth byte codes (Fcodes)
> A small program, usually a bootstrap loader, written in the Forth language and stored in a *PROM* or *EPROM*.

G

gate array
> Also known as an application-specific integrated circuit (*ASIC*). A special type of chip that starts out as a nonspecific collection of logic gates. Late in the manufacturing process, a layer is added to connect the gates for a specific function. By changing the pattern of connections, the manufacturer can make the chip suitable for many needs. After the chip has been configured to meet a specific need, it becomes an ASIC.

Gbyte
> Abbreviation for *gigabyte (Gbyte)*; 1,073,741,824 bytes.

gigabyte (Gbyte)
> One billion bytes. In reference to computers, bytes are often expressed in multiples of powers of two. Therefore, a gigabyte can also be 1024 megabytes, where a megabyte is considered to be 2^{20} (or 1,048,576) bytes.

global
> Having extended or general scope. For example, a global substitution of one word for another in a file affects all occurrences of the word.

global variable
> A variable whose value can be accessed and modified by any statement in a program. That is, the variable is visible to the entire program, including statements and functions.

graphical user interface (GUI)
> A visual, often metaphorical, presentation of features that provides the user with a method of interacting with the computer and its special applications, usually via a mouse or other selection device. The GUI usually includes such things as windows, an intuitive method of manipulating directories and files, and *icons*.

graphics accelerator
> A hardware device dedicated to increasing the speed and performance of graphics. Graphics accelerators calculate pixel values, and write them into the *frame buffer*, freeing up the CPU for other operations.

graphics library

A tool set for application programmers, interfaced with an *application programmer's interface (API)*. The graphics library usually includes a defined set of *primitives* and function calls that enable the programmer to bypass many low-level programming tasks.

group

A collection of users who are referred to by a common name. Determines a user's access to files. There are two types of groups: default user group and standard user group.

group attribute

An attribute attached to a file or directory that determines a user's access. See also *permissions*.

group ID

A number that identifies the default *group* for a user.

GUI

See *graphical user interface (GUI)*.

H

half-word

Half of a *word*. Commonly, a computer's word size is either two or four bytes, and its half-words are, accordingly, one or two bytes. The SPARC workstations use a 32-bit (four byte) word, and therefore have a 16-bit (two byte) half-word. Contrast with *byte* and *word*.

half-word acknowledgment

On the SBus, an acknowledgment to indicate that the slave has read or written a *half-word* of data from the most-significant half-word of the data lines. If the transfer size is greater than a half-word, the master initiating the transfer may perform *bus sizing*.

halt

To intentionally stop the system from running, for example, in preparation for turning off the power.

handle

(1) A number that can be used to access a device or an object such as a file, a window, or a dialog box in a graphical interface. A handle is a means of uniquely identifying an object. (2) In programming, a handle is a pointer to a pointer—that is, a variable that contains the address of yet

another variable. Generally, a handle is a *token* that lets a program access some resource. Programs often receive a handle in response to a request for a resource, and then they use the handle when they need access to the resource. When the program uses the handle, the value of the handle tells the system which resource from the pool of resources maintained by the system to use. See also *pointer*.

hash coding

See *hashing*.

hashing

In database management, an indexing technique in which the value of a key (record identifier) is numerically manipulated to directly calculate either the location of its associated record in a file or the starting of a search for the associated record.

heterogeneous network

A network composed of systems of more than one architecture. Contrast with *homogeneous network*.

high

A term applied to a signal driven to a voltage greater than or equal to V_{OH}.

home directory

The directory assigned to the user by the system administrator; usually the same as the *login directory*. Additional directories the user creates stem from the home directory.

homogeneous network

A network composed of systems of only one architecture. Contrast with *heterogenous network*.

host computer

(1) In a network, a computer that primarily provides services such as computation, data base access, or special programs. (2) The primary or controlling computer in a multiple computer installation.

hostid

See *system ID*.

hung

A condition in which the system is frozen and unresponsive to commands.

I

ID PROM

In the Sun workstation, a PROM (programmable read-only memory) that contains workstation-specification information, such as workstation serial number, Ethernet address, and system configuration information. See also *boot PROM, NVRAM,* and *EEPROM.*

industry standard

Elements of a computer system hardware or software subsystem that have been standardized and adopted by the industry at large. Standardization occurs in two ways: through a rigorous procedure followed by the *ANSI* and *ISO* organizations or through wide acceptance by the industry.

input

Information fed to a command, a program, a terminal, a person, and so on.

installable device driver

A device-control program that can be embedded within an operating system, usually in order to override an existing less functional service, with the purpose of enabling data transfer to and from a device such as a printer, monitor, or disk drive. See also *device driver.*

instruction stream

A set of instructions that must be executed serially, although these instructions can be executed on different processors.

integrated circuit (IC)

In electronics, the packaging of circuit elements, such as transistors and resistors, onto a single chip of silicon crystal or other material. Integrated circuits are categorized by the number of elements they hold, as follows:

small-scale integration (SSI)	fewer than 10
medium-scale integration (MSI)	10 – 100
large-scale integration (LSI)	100 – 5000
very-large-scale integration (VLSI)	5000 – 50,000
super-large-scale integration (SLSI)	50,000 – 100,000
ultra-large-scale integration (ULSI)	more than 100,000

intelligent peripheral interface (IPI)

A device-generic interface used for large capacity, high-performance disks. The IPI supports disk transfer rates at 3 Mbytes per second and above.

intelligent terminal

A terminal with its own memory, processor, and firmware that can perform certain functions independently of its host processor. Contrast with *dumb terminal*.

interactive

(1) Allowing the computer and the user to carry on a dialog. (2) Describes an operating system, such as UNIX, that can handle immediate-response communication between the user and the computer.

internationalization

The process of altering a program so that it is portable across several native languages. This portability supports both different character sets, such as the 8-bit ISO 8859/1 (ISO Latin 1) character set and the 7-bit ASCII character set, and different languages for documentation, help screens, and so on. See also *localization*.

International Organization for Standardization (ISO)

Also known as "International Standards Organization." An international agency that reviews and approves independently designed products for use within specific industries. ISO is also responsible for developing standards for information exchange. Its function is similar to that of *ANSI* in the United States.

interpreter

A program that translates a high-level computer language (such as BASIC) into machine language, a line at a time. Interactive languages use interpreters instead of *compiler*s.

interrupt

(1) To break off a command or other process, thus terminating it. (2) A signal that accomplishes this termination.

interrupt handler

A special routine that is executed when a specific interrupt occurs. Each type of interrupt is mapped to a specific routine such as updating the system clock or reading the keyboard. See also *dispatch table*.

interrupt vector table

See *dispatch table*.

I/O

Input/output. Refers to equipment used to communicate with a computer, the data involved in that communication, the media carrying the data, and the process of communicating that information.

I/O bound

Input/output bound. Describes a situation in which the work performed by a computer's processor is slowed by the lengthy amount of time required for reading from or writing to a storage device, such as a disk drive.

ioctl

I/O control. A function for device control.

ISV

Acronym for independent software vendor. A third-party software developer.

iterative statement

A statement in a program that causes the program to repeat one or more statements.

J

JTAG

Acronym for Joint Test Action Group. JTAG is a boundary-scan test standard adopted by IEEE.

jump table

See *dispatch table*.

K

Kbyte

Abbreviation for *kilobyte (Kbyte)* (1024 bytes).

kernel

The core of the operating system software. The kernel manages the hardware (for example, processor cycles and memory) and supplies fundamental services, such as filing, that the hardware does not provide.

kernel architecture

The type of kernel on a system, such as sun4c for the SPARCstation system.

kill

To terminate a process before it reaches its natural conclusion.

kilobyte (Kbyte)

A unit of measure equal to 1024 bytes.

L

label

(1) In the OPEN LOOK GUI, the title of a *button*, *items*, or *settings* that describes its function. (2) Information written by the format program starting at cylinder 0 of a disk.The disk label describes the size and boundaries of the disk's partitions and its disk type.

large-scale integration (LSI)

A term describing the concentration of between 100 and 5000 circuit elements on a single chip. See also *integrated circuit (IC)*.

latch

A circuit or circuit element used to maintain a particular state, such as on or off, or logical true or false. A latch changes state only in response to a particular input A *flip-flop* is one kind of latch circuit.

latency

The time from when an SBus master request for the bus and the completion of its data transfer.

layer

(1) *window*s and *icon*s that overlap one another on the *workspace*. (2) In communications and distributed processing, a set of structures and routines that handle a particular class of events. For example, in the seven-layer International Organization for Standardization's open systems interconnection model, the *physical layer* deals with the hardware connection, the *data link layer* organizes transmitted signals, and the *network layer* is responsible for routing the signals to their intended recipients. See also *International Organization for Standardization*.

library routines

A series of SunOS functions that can be called by user programs written in C and other compatible programming languages.

lightweight process (LWP)

A class of processes that share resources with each other and therefore use less resources than ordinary processes.

link

(1) An entry in a directory file that links a user-assigned name for a file to the system's identification number for that file. (2) A file name the user gives to a file. See also *symbolic link*.

linker

A program that links compiled modules and data files to create an executable program. A linker can also have other functions, such as creation of libraries.

literal

A value, used in a program, that is expressed as itself rather than as a variable's value or the result of an expression.

little-endian

A format for storage or transmission of binary data in which the least significant byte (bit) comes first. Contrast with *big-endian*.

loadable kernel module

Software used to enhance the system *kernel*.

loading

Putting the machine-language instructions of a program into memory.

local

Having limited scope. Contrast with *global*.

localization

The process of altering a program so that it is specific to a single native language.

locked file

(1) A file upon which one or more of the usual types of manipulative operation cannot be performed. Typically, one that cannot be altered by additions or deletions. (2) A file that cannot be moved or removed, or whose name cannot be changed.

login shell

The name of the default *shell* used when a user logs in.

log out

To end a session on the system, usually when the user finishes work and does not want someone else to have access to the account.

loosely coupled

A computer system architecture characterized by processors that can only access their own memory. Processors do not share a common address space. Contrast to *tightly coupled*.

low

A term applied to a signal driven to a voltage equal to V_{OL}.

LWP

See *lightweight process (LWP)*.

M

machine address

See *absolute address*.

machine language

The basic set of instructions understood by a given computer. These instructions are represented internally by means of a binary code.

macro

(1) A user-defined keyboard shortcut that types text or plays back a sequence of commands. (2) A compound instruction put together from simpler instructions.

makefile

A file used by the `make` command, that describes files that `make` must process and programs that `make` must run.

man pages

UNIX *on-line documentation*. Also referred to as manual pages.

master

An SBus device capable of initiating an SBus transaction. The term *CPU master* is used when a host CPU must be distinguished from a more generic SBus master. The term *DVMA master* is used when explicitly excluding CPU masters. Any SBus master can communicate with any *slave* on the same bus, regardless of system configuration.

MBus

A high-speed, synchronous, circuit-switched interface used to connect SPARC processor modules to physical memory and I/O modules. The MBus specification has two levels of compliance. Level-1 includes the basic MBus signals and transactions needed in a uniprocessor machine. Level-2 has additional signals and transactions for a cache-coherent, shared-memory multiprocessor architecture.

Mbyte

Abbreviation for megabyte; one million bytes.

medium-scale integration (MSI)

A term describing the concentration of between 10 and 100 circuit elements on a single chip. See also *integrated circuit (IC)*.

megabyte (Mbyte)

A unit of measure equal to 1,048,576 bytes or 1024 kilobytes; or roughly 1 million bytes or 1,000 kilobytes.

megaflops

See *MFLOPS*.

memory management

The system functions including the hardware's page mapping and protection. See also *memory management unit (MMU)*.

memory management unit (MMU)

The hardware that supports the mapping of virtual memory addresses to physical addresses. See also *physical address space* and *virtual address*.

message

Information generated by an application that informs users about the status of a process.

MFLOPS

An acronym for millions of floating-point operations per second. MFLOPS are standardized units of execution speed used to rate the floating-point performance of a computer. See also *FLOPS*.

MHz

Megahertz. One million cycles per second.

MIPS

An acronym for millions of instructions per second. MIPS are standardized units of execution speed used to rate the performance of a computer *CPU*. See also *FLOPS* and *MFLOPS*.

MMU

See *memory management unit (MMU)*.

motherboard

(1) The main circuit board containing the primary components of a computer system to which other boards may be attached. See also *daughterboard*. (2) In SBus terminology, a circuit board containing the central processor, SBus controller, and any SBus expansion connectors.

mount

The process of accessing a directory from a disk attached to a machine making the mount request or remote disk on a network. See also *unmount*.

mounting

The process of making a *file system* accessible over the network by executing the `mount` command.

mount point

A directory on a workstation to which you *mount* a *file system* that exists on a remote machine.

MP

See *multiprocessor*.

MSI

See *medium-scale integration (MSI)*.

multiprocessor

A computer employing two or more processing units under integrated control. The processing units are roughly equal and each carries out one or more processes in tandem. In multiprocessing, each processing unit works on a different set of instructions (or on different parts of the same process). The objective is increased speed or computing power, the same as in parallel processing and in the use of special units called coprocessors. In parallel processing, however, multiple processes are carried out simultaneously (rather than concurrently) within a single system, In coprocessing, a separate unit, such as a math coprocessor chip, is designed to handle certain tasks with a high degree of efficiency. Definitions vary, however, and distinctions, particularly between multiprocessing and parallel processing, sometimes blur or overlap.

multitasking

(1) Enabling more than one user to access the same program at the same time. (2) Pertaining to the concurrent execution of two or more tasks by a computer. (3) A mode of operation offered by an operating system in which the computer works on more than one task at a time. There are several types of multitasking. One, *context switching*, is a very simple type of multitasking in which two or more applications are loaded at the same time but only the foreground application is given processing time; to activate a background task, the user must bring the window or screen containing that application to the front. In cooperative multitasking, background tasks are given processing time during idle times in the foreground task (such as when the application waits for a keystroke), and only if the application allows it. In time-slice multitasking, each task is given the processor's attention for a fraction of a second. To maintain order, tasks are either assigned priority levels or processed in sequential order. Because the user's sense of time is much slower than the processing speed of the computer, time-slice multitasking operations seem to be simultaneous.

multithreading

(1) A technique that enables multiprocessing applications to run more efficiently by breaking sequences of instructions (threads) into multiple sequences that can be executed from the kernel simultaneously. See also *asymmetric multiprocessing* and *symmetric multiprocessing*. (2) In data manipulation, a technique in which nodes in a tree data structure contain pointers to higher nodes to make traversal of the structure more efficient.

multiuser system

Any computer system that can be used concurrently by more than one person. Although a microcomputer shared by several people can be considered a multiuser system, the term is generally reserved for machines that are accessed by several or many people through communications facilities or via network terminals. Contrast with *single system*.

mutex lock

A synchronization facilities that allows threads to cooperate in accessing shared data. A mutex lock is one of several kinds of synchronization facilities including in SunOS. A thread can encounter a mutex lock when attempting to update a memory variable. The thread blocks until the mutex is unlocked.

mutual exclusion

A programming technique that ensures that only one program or routine at a time can access some resource (such as a memory location, an I/O port, or a file), often through the use of *semaphores*, which are flags used in programs to coordinate activities of more than one program or routine.

MUX

Short for various forms of the word *"multiplexer"*.

N

named pipe

A *first-in, first-out (FIFO)* file. A UNIX System V process can open the FIFO file, using it for communication just like a *pipe* but between possibly unrelated processes.

native language

1. The language supported by a particular computer system (the host) in the absence of additional software to create the support. Strictly speaking, this would normally be the CPU's machine language, but the term is sometimes applied to a high-level language that is specifically supported

by the operating system, toolbox routines, and native-development systems. 2. In localization, the process of altering a program so that it is specific to a single native language.

NFS

A distributed file system developed by Sun that enables a set of computers to cooperatively access each other's files in a *transparent* manner.

nibble

Half of a *byte* (four bits).

NIS

A hierarchical enterprise naming service for the simplified management of a changing network environment. Also referred to as Network Information Service Plus (NIS+).

nonvolatile memory

A type of memory that retains information when power is removed from the system. A portion of memory (typically RAM), or a dedicated memory subsystem is designated as the nonvolatile memory area for critical data and/or programs.

NVRAM

Nonvolatile random-access memory. A type of *RAM* that retains information when power is removed from the system. See also *EEPROM, boot PROM, ID PROM,* and *nonvolatile memory*.

O

object

A representation of combined states and methods that explicitly embodies an abstraction characterized by the behavior of relevant requests. An object is an instance of an implementation and an interface. An object models a real-world entity, and it is implemented as a computational entity that encapsulates state and operations (internally implemented as data and methods) and responds to requestor services. An object explicitly embodies an abstraction that is meaningful to its clients. Although an object may involve data, an object is not just a data structure or a collection of bits; the purpose of the data is to represent information.

object code

Output from a compiler or assembler that is itself executable machine code or is suitable for processing to produce executable machine code.

object file

A file containing *machine language* code. An executable file.

object management group (OMG)

A consortium established specifically to define the standards required to facilitate object-oriented applications development and use in heterogeneous distributed environments. The goal of OMG is the definition of a Object Management Architecture (OMA) that will enable interoperable applications based on distributed, interoperating objects.

object-oriented graphics

Also called "structured graphics." Computer graphics that are based on the use of graphics primitives, such as lines, curves, circles, and squares. Object-oriented graphics, used in applications such as computer-aided design and drawing and illustration programs, describe an image mathematically as a set of instructions for creating the objects in the image.

ONC

A distributed applications architecture promoted and controlled by a consortium led by Sun Microsystems, Inc.

on-line

Connected to the system and in operation.

on-line documentation

A disk-based form of documentation provided by many application programs, consisting of advice or instructions on using program features. On-line documentation can be accessed directly without the need to interrupt work in progress or leaf through a manual.

open architecture

A term used to describe any computer or peripheral design that has published specifications. A published specification enables third parties to develop add-on hardware for an open-architecture computer or device. Contrast with *closed architecture*.

openboot

With regard to SBus profiles, is the facility by which the *FCodes* program can interrogate the host and determine the state of various parameters it addresses.

open collector

A bipolar bus driver driven only low. See also *open drain*.

open drain

A field-effect transistor (*FET*) bus driver driven only low. See also *open collector*.

OPEN LOOK

A graphical user interface; the name is a registered trademarked of AT&T.

open system

In communications, especially with regard to the ISO open interconnection model, a computer network designed to incorporate all devices—regardless of manufacturer or model—that can use the same communications facilities and protocols. See also *open architecture*.

open systems interconnection (OSI)

An international standardization program to facilitate communications among computers from different manufacturers.

operating system

A collection of programs that monitor the use of the system and supervise the other programs executed by it.

output

Information produced by a command, program, or such, and sent elsewhere; for example, to the terminal, to a file, or to a line printer.

owner

(1) The person who created a file or directory. (2) The attribute of a file or directory that specifies who has owner permissions. (3) A line of data is said to be owned when there is one (and only one) cache in the system that is responsible for writing it back to memory as well as supplying the line when requested by another cache. If no cache is the owner, memory is considered the owner.

P

pack

To store data in a compact form in a storage medium. Packing eliminates unnecessary spaces and other such characters and may use other special methods of compressing data as well. It is used by some programs to

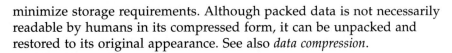

minimize storage requirements. Although packed data is not necessarily readable by humans in its compressed form, it can be unpacked and restored to its original appearance. See also *data compression*.

packed decimal

A method of encoding decimal numbers in binary form that maximizes storage space by using each byte to represent two decimal digits. For example, in binary form, the 1 in the decimal number 12 is represented as 0001, and the 2 is represented as 0010. If one byte is allotted to each decimal digit, decimal 12 is written

00000001 00000010

with extraneous zeros filling the left-most four superfluous bit positions in each byte. In the packed decimal method, however, where each byte represents two digits, the same number is written

00010010

thereby saving one full byte of storage.

packet

A packet is a contiguous sequence of cycles that constitutes the next higher unit of transfer beyond that of a typically bus cycle. The first (header) cycle of a packet carries address and control information, while subsequent cycles carry data. Packets come in two sizes: 2 cycles and 9 cycles. A transaction consists of a pair of packets (request, reply) that together performs some logical function. Packets usually come in request-reply pairs, although there are a few exceptions.

packet switching

A concept wherein a network transmits packets over connections that last only for the duration of the transmission. A packet-switching network handles information in small units, breaking long messages into multiple packets before routing. Although each packet may travel along a different path, and the packets composing a message may arrive at different times or out of sequence, the receiving computer reassembles the original message. This repackaging is called packet assembly and disassembly. Standards for packet switching on networks are documented in the *CCIT* recommendation X.25.

page

(1) A block of 8192 contiguous byte locations used for memory mapping and protection. (2) The data between the beginning of a file and a page marker, or between two markers, or between a marker and the end of the file. (3) To advance text on the screen by one screenful (or page) at a time.

page fault

> The interrupt that occurs when software attempts to read from or write to a virtual memory location that is marked "not present." The mapping hardware of a virtual memory system maintains status information about every page in the virtual address space. A page either is mapped onto a physical address or is not present in physical memory. When a read or write to an unmapped virtual address is detected, the memory management hardware generates the page fault interrupt. The operating system must respond to the page fault by swapping in the data for the page and updating the status information in the *memory management unit (MMU)*.

page frame

> A physical address to which a page of virtual memory may be mapped. In a system with 4096-byte pages, page frame 0 corresponds to physical addresses 0 through 4095. See also *paging* and *virtual memory*.

page mode RAM

> A specially designed *dynamic RAM (DRAM)* that supports access to sequential memory locations with reduced cycle time. This type of access is especially attractive in *video RAM (VRAM)*, where each location is accessed in ascending order to create the screen image. Page mode RAM can also improve the execution speed of code because code tends to execute sequentially through memory.

paging

> The process of replacing the contents of page frame with different pages. A page is a fixed-size unit of memory. The *physical address space* is conceptually divided into page-size units called *page frame*s.

parameter

> A special type of *variable* used within shell programs to access values related to the *arguments* on the *command line* or to the *environment* in which the program is executed.

parameter passing

> In programming, the substitution of an actual value for a formal (dummy) parameter when a procedure or function call is processed.

parent/child

> (1) A term describing the relationship between processes in a multitasking environment in which the parent process calls the child process and most often suspends its own operation until the child process

aborts or is completed. (2) A relationship between nodes in a tree data structure in which the parent is one step closer to the root (that is, one level higher) than the child.

parent directory

A directory containing the working directory or the directory of interest.

parent process

A process from which a *child process* is started.

parity

A method used by a computer for checking that the data received matches the data sent. In typical modem-to-modem communications, parity is one of the parameters that must be agreed upon by sending and receiving parties before transmission takes place.

parse

To break input into smaller chunks so that a program can act upon the information. Compilers have parsers for translating the commands and structures entered by a programmer into machine language. A natural-language parser accepts text in a human language such as English, attempts to determine its sequence structure, and translates its terms into a form the program can use.

partial store ordering (PSO)

A model defining access to memory as implemented by the SPARC reference memory management architecture. Partial store ordering guarantees certain instructions, such as store, FLUSH, and atomic load-store appear to be executed by memory serially in a single order called the memory order.

path name

The location of a file or directory in the UNIX file system.

permissions

The attribute of a file or directory which specifies who has read, write, or execution access.

physical address

An address that corresponds to a hardware memory location. In simple processors (such as the 68000), every address is a physical address. In nearly all recent processors that support virtual memory, programs reference virtual addresses, which are then mapped by memory management hardware onto physical addresses. See also *memory management unit (MMU)* and *virtual memory*.

physical address space

>The set of possible 32-bit or 64-bit physical addresses that can be used to refer to locations in memory (memory space) or I/O space (device registers).

physical memory

>Main memory. The memory connected to the processor that stores instructions, which the processor directly fetches and executes, and any other data the processors must manipulate.

pipe

>(1) Software connection between two programs. (2) To direct the output of one command or program into the input of another. (3) The UNIX operator (|) that directs the output of one command or program into the input of another.

pipeline

>The program linkage established by performing one or more *pipe*s.

PLA

>See *field-programmable logic array (FPLA)*.

platform

>The foundation technology of a computer system. Because computers are layered devices composed of a chip-level hardware layer, a firmware and operating system layer, and an applications program layer, the bottom layer of a machine is often called a platform, as in "a *SPARC* platform." However, designers of applications software view both the hardware and system software as the platform because both provide support for an application.

plug-compatible

>An adjective describing hardware equipped with connectors that are equivalent both in structure and in usage. For example, most modems having DB-25 connectors on their rear panels are plug-compatible; that is, one can be replaced by another without the cable having to be rewired.

pointer

>A table look-up technique as in a pointer pointing to a list of associated functions.

port

>(1) In computer hardware, a location for passing data in and out of a computing device. Microprocessors have ports for sending and receiving data bits; these ports are usually dedicated locations in memory. Full computer systems have ports for connecting peripheral devices such as

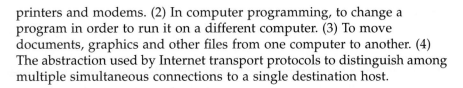

printers and modems. (2) In computer programming, to change a program in order to run it on a different computer. (3) To move documents, graphics and other files from one computer to another. (4) The abstraction used by Internet transport protocols to distinguish among multiple simultaneous connections to a single destination host.

port numbers

Numbers used by *TCP/IP* protocols to identify the endpoints of communication.

POSIX

An acronym created from the phrase "portable operating system interface," an IEEE standard that defines a set of operating-system services. Programs that adhere to the POSIX standard can be easily ported from one system to another. POSIX was based on UNIX system services, but it can be implemented by other operating systems.

power-on self test (POST)

A set of routines stored in a computer's read-only memory (ROM) that tests various system components such as RAM, the disk drives, and the keyboard to see if they are properly connected and operating. If problems are found, the POST routines alert the user by displaying a message, often accompanied by a diagnostic numeric value, to the *standard output* device. If the POST is successful, it passes control to the system's bootstrap loader.

primitive

(1) In programming, a fundamental element in a language that can be used to create larger procedures that do the work a programmer wants to do. (2) At the machine language level, a fundamental machine instruction. (3) Fundamental shapes and objects in computer graphics, used primarily in construction of more complex objects. Graphics primitives include point, line segment, polyline, circle, ellipse, triangle, square, and rectangle.

priority interrupt

Part of the *VMEbus* specification that enables devices that request interruption of normal bus activity to be serviced by an *interrupt handler*. Interrupt requests are prioritized into a maximum of seven levels. The associated functional modules, called interrupters and interrupt handlers, use signal lines called the "interrupt bus."

process

A particular computer activity or job.

process ID

A unique, system-wide, identification number assigned to a *process*.

processor

A hardware device that executes the commands in a stored program in the computer system. In addition to the *central processing unit (CPU)*, many sophisticated graphics systems contain a dedicated processor for use in the *graphics accelerator*.

process status

The current state of a process: running, stopped, waiting, and so on.

program

A sequence of instructions telling a computer how to perform a task. A program can be in *machine language* or it can be in a higher-level language that is then translated into machine language.

PROM

Pronounced "prom." An acronym for programmable read-only memory. A type of read-only memory (ROM) that allows data to be written into the device with hardware called a PROM programmer. After the PROM has been programmed, it is dedicated to that data and cannot be reprogrammed. See also *EEPROM, EPROM,* and *ROM.*

propagation delay

The time needed by a communications signal to travel between two points.

protocol

A formal description of messages to be exchanged and rules to be followed for two or more systems to exchange information.

Q

queue

(1) A line or list formed by items in a system waiting for service. (2) To arrange in, or form, a queue. (3) A multielement data structure from which (by strict definition) elements can be removed only in the same order in which they were inserted; that is, it follows a *first-in, first-out (FIFO)* constraint.

R

RAM

Semiconductor-based memory that can be read or written by the CPU or other hardware devices. The storage locations can be accessed in any order. Note that the various types of ROM memory are capable of random access. The term RAM, however, is generally understood to refer to volatile memory, which can be written as well as read. Compare with *ROM*.

real-time

Term applied to an event or system that must receive a response to some stimulus within a narrow, predictable time frame. Usually, this need requires that the response is not strongly dependent on system performance parameters that are highly variable, such as a processor load or interface *latency*.

record locking

A strategy employed in distributed processing and other multiuser situations to prevent more than one user at a time from writing data to a record. See also *locked file*.

recover

To return to a stable condition after some error has occurred. When a program recovers from an error, it stabilizes itself and continues carrying out instructions without user intervention. When a computer user recovers lost or damaged data, a recovery program searches for and salvages whatever information remains in storage. When a database is recovered, it is returned to a previous stable condition after some problem, such as abnormal termination of the database program, has caused the data to lose its integrity.

recoverable error

A nonfatal error—one that can be successfully managed by software, as when the user enters a number when a letter is required.

recursive

An adjective applied to a computer program that calls itself.

redirection

(1) The channeling of output to a file or device instead of to the *standard output*. (2) The channeling of input from a file or device instead of from the *standard output*.

reduced instruction set computer (RISC)
> A type of microprocessor design that focuses on rapid and efficient processing of a relatively small set of instructions.

reentrant
> The attribute of a program or routine that enables the same copy of the program or routine to be used concurrently by two or more tasks.

reflective memory
> A cache protocol that provides for automatic memory updates upon cache data being marked clean. Operation is dependent upon a memory controller that supports reflective memory.

relational database
> A database in which relationships between data items are explicitly specified as equally accessible attributes.

relative path name
> A series of directory names separated by the slash (/) character that locates a file or directory with respect to the working directory. See also *absolute path name*.

remote file system (RFS)
> A distributed file system, similar to *NFS*, developed by AT&T and distributed with their UNIX *System V* operating system.

remote procedure call (RPC)
> An easy and popular paradigm for implementing the client-server model of distributed computing. A request is sent to a remote system to execute a designated procedure, using arguments supplied, and the result is returned to the caller. There are many variations and subtleties, resulting in a variety of different RPC protocols.

remote shell
> A command interpreter that is initiated on one machine, but that executes on another machine specified on the command line.

remote system
> A system other than the one on which the user is working.

ROM
> Read-only memory. See also *PROM, EEPROM, EPROM,* and *boot PROM*.

root
> See *root file system, root directory, root user name,* and *root user name*.

root directory

> The base directory from which all other directories stem, directly or indirectly.

root file system

> One file system residing on the root device (a device predefined by the system at initialization) designated to anchor the overall file system.

root user name

> SunOS user name that grants special privileges to the person who logs in with that ID. The user who can supply the correct password for the root user name is given *superuser* privileges for the particular machine.

runnable process

> A program that is ready to run, that is, it is not waiting for resources to become available (for example, data from disk or a user).

runtime library

> A file containing one or more prewritten routines to perform specific, commonly used functions. A runtime library, used primarily in high-level languages such as C, enables the programmer to bypass many low-level programming tasks.

S

sample rate

> The frequency of the points used to determine an object's placement on the display device. See *sampling*. See also *sampling rate*.

sampling

> (1) The process of acquiring data from some source. (2) The conversion of analog signals to digital format; samples are taken at periodic intervals to measure and record some parameter, such as a signal from a temperature sensor or microphone. (3) In computer graphics, a procedure that samples many points across an object's lines or surfaces to determine its placement in *pixels*. This occurs during *scan conversion*. See also *sampling rate*.

sampling rate

> The frequency with which samples of a physical variable, such as sound, are taken. The higher the sampling rate (the more samples taken per unit of time), the more closely the digitized result resembles the original. See also *sample rate*.

SBus

> I/O System Expansion Bus. Also IEEE standard 1496-1993 titled, "Standard for a Chip and Module Interconnect: SBus,". SBus is a high-performance I/O interconnect that is optimized for high-speed I/O expansion for desktop and other high performance workstations and servers.

SBus bridge

> A device providing additional SBus slots by connecting two SBuses. In general, a bus bridge is functionally transparent to devices on the SBus. However, in some cases (for example, *bus sizing*) bus bridges can change the exact way a series of *bus cycle*s are performed. Also known as an "SBus coupler."

SBus controller

> The hardware responsible for performing arbitration, addressing translation and decoding, driving slave selects and address strobe, and generating time-outs.

SBus device

> A logical device attached to the SBus. This device can be on the *motherboard* or on an *SBus expansion card*.

SBus expansion card

> A physical printed circuit assembly that conforms to the single- or double-width mechanical specifications and that contains one or more *SBus device*s.

SBus expansion slot

> An SBus slot into which an *SBus expansion card* can be installed.

SBus ID

> A special series of bytes at address 0 of each SBus slave used to identify the *SBus device*.

SBus master

> See *master*.

SBus slave

> See *single system*.

scalar

> A factor, coefficient, or variable consisting of a single value (as opposed to a record, an array, or some other complex data structure).

SCSI

(Pronounced "scuzzy.") See *small computer systems interface (SCSI)*.

segmentation fault

A system fault that occurs when a process has attempted to access an area of memory that is restricted or does not exist. See also *bus error*.

semaphore

In programming, a signal used to govern access to shared resources. A semaphore is a *flag* variable—an indicator—that helps maintain order among processes that are competing for the use of such critical resources as processor time and input/output ports.

serial port

A port for *serial transmission*.

server

(1) In the *client-server model* for file systems, the server is a machine with compute resources (and is sometimes called the compute server), and large memory capacity. Client machines can remotely access and make use of these resources. In the client-server model for window systems, the server is a process that provides windowing services to an application, or "client process." In this model, the client and the server can run on the same machine or on separate machines. (2) A *daemon* that actually handles the providing of files.

server system

A system that is on a *network* and provides resources, such as disk space and file transfers, to other systems.

shell

A programmable command interpreter. The shell provides direct communication between the user and the operating system.

shell procedure

An executable file that is not a compiled program. A shell procedure calls the *shell* to read and execute commands contained in a file. This scheme enables the user to store a sequence of commands in a file for repeated use. It is also called a "shell program" or "command file."

shell script

See *shell procedure*.

shell variable

A UNIX construct that affects how the shell runs and appears. For example, certain variables specify the list of arguments that are listed on the current command line or set the number of command lines saved in a command history.

signal

A C library function; the software signalling facility. A signal is generated by some abnormal event, initiated by a user at a terminal (quit, interrupt, stop), by a program error (bus error, and so forth), by request of another program (kill), or when a process is stopped because it wishes to access its control terminal while in the background. Signals are optionally generated when a process resumes after being stopped, when the status of child processes changes, or when input is ready at the control terminal. Most signals cause termination of the receiving process if no action is taken; some signals instead cause the process receiving them to be stopped or are simply discarded if the process has not requested otherwise.

simulate

To simulate the behavioral characteristics of one system by another. Contrast with *emulate*.

simulation

The representation of physical systems and events typically by computer.

simulator

A program that runs on one computer and imitates the operations of another computer.

single system

A computer system allowing access to only one person at any time. Contrast with *multiuser system*.

slave

An SBus device that responds with an acknowledgment to a slave select and address strobe signal. Any SBus master can communicate with any other slave on the same bus, regardless of system configuration.

slave cycle

That portion of a *bus cycle* that begins with placing an address on the physical address lines and ends with the address strobe signal being asserted.

small computer systems interface (SCSI)
> An industry standard bus used to connect disk and tape devices to a workstation.

SMP
> See *symmetric multiprocessing*.

socket
> A software endpoint for network communication. Two programs on different machines each open a socket in order to communicate over the network. This is the low-level mechanism that supports most networking programs.

source code
> The uncompiled version of a program written in a language such as C or Pascal. The source code must be translated to machine language by a program known as the *compiler* before the computer can execute the program.

SPARC
> The 32-bit scalable processor architecture from Sun. SPARC is based on a *reduced instruction set computer (RISC)* concept. The architecture was designed by Sun and its suppliers in an effort to significantly improve price and performance. SPARC is now a registered trademark of SPARC International, Inc.

SPECmark
> System Performance Evaluation Cooperative (SPEC). Founded in 1988 to establish a set of programs and inputs that comprised a benchmark for performance by measuring the elapsed time of each of 10 benchmark suites.

SPICE
> An acronym for Simulation Program with Integrated Circuit Emphasis.

SRAM
> Acronym for "static random-access memory." See also *dynamic RAM (DRAM)* and *VRAM*.

static allocation
> To reserve memory for use by a program. The memory is set aside when the program starts and remains allocated while the program is running. See also *deallocate* and *pointer*.

static RAM (SRAM)

A form of semiconductor memory (RAM). Static RAM storage is based on the logic circuit known as a *flip-flop*, which retains the information stored in it as long as there is enough power to run the device. See also *dynamic RAM (DRAM)* and *video RAM (VRAM)*.

string variable

A sequence of characters that can be the value of a shell variable. See *variable*.

strong consistency

A memory model that constrain the ordering of operations apply equally to operations on real memory and I/O locations. In addition, the order in which operations to I/O locations by a given processor are executed by memory must conform to the "program order" of these operations for that processor. In Strong Consistency, the loads, stores, and atomic load-stores of all processors are executed by memory serially in an order that conforms to the order in which these instructions were issued by individual processors.

swap

To write the active pages of a job to external storage (*swap space*) and to read pages of another job from external page storage into real storage.

swapping area

See *swap space*.

swap space

The memory used for the transfer of a currently operating program from system memory to an external storage device. Also known as *swapping area*.

symbolic link

An association between entries in a directory or file that a user program has created; links arbitrary symbols to represent addresses in order to facilitate programming. See also *link*.

symmetric application

An application that involves nearly equal use of compression and decompression operations. For example, video mail is a symmetric application because the sender of mail must be able to compress video and audio data, and the receiver must be able to decode that data. Contrast with *asymmetric application*. See also *data compression*.

symmetric multiprocessing

A form of multiprocessing in which more than one processor can run kernel-level code simultaneously. Contrast with *asymmetric multiprocessing*.

synchronous

Under control of a clock or timing mechanism. Contrast with *asynchronous*.

syntax

The order in which the parts of an operating system command are to be typed.

syntax error

An error in the use of language syntax; a statement that violates one or more of the grammatical rules of a language and is thus "not legal."

system

A computer that enables a user to run computer programs.

system administration

The tasks of a person who performs maintenance tasks on systems.

system administrator

The person who performs maintenance tasks on systems.

system ID

A sequence of numbers, and sometimes letters, that is unique to each system and is used to identify that system.

system kernel

See *kernel*.

System V

Pronounced "system five." A version of the UNIX operating system produced by AT&T.

System V Release 4 (SVR4)

Release 4.0 of the UNIX operating system produced by AT&T.

T

table

A display of data in rows and columns.

table look-up

The process of using a known value to search for data in a previously constructed table of values.

table walk

A search performed by the MMU through the address translation tables stored in main memory

task

A standalone application or a subprogram that is run as an independent entity.

task management

The operating-system process of tracking the progress of and providing necessary resources for separate tasks running on a computer, especially in a multitasking environment.

text, data, and stack segment

Elements of the memory segments of a process.In the UNIX system, a process is represented by three memory segments, called the text (or code), data, and stack segments and by a set of data structures collectively known as the process environment. A text segment contains code and constant data, a data segment contains variables, and a stack segment holds a process's stack.

thrashing

The state of a virtual memory system that is spending almost all its time swapping pages in and out of memory rather than executing applications.

thread

(1) In programming, a process that is part of a larger process or program. (2) In a tree data structure, a pointer that identifies the parent node and is used to facilitate traversal of the tree.

three-way handshake

The process whereby two protocol entities synchronize during connection establishment.

throughput

A measure of the amount of work performed by a computer system over a given time (for example, floating-point instructions per second).

tightly coupled
A multiprocessing system architecture where all the processors share common memory and communicate with one another through shared memory.

time-out
A situation in which the SBus controller terminates a bus cycle that a *slave* has failed to acknowledge. In a correctly designed and operating system, time-outs should happen only during system configuration.

time-slice multitasking
See *multitasking*.

timesharing system
A computer with terminals attached to its serial ports. The terminals rely on the workstation for processing power as well as file service and disk storage.

total store ordering
A model which specifies the behavior observed by software on SPARC systems. Total Store Ordering guarantees that the store, FLUSH, and atomic load-store instructions of all processors appear to be executed by memory serially in a single order called the memory order. Furthermore, the sequence of store, FLUSH, and atomic load-store instructions in the memory order for a given processor is identical to the sequence in which they were issued by the processor.

trace
(1) To execute a program in such a way that the sequence of statements being executed can be observed. (2) A simple trace can be implemented by putting numerous output statements in the program, each one writing out (to the screen, to a file, or to some other location) some identifying information and possibly some data values. Many debuggers provide a more sophisticated trace, displaying each statement as it is executed and possibly updating a list of variables and data structures.

trace/breakpoint trap
A trap used for tracing and debugging programs. See also *trace* and *breakpoint*.

trap
A software mechanism that causes control of the machine to be instantly transferred to the kernel, even if a user process is currently running.

U

UART

Universal asynchronous receiver-transmitter. A module, usually composed of a single integrated circuit, that contains both the receiving and transmitting circuits required for asynchronous serial communications.

unasserted

The state of a signal when no action is initiate. Contrast with *asserted*.

UNIX International (UI)

A consortium that coordinates code releases for AT&T's UNIX System Laboratories (USL).

unmount

The process of removing access to a directory on a disk attached to a machine or a remote disk on a network. See also *mount*.

unpack

To recover the original form of the data from packed data.

UUCP

UNIX-to-UNIX copy program. A protocol used for communication between consenting UNIX systems.

V

validate

To have an application verify that the contents of a *text field* are appropriate to the function.

VAR

Value-added reseller.

variable

A symbol with a value that can change when used either in program usage or in the shell. In the shell, the variable is a symbol representing some string of characters. Variables may be used in an interactive shell as well as within a *shell procedure*.

vector

> A line segment on a display surface, especially one of minimum width and solid (no dashing). A vector can also be a conceptual direction (perhaps with length) denoting a direction (of a light ray, for instance) or the boundary of an object; an example is a *normal vector*.

vector architecture

> A vector machine typically consists of an ordinary pipelined scalar unit plus a vector unit. All functional units within the vector unit have a latency of several clock cycles. This allows a shorter clock cycle time and is compatible with long running, vector operations that can be deeply pipelined without generating hazards. Most vector machines allow the vectors to be dealt with as floating-point numbers (FP), as integers, or as logical data. The scalar unit is basically no different from the type of pipelined CPU.

> There are two primary types of vector architectures: vector-register machines and memory-memory vector machines. In a vector-register machine, all vector operations--except load and store--are among the vector registers. These machines are the vector counterpart of a load/store architecture. All major vector machines being shipped in 1990 use a vector-register architecture; these include the Cray Research machines (CRAY-1, CRAY-2, X-MP, and Y-MP), the Japanese supercomputers (NEC SX/2, Fujitsu VP200, and the Hitachi S820), and the mini-supercomputers (Convex C-l and C-2). In a memory-memory vector machine all vector operations are memory to memory. The first vector machines were of this type, as were CDC's machines.

vector table

> See *dispatch table*.

very-large-scale integration (VLSI)

> A reference to the density with which components (transistors and other elements) are packed onto an *integrated circuit (IC)* and to the fineness of the connections between them. VLSI is not precisely defined but is generally considered to range from 5000 to 50,000 components.

video RAM (VRAM)

> A special type of *dynamic RAM (DRAM)* used in high-speed video applications. With conventional DRAM, both the processor and the video circuitry must access RAM by sharing the same control pins on the RAM chips. VRAM provides separate pins for the processor and the video circuitry. See also *static RAM (SRAM)*.

virtual address

> (1) A 16-bit integer identifying a byte "location" in virtual address space. The memory management unit translates the virtual address into a physical address. (2) The address used to identify a virtual block on a mass-storage device.

virtual circuit

> An apparent connection between processes that is facilitated by *transmission control protocol (TCP)*. A virtual circuit enables applications to talk to each other as if they had a physical circuit.

virtual memory

> A system scheme that enables a user program to be larger than physical memory. This is possible through a storage hierarchy in which a virtual image of a program is stored in secondary storage while main memory stores only active program segments.

VLSI

> See *very-large-scale integration (VLSI)*.

VMEbus

> An interfacing system that connects data processing, data storage, and peripheral control devices in a closely-coupled configuration. The VMEbus structure can be described in two ways: mechanically and functionally. The mechanical specification includes physical dimensions of subracks, backplanes, and plug-in boards. The functional specification describes how the bus works, what functional modules are involved in each transaction, and the rules that define behavior.

VRAM

> Acronym for "video random-access memory. See *video RAM (VRAM)*. See also *dynamic RAM (DRAM)* and *static RAM (SRAM)*.

W

wait state

> A pause of one or more clock cycles during which a microprocessor waits for data from an input/output device or from memory. Wait states are most often used to control the speed at which the microprocessor receives data from random-access memory (*RAM*).

whetstone

A general-performance benchmarking test, like the dhrystone, the whetstone is a synthetic floating-point loop benchmark that tries to match the average frequency of operations and operands of a large set of programs. The whetstone program was written before computers with vector instructions were popular, therefore, all whetstone floating-point loops make optimizations via vectorization useless. See *vector architecture*.

window system

A system that provides the user with a multiuse environment on the display device. Separate windows are like separate displays on the monitor screen. Each window can run its own application. The user brings up some number of windows for various applications, and the window system handles the communications between each of the applications and the hardware.

word

The native unit of storage on a particular machine. Depending on the processor, a word can be an 8-bit, a 16-bit, a 32-bit, or larger quantity unit. The Sun SPARCstation uses a 32-bit word.

wrapping

On the SBus, the process, during burst transfers, by which the burst may begin at an arbitrary word boundary within the block, with the address incremented by 4, modulo the size of the burst in bytes.

write

(1) To place text in a file. (2) To use the `write` command to communicate with other users. (3) To write data to memory.

X

XBus

A packet-switched bus that supports multiple buses by way of a cache controller in large multiprocessing configurations.

XDBus

A packet-switched backplane bus that supports multiple boards by way of a large multiprocessing configuration.

XDR

External data representation. A standard for machine-independent data structures developed by Sun. Similar to *ASN.1*.

Xenix

A version of the UNIX system that was originally adapted for Intel-based personal computers.

XGL

Sun graphics library.

XIL

X imaging library. XIL is a platform programming interface for imaging and video support. It provides a common implementation of imaging functionality that is common to multiple higher-level interfaces, provides imaging capabilities that are not currently available, and provides a way for *ISVs* to access low-level and hardware functionality.

X/Open

A group of computer manufacturers that promotes the development of portable applications based on UNIX. The group publishes a document called the X/Open Portability Guide.

Bibliography

For further information consult the following:

SunOS Multithread Architecture, Part Number 91033-002, M.L. Powell, S.R. Kleiman, S. Barton, D. Shah, D. Stein, M. Weeks, Sun Microsystems Inc., Mountain View, CA

Writing Multithreaded Code in Solaris 2.0, Part Number 91003-002, Steve Kleiman, Bart Smaalders, Dan Stein, Devang Shah, SunSoft Inc., Mountain VIew, CA

Beyond Multiprocessing... Multithreading the SunOS Kernel, Part Number 91003-002, J.R. Eykholt, S.R. Kleiman, S. Barton, R. Faulkner, A. Shivalingiah, M. Smith, D. Stein, J. Voll, M. Weeks, D. Williams, SunSoft, Inc., Mountain VIew, CA

Guide to Multithread Programming, part number 801-3176-03, Sun Microsystems, Inc., Mountain VIew, CA

Parallel STREAMS: a Multiprocessor Implementation, A. Garg., Proceedings of the Winter 1990 USENIX Conference.

Virtual Memory Architecture in SunOS, R.A. Gingell, J.P. Moran, W.A. Shannon, Proceedings of the Summer 1987 USENIX Conference.

Realtime Scheduling in SunOS 5.0, S. Khanna, M. Sebree, J. Zolnowski, Winter 1992 USENIX Conference.

SunOS Multi-thread Architecture, M.L. Powell, S.R. Kleiman, S. Barton, D. Shah, D. Stein, M. Weeks, Proceedings of the Winter 1991 USENIX Conference.

Multithreading Techniques used in the SunOS 5.0 Kernel, SunSoft Inc., Summer 1992 USENIX Conference.

UNIX System V Release 4 ES/MP Multiprocessing Detailed Specifications, UNIX System Laboratories.

SunOS 5.2 System Services, Part Number 801-4055-05, SunSoft Inc., Mountain View, CA.

Realtime Scheduling in SunOS 5.0, Khanna, Sebree, Zolnowski, SunSoft Inc., Mountain View, CA.

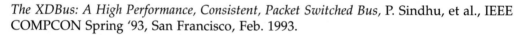

The XDBus: A High Performance, Consistent, Packet Switched Bus, P. Sindhu, et al., IEEE COMPCON Spring '93, San Francisco, Feb. 1993.

A CMOS Low-Voltage-Swing Transmission-Line Transceiver, B. Gunning, et al., ISSCC DIGEST OF TECHNICAL PAPERS, pp. 58-9, Feb. 1992.

The XBus Specification, Xerox Corporation, Palo Alto Research Center, 1992.

A Three-Million-Transistor Microprocessor, F. Abu-Nofal, et al., ISSCC DIGEST OF TECHNICAL PAPERS, pp. 108-9, Feb. 1992.

A BiCMOS 50MHz Cache Controller for a Superscalar Microprocessor, B. Joshi, et al., ISSCC DIGEST OF TECHNICAL PAPERS, pp. 110-111, Feb. 1992.

SBus Specification B.0, Sun Microsystems #800-5922-10, December 1990

The SPARC Architecture Manual (version 8), Prentice Hall, 1992.

The SPARC Technical Papers, B. Catanzaro, Springer-Verlag, ISBN 0-387-97634-5

SuperSPARC User's Guide, Texas Instruments Semiconductor Group, Stafford, TX

LSI Logic L64811, L64831 and SparKIT Technical Manuals, LSI Logic Corporation, Milpitas, CA.

SPARCore Modules Technical Specification, Cypress Semiconductor, 3901 N. First Street, San Jose, CA.

The CRAY S-MP Architecture, CRAY Research Superservers Inc., 3601 S.W. Murray Blvd. Beaveton, OR.

SPARCcenter 2000: Multiprocessing for the 90's, M. Cekleov, et al., IEEE COMPCON Spring '93, San Francisco, Feb. 1993.

IEEE Standard Test Access Port and Boundary-Scan Architecture, P1149.1, IEEE Computer Society Test Technology Technical Committee, New York, Jan. 1989.

Solaris OpenWindows: OpenWindows V3 Collection: Release Reports and White Papers, Part #91021-0, SunSoft Inc., Mountain View, CA

Solaris SunOS 5.0: SunOS 5.0 Multithreading and Real-Time, Part #91025-0, SunSoft Inc., Mountain View, CA

Solaris ONC: Design and Implementation of Transport-Independent RPC, Part #91028-0, SunSoft Inc., Mountain View, CA

Solaris SunOS: SunOS 5.0 Release Report, Part #91023-0, SunSoft Inc., Mountain View, CA

Multithreading and Real-Time in Solaris: Terms and Concepts, Part #91024-002, SunSoft Inc., Mountain View, CA

The ToolTalk Service, Part #91022-002, SunSoft Inc., Mountain View, CA

Introduction to the ToolTalk Service, Part #91031-002, SunSoft Inc., Mountain View, CA

Solaris OpenWindows: ToolTalk in Electronic Design Automation, Part #91032-0, SunSoft Inc., Mountain View, CA

Tool Inter-Operability: A Hands On Demonstration: A Simple Demonstration of How the ToolTalk Service Works, Part #92205-001, SunSoft Inc., Mountain View, CA

Solaris ONC: Network Information Service Plus (NIS+), Part #91027-0, SunSoft Inc., Mountain View, CA

Solaris ONC+: Network Information Service Plus (NIS+): An Enterprise Naming Service, Part #92245-001, SunSoft Inc., Mountain View, CA

Project DOE: Distributed Objects Everywhere, Part #91035-0, SunSoft Inc., Mountain View, CA

The ToolTalk Service: An Inter-Operability Solution, published by SunSoft Press/Prentice Hall, ISBN 013-088717-X.

ToolTalk and Open Protocols: Inter-Application Communication, to be published by SunSoft Press/Prentice Hall, June 1993, ISBN 013-031055-7

The Common Object Request Broker: Architecture and Specification, OMG

Computer Architecture, A Quantitative Approach, John L Hennessy and David A. Patterson. Morgan Kaufmann Publishers, Inc. ISBN 1-55860-069-8

Contacts

Bipolar Integrated Technology

1050 N.W. Compton Drive
Beaverton, OR 97006
(303) 629-5490

Cray Research Superservers Inc.

3601 SW Murray Blvd.
Beaverton, Oregon. 97005
(503) 641-3151

Cypress Semiconductor Corporation

3901 North 1st Street
San Jose, Ca. 95134
(408) 943-2600

Fujitsu Microelectronics, Inc.

Advanced Products Division
50 Rio Roables, M/S 356
San Jose, CA 95134-1806
(800) 523-0034

Institute of Electrical and Electronics Engineers, Inc. - IEEE

445 Hoes Lane
P.O. Box 1331
Piscataway, N.J. 08855-1331
(908) 981-0060

LSI Logic Corporation

1501 McCarthy Blvd.
Milpitas, CA 95035
(408) 433-7627

Ross Technology

7748 Highway 290 West, Suite 400
Austin, TX 78736
(512) 448-8968

SPARC International, Inc.

535 Middlefield Road Suite 210
Menlo Park, Ca.
(415) 321-8692

SunSoft Inc.

2650 Casey Ave.
Mountain View, Ca. 94043
(415) 960-3200

Sun Microsystems, Inc.

Sun Microsystems Computer Corporation
2550 Garcia Ave.
Mountain View, Ca. 94043
(415)960-1300

Systems and Processes Engineering Corporation

1408 Smith Road
Austin, Texas 78721
(512) 385-0318

Texas Instruments Corporation

12203 S.W. Freeway
Stafford, Texas 77477
(713) 274-2000

Xerox Palo Alto Research Center - PARC

3333 Coyote Hill Road
Palo Alto, Ca. 94304
(415) 812-4266

INDEX

Clock speeds, 2, 3
Clock-to-output hold, 386-88
    bused control, 387
    MAD, 387
    point-to-point control, 388
CMU commands, MPSAS, 187
Code locking, 251
Coherency, 157, 158, 161
Coherent Invalidate, 165, 336-38
Coherent Read, 164-65, 168, 335-36, 365-66
    of owned data, 365-66
    of shared data, 365
Coherent Read and Invalidate, 165, 168, 338, 368-69
    of owned data, 368-69
    of shared data, 368
Coherent Write and Invalidate, 165, 338-39, 366-67
Commands, MPSAS, 185-87
    CMU commands, 187
    CPU/FCPU commands, 187
    FPU commands, 187
    module, 187
    Sun4c/Sun4e MMU commands, 187
    universal, 186
Commercial Extensions Products, 24-25
Concurrency strategies, 250
    reentrance, 250-51
    single-lock strategy, 250
Condition variables, 233-36
Configuration address map, MBus, 345-46
Configuration file, 183-85
Connector, MBus, 170, 353-55
    mechanical specifications, 389
    pin assignments, 354-55, 389-91
Consistency quantity, Level 2 MBus, 323
Context numbers, 97-98
Context register, 108
Context table pointer register, 107-8
Control register, 106-7
    E field, 107
    IMPL field, 106
    NF field, 107
    PSO field, 107

reserved field, 107
    SC field, 107
    VER field, 106
Control-transfer instructions, SPARC, 42
Coprocessor architectures, SPARC, 42
Coprocessor operations, SPARC, 41-42
Copy-back protocol, 158
CPU commands, MPSAS, 187
Cray Research S-MP system, 78-79
Cypress 604/605 Cache and MMU Module, 193
Cypress CY7C605 cache controller
    and MMU, 159
Cypress CY7C625 CMTU, 116-17
    block diagram, 116
Cypress CYM6000 series, 273-75
Cypress HyperSPARC modules, 275-77
Cypress/Ross SPARC chipset, 52-54
    cache controller/memory
        management unit, 53
    cache RAM, 53-54
    floating-point unit, 53
    integer unit, 53

D

Data locking, 251
Deadlock, 252-53
DeskSet, OPEN LOOK graphical user
    interface, 24
Diagnostic register, 108-9
Direct data intervention (DDI), 160
DOE, *See* Project DOE (Distributed
    Objects Everywhere)
Dual Serial Port Module, 195

E

EBE (external bus error) field, fault
    status register, 110
E field, control register, 107
Encore Computer/Multimax, 6
ERROR1 (bus error), 341, 360-61
ERROR2 (time-out), 342, 361
ERROR3 (uncorrectable), 342, 362

eXternal Data Representation (XDR), ONC+, 22
External Trap Module, 196

F

Fast SPARC Processor Module, 193
Fault status register, 109-13
AT (access type) field, 110-11
EBE (external bus error) field, 110
FAV (fault address valid bit), 112
FT (fault type) field, 111-12
L (level) field, 110
OW (overwrite) field, 112
FAV (fault address valid bit), fault
status register, 112
FCPU commands, MPSAS, 187
Floating-point architecture, SPARC, 42
Floating point queue (FQ), 33
fork() and fork1(), 242
FPU commands, MPSAS, 187
Framework, MPSAS, 178-83
FT (fault type) field, fault status register, 111-12
Fujitsu MB86900, 49-52
system configuration, 50-52
Fujitsu MB86901, 54

G

Gallium-arsenide (GaAs) SPARC
implementation, 79-80

H

Homogenous modules, Level 2 MBus, 324

I

IMPL field, control register, 106
Indirect data intervention, 160
Input/output (I/O) locations, defined, 85
Instruction-accurate modules, 176-77
Instruction set, SPARC, 33-34, 40-42
arithmetic/logical/shift instructions, 41
control-transfer instructions, 42
coprocessor operations, 41-42

load and store instructions, 41
read/write control register instructions, 42
Intel Scientific Computers/iPSC, 6
Interface Definition Language (IDL), and
DOE, 317-18
Interface specification, MBus, 319-76
International Parallel Machines/IP-1,7
Interrupt Controller Module, 194
I/O adapters, 371
Issuing order, 86

L

L64815 MMU and cache controller, 114-16
block diagram, 115
L64831 SPARC Integrated IU/FPU, 61-67
core system comparisons, 64
HyperSPARC processor, 68-69
MBus-based system, 63
architecture, 66
SBus-based system, 62
architecture, 65
SuperSPARC, 69-72
Level 1 MBus, 127-128, 320
Level 2 MBus, 128, 320-21
cache coherency, 163
cache consistency protocol, 323
cache states, 164
cache write policy, 323
consistency quantity, 323
homogenous modules, 324
signals and transactions, 164-65
Coherent Invalidate transaction, 165,
336-38
Coherent Read and Invalidate
transaction, 165, 168, 338
Coherent Read transaction, 164-65, 168,
335-36
Coherent Write and Invalidate
transaction, 165, 336-38
transaction acknowledgments, 165-66
Iflush command, 91-93
Lightweight processes (LWPs), 212-18, 244-49
preemption, 217
scheduling, 247-49

R

Read/write control register instructions, SPARC, 42

Read/write locks, 237-38

Real memory, 84-85

Real-time scheduling
lightweight processes (LWPs), 248-49
SunOS multithreading architecture, 224-28

Recursive deadlock, 252

Reduced Instruction Set Computer (RISC) *See* RISC architectures

Reference MMU architecture, 93-118
contexts, 97-98
defined, 93
features, 94
functions provided by, 94-95
hardware architecture, 105-13
access to MMU registers, 105-6
context register, 108
context table pointer register, 107-8
control register, 106-7
diagnostic register, 108-9
fault address register, 113
fault status register, 109-13
implementations, 114-19
miss processing, 113
MMU flush and probe model, 102-5
flush operations, 102-4
probe operations, 104-5
Type field, 102
VFPA field, 102
page table descriptor (PTD), 98-99
ET (Entry Type), 99
PTP (Page Table Pointer), 99
page table entry (PTE), 99-102
ACC (Access Permissions), 100
C (Cacheable), 100
ET (Entry Type), 101
M (Modified), 100
PPN (Physical Page Number), 100
referenced/modified bit updates, 114
reset, 113
software architecture, 94-105

Reference MMU implementations, 114-19
Cypress CY7C625 CMTU, 116-17

L64815 MMU and cache controller, 114-16
SuperSPARC TMS390Z50 MMU, 117-19

Reflective memory, 169-70
support, 372-73

Reserved acknowledgment, 342

reserved field, control register, 107

Retry acknowledgment, 342

rflush command, 91-93

RISC architectures, 1, 2
microprocessors, 3

S

SBus, 62, 130-40
architecture, 65
devices/implementations, 133-39
LSI Logic L64853/L64852 controllers, 134-36
Motorola MC92001 Interface Controller, 137-38
Motorola MC92005 slave interface chip (SLIC), 138-39
features, 132-33
overview, 130-32
Sun services for SBus developers, 139-40
See also MBus; XBus; XDBus

SBus Module, 195

Scalability vs. synchronization, 6-7

SC field, control register, 107

Scheduling, lightweight processes (LWPs), 247-49

Second-level caches, 373-74

Self-deadlock, 252

Semaphores, 236-37

Shared bus architecture
See Tightly coupled multiprocessors

Signal grouping, MBus, 347-53

Signals, MBus, 324-33

SIGWAITING signal, 217-18

SIMD (Single Instruction, Multiple Data), 7

Simple architecture, MPSAS, 188

Simple Timer Module, 196

Simulated Disk Module, 195

Simulation levels, MPSAS, 176-77